SOCIOLOGY

Also available from Allen & Unwin

★ Not available from Allen & Unwin in the USA

SOCIOLOGY

*A guide to Problems
and Literature*

Tom Bottomore
*Emeritus Professor of Sociology,
University of Sussex*

THIRD EDITION

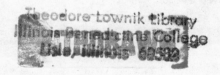
London
ALLEN & UNWIN
Boston Sydney Wellington

© Allen & Unwin (Publishers) Ltd, 1962, 1971, 1987
This book is copyright under the Berne Convention.
No reproduction without permission. All rights reserved.

Allen & Unwin, the academic imprint of
Unwin Hyman Ltd
PO Box 18, Park Lane, Hemel Hempstead, Herts HP2 4TE, UK
40 Museum Street, London WC1A 1LU, UK
37/39 Queen Elizabeth Street, London SE1 2QB

Allen & Unwin, Inc.,
8 Winchester Place, Winchester, Mass. 01890, USA

Allen & Unwin (Australia) Ltd,
8 Napier Street, North Sydney, NSW 2060, Australia

Allen & Unwin (New Zealand) Ltd
in association with the Port Nicholson Press Ltd,
Private Bag, Wellington, New Zealand

First published in 1962
Second edition 1971
Third edition 1987

British Library Cataloguing in Publication Data

Bottomore, Tom
 Sociology: a guide to problems and literature. – 3rd ed.
1. Sociology
I. Title
301   HM51
ISBN 0–04–300108–4
ISBN 0–04–300109–2 Pbk

Library of Congress Cataloging-in-Publication Data

Bottomore, T. B.
 Sociology: a guide to problems and literature.
Bibliography: p.
Includes index.
1. Sociology. I. Title.
HM51.B75 1987   301   86–17278
ISBN 0–043–00108–4 (alk. paper)
ISBN 0–043–00109–2 (Pbk.: alk. paper)

Set in 10 on 11 point Bembo by Computape (Pickering) Ltd
and printed in Great Britain by Billings and Sons Ltd, London and
Worcester.

For Mary

Contents

Preface to Third Edition

In the quarter of a century that has elapsed since this book was first published profound, and often dramatic, social and cultural changes have occurred affecting the development of sociology itself as a body of knowledge and ideas about human society. These changes, however, have not followed a uniform or uni-linear course, and in retrospect the period appears as one of great animation, but also of great confusion, characterized by new departures and sudden arrests or reversals. In my preface to the second edition (1971) I noted that a more radical intellectual temper and new radical movements had emerged during the 1960s, which had made sociologists more aware of the elements of change and conflict in social life, had reawakened their interest in comparative and historical studies, and had directed their attention once more to large social issues of the kind which preoccupied the founding fathers of the discipline in the second half of the nineteenth century.

The radical wave subsided, though it was not wholly quelled, in the 1970s, and a more conservative mood came to prevail, but the political context of sociology has again been changing in recent years as a result of the economic crisis in the Western societies (which also profoundly affects the countries of the Third World), and the growing menace of a military confrontation between the superpowers. One indication of the changing character of sociology over the whole period from the end of the 1950s is the notable revival of Marxist theory which, from being little more than a footnote to the main body of sociological thought (outside the region where 'official Marxism' reigned supreme), has become a major, widely debated paradigm, which is extensively used not only in sociology but in the social sciences more generally (for example, in economics and anthropology), while assuming very diverse forms. At the same time, other new theoretical approaches – among them those of phenomenology and structuralism – have emerged in the process of reorientation of sociological thought, and the diversity of theoretical schemes has provoked an upsurge of methodological disputation. In the present edition, therefore, I consider more fully the various sociological theories, and the ways in which they are grounded or criticized in philosophies of science.

As in the second edition I have again broadened my discussion of the countries of the Third World, but I have retained the specific accounts of Indian society where these illustrate particularly well either some general sociological issues (for example, caste as a type of social stratification, the social influence of religion), or the nature of the changes that have been taking place in the non-industrial and industrializing regions of the world. This attempt – however limited by the extent of my own knowledge and by the scale of the book – to provide a wide-ranging study of culturally and economically diverse societies throughout the world conforms in my view not only with the reality of our present world, in which the interdependence of societies is much greater than ever before in human history, but also with the original and vital conception that has inspired the development of sociology, as a discipline which aims to grasp human life as a whole, to be continually aware of, and to elucidate, the system of social relations, ramifying in time and space, within which every human action is set.

As in previous editions each part of the book is followed by a guide to further reading on the themes discussed. The explosion of sociological writing over the past two decades has made it increasingly difficult to select a few major works in the various fields of study, but I have indicated those which seem to me most likely to be useful to students, and have tried to maintain a balance between earlier 'classical' writings and more recent works.

In the present edition references to works cited in the text are generally given by author and date, with full details of publication provided in the Bibliography at the end of the volume. The original date of publication is usually given, but where page references are indicated these sometimes relate to translations or to later editions, as listed in the Bibliography.

Tom Bottomore
Summer 1985

PART I

The Scope and Methods of Sociology

1   *The Study of Society*

Contemplating all the men of the world, who come together in society to work,
struggle and better themselves, cannot but please you more than any other thing.
           Antonio Gramsci, in a letter from prison to his son Delio

For thousands of years human beings have observed and reflected upon the societies and groups in which they live, yet sociology is a modern science, not much more than a century old. Auguste Comte, in his classification of the sciences, made sociology both logically and chronologically posterior to the other sciences, as the least general and most complex of all, while one of the most eminent of modern anthropologists observed, much later, that 'the science of human society is as yet in its extreme infancy' (Radcliffe-Brown, 1952). It is true that we can find, in the writings of philosophers, religious teachers and legislators of all civilizations and epochs, observations and ideas which are relevant to modern sociology. Kautilya's *Arthasḥástra* and Aristotle's *Politics* analyse political systems in ways which are still of interest to the sociologist. Nevertheless, there is a real sense in which a new science of society, and not merely a new name,[1] was created in the nineteenth century. It is worthwhile to consider the circumstances in which this happened, and to examine the characteristics which distinguish sociology from earlier social thought.[2]

The principal intellectual antecedents of sociology are not difficult to identify. 'Broadly it may be said that sociology has had a fourfold origin in political philosophy, the philosophy of history, biological theories of evolution, and the movements for social and political reform which found it necessary to undertake surveys of social conditions' (Ginsberg, 1947, p. 2). Two of these, the philosophy of history and the social survey, were particularly important at the outset; and they were themselves latecomers in the intellectual history of humanity.

The philosophy of history as a distinct branch of thought is a creation of the eighteenth century, among its founders being the Abbé de Saint-Pierre and Giambattista Vico.[3] The general idea of progress which they helped to formulate influenced profoundly man's conception of history, and is reflected in the writings of Montesquieu and Voltaire in France, of Herder in Germany, and of a group of Scottish philosophers and historians of the latter part of the eighteenth century, Ferguson, Millar, Robertson and others. This new historical attitude is clearly expressed in a passage in Dugald Stewart's 'Memoir of Adam Smith', where he observes:

> When, in such a period of society as that in which we live, we compare our intellectual acquirements, our opinions, manners and institutions, with those which prevail among rude tribes, it cannot fail to occur to us as an interesting question, by what gradual steps the transition has been made from the first simple efforts of uncultivated nature, to a state of things so wonderfully artificial and complicated.

Stewart goes on to say that information is lacking on many stages of this progress, and that its place must be taken by speculation based on the 'known principles of human nature'. 'To this species of philosophical investigation, which has no appropriated name in our language, I shall take the liberty of giving the title of *Theoretical* or *Conjectural* History, an expression which coincides pretty nearly in its meaning with that of *Natural History* as employed by Mr Hume, and with what some French writers have called *Histoire Raisonnée*' (1854–8, Vol. 10, pp. 33–4).

In the early part of the nineteenth century the philosophy of history became an important intellectual influence through the writings of Hegel and of Saint-Simon.[4] From these two thinkers stems the work of Marx and Comte, and thus some of the important strands in modern sociology. We may briefly assess the contributions of the philosophy of history to sociology as having been, on the philosophical side, the notions of development and progress, and on the scientific side, the concepts of historical periods and types of society. The philosophical historians were largely responsible for the new conception of society as something more than 'political society' or the state; they were concerned with the whole range of social institutions, and made a careful distinction between the state and what they called 'civil society'. Adam Ferguson's *Essay on the History of Civil Society* (1767), which in its German translation seems to have provided Hegel with his terminology, and influenced his early writings on society, is perhaps the best example of this approach. In his *Essay*, and in later writings, Ferguson discusses the nature of society, population, family and kinship, the distinctions of rank, property, government, custom, morality and law; that is, he treats society as a system of interrelated institutions. Furthermore, he is concerned to classify societies into types, and to distinguish stages in social development. Similar features are to be found in many of the writings of those whom I have called the philosophical historians; and their work as a whole marks an abrupt change in the intellectual orientation of students of human society. These features re-appear in the nineteenth century in the conceptions of the early sociologists, Comte, Marx and Spencer.

A second important element in modern sociology is provided by the social survey, which itself had two sources. One was the growing conviction that the methods of the natural sciences could and should be extended to the study of human affairs; that human phenomena could be classified and measured. The other was the concern with poverty (the 'social problem'), following the recognition that, in industrial societies, poverty could no longer be regarded as a natural phenomenon, an affliction of nature or of providence, but had to be seen as the result of human ignorance or of exploitation. Under these two influences – the prestige of natural science and the movements for social reform – the social survey came to occupy an important place in the new science of society. Its progress can best be traced in the industrial societies of Western Europe, in such pioneer works as Sir John Sinclair's *Statistical Account of Scotland* (21 vols., 1791–9), and Sir F. M. Eden's *The State of the Poor* (3 vols., 1797), in Condorcet's attempts to work out a 'mathématique sociale' (see Granger, 1956), in Quételet's 'physique sociale' (1835); and in later studies such as Le Play, *Les Ouvriers européens* (1855, 2nd enlarged edn, 1877–9), and Booth, *Life and Labour of the People in London* (1891–1903). The social survey, in diverse forms, has remained one of the principal methods of sociological inquiry.

These intellectual movements – the philosophy of history and the social survey – were not isolated from the social circumstances of the eighteenth and nineteenth centuries in Western Europe. The new interest in history and in social development was aroused by the rapidity and profundity of social change, and by the contrast of cultures which the voyages of discovery brought to people's attention. The philosophy of history was not merely a child of thought; it was born also of two revolutions, the industrial revolution in England, and the political revolution in France. Similarly, the social survey did not emerge only from the ambition of applying the methods of natural science to the human world, but from a new conception of social evils, itself influenced by the material possibilities of an industrial society. A social survey, of poverty or any other social problem, only makes sense if it is believed that something can be done to remove or mitigate such evils; and it was, I think, the existence of widespread poverty in the midst of great and growing productive powers which was responsible for the change of outlook whereby poverty ceased to be a natural problem (or a natural condition) and became a social problem, open to study and amelioration. This was, at the least, an important element in the conviction that exact knowledge might be applied in social reform; and later, that as the human species had established an ever more complete control over its physical environment so it might come to control the social environment.

So far I have considered the liberal and radical elements in sociological thought, which emerged directly from the Enlightenment and the French Revolution. In some recent writings, however, much greater prominence is given to the ideas which were contributed to sociology by the thinkers of the conservative and romantic reaction, especially de Bonald and de Maistre, through their influence upon Saint-Simon, Comte and de Tocqueville. Robert Nisbet (1967), for example, refers to the reorientation of social thought which gave rise to sociology as 'a reaction of traditionalism against analytical reason', and he sums up his view as follows:

> The paradox of sociology . . . lies in the fact that although it falls, in its objectives and in the political and scientific values of its principal figures, in the mainstream of modernism, its essential concepts and its implicit perspectives place it much closer, generally speaking, to philosophical conservatism. Community, authority, tradition, the sacred: these are primary conservative preoccupations in the age . . . (p. 17)

According to Nisbet, they also constitute the important 'unit-ideas' of sociology. A similar argument has been propounded, in another form, by Marcuse (1941, 1964), who contrasts the conservatism of Comte's sociological positivism with the radicalism of 'critical reason' which he takes to be the essential feature of Hegel's social theory, achieving its full expression in Marxist thought.

The influence of the conservative thinkers upon sociology is not in doubt. Saint-Simon's distinction between 'critical' and 'organic' periods in history, and his advocacy of a new moral doctrine to bind men together in the post-revolutionary industrial society, reflect this influence and at the same time prepare the way for Comte's concern with the re-establishment of 'social order'. But Saint-Simon was also the source of other ideas, concerning class and property, which gave rise to a different style of thought in the socialism of the Saint-Simonians and later of Karl Marx. There is a dual tradition in sociological thought, and the diverse elements which went to make it need to be carefully distinguished.

The pre-history of sociology as I have sketched it can be assigned to a period of about 100 years, roughly from 1750 to 1850; or, let us say, from the publication of Montesquieu's *De l'esprit des lois* up to the work of Comte and the early writings of Spencer and Marx. The formative period of sociology as a distinct science occupies the second half of the nineteenth century and the early part of the twentieth century.[5] We can see from this brief survey of its origins some of the characteristics which early sociology assumed. In the first place it was *encyclopaedic*; it was concerned with the whole of human social life and the whole of human history. Secondly, under the influence of the philosophy of history, reinforced later by the biological theory of evolution, it was *evolutionary*, seeking to identify and account for the principal stages in social evolution. Thirdly, it was conceived generally as a *positive science*, similar in character to the natural sciences. In the eighteenth century the social sciences were conceived broadly upon the model of physics. In the nineteenth century, sociology was modelled, to a great extent, upon biology, as is evident from the widely diffused conception of society as an organism, and from the attempts to formulate general laws of social evolution. Fourthly, in spite of its claim to be a general science, sociology dealt particularly with the social problems arising from the political and economic revolutions of the eighteenth century; it was above all *a science of the new industrial society*. Finally, it had an *ideological* as well as a scientific character; conservative and radical ideas entered into its formation, gave rise to conflicting theories, and provoked controversies which continue to the present day.

The wide-ranging claims made by some early sociologists, and notably by Comte and Spencer, provoked criticism and even hostility from those who worked in more specialized fields, among them historians, economists and political scientists, and continued to do so for a long time. But in assessing the contribution of the new discipline in its early phase we should distinguish especially between the claims that were made concerning its field of inquiry and potential scope, and those relating to its actual discoveries. No one believes any longer that the early sociologists discovered precise laws of social evolution; but in attempting to formulate such laws they did contribute significant ideas about the periodization of human history, the processes of social change, and above all the interrelations of different elements of social life in these processes. That is to say, they outlined a conception of human societies as being, in some sense and degree, structured wholes; and this notion of social structure has become an indispensable concept for all the modern social sciences. Moreover, in one particular form, namely Marx's theory of history and society, the conception of distinct social structures undergoing determinate historical changes, acquired – as Berlin (1963, p. 158) has commented – a more rigorous and empirical character, far removed from the vague and abstract systems of Comte and Spencer, and had a profound influence in the creation not only of sociology, but also of modern economic and social history.

Marx, indeed, although he did not use the term 'sociology' in referring to his own work, has come to be regarded as one of the great 'founding fathers' of the discipline, together with Durkheim and Weber, and it is in the writings of these three thinkers that we can best observe how modern sociology was defined and established. Durkheim formulated most explicitly the scope of the new discipline and its relation to other social sciences. Although he was especially concerned to emphasize the autonomy of sociology and to specify the particular range of phenomena with which it should deal (Durkheim, 1895), he did not suppose that sociology could be an encyclopaedic science, or that it could be pursued in isolation from other studies of social life. He envisaged, rather, a gradual diffusion of the sociological approach, and thus a transformation of the more specialized social sciences from within. Only at a later stage did he think that it might be possible to construct a general sociology, comprising more general laws based upon the laws established in particular fields of the special sciences (Durkheim, 1903, 1904). In his editorial preface to the first volume of the *Année Sociologique* (1898), Durkheim explained that

> our efforts will tend especially to promote studies dealing with very limited subjects, and belonging to special branches of sociology. For since general sociology can only be the synthesis of these special sciences, since it can consist only in a comparison of their most general results, it is only possible to the extent that these sciences are developed.

In the event, many French scholars in diverse disciplines were influenced and stimulated by Durkheim's work: in law (Davy, Lévy-Bruhl and Duguit), in economics (F. Simiand), in anthropology (Mauss), in history (Marc Bloch, Granet), in linguistics (Cahen, Meillet) – to mention only the most prominent. Durkheim's ideas were conveyed not only through his own writings but also, and perhaps even more effectively, through the *Année Sociologique* which he founded in 1898. His conception of sociology was, so to speak, incarnated in the organization of the *Année Sociologique*, each issue of which contained one or two original monographs, and a number of surveys from a sociological viewpoint of the year's writing in several distinct fields of social inquiry. Durkheim justified this arrangement by saying: 'Sociologists have, we believe, a pressing need to be regularly informed of researches made in the special sciences, the history of law, customs and religion, social statistics, the economic sciences, etc., for it is here that are to be found the materials from which sociology must be constructed' (Durkheim, 1898).

In Germany, as Raymond Aron (1936) noted, sociology was at first rejected on account of its encyclopaedic character. Here, as elsewhere, an attempt was made to define and limit the field of sociology, in this case by the construction of an abstract science of the 'forms' of social life, largely under the influence of Georg Simmel, who formulated his conception of a science of society in the following terms:

> To separate, by scientific abstraction, these two factors of form and content which are in reality inseparably united; to detach by analysis the forms of interaction or sociation from their contents (through which alone these forms become social forms); and to bring them together systematically under a consistent scientific viewpoint – this seems to me the basis for the only, as well as the entire, possibility of a special science of society as such.[6]

But alongside these endeavours there was a continuing interest in historical interpretation and in the sociology of culture, stimulated especially by Marxism.

Marx, as I have noted, did not call his work 'sociology' and was more inclined to refer to it as a 'science of history' or 'political economy'. But it is evident that his general social theory covers the same field of inquiry as modern sociology, and it soon came to be treated, by the early Marxists as well as by critics, as one of the major sociological systems (Bottomore, 1978a). In Max Weber's work, too, there is no explicit formulation of the field of sociology, or of its relation to other social sciences, but in the first section of Part I of *Economy and Society* (1921) Weber defines sociology in a way which indicates both his relation to the formal sociology of Simmel and others, and his view of the broad scope of sociological analysis:

> Sociology (in the sense in which this highly ambiguous word is used here) is a science which attempts the interpretive understanding[7] of

social action in order thereby to arrive at a causal explanation of its course and effects ... Action is social insofar as, by virtue of the subjective meaning attached to it by the acting individual (or individuals), it takes account of the behaviour of others and is thereby oriented in its course.

Implicitly, Weber claims that sociological interpretation and explanation can be undertaken with respect to every kind of social phenomenon, regardless of whether it is already the object of study of some more specialized science, and his own studies range over many different aspects of social life; particularly in the context of his overriding preoccupation with the 'rationalization' of the modern world (see Löwith, 1932; Brubaker, 1984) which led him to investigate the origins and development of Western capitalism, the relation between religious and economic phenomena, the forms of political domination, the spread of bureaucratic administration, the rationalization of law, and the nature of modern political parties in relation to classes and status groups.

Thus the classical sociologists aimed to establish the scope and methods of the new discipline, to show its worth by the investigation and explanation of major social phenomena, and to associate it closely with other social sciences. Later sociology departed, in certain respects, from these aims. During the 1940s and 1950s there developed, on one side, a preoccupation with the construction of elaborate conceptual schemes, exemplified most fully in the work of Talcott Parsons and his followers;[8] and on the other side, a fascination with the techniques of sociological inquiry, applied to small-scale, and sometimes trivial, problems. At the same time sociologists began to show a preference in their research for 'residual' subjects which did not fall clearly within the sphere of other social sciences, and which could be regarded, therefore, as strictly sociological in rather a narrow sense. A survey of American sociology in 1953–4 revealed that the two main areas of sociological work, in terms of the number of research projects in progress, were urban and community studies, and marriage and the family (Zetterberg, 1956). There was a similar trend in other countries.

These tendencies were encouraged, to some extent, by a desire to establish the autonomy, the 'professional' standing, and the scientific character of sociology as an academic discipline. Their actual result, however, in spite of some real advances (for example, in the study of social mobility), was rather to sow doubts about the value of the contribution which sociology might make either to social thought or to the solution of practical social problems. Not a few sociologists gave the impression of

'lecturing on navigation while the ship is going down', to use
W. H. Auden's phrase quoted by Robert Lynd in his critical
assessment of the social sciences, *Knowledge for What?*, published
in 1939. In this book Lynd outlined an array of problems and a
programme of research which were obviously relevant to the
contemporary economic and political crisis in the Western industrial countries, as well as being close in spirit to the work of the
classical sociologists, but his ideas were largely ignored for the
next twenty years.

Since the late 1950s, however, sociology has again taken new
directions. One major influence upon this development, at the
outset, was the work of C. Wright Mills. In his writings on social
class and power in the USA (Mills, 1951, 1956) he showed the
value of historically informed studies of fundamental structural
elements in a complex industrial society; and in a later work on
method (Mills, 1959) he drew upon his own research experience, as well as upon the sociological tradition of Marx and
Weber in Europe and of Veblen and Lynd in America, to criticize
the prevailing trends in sociology ('grand theory' and 'abstracted
empiricism') and to advocate more adventurous, more imaginative studies of the momentous social and political changes in the
postwar world. In the following decade, partly inspired by
Mills's writing, there was a resurgence of social criticism, and
sociologists began to look again at the larger aspects of social
structure and its changes: to examine the basic characteristics of
industrial societies, to study the social implications of the rapid
advances in science and technology, to investigate the origins and
consequences of social movements and revolutions, to analyse
the processes of industrialization and economic growth. In so
doing they adopted a more radical and questioning attitude
towards social events, much more in the spirit of the early
sociologists, and were no longer satisfied with the received
interpretations of modern societies, or with the mere description
and classification of social phenomena just as they appear in a
moment of time. One indication of this new outlook was the
renewed interest in the historical development of societies;
another, closely connected with it, the revival of Marxism as a
general theory of society.

These developments led to a much wider diffusion of a
sociological approach in other social sciences. In political science,
for example, where there has long been an important area of
sociological research, deriving from the work of Max Weber,
Michels, Mosca and Pareto, as well as from Marxist theory, this
has been greatly extended by numerous studies of political

parties, elites, pressure groups, voting behaviour and bureaucracy; and more recently by studies of social movements (particularly the new radical movements of the 1960s) and of the social context of politics in Third World countries.[9] In economics, on the other hand, the influence of sociology became much less marked with the decline of the German historical school of economics at the end of the nineteenth century, and with the virtual exclusion from academic economics of any consideration of Marxist political economy; though there were some exceptions, notably Max Weber's (1921) study of economy and society and the work of such an eccentric scholar as Thorstein Veblen. This situation began to change, however, as sociological studies of the structure of industrial societies, work and leisure, industrial relations, the administration of industrial enterprises, occupations and education made increasingly important contributions to the study of economic problems. In addition, the extension of economic planning, the concern with economic growth, the widespread recognition of new problems which technological progress and increasing prosperity themselves create, and most recently the reappearance of mass unemployment in the Western capitalist countries, have brought into greater prominence the social aspects of economic activity and stimulated sociological research.

These instances are intended only to illustrate the nature of a sociological approach in the study of society and its place in the social sciences, which will be discussed more fully in Chapter 4 below. Sociology was, with social anthropology, the first science to concern itself explicitly with social life as a totality, with the whole intricate network of social institutions and groups which constitute a society, instead of singling out a particular aspect of society for study. The basic conception, or directing idea, of sociology is, therefore, that of *social structure*; the systematic interrelation of forms of behaviour or action in particular societies and types of society. From this follows the sociologist's interest in those aspects of social life which had previously been studied only in a desultory manner, or which had been the object of philosophical reflection rather than empirical inquiry: the family and kinship, religion and morals, social stratification, urban life. As I noted earlier, the preoccupation with some of the 'residual' subjects may be carried to excess, but the study of such phenomena is an important part of sociology, and properly considered it is inseparable from the study of economic and political institutions.

In these matters social anthropologists have had certain advantages, due in part to the character of the societies which they have usually studied. Dealing with small-scale tribal societies they have been able to view them as totalities, and to investigate every aspect of behaviour, from the economic to the sexual, without fear of encroaching upon the domain of other specialized disciplines. At the same time, however, under the influence of new conceptions of anthropological method which became prevalent in the 1930s and 1940s,[10] they tended to ignore the historical development of societies, and to reject comparative studies in order to concentrate upon giving a very full account of the social life of particular communities. Sociologists, on the other hand, carrying out their studies alongside already established disciplines – economics, political science, law, the history of religion – have made one of their main contributions by showing the connections between particular institutions or areas of social life and other elements in the social structure (for example, between religion and economic life, between property, class and politics), and by emphasizing the need for comparative studies which would reveal the constancy or variability of these connections across different types of society and different historical periods. More recently, sociology and social anthropology have drawn closer together. One important influence has been the rise of new nations from former colonial empires, and the efforts of these economically underdeveloped countries to bring about rapid economic growth, which pose a host of new problems, the study of which requires both knowledge of the traditional form of society and a historical and comparative view of the social process of industrialization; another, the emergence of a vigorous Marxist anthropology in the past decade (Firth, 1972; Godelier, 1973; Bloch, 1975; Seddon, 1978).

The changes in the world situation have brought into prominence another aspect of the study of human society. The great nineteenth-century sociologists have often been criticized for their encyclopaedic and over-ambitious conceptions of the new science. But their view of the subject had one great advantage: it demanded a very wide knowledge of many different types of society and historical periods. Even though sociology was formed in Western Europe, in large measure as a response to the advent of industrial capitalist society, these early scholars did not confine their interest to the European societies. They regarded the whole range of human societies as constituting the subject matter of the science.[11] By contrast, much recent sociology has been characterized by a narrower range of interest. In the 1940s and 1950s particularly, many sociologists were deeply committed to studying very small segments of their own national societies, and during this time the subject took on a distinctly ethnocentric and even parochial character. There were a number of reasons for this situation. The great accumulation of knowledge has undoubtedly made much more difficult the kind of wide-ranging scholarship which was displayed in the work of Max Weber and Durkheim, although a study such as Barrington Moore's *Social Origins of Dictatorship and Democracy* (1966) demonstrates that work of similar scope can still be successfully undertaken. Again, the greater involvement of sociologists in policy-making has meant that they have tended to concentrate upon relatively small-scale practical problems within their own societies. The most important influence, however, was probably a change in the direction of intellectual interest, which showed itself in the adoption of a functionalist approach (involving the study of particular societies, or subsystems within a society, from the aspect of their persistence and immutability), and the consequent abandonment of historical and comparative studies. This change itself was undoubtedly connected with the changed social situation in the Western democracies, which seemed to have attained a condition of relative stability, in their form as developed industrial societies, after the economic and political crisis of the 1930s which culminated in the Second World War.

The recent revival of historical and comparative studies, which I commented upon earlier in this chapter, has been affected profoundly by the rise of the newly independent nations of the Third World. Just as the historian is obliged to take a new view of history as 'world history' in the light of the rise of Asian and African nations (Barraclough, 1964), so also the sociologist has now to conceive his subject matter in a wider context. The formation of new political communities, economic development, urbanization and the transformation of the class structure in the developing countries show many similarities with earlier processes of change in Western societies, but they also have many distinctive features which must be taken into account in any comprehensive theory of social structure and social change. The expansion of sociological studies in the developing countries themselves, in response to their need for an overall view of the radical changes through which they are passing, provides a mass of new material and new ideas which can enter into a reconsideration of some of the fundamental problems of sociology.

The differences between 'encyclopaedists' and 'specialists' in sociology are not likely to be resolved quickly or easily. Human society is, as Comte declared, an extremely complex phenomenon, and the systematic study of it is evidently impossible without specialization. Yet the central ideas from which sociology developed require that each society should be conceived as a totality, itself embraced in the larger totality of an area of civilization and of a continuing historical process. The initial specialization of the social sciences depended upon easily observable and distinguishable features of society; the distinctions, for example, between political, economic, familial and religious institutions. The formation of sociology challenged this division and specialization, but it has nonetheless been reproduced within sociology itself. It may be that these traditional distinctions, in terms of the 'elements of social structure', are the most useful ones, but we should bear in mind two other considerations. First, as Gerth and Mills observed (1954, p. 27), the autonomy of the separate institutions is often limited: 'In "less developed" societies than the mid-nineteenth-century West, as well as in more developed societies, any one of the functions we have isolated may *not* have autonomous institutions serving it. Just what institutional orders exist in a more or less autonomous way is a matter to be investigated in any given society.' Secondly, it is apparent that the increasing scientific concerns with solving theoretical problems, and the interdisciplinary research which this often involves, is tending to bring about a new division of the subject matter, in terms of types of society, of microscopic and macroscopic phenomena, and so on. For purposes of description and exposition it is still convenient to deal with social phenomena under the traditional headings, but we should not assume that the scientific division of labour will always follow these lines, or that the presently existing specialization of research will prove ultimately to be the most fruitful one.

Notes to Chapter 1

1 It was Comte who named the new science *Sociology*. At one time he 'regretted the hybrid character' of the word, derived from the Latin *socius* and the Greek *logos*, but later suggested that 'there is a compensation . . . for this etymological defect, in the fact that it recalls the two historical sources – the one intellectual, the other social – from which modern civilization has sprung' (1851–4, Vol. 1, p. 326).

2 The general histories of social thought have emphasized unduly its continuity; and there have been lacking, in particular, studies of the modern social sciences which would illuminate their origins in the manner of Butterfield's 1950 account of the natural sciences, where

the repercussions of a radical change in men's attitude to the physical world are given prominence. However, in some recent works (e.g. Aron 1965, 1967; Nisbet, 1967; Bottomore and Nisbet, 1978) a similar approach has begun to reveal the sources of sociology by relating its appearance to the rise of industrial capitalism and the changed conception of social life which this provoked.

3   We must except the work of the fourteenth-century Arab philosopher and historian, Ibn-Khaldûn. His *Muquaddimma* (entitled *An Introduction to History* in the English translation by Franz Rosenthal, 1958) is remarkable in expounding a theory of history which anticipates that of the European eighteenth-century writers, and even Marx; but also as the work of an exceptional man who had neither predecessors nor followers. See Issawi, 1955.

4   For accounts of the development of the philosophy of history and studies of some of the writers mentioned above, see Flint, 1893; Bury, 1920; Nisbet, 1980.

5   For accounts of this period see, in addition to the works mentioned in note 2, Aron, 1936; Hughes, 1958; Giddens, 1971.

6   In his essay 'The problem of sociology' (1908). See my discussion of formal sociology in Chapter 3 below.

7   On the concept of 'understanding' (*Verstehen*) see Outhwaite, 1975, and my discussion in Chapter 3 below.

8   For Parsons's original exposition of his conceptual scheme, which he called the 'theory of action', see Parsons, 1937. There is a concise later formulation of the theory in Parsons, 1966. For a brief critical account of Parsons's scheme see my essay in Bottomore, 1975, and for a useful short introduction to his work as a whole Hamilton, 1983. The 'theory of action' and its derivatives in recent sociological thought are discussed more fully in Chapter 2 below.

9   For surveys of political sociology in the 1950s see Dupeux, 1954–5; Bendix and Lipset, 1957; Wiatr, 1964. More recent studies are discussed in Chapter 9 below.

10 The functionalist method, associated particularly with the work of Malinowski and Radcliffe-Brown; see Chapter 3.

11 It is true that they were inclined to attribute a special importance to the Western societies, as having attained a stage of civilization which other societies would eventually reach after going through stages of development. In this way Comte justified the limitation of his main investigation to the 'élite or *avant garde* of humanity' (i.e. the European nations). The view was not entirely unfounded in as much as Western science and technology, and for that matter Western social doctrines such as Marxism and nationalism, have been the principal factors in transforming the modern world.

2   Sociological Theory

There is not today, and indeed there has never been, a body of sociological theory which is universally accepted as valid. As one philosopher of science has suggested, the social sciences, including sociology, are *multiple-paradigm sciences*, a 'state of affairs in which, far from there being no paradigm, there are on the contrary too many' (Masterman, 1970, p. 74). Some earlier sociologists undoubtedly considered that they had discovered fundamental 'social laws', principally laws of social evolution, which constituted a body of theory capable of guiding both thought and action, but their claims were always disputed by other thinkers, as for example in the case of Weber's rejection of 'historical materialism' as a universal science of history. Modern sociologists, for the most part, have set themselves more limited aims and have recognized the existence of two, three or more different 'sociologies' even when they argue for the superiority of a particular paradigm. To a great extent they are concerned primarily to elucidate the character of the sociological approach (i.e. with methodology rather than theory), and to work out more precise concepts and more adequate classifications. In the latter activity they have formulated mainly that kind of limited generalization which is involved in the activity of classification itself. R. B. Braithwaite (1953, p. 1) makes a distinction between sciences at different stages of development, and says:

> If a science is in a highly developed stage, as in physics, the laws which have been established will form a hierarchy in which many special laws appear as logical consequences of a small number of highly general laws expressed in a very sophisticated manner; if the science is in an early stage of development – what is sometimes called its 'natural-history' stage – the laws may be merely the generalizations involved in classifying things into various classes.

Similarly, Nadel (1957, p. 1), in outlining a 'theory of social structure', observes that

> only the most advanced sciences have reached this level of explanatory theory-building. But 'theory' can also be understood in another, less ambitious, sense, namely as a body of propositions (still interconnected) which serve to *map out* the problem area . . . the propositions serve to classify phenomena, to analyse them into relevant units or indicate

their interconnections and to define 'rules of procedure' and 'schemes of interpretation'. 'Theory' here equals conceptual scheme or logical framework, and it is in this sense that the present enquiry can be said to aim at a 'theory'.

As to the so-called laws of social evolution, it seems doubtful whether they should be regarded as laws at all. K. R. Popper (1957, p. 108), in his discussion of 'historicism', observes:

> The evolution of life on earth, or of human society, is a unique historical process. Such a process, we may assume, proceeds in accordance with all kinds of causal laws, for example, the laws of mechanics, of chemistry, of heredity and segregation, of natural selection, etc. Its description, however, is not a law, but only a singular historical statement. Universal laws make assertions concerning some unvarying order . . . i.e. concerning all processes of a certain kind . . . But we cannot hope to test a universal hypothesis nor to find a natural law acceptable to science if we are for ever confined to the observation of one unique process.[1]

This does not mean that the evolutionary scheme has no value. In biology it led ultimately to the science of genetics and the formulation of universal laws of heredity. In sociology, the concept of evolution produced a good deal of confusion (between evolution, development and progress; Ginsberg, 1932) and was frequently a basis for a speculative teleology rather than a scientific analysis.[2] But it led also to some useful attempts at social classification, and to fruitful analyses of the processes of social change; results which the critics of historicism usually overlook. For the rejection of laws of social evolution does not mean that social change cannot be explained in terms of universal laws. Popper himself makes a distinction between 'laws' and 'trends', and suggests that universal laws of the type 'Whenever there are conditions of the kind c there will be a trend of the kind t', can be formulated (1957, p. 129). It would not be difficult to reformulate some propositions of the classical sociologists in such terms. For example, Max Weber's statement of the relationship between the Protestant ethic and capitalism is already close to this formulation and we could reformulate it as saying: whenever there exist economic circumstances a, b, c (to be specified) and a Calvinist-type social ethic (emphasizing the value of secular activity and the duty of abstinence), there will be a trend towards rationalized economic production aiming at maximum output with minimum cost. Similarly, Marx's analysis of the development of capitalism can be regarded as stating a 'trend towards socialism' which results from various tendencies – the centralization and concentration of capital, economic crises, class conflict – within capitalist society. Many familiar sociological propositions could thus be expressed in the form of causal laws (of greater or lesser generality) relating to observable 'trends' or 'tendencies'.[3]

It has been assumed so far that the social sciences are generalizing sciences which aim, like the natural sciences, at the establishment of a theoretical system, but which are as yet at a low stage of development. This is the view which has been taken by many, probably most, sociologists and social anthropologists, most explicitly by Durkheim and Radcliffe-Brown.[4] It has been opposed by those philosophers and social theorists who have tried to make a rigorous distinction between the natural sciences on the one hand, and the historical and cultural sciences on the other, asserting that while the former aim at 'causal explanation' the latter aim at the 'interpretation' or 'understanding' of meaning. A major influence in shaping this second conception of the social sciences is the work of Wilhelm Dilthey, and especially his *Einleitung in die Geisteswissenschaften* (1883).[5] Dilthey's influence was particularly strong in German sociology, as can be seen from the methodological writings of Simmel and Max Weber.[6] In England, Collingwood put forward views similar to those of Dilthey but had little direct influence on the social sciences. However, a number of English writers have claimed the social sciences as historical disciplines.[7] In Italy, Croce's historical philosophy was for a long time the dominant influence in social studies. The more Hegelian Marxist writers have also proposed a philosophical theory of history in opposition to sociology as a generalizing science.[8]

Over the past century this has been one of the fundamental controversies in the social sciences and especially in sociology, but it is too large a question to be examined thoroughly here and it will be convenient to examine some aspects of the problem in discussing sociological methods in the next chapter, since a major part of the dispute turns upon the question of whether the methods of the natural sciences can appropriately be used in studying social phenomena. However, there are some general points which may be rapidly reviewed.

One powerful argument against the scientific character of the social sciences has been that they have not in fact produced anything resembling a natural law. This might be answered (and often is) by referring to the youthfulness of the social sciences, and implying that they will eventually reach a higher theoretical level. But the answer is not entirely convincing; critics would say that the plea of immaturity has been made for a long time, without much sign of growth. Yet the criticism is exaggerated. In sociology, despite the complexity of the subject matter, causal connections and functional correlations has been established with a reasonable degree of probability. Durkheim's study of suicide, or Weber's analysis of the relations between Protestantism and capitalism, may be held (with various qualifications) to establish such connections, and there are other examples which we shall examine later. Moreover, those who dispute the scientific character of sociology are themselves open to criticism. If, as they hold, sociology is concerned with historical interpretation, or with interpreting the social actions of individuals on the basis of introspective knowledge of our own states of mind, the scientific sociologist may ask, in turn, what generally acceptable results have been produced by these methods, and whether in fact they go beyond, or even equal, the insights of poets and novelists.

In any case, those who believe that sociology is a scientific discipline are not obliged to claim that the formulation of laws constitutes its entire value. A part of sociology consists of exact description within an orderly framework of categories which involve only simple theorizing. Descriptive sociology is valuable in two ways. First, in the case of contemporary studies it provides information which is indispensable for the solution of practical problems and for the formulation of, and choice among, rational social policies. Secondly, where historical description or the description of little known societies is concerned it makes an important contribution to humane studies. For if a humane education consists in becoming sympathetically acquainted with a wide variety of human situations, strivings, ideals, and types of personality, then sociological studies are an essential element in such an education. Along with history, literary studies and, I would say, the historical aspects of the natural sciences, but in a more striking way than most of these, sociology makes us aware of the wealth and diversity of human life. It is, or should be, the centrepiece of modern humane studies, and a bridge between the sciences and the humanities.

Between those who regard sociology as a historical discipline and those who consider it a 'natural science of society', there seems to be a third view which, while emphasizing the scientific character of sociology, insists that the study of society requires a different theoretical model and different methods from those of the natural sciences. This point is, in certain respects, trivial. Every science must have an appropriate scheme of explanation and appropriate methods, but there may still be a fundamental unity of scientific method. A more important point is that there may be a radical difference between social laws and natural laws. Many writers have drawn attention to the reflexive character of social laws, in discussing the 'self-fulfilling prophecy' and the 'self-destroying prophecy' (e.g. Merton, 1957). The wider issue involved is whether, and in what sense, men can change the laws of social science. Alan Gewirth (1954), in an essay on this question, concludes that, 'in their *conditional* aspect, social laws can be changed by men in a sense in which natural ones cannot', for men can 'create new correlations of social variables by making new decisions which function as antecedent conditions from which new consequences follow'. The matter can be briefly (though inadequately) summarized as follows: in the natural sciences it is possible to conceive an ultimate closed theoretical system, while in the social sciences this is inconceivable because in human affairs genuine novelty can result from conscious volition.[9] A similar point has been made by Marcuse (1941) in his study of the development of social theory. He condemns sociology, especially Comte's sociology, on account of its search for invariant laws and its conception of a unified science, because this eliminates human freedom and rationality.

These diverse views might lead to various conceptions of sociology: as historical interpretation, or as a 'critical philosophy' (Marcuse), as ultimately reducible to psychology plus historical knowledge, or as a generalizing science whose laws have a very limited range. Some of these points will be considered further in the next chapter. First, however, I propose to examine sociological theory as it has actually developed up to the present time, under three headings: *types of generalization, basic concepts and schemes of classification*, and *explanatory theories*.

Types of Generalization

It is perhaps surprising, in view of the claims sometimes made for the scientific maturity of sociology, that there have been so few attempts to set out in a systematic way, and to evaluate, the different types of generalization to be found in sociological work. One such attempt is the brief discussion by Ginsberg (1947), who finds six types of generalization in social science:

(1) Empirical correlations between concrete social phenomena (e.g. urban life and divorce rates).
(2) Generalizations formulating the conditions under which

institutions or other social formations arise (e.g. various accounts of the origins of capitalism).

(3) Generalizations asserting that changes in given institutions are regularly associated with changes in other institutions (e.g. association between changes in class structure and other social changes in Marx's theory).

(4) Generalizations asserting rhythmical recurrences or phase-sequences of various kinds (e.g. attempts to distinguish the 'stages' of economic development, Bücher, Schmoller and others).

(5) Generalizations describing the main trends in the evolution of humanity as a whole (e.g. Comte's law of the three stages, the Marxist theory of development from primitive society to communist society, Hobhouse's theory of social development).

(6) Laws stating the implications of assumptions regarding human behaviour (e.g. some laws in economic theory).

It will be seen that these types of generalization are very different in range and level; and that they differ also in the extent to which they can be regarded as validated. Those of the first type are empirical generalizations, many of which can be considered well established; but they have not been incorporated in a more general system of laws in such a way as to form part of a scientific theory. The generalizations of types (2) and (3) can be regarded as formulations of universal laws relating to trends, of the kind discussed earlier. Similarly, the generalizations of types (4) and (5) purport to show, and to explain, broad tendencies in social development as a whole, or in some of its aspects; but because of their wide scope, and the difficulties of historical interpretation on this scale, they are much more speculative and have regularly been subjected to detailed criticism, while still providing, in some cases at least, a useful framework for the investigation of particular sequences of change (e.g. the transition from feudalism to capitalism, or the stages in the development of capitalism). Finally, the generalizations of type (6) seem to be mainly confined to some forms of economic theory, particularly that of the Austrian marginalist school (see Hutchison, 1981, chs. 6 and 7), and of the more recent, but affiliated, theories of 'rational action' and 'rational choice' (see Farmer, 1982); and these theoretical schemes have always been strongly contested, not only by Marxist economists, beginning with Hilferding (1904), but by sociologists of various schools as subjectivist and arbitrary in their assumptions about human behaviour.

Sociologists have shown relatively little interest in constructing broader generalizations from the empirical correlations which they have established. Yet it may well be possible to do this, as some examples will show. Durkheim (1897) established a relationship between certain suicide rates and the degree of integration of individuals in a social group, and while his methods and results have been criticized in some respects they have also been found useful and partly confirmed by later studies.[10] There are other social phenomena for which rates can be calculated (homicide and other types of crime, mental illness) that might also be related in various ways to the degree of group integration. Thus, it may be possible to formulate a more general law concerning social integration of which suicide rates would be one instance, and some of the concepts which would enter into such a theoretical scheme perhaps already exist in the shape of Durkheim's notion of 'anomie' and Marx's notion of 'alienation'.

Another example may be taken from the study of social conflict. Simmel (1908b) formulated a number of propositions concerning conflict within and between social groups which have been expanded, reformulated, and related to empirical research by Coser (1956). Coser ends his study with some theoretical reflections upon the functions of conflict, but it seems equally possible to use these propositions in causal explanation and some attempts along these lines have been summarized and examined by Bernard.[11] Here again we can see the possibility of constructing more general laws about the incidence and extent of conflict and, on the basis of such laws, of making statements about trends, or even definite predictions of the occurrence of conflict. Even at the present time it is, I think, possible to make rather simple predictions concerning the effects of particular changes upon the degree of conflict within a group; for example, that if the group becomes engaged in external conflict, the intra-group conflict will usually diminish. Some experimental testing of hypotheses concerning intra-group conflict has been undertaken in studies of small groups, and is referred to in Chapter 6 below.

It may be argued from what has been said above that it would be fruitful to direct sociological theorizing more explicitly to the construction of broader generalizations from the empirical correlations which have been established. These generalizations could then be tested by further research. In this way sociology might come nearer to the cumulative theory construction which characterizes some other sciences, at least in those periods which Kuhn (1970) calls 'normal science'. But this cumulation would need to take place in the framework of a more general theoretical scheme, and the 'progress' of sociology is still likely to differ radically from that of the physical sciences, since in Kuhn's terms there have been no real 'scientific revolutions' in sociology because there has not been, at any stage, a universally accepted paradigm which was subsequently overthrown.

Concepts and Schemes of Classification

It is in the fields of conceptualization and classification that sociology has so far been especially productive. New concepts serve two purposes. In the first place, they distinguish, and draw attention to, classes of phenomena which had not hitherto been considered as forming separate classes. Secondly, the concepts serve as shorthand descriptions of the phenomena and as instruments for further analysis. In the course of this book the principal concepts will be introduced and discussed, but it may be useful to mention some of the more imporant ones at this stage. Such terms as *social structure, social action, role, function, kinship, social class, status, mobility, bureaucracy, ideology, community, domination, conflict,* are regularly and frequently used by all sociologists (and increasingly by other social scientists) and form part of the necessary equipment by means of which they organize their thinking, do research, and communicate the results of research. A large part of the teaching of sociology, in the early stages, consists in showing students how to use such terms appropriately.

It is true, however, that the concepts of sociology are still unsatisfactory. In the first place, it may be suggested that while many useful terms have been defined, we have not yet discovered those central concepts which would be most fruitful in the elaboration of systematic theory.[12] Secondly, it remains the case that many concepts are employed in different senses by different sociologists. Thirdly, the various concepts are not firmly linked by any web of description or explanation. It seems, indeed, that misunderstanding of the use of concepts is a primary source of difficulty. In some attempts to improve the 'conceptual framework' of sociology, and notably in that of Talcott Parsons and his collaborators, the whole emphasis is placed upon definition of concepts rather than upon the use of concepts in explanation.[13] This is a retrograde step by comparison with the work of Marx, Durkheim and Max Weber, all of whom introduced and defined concepts in the course of working out explanatory theories. For example, Weber, in expounding his 'ideal type' method (1904), takes the position that all definitions are in part arbitrary, and that the value of a definition (i.e. of a concept) is only to be determined by its fruitfulness in research and theorizing. Similarly, Marx (1857–8, Introduction) examines concepts or 'abstractions' in the context of his theory of history, and more particularly his theory of 'modern bourgeois production'; while Durkheim demonstrates in all his major studies – of the division of labour, suicide and religion – the close connection between concept formation and an explanatory theory.

In the field of social classification much useful work has been done, although it has not yet resulted in any generally accepted scheme of classification. We may consider first the various attempts to classify whole societies, beginning with those of Comte, Spencer, Marx and Hobhouse. In these attempts different criteria are employed to distinguish one type of society from another; Marx employs an economic criterion, Spencer uses the criteria of size and complexity, while Comte and Hobhouse use principally the criterion of levels of intellectual development. The actual classifications do not differ so widely, however, and all the writers I have mentioned attach importance to the economic structure as an element determining the type of social structure.[14] It may seem doubtful today whether any really useful classification can be developed on the basis of a single criterion; and perhaps no single classification will serve all purposes. It is clear, for instance, that the classifications proposed by the early sociologists derived their meaning from the theories of social evolution with which they were connected. In view of the present-day concern with industrial societies and processes of economic growth, and at the same time with the relative autonomy of economic and political institutions, it might be well to attempt a new classification of societies on the basis of their economic structure and to elaborate this by a sub-classification on the basis of political systems. Such an attempt might be helped by efforts to refine some of the crude classifications which are widely used by sociologists and anthropologists: for example, the distinction between primitive and civilized societies, or that between developed and underdeveloped countries. Much more work has been devoted, in recent years, to such problems of classification, particularly in connection with the distinction between 'industrial' and 'developing' societies.[15]

In the classification of social groups there are many familiar distinctions: face-to-face and impersonal groups, primary and secondary groups, groups and quasi-groups, groups distinguished in terms of size (Simmel), and so on. Many of these distinctions are illuminating and useful in sociological analysis: for example, that made between face-to-face groups and large impersonal associations, or Simmel's (1902) subtle analysis of the connection between the size of groups, their structure, and the relationships among their members. In some more recent writing there have been attempts to advance beyond these elementary distinctions. Thus Gurvitch (1957, Vol. 1, ch. 3) has proposed a complex set of criteria for classifying social groups, including some which were employed by earlier sociologists, such as size, duration and recruitment of members, but also some new characteristics which will be discussed further in Chapter 6 below. Although the scheme is set out in a very abstract fashion Gurvitch shows, by an analysis of social class which is intended to exemplify its use, that it may be fruitful.

Finally, we should consider the attempts to classify social relationships. These have taken many different forms. There are, first, the various accounts of the major types of social bond. Hobhouse made a distinction between three broad 'types of social union', based respectively upon *kinship, authority* and *citizenship.* Durkheim distinguished two principal types of 'social solidarity', *mechanical* and *organic.* Tönnies also distinguished two types of social bond, which he termed *community (Gemeinschaft)* and *society (Gesellschaft).* Similarly, Maine made a distinction between societies based upon *status* and those based upon *contract.* These accounts of the types of social relationship which underly social union are not entirely divergent; there is clearly some affinity between the accounts given by Durkheim, Tönnies and Maine. Hobhouse's distinction is more narrowly political and is thus more similar in its aim to the distinction which Max Weber made between *traditional, charismatic* and *legal-rational* types of authority, but the two schemes of classification are otherwise very different – the type of political system which Hobhouse terms 'citizenship', Weber terms 'legal-rational' (with an emphasis on bureaucracy), and these terms reflect a fundamental divergence in the focus of interest and in philosophical outlook.

If we look at the more general classifications, and especially that of Tönnies, it seems reasonable to suppose that they might be employed in differentiating between social groups, as well as between societies. Tönnies's distinction has in fact been widely used in this way, and it has also been revised and expanded by a number of writers who have sought a more adequate classification of the basic types of social relation. Thus Schmalenbach (1922) distinguished three major types, community, federation and society; and Gurvitch (1957) has proposed a similar classification into communion, community and mass.

In this field of classification of social relations there are, secondly, the attempts to distinguish basic social relationships as such. The forerunner here is Simmel, whose analyses of conflict, competition, authority, subordination, and so on influenced all later German sociologists. Simmel's distinctions were systematized by von Wiese (1933), who attempted to classify all social relationships in terms of their tendency towards association or dissociation, towards diminishing or increasing the social distance between individuals.[16]

Lastly, there are the classifications in terms of 'social action', which play a large part in sociology today. Max Weber (1921, Vol. 1, ch. 1) was the main originator of this way of classifying social relationships, and his distinction between 'traditional action' (determined by long-established customs), 'affectual action' (determined by sentiments), '*wertrational* action' (determined by a belief in the intrinsic value of acting in a certain way), and '*zweckrational* action' (determined by a calculated attempt to achieve desired ends by appropriate means; see Brubaker, 1984, ch. 2) has been the starting point for much later work. The concepts and theories of 'social action' will be discussed more fully in the following section and Chapter 3. Here it may be remarked that while some theorists (e.g. Merton, 1957) have argued that 'social action' is the key concept in sociology, it has in fact been interpreted in diverse ways and has found a place in very different theoretical schemes. The work of Talcott Parsons, who had a dominant influence in the elaboration of a theory of action during the 1940s and 1950s, illustrates one such scheme. In his earlier work Parsons (1937) analysed the concept of social action in the work of Pareto, Durkheim and especially Weber, then went on to expound a 'general theory of action systems' (Parsons, 1951), relating types of action to types of social structure, and finally provided a concise summary of his conceptual scheme (Parsons, 1966, ch. 1), at the same time setting it firmly within a theory of social evolution. This marked a certain rapprochement with the original significance of Weber's work, in which the typology of social action was only one part of a much broader attempt to distinguish and classify social structures and institutions, displaying a sense of history and a range of historical knowledge which were lacking in much of the sociology of the immediate postwar decades.

This brief survey indicates that while many useful distinctions have been suggested, a comprehensive and satisfactory classification of societies, social groups and social relationships has still not appeared. Indeed, the interest shown by sociologists in these problems evidently waned for a long time, one of the last major discussions of the different forms of classification being that by Steinmetz (in the *Année Sociologique*, 1898–9), until the recent revival marked by the works of Parsons (1966, 1971) and Gurvitch (1957, 1958), and by a variety of Marxist reconsiderations of modes of production and social formations. These more recent analyses have no doubt been inspired in part by the social changes occurring in the postwar world, both in the industrial countries and in the new nations of the Third World; and they have not only emphasized fresh distinctions – for example, between industrial and non-industrial, or developed and developing societies – but have located them in revived and modified theoretical schemes of social evolution or development which will be examined in a later chapter.

Explanatory Theories

It may be well to begin with some remarks on scientific explanation. On the whole, recent writers on methodology have followed J. S. Mill's account of explanation:

> An individual fact is said to be explained by pointing out its cause, that is, by stating the law or laws of causation, of which its production is an instance . . . And in a similar manner, a law or uniformity in nature is said to be explained, when another law or laws are pointed out, of which that law itself is but a case, and from which it could be deduced. (Mill, 1879, bk 3, ch. 12)

Braithwaite (1953, ch. 1) says much the same thing, while Popper (1934, 1957) has proposed a modification of Mill's account in respect of 'individual facts'. He argues that a 'causal explanation of a certain *specific event* means deducing a statement describing this event from two kinds of premises: from some *universal laws*, and from some singular or specific statement which we may call the specific initial conditions'. This allows a distinction to be made between two types of causal explanation, scientific and historical; in scientific explanation attention is concentrated upon the relation between a particular fact and a universal law, whereas in historical explanation it is concentrated upon the relation between a particular fact and specific initial conditions.

Scientific explanation is causal in the above sense. But if we conceive explanation more generally as an answer to the question 'Why?', then we can see that it may take either of two forms:

causal explanation which is of the kind 'Because of . . .' and *teleological* explanation which is of the kind 'In order that . . .' (Braithwaite, 1953). The latter kind may be further differentiated, as it is by Peters (1958) who, in the course of a detailed examination of various explanations advanced in psychological theories, distinguishes between causal explanations, explanations in terms of purpose, and explanations in terms of end-states. We have seen that many of the classical sociologists took the view that sociology, as a generalizing science, must aim at establishing causal connections and causal laws. On the other hand, the kind of explanation of human behaviour that first occurs to us is the teleological, in terms of purposes; and it is from this point of view that the advocates of 'interpretation' conduct their argument against a 'natural science of society'.

Between these two, the 'social-causal' and the 'individual-purposive' types of explanation, we may locate those explanations which refer to end-states of society. The functionalist theory purports to explain social phenomena in terms of the part which they play in maintaining the existence of society. This observation should at once be qualified by saying that one version of the functionalist theory, expounded by Malinowski (1939), proposed to explain social phenomena by referring them to individual biological needs and 'derived cultural needs'. In practice, Malinowski oscillated between description and psychological explanations,[17] and the functionalist theory as he propounded it no longer has any adherents. As a sociological theory, functionalism originated with Durkheim, and the classical work of functionalist explanation is *The Elementary Forms of the Religious Life* (1912). It should be noted, however, that Durkheim proposed two incompatible kinds of explanation, *causal* and *functional*, that he never resolved the question as to which of the two was more appropriate in sociology, or considered how they were related, and that for the most part he seemed, indeed, unaware that there was any question to resolve. It is true that in his earlier writings he observed that functional explanation alone was inadequate; the fact that a social phenomenon had a function did not account for its existence, which had to be explained in terms of efficient causes. But in later writings, he simply explained social phenomena by their functions, without qualification. Radcliffe-Brown (1952) largely followed him in this course, advocating causal explanation and a 'natural science of society', but also using the concept of social function, reformulated in a way which he believed, erroneously, eliminated its teleological implications: 'the *function* of any recurrent activity, such as the punishment of a crime, or a funeral ceremony, is the part it plays in the social life as a whole and therefore the contribution it makes to the maintenance of the structural continuity' (of a society). More explicitly than Durkheim, Radcliffe-Brown distinguished different kinds of problems. The systematic investigation of social life involved, he thought, three sets of problems: (1) What kinds of social structure are there? (2) How do social structures function? (3) How do new types of social structure come into existence? But he did not show, any more than did Durkheim, that the answers to such questions could be brought within a single rigorous theoretical system.

After Radcliffe-Brown's work, explanation in British social anthropology (and to some extent in social anthropology generally) came to consist in elucidating the functions of recurrent activities, or institutions, in a social system; and somewhat later, the same kind of explanation became prevalent in sociology through the influence of Talcott Parsons, R. K. Merton and others. In the development of Parsons's theory several phases can be distinguished (Hamilton, 1983). His early work, as I have noted, was concerned with elucidating the concept of social action as it had emerged in a body of European social theory, and with formulating what may be called a 'voluntaristic theory of action'. Then, in the 1950s, he turned his attention to the construction of a theory of 'action systems' or 'social systems', and the theoretical scheme which he developed at that time came to be generally known, and widely influential, as 'structural-functionalism'. Finally, in the 1960s, he became more concerned with problems of social change – rather than the maintenance of structural continuity – and curiously enough reintroduced into sociological theory the evolutionism of Herbert Spencer, conceiving the process of change mainly as one of increasing differentiation. Parsons's later work, like that of Durkheim, raises problems about the relation between functional and causal accounts of social phenomena, which are left unresolved. Merton, on the other hand, followed a different direction and came to regard functionalism less as a theory than as a method or 'approach' (in which form it will be discussed in the next chapter).

It may indeed be questioned whether functionalism is a theory at all. First, it can be argued that the postulation of end-states may *never* be explanatory and that it is certainly *not always* explanatory. What we are given is description or re-description (Peters, 1958). It may be noted here that in the biological sciences, where the notion of function has mainly been used, there has been a consistent development from functional description to causal explanation. Secondly, because the concept of function is based upon an analogy between social life and organic life, it may be argued that the analogy is not sufficiently close for functionalism, so far as it provides explanations at all, to provide valid explanations for social phenomena. The analogy presents several difficulties: societies change their structure while organisms do not; it is impossible to determine the health or sickness of societies in the way that this can be done for organisms, and consequently it is impossible to speak precisely about the 'normal' and 'pathological' functioning of the 'organs', or about 'function' and 'dysfunction' (in fact, all such ways of speaking about societies involve value judgements); it is difficult to determine the function of a social activity or institution with the same precision as the function of organs is determined in biology by the examination of numerous instances (and in the organic world there is, moreover, a one-to-one correspondence between organ and function which does not seem to hold in the social world). It follows from these difficulties: (1) that even if some functional explanations of social phenomena were valid, the range of explanation would be severely limited since the important phenomena of structural change could not be so explained; (2) that we cannot in fact decide in many cases the contribution which a social activity makes to the maintenance of the social system, except in evaluative terms; and (3) that we cannot easily assign a specific function to a particular social activity. On the last point Gellner (1958) has observed that there may exist in human societies 'functionless appendices', and that, in general, comparative study (including historical study) is necessary if we are even to attempt to verify a statement about the real function of an activity in any given society.[18]

In fact, functionalism as a theory in the sense which Durkheim, Radcliffe-Brown or Parsons gave to it has been largely abandoned, and it never became a really dominant paradigm (except possibly in American sociology during the 1950s), but always co-existed, in a state of controversy, with other theoretical schemes. Among the latter it will be convenient to begin by discussing the theories of social action, which are directly related to the work of Weber and Parsons and also express the increasing emphasis upon 'human agency' in much recent sociology. One of the criticisms brought against Parsons's theory in its later form is that it departs from a voluntaristic conception of social action and culminates in the notion of a dominating and constraining social system. Thus Dawe (1978, ch. 10), in a critical review which concentrates on Weber and Parsons, counterposes 'two sociologies' – the sociology of social system and the sociology of action – and argues strongly in favour of the latter as a conceptualization of society 'as the derivative of social action and interaction, a social world produced by its members, who are thus pictured as active, purposeful, self- and socially-creative beings' (p. 367). This emphasis on the human agent as the creator, rather than the creature, of society has taken many different forms, in the phenomenological sociology deriving mainly from the work of Schutz (1932) and leading in one direction to ethnomethodology (Garfinkel, 1967), and in some versions of Marxist theory which will be considered later.[19] At the same time there have been various attempts to bring the ideas of 'human agency' and 'social system' together in some more comprehensive theoretical scheme; for example, in the work of Touraine (1965, 1973) on the 'sociology of action' and the 'self-production of society', and in much of the writing of Giddens (1979, 1984) who has elaborated the ideas of 'destructuration' and 'restructuration' first formulated by Gurvitch (1958) and has critically examined the diverse sociological methods of the present time (Giddens, 1976).

The recent debates have brought to the forefront again a long-standing fundamental problem of sociological theory, concerning the relation between individual and society, which received its classic formulation by Simmel (1908a, pp. 350–1):

> The individual is contained in sociation and, at the same time, finds himself confronted by it. He is both a link in the organism of sociation and an autonomous organic whole; he exists both for society and for himself . . . His existence, if we analyze its contents, is not only partly social and partly individual, but also belongs to the fundamental, decisive, and irreducible category of a unity which we cannot designate other than as the synthesis or simultaneity of two logically contradictory characterizations of man – the characterization which is based on his function as a member, as a product and content of society; and the opposing characterization which is based on his functions as an autonomous being, and which views his life from its own centre and for its own sake.

Another recent theoretical scheme, structuralism, stands entirely opposed to those theories of action which attribute an absolute pre-eminence to the individual human agent as the creator of society. Structuralist sociology takes as its object of investigation a 'social system', and in its more extreme forms (largely in Marxist structuralism) claims to eliminate the human subject entirely from social theory and to construct a science of various 'levels' of human practice which are inscribed in the structure of a social totality (Althusser, 1965; Althusser and Balibar, 1970). But structuralism, like the theories of social action, is quite diverse – a congeries of theories or a very broad paradigm rather than a uniform theoretical standpoint (see Bottomore and Nisbet, 1978, ch. 14). Originating in linguistics, and then making its way into literary criticism, aesthetic theory and the social sciences, modern structuralism has emphasized the importance of disclosing the 'deep structure' which underlies and produces observable phenomena. In anthropology structural analysis is particularly associated with the work of Lévi-Strauss,[20] and in this form it stimulated the development of a Marxist anthropology; thus Godelier (1973), in his argument against empiricism and functionalism in anthropology, observes that for Lévi-Strauss, as for Marx, 'structures are not directly visible or observable realities, but levels of reality which exist beyond man's visible relations and whose functioning constitutes the deeper logic of a social system'. This idea of a real structure behind appearances has also profoundly influenced Marxist political economy, where Marx's analysis of the commodity in *Capital* is seen as an exemplary instance of structural analysis, and Marxist sociology, particularly in the study of social classes and the state (Poulantzas, 1968).

Structuralism, especially in its Marxist form, has had to confront the problem of the relation between structural and historical analysis in social theory. Some Marxists (e.g. Hindess and Hirst, 1975) argued that there is no real object 'history' open to scientific study (only an 'ideological non-subject'), but others endeavoured to combine structuralist and historical conceptions, notably Goldmann (1970) in his 'genetic structuralism' (much influenced by Lukács and Piaget) which he formulated thus: 'From this standpoint the structures which constitute human behaviour are not in reality universally given facts, but specific phenomena resulting from a past genesis and undergoing transformations which foreshadow a future evolution.' These controversies, another aspect of which is to be seen in the opposition between Sartre's 'dialectical reason' and Lévi-Strauss's 'analytical reason' (Lévi-Strauss, 1962, ch. 9), have provoked fresh reflection on the possibility of a sociological theory of history, in relation not only to Marx's 'historical materialism' but to the more general revival of evolutionist or developmental conceptions.

It will be evident from the foregoing discussion that Marxist thought, which was ignored or dismissed for long periods, has come to exercise a major influence upon the social sciences and historical studies. Marxism is, in fact, the most comprehensive and ambitious social theory that has yet been constructed, and as Schumpeter (1942) claimed: 'the so-called Economic Interpretation of History, is doubtless one of the greatest individual achievements of sociology to this day'. But the Marxist theory presents many difficulties of interpretation, as incessant debate over the past century attests. In the first place, the very breadth of Marx's thought, and the course which it followed, raises questions about whether it should be regarded as primarily constituting a sociological theory, political economy, a critical philosophy of history, or a unique and complete intellectual world of its own which transcends existing disciplines.[21] And if Marxism is regarded as being essentially a sociological theory, contesting and contested by other theories, then it has to be recognized, first, that there are many incomplete elements and unsettled questions within it – concerning social classes, the state, the role of class conflict in history, the development of modern capitalism; and secondly, that Marx's own thought has been presented and developed by later Marxists in very diverse ways, and has been greatly influenced by ideas originating in the social sciences and the philosophy of science outside its own sphere. Thus in the Marxist thought of the past few decades there has emerged, for example, a very clear distinction between a 'sociology of social system' and a 'sociology of action', which I have described elsewhere (Bottomore, 1981) as a distinction between 'scientific' and 'humanist' Marxism. What is incontestable, however, is that Marxist sociology has been for a long time a major factor in directing historical and sociological research to the investigation of major problems, and in provoking the construction of alternative theories (most directly and obviously in the case of Max Weber); and that it is still today a principal source of the continuing reflection on the nature, scope and limits of social knowledge, or a science of society. In this sense at least Marxism has been an obscurely dominant paradigm.

This chapter may fittingly conclude with some general reflections on the formulation of theoretical problems and theory construction in sociology. The questions which provoke theoretical analysis – and hence those activities of concept formation, generalization, interpretation and construction of broad explanatory schemes, which I have discussed – may derive from various sources. As I have already noted, sociology itself emerged as a response to the social and intellectual concerns aroused by the economic and political revolutions which created modern capitalist society. The broadest theoretical questions were posed in terms of the origins and development of this new social system, the character of the new social groups (above all, social classes) which appeared in it, and the changes which it brought about in traditional social institutions and in social consciousness. Similarly, at the present time, theoretical questions may arise from philosophical or speculative thought about social trends in the advanced industrial societies – about mass society and alienation, the prospects for democracy or socialism in relation to the actual historical development of collectivist societies, the nature and aims of new social movements and the significance of the utopian political ideas which they often express – or, on the other hand, from problems in the development or 'modernization' of the nations in the Third World.

A second source of theoretical problems, related to the foregoing, is provided by previously elaborated theories, which may be rejected or revised in the light of new discoveries and interpretations. Thus Marx's theory of the development of production and the formation of social classes, Durkheim's theory of the division of labour and social solidarity, and Weber's theory of a comprehensive movement towards the total rationalization of social life have all given rise to intense theoretical controversies from which the construction of new theories may begin.

Finally, theoretical questions may emerge from practical problems, especially when these are connected with broader issues of social policy. For example, the concern of social reformers with poverty in the nineteenth-century Western capitalist societies led to investigations which revealed both the extent of poverty and some of its principal causes, notably prolonged ill-health and unemployment; and these inquiries helped to stimulate thought about the causes of unemployment, in the context of more general theories of the business cycle and of the operation of capitalist economies.

Undoubtedly there has been some progress in sociological theory, at least in the sense of greater conceptual clarity and systematization; but sociology, like other social sciences, is still characterized by the co-existence of numerous alternative paradigms, and an absence of those 'scientific revolutions' in which one reigning paradigm is more or less definitively overthrown and replaced by another. This state of affairs is closely related to the profound involvement of the social sciences with their social and cultural milieu, so that it may be argued that every sociological theory rests ultimately upon a 'philosophical anthropology', upon some extra-scientific image of human nature and society which is expressed in distinct 'value-orientations' and is strongly influenced by general changes in cultural values. In this vein Weber (1904, p. 112) observed, at the end of his essay on 'objectivity':

> All research in the cultural sciences in an age of specialization, once it is oriented towards a given subject matter through particular formulations of problems, and has established its methodological principles, will regard the analysis of this subject matter as an end in itself . . . it will cease to be aware of its rootedness in ultimate value ideas. And it is good that this is so. But a time comes when the atmosphere changes. The significance of the unreflectively used points of view becomes uncertain . . . The light of the great cultural problems has moved on. Then science too prepares to change its standpoint and its conceptual apparatus . . .

Whether sociological theory is in this way inescapably 'value impregnated', as well as 'value impregnating' (Bhaskar, 1979), will be examined more closely in the next chapter.[22]

Notes to Chapter 2

1   Durkheim, in his criticism of Comte, expressed a similar idea, remarking that Comte's 'law of three stages' was not only *not* a law, but was not even a reasonable hypothesis (since it could not be tested).

2   For further discussion see Chapter 17 below.

3   On the notions of 'law' and 'tendency' in relation to the problems of determinism in Marxist theory see the entry 'Determinism' in Bottomore, 1983.

4   See Durkheim, 1895, where it is argued forcefully that the business of the sociologist is to establish causal connections and causal laws; and Radcliffe-Brown, 1957, p. 3: 'The theses to be maintained here are that a theoretical science of human society is possible; that there can only be one such science . . .'

5   Dilthey's works are not available in English, but there is a good exposition and discussion of his views, with some excerpts from his writings, in two books by Hodges (1944, 1952).

6   See particularly the essays translated in Simmel, 1980, and the editor's introduction to the book, and Weber's 'critical studies in the logic of the social sciences' in Weber, 1949. But Weber also believed that causal explanation was possible and necessary in sociology: 'it cannot be too strongly emphasized that any understanding of, or insight into, the [human] action in question must be carefully verified by the customary methods of causal inference'. For a general discussion of the 'method of understanding' see Outhwaite, 1975.

7   For example, Evans-Pritchard, 1951, p. 60, says: 'In my view [social

anthropology] is much more like certain branches of historical scholarship – social history and the history of institutions and of ideas as contrasted with narrative and political history – than it is like any of the natural sciences'; and Carr-Saunders, 1958, in a lecture on this theme, argues that:

> Social science aims at interpreting social facts, that is the actions of men in relation to things, and to one another. These facts are entangled in a network so intricate that an attempt to discover invariable sequences must meet with failure. Such sequences, however, if discoverable, would not yield an interpretation of social facts in the light of our knowledge of people, and that is the interpretation which social science seeks. (p. 11)

He concludes the lecture by asserting a close affinity between social science and history; and 'since no one doubts that the place of history is among the humanities, the place of social science must be there also' (p. 15).

8   One of the most influential writings of this tendency is Lukács, 1923. See also the critical examination of sociology from this point of view in Marcuse, 1941.

9   For a more extensive discussion of this issue, in the context of a realist philosophy of science, see Bhaskar, 1978, especially ch. 2.

10   See particularly Douglas, 1966, and Giddens, 1966.

11   In *The Nature of Conflict* (UNESCO, 1957), pp. 33–117. See also Bernard, 1954.

12   Radcliffe-Brown, 1957, while claiming that a theoretical science of human society is possible, goes on to say that 'such a science does not yet exist except in its elementary beginnings' and also that 'we have not yet thought of the important concepts for social science'.

13   For a critical view of this tendency, see Bottomore, 1975b, and for a more general discussion of the problem of concept formation, Outhwaite, 1983a.

14   Hobhouse, Wheeler and Ginsberg, 1915, used an economic criterion exclusively in their attempt at a subclassification of primitive societies; and Comte and Spencer both proposed, besides their other classification, a distinction between 'militant' and 'industrial' societies which rests upon economic differences.

15   See Aron, 1961, 1966; Gellner, 1964. On the Marxist classification see Hobsbawm, 1964; Avineri, 1968b; Hindess and Hirst, 1975; and for a highly critical account of sociological conceptions of 'development' and 'modernization', Frank, 1967. The types of 'global society' are discussed in a more general way by Gurvitch, 1958, Vol. 1, ch. 7.

16   For an English version of von Wiese's sociology see Becker, 1932, and also the discussion in Aron, 1936, ch. 1.

17   For an acute criticism along these lines see Gluckman, 1949.

18   Diverse critical assessments of functionalism are collected in the work edited by Demerath and Peterson, 1967.

19   There is a good general review of what may be broadly termed 'phenomenological sociology' in Wolff, 1978, ch. 13.

20   For an exposition of the principles of structural anthropology see
     Lévi-Strauss, 1958; Leach, 1970.
21   I have examined the different views of Marxist thought in relation
     to sociology in Bottomore, 1975a, and have outlined the main
     elements of a Marxist sociology in Bottomore, 1973; Bottomore
     and Goode, 1983.
22   For a general account of some of the main issues discussed in this
     chapter see Bottomore, 1984a, ch. 2; Bottomore and Nisbet, 1978,
     Introduction; Bottomore, Nowak and Sokolowska, 1982, Intro-
     ductions.

3 *Sociological Methods*

The French mathematician, Henri Poincaré, once referred to sociology as 'the science with the most methods and the fewest results'. This is an unduly harsh judgement. As I have shown in the previous chapter, sociological theory has produced an important body of concepts and classifications, a large number of generalizations which connect different phenomena of social life and to some extent explain their occurrence or frequency, and some more inclusive theoretical schemes which, for all their deficiencies, have illuminated a variety of problems. Sociological research, guided by these theoretical constructs, has provided not only the material for testing generalizations and attempting further correlations, but descriptive accounts of social situations that are indispensable for coherent policy-making. The truth in Poincaré's observation is that there has been much dispute, increasing in intensity again in recent years, over the proper methods of sociology, and recurrent formulations of 'new rules of sociological method'.[1]

It will be useful to begin by outlining the controversy between those who think of sociology in terms of natural science and those who think of it as being quite different from any natural science and perhaps more like history or philosophy. What are the differences between 'nature' and 'society' which would require radically different methods of inquiry? They were first clearly stated by Dilthey (1883) and were then widely discussed by German historians and philosophers, especially Windelband and Rickert.[2] There are two major differences between the natural world and the socio-cultural world. First, the natural world can only be observed and explained from the outside, while the world of human activity can be observed and comprehended from within and is only intelligible because we ourselves belong to this world and have to do with the products of minds similar to our own. Secondly, the relations between phenomena of the natural world are mechanical relations of causality, whereas the relations between phenomena of the human world are relations of meaning, value and purpose. It follows from this, in Dilthey's view, that the 'human studies' should be concerned, not with the establishment of causal connections or the formulation of universal laws, but with the construction of typologies of personality and culture which would serve as the framework for understanding human strivings and purposes in different historical situations. I cannot here examine, in all its complexity, Dilthey's account of the methods of the 'human studies'. His approach has been re-stated recently, in an extreme form, in the arguments of Hayek (1952) against 'scientism', and it is implicit in the views of Evans-Pritchard and Carr-Saunders which were quoted earlier. Dilthey's ideas are relevant to the distinction between causal explanation, explanation in terms of purpose, and explanation in terms of end-states which we have already examined, and much 'functional explanation' in social anthropology seems consonant with his conception of method. For example, Malinowski related the function of institutions to biological needs as modified by conscious purpose, and many later functionalists, though remaining on the level of sociological explanation without recourse to psychology or biology, interpreted social institutions in terms of the values and purposes of individuals in the communities they studied.

This *Methodenstreit* between positivists and anti-positivists, which began in Germany in the latter part of the nineteenth century and is reflected very clearly in Max Weber's methodological writings (1949), has been vigorously resumed in recent decades, in a number of different forms.[3] In Britain, several writers have attempted to reformulate a sharp distinction between the methods of the social sciences and those of the natural sciences. Winch (1963) starts from Wittgenstein's philosophy and the notion that language expresses a way of life in order to argue that since sociology is concerned with the study of ways of life its method is close to, or indistinguishable from, that of linguistic philosophy. Another, less restrictive, philosophical view of the social sciences is provided by Louch (1966), who argues persuasively that the sciences which deal with human action are 'moral sciences', which require, not measurement and experiment, but appraisal, reflection and detailed accounts of action in particular contexts. This has affinities with the approach of 'methodological individualism', which arose out of Popper's writings on the logic of the social sciences and was widely discussed in the 1960s (see Agassi, 1966). One of the best short statements of an anti-positivist view has been given by Isaiah Berlin (1969) in an essay on Vico:

> Vico ... uncovered a species of knowing not previously clearly discriminated, the embryo that later grew into the ambitious and luxuriant plant of German historicist *Verstehen* – empathetic insight, intuitive sympathy, historical *Einfühlung*, and the like ... This is the

sort of knowledge which participants in an activity claim to possess as against mere observers; the knowledge of the actors, as against that of the audience, of the 'inside' story as opposed to that obtained from some 'outside' vantage point; knowledge by 'direct acquaintance' with my 'inner' states or by sympathetic insight into those of others, which may be obtained by a high degree of imaginative power; the knowledge that is involved when a work of the imagination or of social diagnosis, or a work of criticism or scholarship or history is described not as correct or incorrect, skilful or inept, a success or a failure, but as profound or shallow, realistic or unrealistic, perceptive or stupid, alive or dead.

In France and Germany the revival of this methodological controversy has taken place largely in the context of Marxist thought. Sartre (1960) draws upon Marxism and existentialism in order to establish the value of a dialectical method – opposed to positivism – which consists in the interpretation of individual action (man's *project*) in relation to social groups, and of group action in relation to a whole society, itself conceived as part of a historical totality.[4] The debate in Germany has been animated principally by the thinkers of the Frankfurt School, Adorno, Horkheimer and Marcuse, and in the second generation Habermas.[5] Their work has taken up again the issues raised in the earlier methodological writings of Dilthey, Rickert and Weber, but in a more specifically Marxist context, with an emphasis on the place of values in social science, and on the opposition between a 'critical theory' of society (derived from Hegel and Marx) and a positivist, 'value-free' sociology.[6] More recently, as I indicated in the previous chapter, there has been another revival of the criticism of positivism (or more broadly of 'scientism' or 'naturalism') in the theories of social action which assert the importance of 'human agency'; and the influence of phenomenology in forming this new approach will be considered later.

It should be observed here that Dilthey did not aim to create an abyss between the natural sciences and the human studies. In his view they are related, and up to a point they use the same methods of investigation, but the human studies also use *other* methods and they arrive at different results. Subsequently, Weber adopted a similar standpoint, though with a much stronger emphasis on causal explanation, which is expressed throughout his major methodological essay on 'objectivity' (1904), summarized in his definition of sociology as a science which 'attempts the interpretive understanding of social action in order thereby to arrive at a causal explanation of its course and effects' (1921) and exemplified in his study (1904–5) of the relation between Protestantism and capitalism, where he offers a historical causal explanation of the development of Western capitalism[7] and at the same time presents the explanation in such a way that we 'understand' the affinity between the Protestant ethic and the 'spirit of capitalism'.

The controversies about the nature of the social or cultural sciences have continued in diverse forms for more than a century and show no sign of abating, with 'naturalist' or 'anti-naturalist' conceptions in the ascendant at different times. Hughes (1958), in his study of the reorientation of European social thought at the end of the nineteenth century, described the 'revolt against positivism' while recognizing that important centres of positivist thought continued to flourish, notably in Vienna under the influence of Ernst Mach's philosophy of science. The Austro-Marxists, and in particular Max Adler, sustained a neo-Kantian positivist outlook within Marxism (Bottomore and Goode, 1978, Introduction) and there was a considerable revival of positivism in a new form during the 1920s in the work of the Vienna Circle, one of whose leading members, Otto Neurath, in a monograph on empirical sociology (1931), argued forcefully that Marxism was the most complete of all the attempts so far to create what he called 'a strictly scientific unmetaphysical physicalist sociology'. In the past few decades new forms of 'naturalism' have emerged in sociology, often critical of the earlier doctrines of positivism and empiricism, the most important of them being 'structuralism' and 'scientific realism'. At the same time, new 'anti-naturalist' doctrines have been formulated, largely influenced by phenomenology, in particular in the theories of social action and the existentialist Marxism of Sartre and Marcuse. One evident consequence of the latest methodological disputes is that sociological thought has become deeply involved with metatheoretical issues in the philosophy of science, and it will be necessary to consider later in this chapter some of the fundamental questions which have been raised. First, however, I propose to outline some of the principal methods or approaches which seem to have directed sociological inquiry up to the present time.

Historical Sociology

The historical approach has taken two principal forms, the first being that of the early sociologists, influenced by the philosophy of history and afterwards by the biological theory of evolution.

This involves a certain order of priorities in the problems for research and theory, concentrating upon problems of the origins, development and transformation of social institutions, societies and civilizations. It is concerned with the whole span of human history, and with all the major institutions of society, as in the work of Comte, Spencer and Hobhouse, or with the whole course of development of a particular social institution, as in Westermarck's (1926) study of marriage or Oppenheimer's (1907) work on the state. It was argued earlier that there is no 'law of evolution', but that these evolutionist works are in fact historical descriptions and interpretations set in a teleological framework. A severe critic has remarked that 'the evolutionist comparative method had achieved a kind of massive futility in the vast tomes of Frazer and Westermarck' (Leach, 1957), and it is unlikely that sociologists will, in the future, be much concerned with such comprehensive schemes. The work of the evolutionists was bound up with the eighteenth- and nineteenth-century controversies over social progress, and was done under the influence of that 'animating and controlling idea', as Bury (1920) called it. Ginsberg (1932) replied to some detailed criticisms of the evolutionist approach, and justified the concept of evolution in sociology by its relevance to our concern with the overall direction of human development, but such preoccupations have, I think, largely passed away. The present interest in problems of social development is almost entirely focused upon industrialization and economic growth; it is concerned, therefore, with a particular historical phenomenon and also recognizes that there are diverse starting points and lines of development, as well as different possible outcomes. In any case, it is difficult to see that much would be added to our understanding of social changes in the modern world by the attempt to bring them within a comprehensive scheme of the whole process of human social development. It should also be frankly recognized that there are many divergent evolutionary schemes, and that in some cases they acquired a dogmatic character which obstructed thought and research. An obvious example is that 'official' Marxism, now happily less prevalent, in which the 'guiding thread' that Marx followed in an original study of modern capitalism was transformed into a doctrine of social evolution, tediously reiterated and carefully secluded from the kind of misfortune envisaged by Spencer, 'a deduction killed by a fact'.

This is not to disparage the genuine achievements of the early evolutionists. They classified in illuminating ways a mass of ethnographic and historical materials, outlined possible typologies of human society, and made important contributions to our knowledge of social change. On the basis of their work we can distinguish some of the factors which produce change in social structures, and perhaps formulate, in place of a general account of social evolution, laws and conditions relevant to particular kinds of change. In the case of Marx, in particular, his theory of history stimulated a great variety of original and important historical and sociological researches.

In another form the historical approach is characteristic of the work of Max Weber, and of a number of later sociologists influenced by him. Criticizing the Marxists of his time, Weber (1904, p. 68) argued that 'the so-called materialist conception of history, as a *Weltanschauung* or as a formula for the causal explanation of historical reality, has certainly to be rejected. But the advancement of the economic *interpretation* of history is one of the most important aims of our journal.' Here Weber seems to be advocating 'interpretation' as against causal explanation, but as I have shown he himself emphasized the importance of the latter, and his comments on Marx's historical materialism should be seen rather as raising questions about the possibility of a scientific theory of the historical process as a whole. His own historical approach is exemplified especially in his studies of the origins of capitalism, the development of modern bureaucracy, and the economic influence of the world religions. The main methodological features of these studies are that particular historical changes of social structures and types of society are investigated (and these are compared in certain respects with other types of change and of society); and that both causal explanation and historical interpretation find a place. It is also implicit in Weber's work that the general sociological propositions refer only to trends, while their application to particular societies and situations involves historical study in detail (as Marx also contended), and even then finds a limit imposed by human creativity, the results of which neither the sociologist nor the historian can predict.

In more recent sociology, this historical approach directed the work of Mills (1951) and Aron (1958, 1967), both of whom also devoted essays to Weber's methodology (Gerth and Mills, 1947, Introduction; Aron 1936, 1967). There has also been a notable revival of historical sociology in a broadly Marxist framework, in studies of the development of modern societies, or more specifically modern capitalism (Moore, 1966; Wallerstein, 1974, 1980; and for a critical assessment of recent work Holton, 1985), and in the analysis of underdevelopment and development in the present-day world, which will be discussed in a later chapter (Part V below).

The Comparative Method

The comparative method was for long considered the method *par excellence* of sociology. It was first used by the evolutionist sociologists, but its use does not involve a necessary commitment to an evolutionary approach (Ginsberg, 1947, pp. 39–41). Durkheim (1895) first set out clearly the significance of the method. After claiming that sociological explanation 'consists entirely in the establishment of causal connections' he observes that the only way to demonstrate that one phenomenon is the cause of another is to examine cases in which the two phenomena are simultaneously present or absent, and thus to establish whether one does depend upon the other. In many of the natural sciences the establishment of causal connections is facilitated by experiment, but since experiment is impossible in sociology we are obliged, says Durkheim, to use the method of indirect experiment, that is, the comparative method. Even if there is some doubt as to whether causal connections can be rigorously demonstrated in the social field, it may at least be claimed that systematic comparisons are illuminating in so far as they show that certain social phenomena are frequently associated with each other, or frequently occur in a regular order of succession.

But as Radcliffe-Brown (1957, p. 79) observed, 'the comparative method alone gives you nothing. Nothing will grow out of the ground unless you put seeds into it. The comparative method is one way of testing hypotheses.' The difficulties when using the comparative method seem to be due in part to the absence of hypotheses, or of clearly formulated hypotheses, at the outset, and in part to the problem of defining the unit of comparison. Thus, for example, Comte's use of the comparative method to establish his 'law of three stages' is based, not upon a scientific hypothesis but upon a philosophical view of the development of humanity as a whole. A similar criticism may be brought against much of the work of Hobhouse; in *Morals in Evolution* (1906), for example, he is not so much concerned with comparing social institutions in different types of society in order to test limited hypotheses as with tracing the general development of the different social institutions in terms of a philosophical conception of progress.

In defining the unit of comparison, other difficulties arise.

There are formidable problems in comparing whole societies with each other, and a common procedure has been to compare a particular social institution, or the relationship between two institutions, in different societies. Critics of the comparative method, however, have pointed out that what appear superficially to be similar institutions may in fact be very different in the societies being considered, and secondly, that an institution detached from the context of the whole society in which it functions may easily be misunderstood.[8] These objections indicate real difficulties. They can perhaps be overcome by limiting the range of comparisons to societies which are broadly similar, that is, societies of the same type, as determined by a prior classification. The classification itself, of course, involves comparison but only of a very broad and general kind. The detailed comparisons involved in testing hypotheses could then be undertaken with some assurance that the units of comparison were not totally dissimilar or radically misinterpreted. In fact, the comparative method has often been fruitfully used in this way, as a number of studies, some old and some recent, illustrate. Hobhouse, Wheeler and Ginsberg (1915) made a systematic comparative study of some major institutions in tribal societies. Their method was to distinguish in these societies different types of economic system, and then to examine how far variations in the institutions of government and social stratification were correlated with the economic differences. More recently, studies of social stratification and social mobility in industrial societies, sponsored by the International Sociological Association (1954, Vol. 1; 1956, Vol. 3), although conducted independently, were broadly planned to facilitate comparisons and deliberately employed similar methods and categories of analysis.

In neither of these instances is there much attempt to test clearly formulated hypotheses, but the studies are in fact connected with implicit hypotheses, and indeed with more general theories, of social development in the one case and of social class in the other. Some other recent studies concerned with the characteristics of industrial societies have aimed more deliberately at testing hypotheses by comparative inquiry; for example, concerning the degree, causes and consequences of social mobility (Lipset and Bendix, 1959), or the social prerequisites of democratic government (Lipset, 1960). Comparisons have also been made between different capitalist societies (e.g. Dore, 1973), and more broadly between capitalist and socialist countries in the present-day world.[9] As I noted earlier, in discussing historical sociology, there have been renewed attempts to compare the course of development of the modern industrial societies, notably in the study by Moore (1966), and comparative historical investigations have regained the importance which they had for Weber in his studies of the 'economic ethic' of the world religions or of the differences between the occidental and oriental city. But the comparative method can also be used in investigating variations within a particular society, as in Durkheim's classic study (1897) which aims to discover the social causes of suicide by relating the rates of suicide in different social groups to other characteristics of the groups;[10] and a great deal of sociological research in many fields makes explicit or implicit use of such comparisons.

The nineteenth-century advocates of the comparative method regarded it as a method of general application, and Freeman (1873) claimed that 'the establishment of the comparative method of study has been the greatest intellectual achievement of our time', citing in particular its results in the study of language and going on to show how it might be applied in the study of social institutions. As I have indicated, the comparative method has been extensively used in small-scale studies within particular societies, and in cross-national investigations of specific phenomena, with greatly improved techniques of research; but there has also been a renewal of attempts to make much broader comparisons. At these different levels the comparative method clearly remains a fundamental method for any sociology which intends or claims to be a generalizing science.

Functionalism

The functionalist approach, in sociology and social anthropology, appeared initially as a reaction against the methods and claims of the evolutionists. It was a criticism of naive and superficial uses of the comparative method, and of the methods of 'conjectural history', which employed unverified and unsystematic data on contemporary tribal societies for reconstructing the early stages of human social life. It was also a criticism of the intention or claim of the evolutionists to give a scientific account of the whole social history of mankind.

The notion of 'social function' had, of course, been formulated in the nineteenth century, most explicitly by Herbert Spencer. It is based upon an age-old analogy between a society and an organism, but it could be presented in a more scientific guise after the development of modern biology. Spencer, however, like most of those influenced by biological conceptions, was most concerned to work out a theory of social evolution, and his analyses of social structure and social function in the *Principles of Sociology* (1876–96), though of some interest, are brief and unconvincing.[11] It was Durkheim, as Radcliffe-Brown insists,[12] who first gave a rigorous formulation of the concept of social function in *The Division of Labour in Society* (1893) and in *The Rules of Sociological Method* (1895).

Durkheim defined the function of a social institution as the correspondence between it and the needs of the social organism. It has been shown earlier, in considering functionalism as a theory, what difficulties arise from this analogy between society and an organism, and from attempts such as Durkheim's to distinguish between the 'normal' and the 'pathological' functioning of institutions. As a method, functionalism cannot be entirely detached from its theoretical imperfections; yet it has some features which we may consider independently. The extreme form of the functionalist approach, as propagated by Malinowski, was influential in persuading many social anthropologists to devote themselves to the detailed and meticulous description of actual social behaviour in particular societies, and to forsake and condemn both the historical approach and the comparative method. Similar results followed the later adoption of the functionalist approach in sociology, although here, because of the difference in scale of the societies studied, it often meant limiting inquiry to village and community studies. This redirection of interest brought some obvious gains, especially in the study of primitive societies, by its emphasis on field work involving exact observation and recording of social behaviour.

But again, in the work of Malinowski, the functionalist approach involved the dogmatic assertion of the functional integration of every society rather than the tentative formulation of a hypothesis about the interrelation of institutions. Thus every social activity had a function by virtue of its existence, and every activity was so completely integrated with all the others that no single phenomenon was intelligible outside the whole social context. This also meant that it was difficult, if not impossible, to give an explanation of social change in a society except in terms of external influences.

In the course of time the functionalist approach has been modified, so as to become less dogmatic and less exclusive. Merton (1957, ch. 1) presents it as *one* possible approach to the study of social behaviour, and attempts to make it more useful by introducing a number of qualifications. One of these, the distinction between function and dysfunction (which is intended to allow for endogenous social change and to rebut the charge that functionalism expresses a conservative political ideology), however, is no more acceptable than Durkheim's distinction between 'normal' and 'pathological' functioning, from which it derives, since it claims to discriminate scientifically between activities which, in most cases, are matters of moral evaluation. Merton's other important distinction, between manifest and latent functions, is an elaboration of Durkheim's principle that the functions of social institutions are by no means obvious, and are not always what they seem to be. It directs us to more careful, and also more imaginative, study of the actual working of social institutions, as against the received interpretations of their working. It also indicates that any institution may have several functions, any one of which may be of crucial importance in a particular society. This point is made in another way in Merton's criticism of Durkheim's theory of religion. Durkheim claimed to have discovered *the* social function of religion: the expression and reinforcement of social solidarity. This may be so in some societies, but religion has also frequently been a source of discord and social conflict. It follows that historical and comparative inquiry is necessary to discover the range of functions of a social institution – and also that we have to do here with a phenomenon which is very different from 'function' in the biological sense, and which we might do better to call the 'working' of an institution or the 'way in which it is connected with other specific social institutions or activities'. What is most valuable in the functionalist approach is the greater emphasis and clarity given to the simple idea that in every particular society the different social activities are interconnected. It still remains to discover, however, in each case, *which* activities are closely related, and *how* they are related.

Formal Sociology

Formal or systematic sociology also represented a reaction against the evolutionary and encyclopaedic science of the early sociologists. Its originator was Georg Simmel, and it remained very largely a German approach to sociology. The controversy about the status of the social sciences in relation to the natural sciences, and the philosophical school of phenomenology, were important influences upon its development,[13] but its immediate source was the concern to define the field of sociology in relation to the existing social sciences. Simmel's conception of sociology, although it was much discussed in his own time, was not attentively studied by later sociologists until two decades or so ago.[14] It is expounded chiefly in the first essay, 'The problem of sociology' (1908a), in his *Soziologie*, where Simmel argues that sociology is a new *method*, a new way of looking at facts which are already treated by the other social sciences, this new approach consisting in considering the 'forms' of sociation or interaction as distinguished from the historical content; and he justifies this distinction as follows:

> Superiority, subordination, competition, division of labour, formation of parties . . . and innumerable similar features are found in the state as well as in a religious community, in a band of conspirators as in an economic association, in an art school as in a family. However diverse the interests which gave rise to these sociations, the forms in which the interests are realized are identical. On the other hand, an identical interest may be embodied in very different sociations. Economic interest is realized both in competition and in the planned organization of producers . . . The interests upon which the relations between the sexes are based are satisfied by an almost endless variety of family forms . . . (p. 317)

He then goes on to suggest that sociology is also concerned with forms of interaction which have not been studied at all by the traditional social sciences, forms which appear not in major institutions such as the state, the economic system, and so on, but in minor and fleeting relationships between individuals. Nevertheless, Simmel claims, the latter are important in the mass and exhibit society *statu nascendi*.

So far as Simmel's work was continued by later thinkers it became divided between these two aspects. Von Wiese (1933) elaborated the method, and attempted to construct a general sociology on the basis of relational concepts such as 'social distance', 'approach' and 'withdrawal'. More recently some sociologists, among them Homans, came to devote their attention particularly to the 'elementary forms of social behaviour' (or interaction in small groups, which will be discussed further in Chapter 6 below), but their work has often diverged from Simmel's intention by reducing the analysis of the relationships to psychological terms.

Simmel's sociology had a wider range and significance than is suggested by some of the later studies in which his influence is apparent. In his *Soziologie* he was concerned with 'minor' forms of interaction, but in the *Philosophy of Money* (1907) he examined major social relationships, especially in the modern capitalist societies. It also deserves notice that among the propositions that can be produced to demonstrate the character of sociology as a generalizing and explanatory science, several are due to Simmel; for example, those on the incidence and intensity of conflict, and on the effects of changes in the size of social groups. Finally, Simmel's sociology has some affinities with modern structuralism; Tenbruck (1954, pp. 85–6) argued that the forms 'exert constraint in the structuring of actions ... [and] in that they recurrently bring about typical situations and typical changes, forms provide a basis upon which predictions can be made', and Aron (1936) had earlier noted that one consequence of formal sociology was to give the concept of society an increasingly abstract and relational character.

Structuralism

In the 1960s a new 'structuralist' method came into prominence in the social sciences. Originating in linguistics, as I noted in the previous chapter, its main influence was in social anthropology, through the work of Lévi-Strauss; but it is still not clear what that influence may be in the long term. Leach (1967), in his introduction to a symposium on structural analysis – some of which was highly critical of the method – claimed only that Lévi-Strauss 'has provided us with a new set of hypotheses about familiar materials. We can look again at what we thought was understood and begin to gain entirely new insights.' One significant feature of the structuralist method as expounded by Lévi-Strauss is that it aims to discover universal elements in human society, and these elements appear to be basic characteristics of the human mind itself, which are seen as determining the possible varieties of social structure. Thus, in this form at least, structuralism seems to involve a psychological reductionism.

More generally, in so far as structuralism concentrates on universal timeless elements it stands opposed to a historical approach to social structure, and this feature raised particular difficulties in the context of Marxist thought, where the structuralist method came to have its greatest influence, both in anthropology (see Godelier, 1973) and in sociology through the work of Althusser (1965; Althusser and Balibar, 1970), Poulantzas (1968), and Hindess and Hirst (1975, 1977). In the controversies about structure and history, some of which began much earlier (for example, in the exchange between Lévi-Strauss, 1953, and Gurvitch, 1958), Goldmann (1970) proposed a method – which he

called 'genetic structuralism' – that would in some way combine
historical and structural analysis, and in a recent work Habermas
(1981), starting from a very different tradition of social theory,
has also described his approach as 'genetic structuralism'.[15] The
Marxist structuralism inspired by Althusser has been strongly
criticized from several aspects during the past decade, and some
of the major questions that have been raised will be considered in
the next section.

As a particular approach to the study of society, structuralism
had a profound influence on methodological controversies by
reanimating the discussion of the concept of 'social structure',
and the whole debate about the possibility of a natural science of
society (in which context its relation to 'scientific realism' as a
philosophy of social science will be examined later). Since the
1970s there has been a reaction against structuralism in its
broadest sense in a new movement of thought which has come to
be known as 'post-structuralism' or 'deconstruction', but the
influence of the latter has been mainly in the field of literary
theory (Eagleton, 1983) and its influence on the social sciences is
as yet imperceptible.[16]

Marxism

The revival of Marxist thought in the social sciences, as I noted
earlier, is perhaps the most prominent feature of the postwar
development of these disciplines. But as I also observed,
Marxism is by no means a uniform, sharply defined body of
theory and method, and in the past few decades very diverse
conceptions of Marxist method have been formulated, frequently
influenced by ideas which have their source outside Marxism
itself. It is far from easy to find a way through this labyrinth, but a
beginning may be made by distinguishing between two main
currents of Marxist social theory which I have elsewhere called
the 'humanist' and the 'scientific' (Bottomore, 1981).

What characterizes humanist Marxism is its emphasis on
consciousness and action, or 'praxis', rather than 'laws of development'. Thus Lukács (1923) and Korsch (1923) both argued that
Marxism is the expression of the (rational) class consciousness of
the proletariat, and Gramsci (1929–35), in a similar fashion,
opposed Marxism to sociology ('vulgar evolutionism') as the
philosophical world view of the proletariat, containing within
itself 'all the fundamental elements needed to construct a total and
integral conception of the world ... an integral civilization'.

Somewhat later the thinkers of the Frankfurt School developed their 'critical theory' in which the criticism of bourgeois culture and the crucial role of intellectuals in fashioning a new consciousness became fundamental themes. The later critical theory of Habermas has continued these themes (and the opposition to 'scientism') though with some significant modifications, and in particular an increasing attention to economic and political trends. Another important centre of humanist Marxism has been the group of Yugoslav philosophers and sociologists associated with the journal *Praxis*, whose work emphasizes 'human needs' and normative conceptions of 'human nature'.[17]

Scientific Marxism has also developed in a variety of forms, the earliest being the neo-Kantian positivism of the Austro-Marxist school, expounded as the fundamental Marxist method by Max Adler, which produced major studies of changes in the capitalist economy, of nationalism, and of law (Bottomore and Goode, 1978, Introduction). From the 1920s onwards much Marxist work followed a broadly positivist orientation, one theoretically insignificant but ideologically potent influence being Stalin's (1938) codification of historical materialism as a crude evolutionist theory. More interesting, however, is the postwar influence of structuralism, and of the tradition of French rationalism, in Althusser's (1965, 1970) presentation of Marxism as a 'new science' characterized by two fundamental methodological conceptions: first, that science is a theoretical activity in which the crucial factor is the construction of a 'problematic' (i.e. a conceptual or theoretical scheme), and secondly, that explanation consists in disclosing 'the effectivity of a structure on its elements'.[18] The latter notion was particularly important in the attempts to modify, and to resolve the problems inherent in, the strict economic determinism implied or stated by the traditional Marxist model of 'base and superstructure',[19] though it may be questioned how far the notions of structural causality and of the 'relative autonomy' of the different levels of social structure actually go beyond the qualifications already introduced by Engels in the 1890s.[20] The structuralist wave of the 1960s and 1970s has now receded somewhat, but the ideas which it fostered are still important and influential in the social sciences, both for defining the central preoccupation with social structure and for their contribution to the realist philosophy of science.

There have always been Marxists who have argued that the contrast or opposition between a 'humanist' and a 'scientific' approach to the study of human society is actually overcome by Marxism, which has its own distinctive – dialectical – method; or in other words that there are 'three sociologies', as suggested by Benton (1977), who is, however, highly critical of dialectical 'mumbo-jumbo' and founds his own conception of Marxist sociology on materialist and realist theories. The difficulty with presenting Marxist sociology in terms of a unique dialectical method is that dialectics itself has long been a highly contentious issue in Marxist thought, very diversely interpreted, and where its originality is stressed often seeming to diverge widely from Marx's own method which, it can be claimed, has marked affinities with positivism and is at all events naturalistic and empirical (Bhaskar, 1983; Wellmer, 1969, ch. 2).

It will be evident that the general sociological controversies about method have been replicated in a distinctive form within Marxism, while Marxist debates have in turn entered the sociological discussions. In the following section I shall consider a methodological orientation which has been one of the principal sources of the 'humanist' approach to the subject matter of the social sciences.

Phenomenology and Sociology

As a philosophical movement phenomenology, 'with the revival of Existentialism as its offshoot, was the dominant philosophy on the European continent during the first half of this century' (Ayer, 1982).[21] Its influence upon sociology was more widespread and led in various directions. The Frankfurt School thinkers, while critical of Husserl's ahistorical conception of 'essence', and his exclusive analysis of thought and consciousness, found merit in his 'freeing of critical reason from the prejudices contained in the naive and uncritical religion of "facts"' (Adorno, 1940);[22] and Marcuse in particular, it may be claimed, attempted in his earlier writings some kind of synthesis of phenomenology and Marxism.[23] Sartre, in his early philosophical works, concentrated on a phenomenological analysis of 'existential subjectivity', but later on he too was led to attempt a reconciliation of this approach with Marxism, the 'unsurpassable' philosophy of our time. Accepting historical materialism as the only valid interpretation of history Sartre then claimed for existentialism simply the task of 'humanizing' Marxism (which, in its 'official' versions has 'completely lost the sense of what it is to be a man'), and tried to bring together subjective freedom and historical necessity in a new conception of *praxis* (Sartre, 1960).[24]

But the most direct, and especially in the United States the most powerful, phenomenological influence has come from the work of Alfred Schutz, whose starting point was Weber's 'central concept' of subjective meaning, elaborated in the light of Husserl's philosophy (Schutz, 1932). This elaboration involves, as Wolff (1978) indicates, a considerable revision of Weber's ideas, by eliminating his second central concept (causal explanation) and also historical analysis, which constituted a major part of his substantive studies. It may be added that phenomenological sociology, in the form given to it by Schutz, has been generally indifferent to large-scale social and political phenomena; it is above all a method – especially in one of its later manifestations, ethnomethodology – for studying and describing minor social relationships, to some extent in the style of Simmel in some of his work, but never in such an interesting way.

Phenomenology is only one, though an important, element in a broader stream of thought about the methods of the social sciences which has come to be known as 'hermeneutics' – that is, the understanding or clarification of the meaning of (conscious, purposive) human action – the various forms of which have been carefully distinguished by Bauman (1978) and are described by Wolff (1978) as sharing a 'humanistic-culturalistic' rather than a 'positivistic-naturalistic' approach. The basic common assumption, according to Morris (1977, p. 8), is 'that human beings are not merely acted *upon* by social facts or social forces; that they are constantly shaping and "creating" their own social worlds in interaction with others; and that special methods are required for the study and understanding of these uniquely human processes'. A similar view is pithily expressed in the influential book by Berger and Luckmann (1966), but with an emphasis on both aspects of the individual/ society relation, which they call the 'social dialectic': '*Society is a human product. Society is an objective reality. Man is a social product*' (p. 79). This recapitulates the idea formulated by Simmel (see p. 32 above), and highlights a fundamental question of sociological theory and method, particularly in the context of phenomenology: namely, the modes of 'understanding' the subjective meaning of individual action on one side, and the meaning of 'objective culture' or institutional structures on the other, and the sense, if any, in which the objective structures may be regarded as possessing 'causal powers'.

Sociology and the Philosophy of Science

The seemingly irreducible multiplicity of paradigms, and the intense methodological debates, have led sociological thinkers into an increasing involvement with the philosophy of science. Indeed, it may sometimes appear that too little attention has been given, in recent decades, to the development of sociological theory as such, and too much to reflection on the philosophical foundations of any possible science of society. In principle the philosophy of science is a second-order discipline which describes and analyses the practices of already constituted sciences that have produced a body of generally recognized knowledge and are engaged in revising and extending it through a process of *discovery* (as Popper argues). But it may diverge into *prescription*,[25] and this occurs much more easily in the social sciences where there is widespread uncertainty about the validity of the concepts, methods and theoretical schemes that are used. Hence social scientists, unlike natural scientists, may be tempted to think that in order to form concepts and construct theories, and then defend their theoretical stance, they must first establish or adopt some secure philosophical basis for their work; and although this seems to me both mistaken and mischievous as a general view, it may still be acknowledged that the social sciences engender, in specific and distinctive ways, the kind of conceptual questions with which philosophers are concerned, and that it is at least difficult to establish a sharp disjunction between philosophy of science and social theory (Outhwaite, 1983a).

However, there are various philosophies of science, and I propose now to examine briefly what some of the major ones have to say about the problems of sociological theory and method. Benton (1977) distinguishes three alternative 'philosophical foundations' of sociology: positivist, humanist and Marxist (in a realist sense). Positivism has been conceived in various forms, from Comte to the Vienna Circle, and the objections to it are equally diverse (Giddens, 1978). One criticism, which we have already encountered in the work of Marcuse, is that the positivist emphasis on the discovery of 'social laws' excludes the possibility of changing the social system (Marcuse, 1941, pp. 343–4); but this is scarcely the case if, as with Marx, the laws that are formulated are laws of contradiction, conflict and necessary transformations of society. More broadly, it has been argued that a positivist social science implies the notion of a 'scientific politics'; that is to say, it reduces politics to a matter of technocratic policy-making by experts, and leads to a new form of domination. This is the theme of much Frankfurt School theory, notably in the later writings of Marcuse (1964) and in the essays of Habermas (1968–9) on the scientization of politics; and it is summarized in the argument by Fay (1975, ch. 2) that 'a positivist conception of social science contains within itself the idea of technical manipulation'. But positivism has also been strongly defended against such criticisms, for example by Keat (1981, ch. 1), who argues that 'neither scientism nor the positivist view of science entail the possibility of a scientific politics, since both are consistent with the claim that political decisions cannot be made solely by reference to scientific knowledge', and goes on to reject the view common to the Frankfurt School thinkers (Bottomore, 1984b) that the strict separation of 'fact' from 'value' in positivist conceptions of science entails treating judgements about values and social norms, in the manner of Max Weber, as being arbitrary, non-rational and resting only on 'decision': the proponents of positivism 'need not regard politics as inherently non-rational, since they may accept that science is not the only form of human knowledge or rational enquiry' (Keat, 1981, p. 21).

In its wider sense positivism may be equated with 'naturalism' (i.e. the view that a 'natural science of society' is possible), and in this form it has been expounded in several recent philosophies of science, one of the most prominent and influential being 'realism' (Bhaskar, 1978, 1979; Harré, 1979; Keat and Urry, 1982). Benton (1977), in discussing Marxism as his third 'philosophical foundation' of sociology, treats it as a realist philosophy of science, and realism has indeed been closely related to Marxism, and more particularly to Marxist structuralism. Thus Bhaskar (1983) argues that Marx was committed to realism at two levels: to 'common sense realism, asserting the reality, independence, externality of objects', and to 'scientific realism, asserting that the objects of scientific thought are *real structures* irreducible to the events they generate'; and in his study of the modern human sciences (Bhaskar, 1979) he examines in detail the extent to which society can be studied in the same way as nature, through the Marxist conception of an underlying real structure of social life. Similarly, Keat and Urry (1982, Postscript) examine particularly the relation of scientific realism (or 'theoretical realism' in their terminology) to narrower forms of positivism and to Marxist social theory.

Another form of naturalism is Popper's 'critical rationalism', the particular interest of which for sociology is its emphasis on the analysis of individual action and its rejection of 'holism'. Popper rejects 'psychologism' (i.e. the doctrine that 'all laws of social life must be ultimately reducible to the psychological laws of "human nature" '), but notes its

> great merits . . . in propounding a methodological individualism and in opposing a methodological collectivism; for it lends support to the important doctrine that all social phenomena, and especially the

function of all social institutions, should always be understood as resulting from the decisions, actions, attitudes, etc. of human individuals, and that we should never be satisfied by an explanation in terms of so-called 'collectives' (states, nations, races, etc.). (1945, Vol. 2, ch. 14)

Psychologism can be avoided, in Popper's view, by combining the analysis of individual action with an analysis of the 'logic of social situations', and in a later formulation (1974, sect. 24) he says that his method 'consists of constructing a *model of the social situation*, including especially the institutional situation, in which an agent is acting, in such a manner as to explain the rationality ... of his action',[26] and is the outcome of 'an attempt to generalize the method of economic theory (marginal utility theory) so as to become applicable to the other theoretical social sciences'. Leaving aside the more general questions that have been raised about Popper's philosophy of science (e.g. the criterion of 'falsifiability'), there are specific problems with 'methodological individualism'; on one side, what exactly is to be included in the 'model of the social situation' (and from a Marxist standpoint the significance of ownership of the means of production, classes, and class power, which do not usually figure in the 'individualistic' accounts), and on the other side, how one could give a non-social explanation of individual behaviour when the designation of the properties of individuals presupposes a social context (Bhaskar, 1979, ch. 2, sect. 2). Nevertheless, methodological individualism does raise again in a new way the long-standing problem of the relation between human agency and social determinism, and it has an important place in the renewed controversies about this central issue of sociological theory.

A second important 'philosophical foundation', which may be called 'humanist' (Benton, 1977, ch. 6) or 'hermeneutic' (Bhaskar, 1979, ch. 4; Giddens, 1979, ch. 1), has diverse sources, in phenomenology and existentialism, in Hegel and Wittgenstein, and in some forms of Marxist thought (notably the Frankfurt School).[27] The hermeneutic approach is defined by Keat (1981, Introduction) as 'the interpretive understanding of meanings', in which the significance of language or communicative interaction is emphasized, and 'social reality is seen to consist in rule-governed, meaningful activity'; but within this broad 'interpretive' approach there is a considerable variety of positions, carefully distinguished and analysed by Outhwaite (1975), among which three of the most influential may be briefly considered here.

Winch (1963) derived from Wittgenstein's later philosophy an idea of the social sciences (rigorously separated from the natural sciences) according to which they are concerned with meaningful, rule-following behaviour and are based on the method of 'understanding' the rules that constitute 'forms of life', which involves essentially conceptual analysis of internally related elements. Winch's argument has been strongly criticized by Gellner (1968) and Bhaskar (1979, ch. 4); their most general objection is that it seems to take the position that society is entirely conceptual in character, hence a field of study amenable only to philosophical analysis, and that there are features of the real world quite incompatible with such a model. Clearly, the adoption of Winch's position would destroy the greater part of the social sciences as they have actually been practised, reabsorbing them into a pre-scientific philosophy; and most social scientists have happily ignored his prescriptions, the main influence of which has been to focus attention, in the recent methodological debates, on the specific nature of social causation as being conceptually and linguistically mediated (Bhaskar, 1979, pp. 173–4).[28]

A more powerful direct influence upon sociology, as I noted earlier in this chapter, came from the work of Schutz, but phenomenology does not seem to have had a major impact on the philosophy of science[29] and if anything its influence has waned in recent years, as the eclipse of existentialism illustrates. There are some similarities between the views of Schutz and Winch (Keat and Urry, 1982), but the principal development of a philosophy of science inspired in part by phenomenology, and belonging to the 'humanist' tradition, is to be found in the 'critical theory' of Habermas, which is, however, critical both of positivism and of a purely hermeneutic social theory (Fay, 1975, ch. 5; Keat, 1981, Introduction). Habermas's conception of the methodology of the social sciences is extremely complex, and has undergone significant changes over the past two decades; but its main themes can be briefly indicated.[30] Starting from the work of the Frankfurt School, Habermas first elaborated the critique of positivism and then went on to distinguish three 'knowledge-constitutive interests': a 'technical' interest which constitutes the domain of empirical-analytic science, a 'practical' interest in communicative understanding which constitutes the domain of historical-hermeneutic knowledge, and an 'emancipatory' interest which constitutes the domain of self-reflective or critical knowledge (Habermas, 1968). His general argument is that all three kinds of knowledge are involved in the social sciences (unlike the natural sciences), but in his more recent work this theory of knowledge has receded into the background, and greater weight seems now to be given to empirical–analytical knowledge and to substantive issues arising from Marxist social theory (Habermas, 1973, 1976).

The third 'philosophical foundation' of modern sociology distinguished by Benton (1977) is Marxist thought, but his exposition presents Marxism as a realist philosophy of science, and as I have shown earlier it has also been interpreted in many other ways, in terms of other philosophical standpoints. Marxism is not, in my view, a distinctive method, but a body of distinctive theoretical ideas and knowledge which, like other sociological paradigms, should be assessed in two ways: as an accumulated and developing sum of empirical statements, explanations and interpretations; and as embodying a particular conception of the nature of social knowledge (a theory of knowledge) which is properly the object of philosophical analysis. It may be that the Marxist theory is best comprehended – and this is indeed my own view – in terms of a realist philosophy of science, but the latter is not itself Marxist in provenance.

In the light of this review of methodological positions and disputes what are we to conclude about the nature of sociology as a 'science'? My own conception, sustained by a realist philosophy of science and by the body of sociological knowledge that has actually been produced (which forms the substance of the following chapters), is that the discipline is scientific in its method and intention. The important features of method are: (1) that it is concerned with facts, not with value judgements upon them (while recognizing that facts may be, in very complex ways, 'value-impregnated' or 'theory-dependent');[31] (2) that it brings empirical evidence in support of the statements made; (3) that it is objective (in the sense that no one is prevented from basing his statements upon consideration of the evidence). In its scientific intention, sociology aims at (1) exact description, by the analysis of the properties and relations of social phenomena, and (2) explanation, by the formulation of general statements about causal factors or 'powers'.[32] It may be readily admitted that sociology as a scientific pursuit encounters great difficulties in all these respects; but the wide-ranging discussions of the difficulties only confirm that the discipline exists because it strives to be a science – factual, empirical, objective, descriptive and explanatory.

We may conclude here by considering briefly what the sociological methods of inquiry can accomplish and what are their limitations. First, the sociologist can assemble empirical data which make possible more rational judgement upon practical issues than can be derived from traditional ideas. Secondly, he can sometimes make reasonable predictions even when he is not able to give an explanation of the phenomena. Thirdly, he can explain some social phenomena, that is, subsume statements about them under more general statements. It is in the last case that sociological methods have their most serious limitations, because of the complexity of social happenings and the effects of human creativity. It follows that sociological generalizations only describe trends or tendencies. Like all scientific generalizations they are corrigible by the discovery of new instances, but they are *also* corrigible by the *creation* of new instances which results, as Marx maintained, from human beings making 'their own history', even though they do not make it 'just as they please'. Hence when such generalizations are used to account for specific instances they need to be supplemented by detailed historical inquiry which may reveal unique features in the situation.

The ultimate test of the various methodological approaches considered in this chapter is whether they help to generate an adequate general scheme of ideas and procedures which makes possible a more realistic investigation and a fuller understanding of particular social events or processes at different levels of complexity. At the same time the controversies between adherents of different methods may be valuable in their own right in so far as they oblige us to look more closely at the difficulties inherent in our subject matter and induce us to adopt a more critical approach in our own investigations.

Notes to Chapter 3

This chapter deals with methods in the sense of scientific method, or the logic of sociology; not with the techniques of research. On the latter subject there is now a large literature, but the following works provide useful introductions: Moser and Kalton, 1971; Goode and Hatt, 1952; and Galtung, 1967, which is particularly interesting in that it connects research methods with theory construction.

1 See especially Giddens, 1976, who reviews some of the major disputes of the past few decades.
2 Some aspects of this debate are considered in Collingwood, 1946, pp. 165–82.
3 For a lucid account of the positivist view and its critics see Giddens, 1978.
4 See also the useful study of Sartre's Marxism by Desan, 1965.

5   For a sympathetic introduction to their ideas see Held, 1980, and for a more critical account Bottomore, 1984b.

6   The most important early statement of 'critical theory' is that by Horkheimer, 1937; for more recent expositions see Habermas, 1968; Adorno *et al.*, 1969; Wellmer, 1969.

7   The causal explanation is still more prominent in Weber's later account of the origins of Western capitalism, 1923, pt. 4.

8   Malinowski made a major criticism along these lines in his article on 'Culture' in the *Encyclopaedia of the Social Sciences* (1930).

9   There is now a vast literature on this subject, ranging from comparisons of economic performance in terms of 'planned' and 'market' economies to debates about totalitarianism and democracy. One useful general study (though now outdated in certain respects) is Aron, 1961. There is an interesting account of recent comparative research in Eastern and Western Europe, under the auspices of the UNESCO Vienna Centre, in Szalai and Petrella, 1977.

10 For a critical review of Durkheim's study, and an account of later research, see Douglas, 1966, and Giddens, 1966.

11 The most elaborate, and also most fantastic, presentation of the analogy between society and an organism, influenced by Spencer's ideas, is in Schäffle, 1875–8.

12 Radcliffe-Brown, 1952, ch. 9, provides the best short account of the functionalist approach.

13 Dilthey regarded Simmel's sociology with favour because it rejected any attempt to explain the whole cultural life of mankind and aimed, at the most, to establish a typology of social relationships.

14 The revival of interest in Simmel began with the publication of the centenary volume edited by Wolff, 1959, which provided a comprehensive account of Simmel's major writings and translations of some important texts. Among the subsequent literature may be noted the volume of essays edited by Coser, 1965; the excellent introduction by Oakes (noteworthy especially for the thorough discussion of the idea of 'interpretation') to Simmel, 1980; and the short study of Simmel's life and work by Frisby, 1984.

15 See also the general account of structuralism by Piaget, 1968, which expresses a similar standpoint.

16 Nevertheless, the 'deconstruction' practised by Derrida, Foucault and others impinges upon social theory at several points, and it has been rigorously criticized from this aspect by Rose, 1984.

17 On the diverse forms of humanist Marxism see Bottomore, 1975a, ch. 3, and 1984b; Marković and Petrović, 1979; Jacoby, 1983.

18 On Althusser's work see Geras, 1983 and the highly critical account by Kolakowski, 1971. There is a clear and forceful exposition of Marxist structuralism, in relation to anthropological studies, in Godelier, 1973, pt. 1.

19 For a discussion of these issues see Larrain, 1983, 1986, and Giddens, 1981.

20 See especially the comments by Kolakowski, 1971, and also the controversies about the 'relative autonomy' of the state which are discussed in Chapter 9 below.

21 Pivčević, 1970, provides a useful introduction to the work of Husserl and later developments, together with a critical assessment.

22 See Wolff, 1978. But it should also be noted that the work of the Frankfurt School can itself be criticized for its unhistorical character and its pre-eminent concern with consciousness and culture (Bottomore, 1984b), which suggests a closer affinity with phenomenology than has always been recognized.

23 See also his later essay (Marcuse, 1965).

24 See also the commentaries by Desan, 1965, and Pivčević, 1970.

25 As was suggested by Feyerabend in a symposium on Kuhn's philosophy of science (Lakatos and Musgrave, 1970).

26 See also the exposition of 'methodological individualism' by Agassi, 1966, in which the method is critically related to Weber's 'ideal type', viewed as being 'on the borderline between psychologism and institutionalism'.

27 Benton traces the relation of the humanist tradition to Kant and neo-Kantianism, but it should be noted that there was also a neo-Kantian positivism, most evident in Austro-Marxism (Bottomore and Goode, 1978, Introduction).

28 As was argued earlier by Max Adler, particularly in his work on causality and teleology (1904), his essays on problems of Marxism (1913), and his critique of Othmar Spann's sociology (1927), selections from which are translated in Bottomore and Goode, 1978.

29 Its relevance to the social sciences, in this respect, is well set out in Natanson, 1973; and see also the general account by Wolff, 1978.

30 I have discussed it more fully in a general study of the Frankfurt School (Bottomore, 1984b). There is a more comprehensive account in Held, 1980, pt. 2, and a sharply critical assessment in Kolakowski, 1978, Vol. 3, ch. 10). Much can be learned about the development of Habermas's thought from an interview with him published in *New Left Review*, no. 151 (May/June 1985).

31 For further discussion of these issues see Mulkay, 1979, and Bhaskar, 1979, ch. 2.

32 This account follows, in the main, that given by Gibson, 1960, and my general position is close to that expounded by Keat and Urry, 1982.

4 The Social Sciences, History and Philosophy

Sociology does not claim to be a potentially all-inclusive and all-sufficing science of society which might eventually absorb the more specialized sciences; but it *is* synoptic, taking as its field of study all social relations and structures irrespective of their particular content, as Simmel suggested. Nothing social – and more broadly, nothing human – is alien to it. We need, therefore, to consider in somewhat more detail than in the first chapter how it is or should be related to the other social sciences, and to some other disciplines that concern themselves with the human condition. In the following pages I shall discuss its relations first with two other general sciences, social anthropology and psychology, then with two of the special social sciences, economics and political science, and finally with history and philosophy.

Social Anthropology

It is often said that although sociology and social anthropology had quite different origins (one in the philosophy of history, political thought and the social survey, the other in physical anthropology and ultimately in biology) they are now practically indistinguishable. But if one examines the concepts, methods of investigation and analysis, and directions of interest of the two disciplines, it soon becomes apparent that they are still widely separated. Nevertheless, looking at the history of their relations, it can be seen that after an early period of close connection, where individual work could not easily be assigned to one or the other (e.g. Tylor, Spencer, Westermarck), there was a period of extreme divergence when the functionalist approach was generally adopted in anthropology while much sociology (at least in the European countries) continued to be historically oriented and concerned with problems of social development; and that finally, in recent years, there has been a new convergence of the two disciplines. The broad differences between sociology and social anthropology that emerged during the period of divergence can be related to differences in the object of study. Social anthropologists, once field work had become a fundamental requirement, were involved in studying small societies, of a very different character from their own, relatively unchanging, and for the most part lacking historical records. Such societies could be observed as functioning wholes, they could apparently be described and analysed in ethically neutral terms since the anthropologist as an outsider was not involved in their values and strivings,[1] and since they changed little and had few records of past changes a historical approach seemed unnecessary and more or less impossible.

This situation has now radically altered; many if not most tribal societies have been changing under the influence of Western ideas and technology, larger groupings now predominate over tribal societies, and social and political movements are developing which involve the social anthropologist in the same kind of value problems which the sociologist has had to face in studying his own society, or societies of the same civilization.[2] In brief, we can see that the object of study now is societies in the process of economic growth and social change, and that sociologists and social anthropologists work increasingly in Africa and Asia upon the same kinds of problems.[3] It may be added that as tribal societies, regarded as the preserve of the social anthropologist, have more or less disappeared, so to some extent the special prerogatives of the sociologist in studying advanced societies have been challenged, and there is an increasing number of anthropological studies, of the 'little community', kinship groups, and so on, in industrial societies.

One major influence in furthering this *rapprochement* between sociology and social anthropology has been the recent diffusion of Marxist thought, as a result of which some general concepts, such as 'mode of production', have come to be used in both disciplines (Bloch, 1975; Seddon, 1978), and a Marxist structuralist approach has been widely employed (Godelier, 1973). This convergence, on the basis of Marxist theory, is particularly evident in the study of 'developing societies' (Taylor, 1979), which will be discussed more fully in Chapter 17, and in the analyses of 'post-colonial societies' (Alavi, 1983).

More broadly it should be noted that many developing countries, of which India is an example, are 'peasant' or 'agrarian' societies, and as such have long been studied both by sociologists and by social anthropologists (Wolf, 1966; Shanin, 1971). In recent decades the impact of industrialization on village communities and traditional forms of social stratification, and the role of the peasantry in political movements, have been intensively studied in ways which bring together the work not only of sociologists and social anthropologists, but also of political scientists and economists, and the gap which existed between the various social sciences has often been successfully bridged.

Psychology

The problem of the relation between psychology and sociology, and of the status of social psychology in relation to both, is difficult and unsettled. There are two extreme views. J. S. Mill (1879, Vol. 2, p. 469) believed that a general social science could not be considered firmly established until its inductively established generalizations could be shown to be also logically deducible from the laws of mind: 'Human beings in society have no properties but those which are derived from, and may be resolved into, the laws of the nature of individual man.' Durkheim (1895), on the other hand, made a radical distinction between the phenomena studied by psychology and sociology respectively. Sociology was to study *social facts*, defined as being external to individual minds and exercising a coercive action upon them; the explanation of social facts could only be in terms of other social facts, not in terms of psychological facts.

> Society is not a simple aggregate of individuals; the system formed by their association represents a specific reality possessing its own characteristics . . . In short, there is the same discontinuity between psychology and sociology as there is between biology and the physico-chemical sciences. Consequently, whenever a social phenomenon is directly explained by a psychological phenomenon one can be sure the explanation is invalid. (pp. 103–4)

The opposed views of Mill and Durkheim still have their partisans today, but they have also been strongly criticized,[4] and most sociologists seem to have adopted various intermediate positions. Some would hold that many sociological generalizations can be more firmly established by being related to general psychological laws, but that there may also be sociological laws *sui generis* (Ginsberg, 1934, ch. 1). Similarly, Nadel (1951, ch. 8) argued that some problems posed by social inquiry might be 'illuminated by a move to lower levels of analysis – psychology, physiology and biology'. Under Dilthey's influence, many German sociologists, including Max Weber, came to hold the view that even where strictly sociological explanation is possible, the sociologist gains an additional satisfaction or conviction in being able to 'understand' the meaning of individual action, which must also be the starting point of his analysis. Such understanding was conceived in terms of 'common sense psychology', but neither Dilthey nor Weber was hostile to the development of a scientific psychology in a broad sense, and Weber was sympathetic to some of Freud's ideas. Freud's psychology, although it emphasized the role of individual and biological factors in social life, nevertheless recognized that the innate impulses were transformed in various ways before they became manifest in social behaviour; and in the work of the post-Freudian school – especially Karen Horney and Erich Fromm – the influence of society in moulding individual behaviour is given still greater prominence. In an early essay Fromm (1932) set out to establish a relation between psychoanalysis and Marxism by locating the family in a historically created class structure, and his later concept of the 'social character' was intended precisely to relate individual psychological characteristics to the characteristics of a particular social group or social system (Fromm, 1942, Appendix).

Other thinkers, however – and notably the Frankfurt School, who had themselves started out from a Marxist position – have criticized such sociological interpretations of psychoanalysis, and their own studies concentrated upon the psychology of the individual (Adorno *et al.*, 1950) and the idea of a universal human nature (Marcuse, 1951). The latter notion has indeed been prominent in diverse forms of recent social theory; for example, in the theories of action which emphasize the importance of 'human agency', though without much direct recourse to psychological analysis (Dawe, 1978), and also in the structuralism of Lévi-Strauss in so far as this aims to relate universal structural characteristics of human society to universal structures of the human mind itself.[5]

In spite of the wide recognition that sociological and psychological explanation may complement each other, the two disciplines are not, in practice, closely associated, and the place of social psychology, which ought to be especially close to sociology, is still disputed. It is easy to say that social psychology is that part of general psychology which has a particular relevance to social phenomena, or which deals with the psychological aspects of social life. In fact, all psychology may be considered 'social' in some degree, since all psychic phenomena occur in a social context which affects them to some extent; and it becomes difficult to mark out even roughly the boundaries of social psychology. This means that social psychologists have usually felt a closer association with general psychology than with sociology, have been bound to a particular method (emphasizing experiment, quantitative studies, etc.) and have often ignored the structural features of the social milieu in which their investigations are conducted. This divergence between sociology and social psychology can be illustrated from many fields. In the study of conflict and war there have been mutually exclusive sociological and psychological explanations (Ginsberg, 1947, ch. 9; UNESCO, 1957; and see also the discussion in Chapter 12 below). In studies of social stratification, the psychological approach seems to have produced a particular account of class and status in subjective terms, which is contrasted with the sociological account in terms of objective factors, rather than systematic investigation of the psychological aspects of a significant element in the social stucture. The 'psychology of politics' hardly deserves to be mentioned, so remote does much of the writing appear to be from the most obvious facts of political structure and behaviour. In almost every field of inquiry it could be shown that psychology and sociology constitute for the most part two separate universes of discourse.

There have, of course, been many declarations in favour of closer association between the two disciplines, and some attempts to bring them together. One body of ideas which subsequently became influential is that propounded by G. H. Mead (1934), who made a distinction between the 'I' (the individual organism) and the 'Me' (the 'generalized other' formed by social experience) and argued that 'we are individuals born into a certain nationality, located at a certain spot geographically, with such and such family relations, and such and such political relations. All of these represent a certain situation which constitutes the "me"' (p. 182). But Mead concentrated on the analysis of the 'self' rather than social structure, so that although his concept of the 'me' resembles Fromm's 'social character', it is not linked in the same way with a distinct theory of society; and the later influence of Mead's thought, in one version of 'interactionism' (Fisher and Strauss, 1978), has been more psychological than sociological.

Another attempt to relate social psychology to sociology (Gerth and Mills, 1954), which owes something to Mead's work, does pay much closer attention to social structure, however. The authors argue that:

> The social psychologist attempts to describe and explain the conduct and motivations of men and women in various types of societies. He

asks how the external conduct and inner life of one individual interplay with those of others. He seeks to describe the types of persons usually found in different types of societies, and then to explain them by tracing their inter-relations with their societies. (p. 3)

The field of study of social psychology is thus the interplay between individual character and social structure and, as Gerth and Mills say, it can be approached either from the side of biology or from the side of sociology. In the recent past the trouble has been that those coming from either side remained largely ignorant of what was being done on the other side, and were enclosed in their own world of academically approved terminology and method. Gerth and Mills attempt to bridge the gap by using the concept of 'role' as the key term both in their definition of the person and in their definition of institutions. Social role represents the meeting point of the individual organism and the social structure, and it is used as the central concept in a scheme which makes possible an analysis of character and social structure in the same terms.

This is quite similar to Fromm's conception of the 'social character', and Gerth and Mills, like Fromm, take up again the fundamental problem of the relation between the individual and society, which was earlier examined by Ginsberg (1921) in an illuminating study dealing with the respective influence of instinct and reason in social life, with theories of the 'group mind', and with problems of public opinion and organized group behaviour. More recently Hirst and Woolley (1982) have explored these issues in the light of debates about nature and culture, cultural relativism and rationality, in an attempt 'to illustrate the influence of social relations on human activities, abilities and attributes in a way which challenges established "common sense" prejudices and which does not reject, but makes use of, biological and psychological knowledge', and they define their approach as being 'equally opposed to concepts of a fixed "human nature" and to extreme sociologistic views of humans as infinitely malleable social products'. Marxism has strongly influenced some recent studies: for example, Sartre's (1960) exposition of 'dialectical reason', which aims to clarify the relation between structural conditions and intentional actions and to incorporate in Marxist theory elements of the individualistic and humanist outlook of existentialism; and Sève's (1974) construction of a psychology of personality which is integrated with historical materialism.

However, these sociological and Marxist excursions into the psychological field seem as yet to have had little impact on the mainstream of work in social psychology, which remains largely committed to statistical and experimental inquiries that are chiefly concerned with the individual or with simple aggregates of individuals and have only a distant relationship with sociology. In practice, it must be recognized, sociology and psychology offer alternative accounts of behaviour, and as the recent literature shows there are substantial difficulties in bringing them together in any comprehensive and rigorous theoretical scheme.

Economics

Alfred Marshall, in an inaugural lecture delivered in Cambridge in 1885, referring to Comte's idea of a general social science, observed: 'No doubt if that existed Economics would gladly find shelter under its wing. But it does not exist; it shows no signs of coming into existence. There is no use in waiting idly for it; we must do what we can with our present resources' (Pigou, 1925, pp. 163–4). Would this judgement still be true today? I do not think so. Sociology is now firmly established as a social science, and sociologists have both critically examined the limitations of economic theory and made contributions to the study of economic phenomena. On the other side, economists themselves seem to have become weary of the frequency with which the phrase 'other things being equal' recurs in economic analysis, and some of them have attempted to go beyond description (which forms a large part of most economic textbooks) or deduction from a small number of simple presuppositions about human behaviour. They have also had to face the difficulty that many major economic phenomena – transformations of the structure of production or of the whole economic system, economic crises, the incidence of industrial conflict, levels of productivity and growth – are resistant to any purely economic analysis.

We may consider first those critical studies which suggest that economics cannot be an entirely autonomous science. One early work of this kind is that by Simiand (1912), a collaborator of Durkheim in the *Année Sociologique*, who persuasively advocated a sociological approach to economic problems, arguing that the 'first principles' of economics are hypotheses which need to be tested by sociological research, rather than being taken as the starting point for deductive reasoning that leads to conclusions no more certain than the original hypotheses. A later study (Löwe, 1935) examines the 'significance and limits of pure economics' and discovers two sociological principles which underly (as logical conditions) the classical laws of the market – 'economic man', and competition or mobility of the factors of production – and goes on to suggest fruitful areas of co-operation between economics and sociology. Also to be considered here are those works which treat economic relationships within the framework of general sociology. The classic study in this field is Weber's *Economy and Society* (1921–2), which aimed 'to analyse certain of the simplest sociological relationships in the economic sphere' through an examination of the main features of rational economic action; while a later work (Parsons and Smelser, 1957) set out, on Weberian lines but in a more ambitious way, to present economic theory as a part of general sociological theory. A number of other studies have expounded principles of economic sociology or anthropology (Goodfellow, 1939; Herskovits, 1952), and particularly, in recent years, from the perspective of Marxist theory (Seddon, 1978).

A second contribution of sociology to economic analysis is to be found in the studies devoted to specific problems of economic life. Thus Simiand (1932) examined empirically the relation between wage and price levels and advanced a sociological theory of wages; and a later work in the same field (Wootton, 1955), after analysing the inadequacies of the classical economic theory of wages, went on to present a sociological account of the determinants of wage and salary differentials, based upon the data for Britain. There are numerous other sociological studies of this kind (some of which will be referred to in Chapter 8 below), perhaps the best known being those concerned with the theory of the firm, such as Veblen's classical work (1904) on business enterprise, and many later studies of the modern corporation by sociologists or sociologically minded economists (Berle and Means, 1934; Schumpeter, 1942; Galbraith, 1971; Scott, 1979).

Finally, in their studies of the general characteristics of different economic systems sociologists have investigated aspects of economic behaviour that are either neglected or treated in a cursory fashion by economists. Among the major writings of this nature are, clearly, the works of Marx and later Marxist political economists, of Weber on the origin and development of capitalism (1904–5, 1923), of the German historical school of economics and in particular Sombart (1902), and more recently the studies of 'industrial' or 'post-industrial' society (Aron, 1962; Touraine, 1969). Other writings have dealt with the later development of capitalism (Schumpeter, 1942; Mandel, 1975) and with socialist economies (Horvat, 1982), but there is also a considerable literature on earlier types of economic system, including tribal economies (Mauss, 1925; Firth, 1939; Seddon, 1978).

It may reasonably be claimed that sociology and economics, which were closely associated at their origins, for example, in the work of Quesnay and Adam Smith, of Saint-Simon and Marx, but then diverged, have begun to come closer together again in recent years. Two factors account for this tendency. One is the change in the character of present-day economic systems: on one side, the greatly enhanced importance of planning in national economies and to some extent in the world economy; on the other, the emphasis on economic development, and the social factors which affect it, in the countries of the Third World. This has resulted in a shift of interest towards macro-economic questions, and an approach which more closely resembles that of classical political economy, one form of which was Marx's economic theory. The revival of Marxist political economy – which is inherently sociological by virtue of its fundamental concepts of modes of production, forms of society, classes and historical transformations – is a second factor which has brought about a certain convergence of economics and sociology, as is noted in some recent literature (Horowitz, 1968; Kühne, 1972). There has also been convergence in a different fashion through the diffusion of economic models of the 'rational actor' into other social sciences (Barry, 1970; Farmer, 1982; Hindess, 1984).

Although economics and sociology remain widely separated in many respects there are now, as I have indicated, important areas of overlapping interest, in problems of economic growth and rival forms of economic organization, and in the debates about method which raise many of the issues – about structural analysis, methodological individualism and so on – which I discussed in the previous chapter. It seems likely, therefore, that a more fruitful interaction will develop in the future between economists and sociologists, to the benefit of both disciplines.

Political Science

Traditional political science had three main aspects: *descriptive* (accounts of the formal organization of central and local govern-ment, and historical studies of the development of such organi-zation); *practical* (the study of current problems of organization, procedure, etc.); and *philosophical* (the mingling of descriptive and evaluative statements in what is called, in a broad sense, political theory). In most political science of this kind there was little attempt at generalization beyond that which is involved in an elementary classification of the types of political regime, largely in terms of their formal characteristics.

The influence of sociology in the field of political studies has been to direct attention towards *political behaviour* as an element in a social system, rather than the formal aspects of political systems considered in isolation, and to encourage attempts at scientific generalization and explanation. This influence began to be felt at an early stage in the development of sociology, largely through the work of Marxist thinkers, since in Marx's theory political institutions and behaviour are closely linked with the economic system and with social classes, and have to be analysed in this general social context. It was Marxist thought which provoked, at the end of the nineteenth century, the political sociology of Michels, Max Weber and Pareto, and thus led directly to the modern studies of political parties, elites, voting behaviour, bureaucracy and political ideologies.

Another, quite different, sociological influence is to be seen in the development of behaviourism in American political science. This may be dated roughly from Charles Merriam's Presidential Address to the American Political Science Association in 1925, in which he said: 'Some day we may take another angle of approach than the formal ... and begin to look at political behaviour.' Thereafter, a behaviourist approach developed rapidly at the University of Chicago, and although it was aided in the 1930s by an influx of European scholars who brought their own socio-logical orientation, derived from Michels and Weber, it took quite a different direction from that in Europe, being largely unaffected by Marxist ideas and having as its principal aim the creation of a strictly 'scientific' (and to some extent, quantitative) discipline (Crick, 1959).

In recent years the sociological influence upon political science has become even more marked. First, there has been a direct borrowing of explanatory schemes and models; for example, of functionalism, as in Almond and Coleman (1960), or of the idea of a 'social system', as in Easton (1965). There has also been a renewal of Marxist sociological ideas, inspired on one side by the revolutions in developing countries (Gough, 1967; Miller and Aya, 1971) and on the other side by the new social movements which have emerged in the advanced industrial countries (Botto-more, 1979, ch. 2).

Studies of the political development of 'new nations', because of the nature of the problems which are raised, have brought together the work of political scientists and sociologists (and frequently of anthropologists as well). The forces at work, and the changes which take place, in a peasant society, in a society made up of tribal units, or in a society organized in a caste system belong more to the sphere of knowledge of the sociologist and anthropologist than to that of most political scientists; and to study political processes in such societies requires extensive borrowing from these other disciplines.

Finally, there has been a continuation and extension of work in fields which I have already mentioned: on political parties and pressure groups, on the relation between class and politics, on elites, and on the processes of government and administration. A particular feature of these studies is that they are carried out increasingly on a comparative basis, with the aim of arriving at some general statements about political organizations and political action, at least within the limits of a specific type of society (e.g. Western industrial society).

The orientation of theory and research in political science over the past decade has made it increasingly difficult to distinguish the subject from political sociology. The behaviourist approach which was characteristic of American political science has been severely criticized and in part abandoned, but other general schemes of thought have been adopted from sociology – including those derived from Marxism – and the objects of research are increasingly sociological in kind. Some differences perhaps remain. Political scientists still devote a good deal of attention to the formal structure of government, which sociologists sometimes unwisely neglect. Political theory is still seen by many as being closely associated with philosophical ideas and problems, but here the case of sociology is hardly different, as I shall argue later; though its philosophical connections have not, perhaps, been so fully recognized. In general, we may say that the trend in political science, unlike that in economics, has been towards a merger with sociology in many of the most significant fields of research.

History

In an earlier chapter some account was given of that view of the social or cultural sciences which regards them as being of the same general character as history, or even as being a kind of historical study. This seems to me mistaken. Sociology and history may overlap in one area but diverge widely in another. I should like here to examine briefly some aspects of their relationship.

The first and simplest point is that the historian frequently provides the material which the sociologist uses. The comparative method often requires, and historical sociology always requires, data which only the historian can supply. It is true that the sociologist must sometimes be his own historian, amassing information which had not previously seemed worth collecting, but he cannot always be so – time does not allow.

But the historian also uses sociology. Until the present century it was perhaps from philosophy that the historian took his clues to important problems, as well as many of his concepts and general ideas; these are now drawn increasingly from sociology. Indeed, we can see that modern historiography and modern sociology have both been influenced, and in similar ways, by the philosophy of history. The latter established the conception of historical periods, and thus bequeathed to historiography theoretical ideas and concerns which were entirely absent from the work of the earlier narrative historians, the chroniclers and annalists. It bequeathed to modern sociology the notion of historical types of society, and thus the first elements of a classification of societies. In much recent historiography and sociology it seems to me that the same basic framework of reference, to types of society, is employed. In the historical field, the connection is most evident where economic and social history (especially the latter) are concerned. It is worthy of note, for instance, that the editors of one of the leading journals of social history, the *International Review of Social History*, defined the scope of the review in its first number in the following terms: 'Social history is taken to mean the history of estates, classes, social groupings regardless of name, seen both as separate and as mutually dependent units' (1956, vol. 1, pt 1, p. 4). In only slightly different terms this could also define an important part of historical sociology. At the present time there is, in several countries, evidence of co-operation and even trespassing into each other's territory by sociologists and social historians. The *Annales* school of historians in France, originating in the work of Lucien Febvre and Marc Bloch, and continued pre-eminently by Fernand Braudel, has established a new kind of 'structural history' which is close to sociology and strongly influenced by Marxist conceptions.[6] Braudel's study (1979) of civilization and capitalism is a massive contribution to the investigation of the origins and development of capitalism; a field of inquiry which has long been shared by historians and sociologists (Holton, 1985). Another example of a wide-ranging debate involving both disciplines is to be found in the discussions of the significance of the frontier in American history (Hofstadter and Lipset, 1965). There has also been a notable convergence of interests in some more specialized areas: in Britain, for example, in historians' accounts of the social structure of nineteenth-century towns, or the characteristics of the medieval peasantry or the eighteenth-century nobility, and in sociologists' studies of the social history of various professions (Briggs, 1966).

In what ways, then, do historiography and sociology differ? It used to be said that the historian describes unique events, while the sociologist produces generalizations; but this is far from being always the case.[7] The work of any serious historian abounds in generalizations, while many sociologists have been concerned with describing and analysing unique events or sequences of events. Perhaps we should say that whereas the historian usually sets out to examine a particular sequence of events, the sociologist usually begins with a generalization, which he proposes to test by the examination of a number of similar sequences of events. In short, the intention is different. But even this qualified distinction is not wholly true. It depends very much upon the kind of historiography (e.g. it is most true of diplomatic history) and the kind of sociology (where it is most true of comparative studies). Making a still weaker distinction, we might say with Trevor-Roper (1957, Introduction) that the historian is concerned with the interplay between personality and massive social forces, and that the sociologist is largely concerned with these social forces themselves.

The more the distinction is refined to take account of the actual work of historians and sociologists the clearer it becomes that the two disciplines cannot be radically separated. They deal with the same subject matter – human beings living in societies which undergo historical changes – sometimes from different points of view, sometimes from the same point of view. As a recent study (Burke, 1980, p. 13) has suggested: 'Each discipline can help to free the other from a kind of parochialism.' And certainly two of the least parochial of sociologists, Marx and Weber, were themselves historians of no mean stature.

Philosophy

Sociology originated largely in a philosophical ambition: to account for the course of human history, to explain the social crisis of the European nineteenth century, and to provide a social doctrine which would guide social policy. In its recent development sociology has for the most part abandoned such aims; and some would say that it has abandoned them too completely. However this may be, there remain connections between sociology and philosophy in at least three respects.

First, as I showed in the previous chapter, sociology is closely associated – and increasingly so – with the philosophy of science, because of the difficulties peculiar to the human sciences in concept formation and theory construction.

In the second place, there is a close relationship between sociology and moral and social philosophy. The reality studied by sociology and other social sciences – human social relations – embodies meanings and values which are expressed both in conceptions of the world, social doctrines and political ideologies, and in actions governed by choices and decisions. The sociologist, it has generally been claimed, studies values, the courses of action influenced by them, and the structures created, modified or sustained by individual and collective action, as *facts*; and makes a sharp distinction between the description or analysis of social facts and any kind of valuation of them. This, at least, is the view taken by Durkheim (1895), Weber (1904, 1917), Marx (in some interpretations, such as that of the Austro-Marxists), and in very diverse ways by positivists, structuralists and adherents of the realist philosophy of science (Keat and Urry, 1982, ch. 9 and Postscript). On the other side it has been argued in various forms that the fact/value distinction cannot be upheld in the social sciences; that knowledge, science and truth are themselves human values, that the social scientist as a member of society cannot fully detach himself from the reality he studies, that descriptions and theories of social phenomena necessarily involve evaluations (Strauss, 1953; Taylor, 1967), and in some conceptions of social action, that human agency can only be understood as moral action and moral community (Dawe, 1978), or that knowledge of human social life is constituted not only by empirical-analytic sciences, but by the interpretation of communicative interaction and by self-reflection based upon an emancipatory interest (Habermas, 1968). The complex and continuing debate about fact and value, closely related to controversies in the philosophy of science, is a principal meeting ground of sociology and philosophy; and any kind of sophisticated theory construction in sociology is inconceivable without some comprehension of the philosophical issues that have been raised.

Finally, it may be held that sociology leads on directly to philosophical thought. This was, for instance, the view of Durkheim (1909), who wrote: 'I believe that sociology, more than any other science, has a contribution to make to the renewal of philosophical questions ... sociological reflection is bound to prolong itself by a natural progress in the form of philosophical reflection'; and in his own study of religion (1912) such a prolongation can be seen in the transition which he makes from a discussion of the social influences upon the categories of thought to an epistemological discussion. Mannheim was concerned with a similar question, and considered that his sociology of knowledge had implications for epistemology, which he stated in detail (Mannheim, 1952, pt 5). More recently Habermas (1981) in a considerably revised exposition of 'critical theory' which gives greater weight to the construction of an empirical science, has suggested that 'the social sciences can enter into a cooperative relationship with a philosophy which assumes the task of contributing to a theory of rationality' (Vol. 2, p. 584).[8]

In this context it is worth reiterating that much of what is important in sociological thought originates in philosophical reflection as well as being prolonged in it; and the point I made earlier about the value of connection between political science and political philosophy applies over a much wider field. Sociological research may easily become trivial and useless if it ignores the larger problems of social life which are formulated in philosophical world views and social doctrines. The immense influence of Marxist thought is due in great measure to the fact that it brings together a sociological theory and a social philosophy or 'philosophical anthropology'; and in less obvious ways the work of other major sociological thinkers, especially Max Weber,[9] has been influential for the same reason.

The preceding discussion should have given some indication of the ramifications of sociological thought, of its contribution to other disciplines and at the same time its dependence on them. Sociology, as a synoptic social science, provides models of social structure within which particular social relations can be located and analysed; it depicts and suggests explanations of broad tendencies of development in different forms of society and in different epochs; it draws attention to, and elucidates, connections between social phenomena which more specialized inquiries would ignore (e.g. between religious beliefs and economic behaviour, between social stratification and political events, between law and other forms of social control); it brings out the significance and the problematic character of the relation between the individual as an organism and as a social being which other human sciences tend to ignore; and more generally it raises a series of fundamental methodological issues for debate. But sociology, as I have shown, also depends heavily upon the knowledge produced by other disciplines, and sociologists themselves, for the most part, need to specialize in particular fields of inquiry (in law, religion, economics, politics); the more they do so, within the framework constituted by conceptions of social structure and social action, the more fruitful and illuminating are their researches likely to be.

Notes to Chapter 4

1 It was, however, a very limited, and often deceptive, neutrality. Many of the societies studied were under colonial rule, and the anthropologist might well find himself obliged to take sides, with or against the colonial rulers.

2 For example, both sociologists and anthropologists have to face the fact of revolutionary movements in the Third World. A radical view of these issues is vigorously expounded by Kathleen Gough, 1967.

3 See, for example, the study by Lloyd, 1982, which examines the applicability of the concept of 'social class' in studies of Third World countries, and in particular the question of whether an urban proletariat is emerging there.

4 On Durkheim's 'sociologism' see Lukes, 1973, pp. 16–22, and for a critical discussion of Mill and 'psychologism' Popper, 1945, Vol. 2, ch. 14.

5 See also the recent discussions of 'human needs', which are usefully reviewed and criticized in Springborg, 1981, and the article on human nature by Marković, 1983.

6 For a comprehensive account of the *Annales* school and its influence see the issue of *Review*, vol. 1, no. 3/4 (1978).

7 Although it has been claimed recently (Stone, 1979) that there is a certain revival of 'narrative history' which is descriptive rather than analytical and focused on man, not circumstances. Hobsbawm, 1980, in commenting on this claim, emphasizes the extent to which historians still believe in 'the possibility of generalizing about human societies and their development'.

8 See also the discussion of this question by MacIntyre, 1971, ch. 21.

9 For a comparison of Weber and Marx from this point of view, see Löwith, 1932.

Notes on Reading for Part I

I The Background of Sociology

Bierstedt, Robert, 'Sociological thought in the eighteenth century' (1978).
Bramson, L., *The Political Context of Sociology* (1961).
Bryson, Gladys, *Man and Society: The Scottish Inquiry of the Eighteenth Century* (1945).
Bury, J. B., *The Idea of Progress* (1920). An excellent short account of the philosophy of history and theories of progress from the seventeenth century up to the theories of Comte and Spencer. See also the study by Kenneth Bock, 'Theories of progress, development, evolution' (1978), which relates the idea of progress to more recent theories.
Durkheim, Émile, *Montesquieu and Rousseau: Precursors of Sociology* (1960). The first essay examines Montesquieu's conception of social types and social laws, and his use of the comparative method.
McLellan, David, *The Young Hegelians and Karl Marx* (1969).
See also the general histories of sociological thought mentioned in the text (Chapter 1 above).

II Sociological Theories and Methods

1 *General*

Benton, Ted, *Philosophical Foundations of the Three Sociologies* (1977).
Durkheim, Émile, *The Rules of Sociological Method* (1895).
Giddens, Anthony, *New Rules of Sociological Method* (1976).
Keat, Russell and Urry, John, *Social Theory as Science* (1982).
Mill, J. S., *A System of Logic* (1879), bk 6, 'On the logic of the moral sciences'.
Weber, Max, *The Methodology of the Social Sciences* (1949). English translation of some of Weber's most important methodological essays.

2 *Historical and Comparative Methods*

Aron, Raymond, *Introduction to the Philosophy of History* (1938). Section III examines the notions of historical and sociological causation.
Bloch, Marc, 'A contribution towards a comparative history of European societies' (1928).
Durkheim, Émile, *The Rules of Sociological Method* (1895), ch. 6.
Ginsberg, M., 'On the concept of evolution in sociology' (1956).

Hofstadter, Richard, *Social Darwinism in American Thought* (1955).
Popper, Karl R., *The Poverty of Historicism* (1957).
Radcliffe-Brown, A. R., 'The comparative method in social anthropology', in Radcliffe-Brown, 1958, ch. 5.

3 *Functionalism*

Demerath, N. J. and Peterson, R. A. (eds.), *System, Change and Conflict* (1967).
Malinowski, B., *A Scientific Theory of Culture and Other Essays* (1944).
Merton, R. K., *Social Theory and Social Structure* (1957), ch. 1, 'Manifest and latent functions'.
Radcliffe-Brown, A. R., 'On the concept of function in social science', in Radcliffe-Brown, 1952, ch. 9.

4 *Structuralism*

Bottomore, Tom and Nisbet, Robert, 'Structuralism', in Bottomore and Nisbet, 1978.
Lévi-Strauss, Claude, *Structural Anthropology* (1958), chs. 2, 15.
Piaget, Jean, *Structuralism* (1968).
Robey, David (ed.), *Structuralism: An Introduction* (1973).

5 *Marxism*

Avineri, S., *The Social and Political Thought of Karl Marx* (1968a).
Bottomore, Tom, *Marxist Sociology* (1975).
Bottomore, Tom, 'Marxism and sociology', in Bottomore and Nisbet, 1978.
Godelier, Maurice, *Perspectives in Marxist Anthropology* (1973).
Goldmann, Lucien, *Marxisme et sciences humaines* (1970).
Löwith, Karl, *Max Weber and Karl Marx* (1932).
Schumpeter, J. A., *Capitalism, Socialism and Democracy* (1942), ch. 2, 'Marx the sociologist'.

6 *Phenomenology and Hermeneutics*

Bauman, Zygmunt, *Hermeneutics and Social Science* (1978).
Luckmann, Thomas (ed.), *Phenomenology and Sociology* (1978).
Outhwaite, William, *Understanding Social Life* (1975).
Wolff, Kurt H., 'Phenomenology and sociology' (1978).

III The Social Sciences, History and Philosophy

1 *Economics*

Hardach, Gerd and Karras, Dieter, *A Short History of Socialist Economic Thought* (1978).

Löwe, Adolf, *Economics and Sociology* (1935).
Perroux, François, *Économie et société* (1960).
Smelser, Neil J., *The Sociology of Economic Life* (1963).
Weber, Max, *Economy and Society* (1921), pt 1, ch. 2.

2   Political Science

Barry, Brian, *Sociologists, Economists and Democracy* (1970).
Bottomore, Tom, *Political Sociology* (1979).
Giddens, Anthony, *Politics and Sociology in the Thought of Max Weber* (1972).
Lipset, S. M. (ed.), *Politics and the Social Sciences* (1969).

3   Psychology

Billig, Michael, *Ideology and Social Psychology* (1982).
Fromm, Erich, 'The method and function of an analytic social psychology: Notes on psychoanalysis and historical materialism' (1932).
Fromm, Erich, *The Fear of Freedom* (1942), Appendix, 'Character and the social process'.
Ginsberg, M., *The Psychology of Society* (1921).
Mead, G. H., *Mind, Self and Society* (1934).
Sève, Lucien, *Man in Marxist Theory and the Psychology of Personality* (1974).

4   History

Braudel, Fernand, 'Histoire et sociologie' (1955).
Briggs, Asa, 'History and society' (1966).
Burke, Peter, *Sociology and History* (1980).
Carr, E. H., *What is History?* (1961).
Ginsberg, M., 'History and sociology' (1932).
Lipset, S. M., *Revolution and Counterrevolution* (1968), ch. 1.

5   Philosophy

Bhaskar, Roy, *The Possibility of Naturalism* (1979).
Durkheim, Émile, *Sociology and Philosophy* (1924).
Myrdal, Gunnar, *Value in Social Theory* (1958).
Ryan, A., *The Philosophy of the Social Sciences* (1970).
Wright, G. H. von, *Explanation and Understanding* (1971).

PART II

Population and Social Groupings

5   Population and Society

The phenomena of population constitute the domain of a special science, demography, which was one of the earliest of the modern social sciences to emerge. It played an important part in the eighteenth century in stimulating the growth of other social sciences, and it has remained closely associated with sociology. The demographer, as soon as he goes beyond measurement and calculation to study the causes or consequences of population changes, differential fertility and mortality, and similar problems, enters the domain of sociology. The most interesting demographic questions have always involved social factors of the kind with which sociology is concerned.

At the same time, it is evident that for the sociologist the size, distribution and qualities of the population are basic data. Durkheim made population size one of the principal elements in that branch of sociology which he called morphology. Societies can be classified according to their *volume* and *density*. By volume Durkheim meant the number of 'social units' (i.e. individuals) in the society. By density he meant the 'number of social relationships' in a society; distinguishing between *material density* influenced by the concentration of population, the growth of towns and the development of means of communication, and *moral density*, which is measured by the number of individuals who effectively have relations (not merely economic but cultural relations) with each other. Durkheim thought that increased volume generally brought about increased density, and that the two factors together produced variations in social structure. In *The Division of Labour in Society* (1893) he set out to show that increase of population produces, through the division of labour, a change from a type of society based upon 'mechanical solidarity' to one based upon 'organic solidarity'. Recent sociology has been little concerned with such general relationships between population size and type of social structure, though the problem has been taken up in a different way by Riesman (1950).

More usually, in sociology and other social sciences, population size and population changes have been related to particular aspects of social structure or to particular social phenomena. Thus, a number of sociologists have been concerned with the relation between demographic changes and war.[1] There have also been many discussions of the relations between demographic change and economic activity, from Malthus's *Essay on Population* up to recent studies of the influence of population movements upon economic growth, as in Lewis (1955, ch. 6).[2]

It has always been recognized that there is a reciprocal relation between population and social structure; that is, that the social structure influences population changes as well as being affected by them. Indeed, sociological study in this field has been predominantly concerned with the social influences upon population size. There is now a very large literature on these questions, and it is impossible to do more than summarize the principal results. The actual problems vary, of course, from one type of society to another. In the 1940s and 1950s Western demographers and sociologists were chiefly interested in the social factors influencing the decline in the birth rate, which slowed down the rate of population growth in the interwar years and at one stage seemed likely to produce stationary or even declining populations. The various social factors have been distinguished and analysed in a large and increasing literature, which includes Alva Myrdal (1945), Glass (1940), and the study made in Britain by the Royal Commission on Population (1949). The Royal Commission's report lists and examines some of the influences which promoted family limitation; the references are to British experience but very similar influences must have been operative elsewhere. It is clear that improved methods of birth control and more general knowledge of such methods were imporant in making family limitation easy. But the *desire* to limit family size had other causes, among them the resentment felt by women to excessive child bearing and the greater emancipation of women which allowed their protest to become effective, the declining importance of the family as a productive unit and the increasing economic burden of children (as a result of restrictions upon child labour and the spread of compulsory education), the growth of new wants which competed with the desire for children, the raising of standards of parental care and especially the desire of parents to give their children the best possible start in life. The last influence was itself affected by the opportunities for social mobility in an expanding economy and a less rigidly stratified society; only by limiting births could each child be given the fullest opportunities to rise in the social hierarchy. Many studies have demonstrated the advantages, in this respect, of the child from a small family. One other feature of family limitation is apparent from all studies: it began in the higher strata of society, and only gradually spread to the lower strata. This could be explained partly in terms of differences in knowledge, but the adoption of birth control in the higher strata still needs some other explanation. One well-known study (Banks, 1954) suggests that, in Britain, family limitation in the middle classes began with the economic recession of the 1870s which threatened their new standards of comfort. Its gradual extension to other strata could then be explained by imitation of a social model, as well as by the perception of the advantages of a small family in the competitive struggle for economic and social advancement.

More recently the concern with population size has taken a different direction, with the emphasis now upon the rapid growth of population, in particular countries and in the world as a whole. In 1950 the world population was 2,500 million, by the early 1980s it had reached 4,500 million, and it is expected to reach 8,000 million by the year 2025, though there are some indications of a deceleration of the rate of growth. In the industrial countries, during the period of rapid growth, the main concern was with its social consequences, with congestion and environmental damage.[3] In the developing countries, on the other hand, the major problem has been seen as the impact of population growth on economic development and social welfare. Gunnar Myrdal (1968), in his large-scale study of poverty in the countries of South Asia, observed that there had been much discussion a decade or so earlier about whether these countries were faced with a problem of excessive population growth, and concluded: 'By now, it is commonly recognized that all the countries in the region have entered a critical phase of sharply accelerated population growth, and that the prospects for successful economic development are crucially related to population trends' (Vol. 2, pp. 1389–90).

Indeed, in all the less developed regions of the world, since the end of the Second World War, there has been a population explosion determined by high fertility and declining mortality as a result of improvements in nutrition and medical care. Thus in India the population increased from 315 million in 1941 to 436 million in 1961, and 684 million in 1981. But the most rapid growth is taking place in Africa, where it is expected that the population will more than treble from 470 million in 1980 to 1,544 million in 2025, increasing the already evident threat of extreme poverty and starvation, and in Latin America, where the population is projected to more than double from 364 million (in 1980) to 865 million in 2025 (Tabah, 1982). One consequence of these differential rates of population growth is that the distribution of the world's population will be very different in 2025; Europe, which now accounts for about 10 per cent of the total, will have only 6.4 per cent in 2025, while the share of Africa will rise from about 11 per cent to nearly 19 per cent. In general, the population of the less developed regions is likely to increase from about 75 per cent to 83 per cent of the world total (Tabah, 1982, p. 180).[4]

Clearly, such rapid population growth has important consequences for economic development, particularly, as Myrdal argued (1968, Vol. 2, ch. 28), through the skewed age structure which produces a high dependency burden and diverts resources from productive investment to the provision of extensive social services.[5] These consequences have to be seen in the context of other influences on the economic development of Third World countries, which will be considered in a later chapter (Chapter 17 below), but their independent significance is now generally recognized, as is shown by the widespread adoption in less developed countries of population policies designed to reduce fertility, and by the international support for such policies. In India there have been several attempts over the past few decades to limit family size, but these have had as yet relatively little impact, and the population is still expected to increase to some 1,234 million by the year 2025. The most drastic policy, as yet, to reduce fertility is that adopted in China, where a combination of financial incentives and a massive publicity campaign aims to establish the single-child family as a norm, but the present population of 1,000 million may still increase to almost 1,500 million by 2025 (though this is a considerably lower rate of increase than that in most Third World countries). In recent years fertility has declined in many countries, and some demographers have anticipated a fairly rapid convergence to replacement level fertility during the next few decades, but Demeny (1982) concludes his account of population policies on a cautious note:

> no claim can be made that such convergence is assured or even highly probable ... Sixty years of socialist rule have left the fertility of the Muslim populations of the Soviet Union virtually unchanged. In 1980, World Bank projections anticipated that Iran's population would stabilize at 102 million; in 1981 the figure was changed to 140 million, presumably to reflect the hostility of the new regime towards family planning. In sub-Saharan Africa and in much of South Asia, fertility decline has not yet begun, and no solid theory explains why it should start tomorrow. If the past is a guide to the future, a significant reversal of recent Chinese fertility trends is by no means impossible ... Policy makers' ability to influence fertility trends remains tenuous within countries; the proposition applies with double force to the global scene. (pp. 226–7)

Demographers and sociologists have been concerned with the distribution of the population, as well as with its size. The outstanding phenomenon of recent times, in Western Europe and America, but increasingly throughout the world, is the growing concentration of population in urban areas, as one effect of economic development. This has encouraged studies of the conditions favourable to the growth of towns, and attempts to construct a typology of towns by comparative inquiry. It has been recognized that the existence of towns depends in the first place upon the existence of an economic surplus, and that their growth is affected by the growth of industry, trade and administration. The relations between urban centres and the countryside have varied from one type of society to another. At most times towns have been dependent upon the country, they have not been dominant in the society as a whole, and they have been subject to variations in size and importance. Only in modern industrial societies has urbanism become the predominant way of life. In many societies, too, there has been conflict between town and country; Pirenne (1925) showed the role played by the European towns, especially in the fourteenth to sixteenth centuries, in dissolving feudal social relationships and challenging the feudal social order. Ibn-Khaldûn, in his *Muquaddima (An Introduction to History)* (1377–1404), contrasted tribal with city life and outlined a theory of conflict between sedentary city dwellers and nomadic tribes to explain the rise and decay of Arab cities.

In another aspect demography has extended into human geography and urban sociology, with the study of social phenomena in relation to the concentration of population. The major characteristics are the existence of distinct zones and sectors in urban areas, distinguished by economic, class, ethnic and other features, differences between urban and rural areas in respect of such phenomena as crime, divorce and suicide, and also more generally in the types of social relationship and in cultural outlook. The notion of zones and sectors in the city was developed largely by Park, Burgess and others belonging to what came to be called the 'ecological school' in the USA. Park (1926) distinguished many different regions within the American city:

> There are regions . . . in which there are almost no children . . . regions where the number of children is relatively very high: in the slums, in the middle class residential suburbs . . . There are other areas occupied almost wholly by young unmarried people . . . There are regions where people almost never vote . . . regions where the divorce rate is higher than it is for any state in the Union, and other regions in the same city where there are almost no divorces . . . There are regions in

which the suicide rate is excessive; regions in which there is ... an excessive amount of juvenile delinquency.

Another member of this school, H. W. Zorbaugh, in *The Goldcoast and the Slum* (1929) studied two extreme regions of Chicago and contrasted their social characteristics. More recent ecological studies of the city have attempted to provide a general classification into regions combining the notion of concentric zones with that of sectors. One example is Chombart de Lauwe's (1952) study of Paris, in which concentric zones, elementary units (districts) and the distribution of social classes are treated separately and then combined in a general typology.

Urbanism as a way of life has attracted many students. It is evident from a number of indices – divorce rates, suicide rates, and so on – that there are important differences between town dwellers and those who live in rural areas; and the greatest divergence is to be found in the great cities. Sociologists have attemped to explain these differences in terms of the social situation and group affiliations of town dwellers, but also in terms of the culture of cities. Simmel, in a classical study (1903), showed how city life favoured the intellectual development of the individual and produced a distinct type of person. A more pessimistic account is that of Lewis Mumford, in his *Culture of Cities* (1940), where the pathological features of city life are emphasized; the isolation of the individual, the fragmentation of his social contacts and his personality, the growth of ennui, frustration and a sense of futility. The principal features of urban life were examined in a more general way in Wirth's frequently cited essay, 'Urbanism as a way of life' (1938).

In recent years the study of urban life and urbanization has taken some new directions. One is the attention given to the rapid growth of very large cities and mega-cities, both in the industrial countries and in the developing countries. A study of India's urban future (Turner, 1962) gave some startling 'high estimates' for the growth of Calcutta, Delhi and Bombay up to the year 2000, and although these now seem exaggerated, the growth of large cities in the developing world will nevertheless be very rapid. As Tabah (1982, p. 199) writes:

> By the end of the century, the developing world will have huge urban conglomerates of a sort never encountered in the industrialized countries. According to United Nations projections for the year 2000, the population of Mexico City will be 31 million; Sao Paulo, 26 million; Shanghai will hold 24 million; Beijing, 21 million; Rio de Janeiro will have 19 million inhabitants and Bombay and Calcutta will have 17 and 16 million respectively.

Africa is as yet less urbanized than other developing regions, but has the highest rate of urban population growth, with some cities doubling in size every six or seven years. Tabah concludes that the situation is rapidly deteriorating in the Third World countries: 'In the large metropolises, uncontrolled migration concentrates the inequalities in regional development, creates crises in municipal finance and ultimately erects obstacles to the development of the entire country.'

Of course, the growth of towns creates opportunities as well as problems. The towns are centres of innovation, of economic growth and political change, and the new values and attitudes which develop there may have an important influence upon the rural population. A study by Dube (1955) shows the influence of Hyderabad upon the political structure, caste relations, and social attitudes in a village within its orbit; and another study by Bailey (1957) of a village in the Orissa hills more remote from an urban centre shows how even there the influence of the urban economic system leads to a growth of commerce, while the development of national administration results in a breakdown of political isolation, with important effects upon village organization. At the same time, however, rural attitudes affect the towns, for a large proportion of the town population consists of recent immigrants from the countryside. As Lloyd (1967, p. 110) observes of some African towns:

> Here the individual may escape the restraint of his family and kin, of traditional elders and tribal values. How many men choose to do so is another matter; for ... the African townsman tends to remain in a very close relationship with his kin and community of origin.

A study of immigrant workers in Bombay (Prabhu, 1956) revealed a similar attachment to the villages of origin. Nearly half the sample studied visit their village once a year, and almost all would have liked to pay more frequent visits. Those with families send them on visits to the village as often as they can. The immigrant workers live between two cultures, urban and rural, and urban values are not yet completely predominant, though they are gradually tending to prevail: in the city women acquire greater freedom, there are changes in dress and in the value of education, and caste rules are not so strictly observed. On the other hand, the joint family continues to be highly regarded; it still has a function in the city as a system of mutual aid, and it maintains the link between the immigrant and his village.

These are phenomena of a period of transition – which may be very long – in the largely peasant societies of Asia and Africa which are now becoming more industrial and urban. Since 1945 a number of Third World countries, and notably China, have been transformed by peasant-based revolutions, inspired and led largely, it is true, by urban intellectuals, but this is less likely to be the case in the future. There may not be, as yet, a Third World proletariat in a Marxist or Weberian sense (Lloyd, 1982), although it is much more evident in Latin America than in Africa; but there is, in the rapidly growing cities, a large mass of the semi-urban poor living in 'shanty towns', who form one important basis for new radical movements, and there is a growing middle class, sections of which may well adopt reformist or radical policies. The class structure and political movements in the developing countries will be examined more fully in later chapters.

In the industrial countries, although some attention is given to the growth of mega-cities, the principal focus of recent interest has been elsewhere. These countries are overwhelmingly urban, and the urban/rural contrast has lost much of its significance; instead, partly under the influence of Marxist theory (especially in the work of Castells, 1976), attention has come to be concentrated on 'collective consumption' (e.g. housing, transport, land use) and its determination by the 'urban social structure', that is to say, mainly by the class structure, by urban politics, the 'local state' and the various 'managers' of urban resources (Pahl, 1975). Studies of this kind merge into more general analyses of property ownership, class relations, and political conflict, and they will be considered later in that context.

The qualitative aspects of population attracted much attention in the nineteenth century, and were studied from two points of view. First, there were the attempts to distinguish between societies in terms of racial or national characteristics, conceived as innate qualities. This approach has generally been abandoned, for little connection has been found between race as defined by physical anthropology and intellectual or temperamental qualities of interest to the psychologist and sociologist. Modern sociological studies of race are concerned with race prejudice and race relations,[6] while national character, so far as it is studied at all, is conceived as the outcome of the institutional arrangements of a society, or of the 'culture pattern' reflected in individual upbringing, or most frequently as the product of both together.

Secondly, there were studies of presumed innate differences between individuals or groups within society, which were connected with elite theories (Pareto) or arose from concern about the effects of differential fertility on the quality (physical or intellectual) of the population. In England, the latter concern crystallized in the eugenics movement started by Francis Galton, and continued by Karl Pearson from his position as professor of eugenics in the University of London. All this was connected with a wider intellectual movement of 'social Darwinism' influenced by the unfortunate biological analogies formulated by Herbert Spencer. Eugenics has little connection with modern sociology, but one particular problem continued to arouse discussion: namely, the assumed relation between differential fertility and the trend of national intelligence. It was supposed that the declining birth rate in the upper strata of society, resulting in their failure to reproduce themselves, might bring about a gradual decline in the general level of intelligence. The problem was reviewed by Burt (1950), and investigated in a comprehensive survey conducted by the Scottish Council for Research in Education (1949, 1953) which showed a rise in the general level of intelligence between 1932 and 1947. It seems likely that the improvement in general welfare was an important factor in the result shown by the Scottish survey. Differential fertility may, of course, play a part in determining the cultural characteristics of a society: for example by changing the relative size of various ethnic or religious groups in the population, but its effects on the *quality* of a population (in terms of intelligence, or of even more nebulous features such as the honesty, enterprise, public spirit, and so on of the citizens) appear to be slight or non-existent when compared with the influence of improved standards of nutrition, medical care, housing and education.

The preceding discussion will have indicated that population questions have a great complexity, which arises from the numerous and diverse interrelations between population and social structure. As Marx (1857–8) observed in his critique of the method of political economy 'the population is an abstraction . . . a chaotic conception of the whole' unless we take account of its distribution among classes, town and country, different branches of production, and so on. This is the theme of the following chapter.

Notes to Chapter 5

1 For a general discussion of different theories of war, including demographic theories, see Quincy Wright, 1942.
2 There is a general survey of population theories with reference to 'optimum population' and resources in Penrose, 1934.
3 See, for a discussion of the situation in Britain, Taylor, 1970. The

essay by Eversley in this volume, however, makes the point that population management is a very inexact science, largely because of unforeseen fluctuations in the birth rate. In Britain the birth rate has been falling again since 1964, and in due course there could conceivably emerge pro-population rather than anti-population campaigns.

4 There are also considerable differences within regions. A recent demographic survey by the EEC estimates that in the ten member states (as of 1985) population will increase by only 2.5 per cent up to the year 2000 (and in Germany and Denmark will actually decline), whereas in the two new member states, Spain and Portugal (from 1986), it will increase by 14–16 per cent. It may be noted briefly here that changes in relative population size may also have political consequences; see Demeny, 1982, pp. 210–12.

5 For a review of various approaches to the economic effects of population changes, see Myrdal, 1968, Vol. 3, Appendix 7. See also the discussion in Demeny, 1982, pp. 213–16.

6 There is an excellent short survey of the sociological aspects of race in Firth, 1956, ch. 1. In the 1960s the whole subject of race and racism began to be studied in a more critical way, partly under the influence of political movements such as the Black Power movement in the USA (Barbour, 1968; Carmichael and Hamilton, 1967). There is a good collection of critical essays in Zubaida, 1970.

6   *Types of Social Group*

The distribution of the population in social groups, and the size, number and characteristics of such groups, are important features of the structure of a society. According to Ginsberg (1939), 'The description and classification of the principal types of social groups and institutions' make up the study of social structure, and Firth (1956, p. 98) writes similarly that 'The social structure of a community includes the different types of groups which the people form and the institutions in which they take part'. It is difficult, and probably undesirable, to make a rigid distinction between the study of groups and the study of institutions, since the latter (which may be defined as enduring patterns of behaviour) arise out of the activities of groups and in turn guide and constrain those activities. But for purposes of exposition it is convenient to deal first with the different groupings which may be found either in all societies or in particular types of society.

We may begin by distinguishing between social groups proper, and the looser associations which have been termed by some writers 'quasi-groups'. A social group may be defined as an aggregate of individuals in which (1) definite relations exist between the individuals comprising it, and (2) each individual is conscious of the group itself and its symbols. In other words, a social group has at least a rudimentary structure and organization (including rules, rituals, etc.), and a psychological basis in the consciousness of its members. A family, a village, a nation, a trade union, or a political party is a social group in this sense. A quasi-group, on the other hand, is an aggregate which lacks structure or organization, and whose members may be unaware, or less aware, of the existence of the grouping. Social classes, status groups, age and sex groups, crowds, are examples of quasi-groups. But these examples suggest that the frontier between groups and quasi-groups is fluid and variable. Quasi-groups may become more organized themselves or may give rise to organized social groups, as for example, the working class in modern capitalist society has brought into existence the 'labour movement', the feminine sex group has created the 'women's movement', and generations have sometimes produced 'youth movements'; or they may become fully organized and institutionalized, as is the case with age groups which become formal 'age sets' in some tribal societies.

Social groups can be classified in a variety of ways. We may consider first the character of the relationship between the members. The best-known distinction here is that first proposed by Tönnies (1887) between *Gemeinschaft* (community) and *Gesellschaft* (society or association). Community is defined as 'intimate, private, and exclusive living together', and Tönnies gives as examples of groups based on this type of relationship the family or kin group, the neighbourhood (rural village), and the group of friends. Association is defined as 'public life', as something which is consciously and deliberately entered upon; and Tönnies mentions as examples principally those groups which are concerned with economic interests. Two major criteria are used by Tönnies in defining community and association. First, in communities individuals are involved as complete persons who can satisfy all or most of a wide range of purposes in the group, while in associations individuals are not wholly involved but look to the satisfaction of specific and partial ends. Secondly, a community is united by an accord of feeling or sentiment between individuals whereas an association is united by a rational agreement of interest.

In Tönnies's own work the distinction between community and association was applied both to the social groups within a society, and to societies themselves. In the latter sense it has an affinity with some other distinctions between two broad types of society, which will be discussed in the next chapter. As applied to social groups it resembles the distinction made by Cooley (1909) between 'primary groups' and others (which have been called 'secondary groups' by later sociologists):

> By primary groups I mean those characterized by intimate face-to-face association and co-operation. The result of intimate association, psychologically, is a certain fusion of individualities in a common whole, so that one's very self, for many purposes at least, is the common life and purpose of the group ... it involves the sort of sympathy and mutual identification for which 'we' is the natural expression. (p. 23)

Cooley's definition of the primary group, as has been pointed out (Davis, 1948, ch. 11), implied three conditions: physical proximity of the members, smallness of the group, and the enduring character of the relation. Tönnies, on the other hand, intended his distinction to apply to all social groups, but it is worthy of note that his examples of 'community' (family, village, group of friends, medieval town) also imply, in varying degrees, these three conditions.

Thus we have a number of criteria which can be applied in the classification of social groups: the end for which the group exists, the emotional or intellectual character of the relations between members of the group, the personal or impersonal nature of their relations, the size of the group, and its duration. Some of these factors have received more attention than others. The size of groups has been studied from different points of view. Simmel (1902), in a well-known essay, examined the relationship between the number of members and the structure of a group. In another study (1903), he showed how the concentration of population in cities changed the nature of social relationships. Other sociologists have discussed the general problem of changes in the scale of social organization. Durkheim, as we saw earlier, explained the division of labour and the emergence of a new form of society based upon organic solidarity by the growth of population. Hobhouse took increase in scale as one of his criteria of social development, but at the same time examined the repercussions of this increase upon other factors in development. It is evident that one major problem of social life has been that of establishing and maintaining social solidarity in large groups, where the intimate relationships of primary groups are impossible (Homans, 1948, ch. 16; Angell, 1941).

Recent studies of social groups have taken a number of different directions. There have been several attempts at a more systematic typology of groups. One of the most comprehensive is that of Gurvitch (1957, Vol. 1, ch. 5) who proposed fifteen criteria of classification: content, size, duration, rhythm, proximity of members, basis of formation (voluntary, etc.) access (open, semi-closed, closed), degree of organization, function, orientation, relation with the inclusive society, relation with other groups, type of social control, type of authority, degree of unity. This scheme of classification incorporates many of the distinctions which we have already discussed; it has still to be seen whether the additional criteria make possible a typology in which the significant differences between groups would be revealed.

A second approach is best illustrated in the study of primary groups by Homans (1948) who suggests a number of reasons for studying such groups, among others that 'perhaps we cannot manage a sociological synthesis that will apply to whole communities and nations, but it is just possible we can manage one that will apply to the small group'. Thus he aims at formulating generalizations which will apply to small groups, on the basis of re-analysis of data from a number of detailed empirical studies. The emphasis throughout is upon the similarities between groups, and not upon the differences, as it is in the case of attempts at a typology. While the analysis and interpretation of material provided by the original studies are often illuminating, the resulting generalizations are disappointing in respect of their importance or probable validity. It is difficult to take seriously the proposition that 'the more frequently persons interact with one another, when no one of them originates interaction with much greater frequency than the others, the greater is their liking for one another and their feeling of ease in one another's presence' (p. 243). The example given of relations between brothers is unfortunate, since it is between siblings that some of the most violent antipathies arise, and the portrayal of family life in the novels of Ivy Compton-Burnett seems equally plausible.

Homans's work, however, revived interest in the study of primary groups, and the interest was reinforced by other developments such as Moreno's (1953) sociometric studies. One of the attractions of small group studies is the possibility of experiment, and some useful if limited work has been done on these lines; for example, in the experiments on group leadership (Argyle, 1957, pt 2, ch. 5).

Homans makes clear that the study of small groups is only one possible approach to the study of society, but in other cases enthusiasm for small group analysis has led to distortion. The work of Cooley already foreshadowed one error; he wrote that primary groups 'are primary in several senses, but chiefly in that they are fundamental in forming the social nature and ideals of the individual', and again that 'they do not change in the same degree as more elaborate relations but form a comparatively permanent source out of which the latter are ever springing ... [they] are springs of life, not only for the individual but for social institutions' (Cooley, 1909, pp. 23, 26–7). Cooley and some recent sociologists seem to imply that it is possible to move directly from the study of small groups to the study of inclusive societies. This is associated with the view that small groups have a determining influence upon social life. Yet all the evidence points to the opposite conclusion. Historically considered, small groups have been shaped by society much more than they have shaped it. The modern Western family, for example, is the product of industrialism, and the transformation of the rural village is likewise due to more general changes in the inclusive society.

Another approach to the study of groups is that suggested by

Redfield (1955), who justifies the choice of this area of study in much the same terms as Homans. He writes:

> The little community has been chosen because it is a kind of human whole with which students of man have a great deal of experience, and because it is easier to develop a chain of thought in relation especially to villages and bands than to try to do so also in relation to personalities and civilizations and literatures. (p. 2)

Moreover, 'the small community has been the very predominant form of human living throughout the history of mankind ... One estimate is that today three-quarters of the human race still live in villages'. Redfield defines the little community by four characteristics: (1) *distinctiveness* – 'where the community begins and where it ends is apparent'; (2) *smallness* – 'either it itself is the unit of personal observation or else, being somewhat larger and yet homogeneous, it provides in some part of it a unit of personal observation fully representative of the whole'; (3) *homogeneity* – 'activities and states of mind are much alike for all persons in corresponding sex and age positions; and the career of one generation repeats that of the preceding'; (4) *self-sufficiency* – it 'provides for all or most of the activities and needs of the people in it. The little community is a cradle-to-the-grave arrangement' (p. 4).[1]

Having defined the object of his study Redfield goes on to analyse it in terms of the general concepts which have been applied to all types of groups and inclusive societies: ecology, social structure, life cycles, personality, cultural values, social change. His study clarifies, and suggests modifications of, some of these concepts. In the later chapters he examines directly the problem we have raised about the relation between small groups and the larger communities, up to the inclusive society, within which they exist. First, there are different types of relation. The Siriono Indians are a very distinct and self-sufficient group, having only slight contact with other Indian bands and avoiding contacts with white men. On the other hand, the relations of the Nuer (described by Evans-Pritchard) with the larger society can be represented by a diagram of concentric circles. The village of Chan Kom (studied by Redfield) has more complex relations with the state of Yucatan and with Mexico as a whole. There is 'a complex aggregation of settlements to which any one village ... would be related in a number of kinds of relationships and functions' (p. 122).

Redfield suggests that we need 'a recognition of a series or range of kinds of communities according to their degree of independence from city, manor, national state, or other centre of a different or more developed mode of living' (p. 124). He goes on finally to propose, with reference to peasant communities or partly urbanized rural communities, a distinction between abstract kinds of living; between folk society and civilization. Here he encounters the preoccupations of earlier sociologists, Maine, Tönnies and Durkheim, whose dichotomies I have already briefly discussed.

The problem of the relationship between social groups and the inclusive society can be put in another form. We may ask how, and to what extent, types of societies can be distinguished in terms of the social groups which exist within them. There is one very familiar distinction, between 'primitive' and 'civilized' societies, in terms of the *number* and *diversity* of the social groups within them. Spencer, and especially Durkheim, made use of this characteristic in their classifications of societies. Tribal societies are no longer regarded by anthropologists as simple, but they are certainly less differentiated. The contrast which Durkheim draws in *The Division of Labour in Society* (1893) is broadly accurate; and there is much to be said for his association of individualism with increasing social differentiation, ultimately based upon the more extensive division of labour.

Another approach would be to classify societies in terms of the predominant types of social groups. This has been attempted in various ways. One of the best-known distinctions is between societies in which primary groups predominate and those in which secondary groups predominate. Since Tönnies's original distinction between 'community' and 'association', many sociologists have employed this criterion, with slight variations in meaning. It is a commonplace of modern sociology to refer to the impersonal, rationalized and segmentary relationships between individuals in urban industrial societies, and to contrast these with the relationships existing in tribal and non-industrial societies. Yet all such dichotomies appear much too simple; for in spite of all the sociological research we still know relatively little, in detail, of the social relations in modern societies and can still be surprised by the importance of kinship and other primary groupings (see Chapter 10 below). Perhaps a more useful classification would result from identifying the specific types of group which are characteristic of different societies. This can be illustrated by a comparison between India, as an example of an agrarian society, and a Western industrial society.

It is not difficult to identify the major types of group in traditional Indian society; they are the village community, the caste group, and the joint family. By contrast, the types of group which are characteristic and important in Western industrial societies seem to be the economic, occupational and political organizations, social classes, and the nuclear family. In addition, the inclusive society itself (as a nation–state) has much greater significance. What can be said about Indian society in terms of these characteristic groups? I shall refer later to the joint family (Chapter 10) and the caste groups (Chapter 11). Here it will be useful to say something about the village community, which has often been regarded as the most important feature of the social structure, and which raises many issues in connection with the process of urbanization which I discussed earlier.

The early studies of the Indian village emphasized its self–sufficiency and its stability. Self–sufficiency meant that the village had its own political, as well as economic, institutions. 'The village communities are little republics, having nearly everything they want within themselves, and almost independent of any foreign relations. They seem to last where nothing else lasts' (Metcalfe, 1855). Maine (1861, p. 153) referred to the Indian village constitution as

> the least destructible institution of a society which never willingly surrenders any one of its usages to innovation. Conquests and revolutions seem to have swept over it without disturbing or displacing it, and the most beneficent systems of government in India have always been those which have recognized it as the basis of Indian administration . . .

Marx (1867, ch. 12), emphasizing the economic self–sufficiency of the village, found in this a clue to the unchanging character of Indian and other Asian societies:

> The simplicity of the organization for production in these self–sufficing communities that constantly reproduce themselves in the same form, and if destroyed by chance, spring up again on the same spot and with the same name – this simplicity supplies the key to the secret of the *unchangeableness* of Asiatic *societies*, an unchangeableness in such striking contrast with the constant dissolution and refounding of Asiatic *states*, and the neverceasing changes of dynasty. The structure of the economic elements of society remains untouched by the storm clouds of the political sky.

Indian villages remained in certain respects self–sufficient and autonomous until well into the nineteenth century, when the development of capitalism under British rule began to exert its influence.[2] The more rapid industrialization and urbanization since 1947 have certainly brought about great changes. A number of village studies give some indication of the nature of these changes. Dube (1955) has shown the increasing influence of Hyderabad town upon the village of Shamirpet (twenty-five miles away) through the development of transport, making for greater mobility, and the attraction of urban educational facilities. Other influences are the government welfare agencies, the activities of nationwide political parties, and national development programmes (Dube, 1958). The outcome of these more intensive contacts with the larger society is a change in the social and political hierarchy of the village; wealth, education and position in the government service are among the new sources of prestige and influence. Redfield and Singer, in their foreword to a collection of studies on India's villages (Marriott, 1955), observed that: 'In village India the traditional landmarks lose their outlines – caste, joint family, festivals, and religious beliefs. The school, the political party, the movie, the community plan, begin to reach even remote villages.' At the same time the traditional groups do not disappear, and they reappear, sometimes in a modified form, in urban areas. The joint family survives in Indian towns, and caste associations are formed which provide housing, employment and other welfare services for their members.

Similarly, in the new African states, village, kinship and tribal bonds remain strong, and as Lloyd (1967, ch. 12) suggests, 'tribalism' develops as an urban phenomenon (in much the same way as caste) because it is a familiar way of categorizing oneself and receiving support from others in a strange and complex environment. Thus the traditional social groups give way only slowly to those which arise in a modern industrial society – occupational groups, trade unions, classes, political parties, and a variety of voluntary associations – except in those countries where, as in China, a revolution has accomplished a much sharper break with the past.

Even at a more advanced stage of industrialization the constellation of groups in some of the countries of the Third World may differ considerably from that in the industrial countries of Europe and North America, for these countries are creating new forms of society on the basis of their own heritage of thought and institutions. In India, Gandhi's ideas entered into more recent political doctrines, as in the proposal by Jaya Prakash Narayan (1959), a former leader of the Praja Socialist Party, that the village community, expressing the two ideals of the voluntary limitation of wants and of unanimity in social and political views, should be preserved and strengthened as a fundamental element in the

Indian political system; but the Gandhian influence seems to have diminished considerably in the past two decades. In Africa, some exponents of 'African socialism' have emphasized the distinctive 'communitarian' character of traditional African society, and have urged that this should be preserved in the process of economic growth, by embarking upon *gradual* industrialization combined with decentralization and the maximum possible participation of workers and peasants in the planning and execution of development projects (Worsley, 1967, ch. 4; Mohiddin, 1981, Introduction). One of the best known forms of socialist development in Africa, the 'Ujamaa' socialism of Tanzania, strongly emphasizes co-operative village agriculture as the basis of economic development (Mohiddin, 1981, ch. 3; Yeager, 1982).

On the other hand, it is evident that new social classes and elites, similar to those in the industrial societies, have acquired increasing importance in the developing countries (Bottomore, 1964, ch. 5); but with some significant differences. For various reasons, the military has been a major force in many developing countries (Janowitz, 1964; Huntington, 1968, ch. 4; Luckham, 1977), while elsewhere unified political elites emerging from national liberation struggles or revolutions have established their dominance in one-party regimes. But other modern social groups – bureaucrats, entrepreneurs, trade unions, technologists – still play an important part, alongside the more traditional groups of kin, tribe or village.

The discussion of types of social group should not be limited, therefore, simply to the contrast between folk and urban, traditional and modern, agrarian and industrial, societies. These distinctions are important since there correspond to them, as I have shown, differences in the kind of social group which is predominant; but there are also other distinctions to be made between types of society (as will be considered in the next chapter), the variety of social groups is greater than these simple dichotomies suggest, and in the course of a society's development new types of social group and social relationship are always being created.

Notes to Chapter 6

1   Thus Redfield (in contrast with Homans) is concerned with one fairly definite type of small group, and his descriptions and generalizations are all the more valuable for this limitation.
2   These changes are discussed in Desai, 1948. The self-sufficiency of the village in modern times has probably been exaggerated; for criticism of the idea see Srinivas, 1954.

Notes on Reading for Part II

I Population and Society

1 General

Faaland, Just (ed.), *Population and the World Economy in the 21st Century* (1982).

Myrdal, Alva, *Nation and Family* (1945). A pioneer study of the modern family and Swedish population policy.

Penrose, E. F., *Population Theories and Their Applications* (1934).
Reviews the main theories of population and discusses the relation between population and resources.

Sauvy, A., *Théorie générale de la population* (2 vols., 1952, 1954).
The first volume deals in detail with the relation between population and the economy.

United Nations, *The Determinants and Consequences of Population Trends* (1954).
A summary of numerous studies made by the United Nations, which briefly presents the available information on population in relation to social, cultural and economic factors.

United Nations, *Demographic Yearbook* (annually).

Wrigley, E. A., *Population and History* (1969).

Wrong, Dennis, *Population and Society* (1967). A useful short introduction.

2 Population Problems in Developing Countries

Cassen, Robert H., 'Population and development: A survey' (1976).

Coale, A. J. and Hoover, E. M., *Population Growth and Economic Development in Low-Income Countries* (1958).

Davis, Kingsley, 'The world's population crisis' (1966).
Deals with the world situation, but with special emphasis on developing countries.

II Urbanism

1 General

Castells, M., *The Urban Question* (1976).

Fustel de Coulanges, N. D., *The Ancient City* (1864). A pioneering work on the institutions of Greek and Roman cities.

Lynd, R. A. and H. M., *Middletown* (1929) and *Middletown in Transition* (1937). Two pioneer studies of an American town.

Mingione, Enzo, *Social Conflict and the City* (1981).
Pahl, R. E., *Whose City?* (1975).
Pirenne, H., *Medieval Cities* (1925). A classical study of the emergence, growth and role of towns in medieval Europe.
Saunders, P., *Social Theory and the Urban Question* (1981).
Simmel, G., 'The metropolis and mental life' (1903). English trans. in Hatt and Reiss (eds.), *Cities and Society* (1957).
An illuminating essay on the cultural effects of city life.
Wirth, L., 'Urbanism as a way of life' (1938). Reprinted in Hatt and Reiss, 1957. A well-known study of the sociological problems of urbanism, which outlines a typology of cities.

2 Urbanization

Abu-Lughod, J. and Hay, R. (eds.), *Third World Urbanization* (1977).
Friedmann, J. and Wulff, R., *The Urban Transition* (1975).
McGee, T. G., *The Urbanization Process in the Third World* (1971).
Mumford, Lewis, *The City in History* (1961).
Turner, Roy (ed.), *India's Urban Future* (1962).

III Social Groups

1 General

Argyle M., *The Scientific Study of Social Behaviour* (1957) pt 2, ch. 5, 'Small social groups'.
Gurvitch, G., *Traité de sociologie* (1958), Vol. 1, sect. 2, ch. 3.
Homans, G. C., *The Human Group* (1948).
Redfield, R., *The Little Community* (1955).

Among the studies of particular primary groups the following provide good examples of this kind of research:

Thrasher, F. M., *The Gang* (1936).
Whyte, W. F., *Street Corner Society* (1943).

2 Studies of Villages and Rural Groups

Dube, S. C., *India's Changing Villages* (1958).
Maine, H. S., *Village Communities in the East and West* (1871).
Marriott, McKim (ed.), *Village India: Studies in the Little Community* (1955).
Myrdal, Jan, *Report from a Chinese Village* (1965).
Wolf, Eric, *Peasants* (1966).

For studies of other types of group (the family, elites, etc.) see the relevant Notes on Reading in Part III.

PART III

Social Institutions

7 Social Structure, Societies and Civilizations

'Social structure' is one of the central concepts of sociology, but it has not been employed consistently or unambiguously. Herbert Spencer (1876–96, Vol. 1, pt 2), who was one of the first writers to use the term, was too much fascinated by his biological analogies (organic structure and evolution) to make clear what he meant by the structure of society. Durkheim (1893, ch. 6; 1895, ch. 4) also left the term vague. Many later sociologists and social anthropologists have tried to give a more precise meaning, but their conceptions of social structure diverge widely. Thus Radcliffe-Brown (1952) regards as 'a part of the social structure all social relations of person to person ... In the study of social structure the concrete reality with which we are concerned is the set of actually existing relations, at a given moment of time, which link together certain human beings' (pp. 191–2). But he goes on to say that the object which we attempt to describe and analyse is *structural form*, that is, the general relationships, disregarding slight variations and the particular individuals involved. It is this structural form which most writers have designated social structure. But Radcliffe-Brown's definition is very broad, as Firth (1951, ch. 1, p. 40) has pointed out: 'It makes no distinction between the ephemeral and the more enduring elements in social activity, and it makes it almost impossible to distinguish the idea of the structure of a society from that of the totality of the society itself.'

Other writers have restricted the term to the more permanent and organized relationships in society. Thus Ginsberg (1939) regards social structure as the complex of the principal groups and institutions which constitute societies. This conception is also important for the connection which it emphasizes between the abstract social relationships and the social groups which give rise to or are involved in them. From this point of view, the study of social structure can be undertaken in terms of institutional arrangements, or of the relations between social groups, or of both together, as I noted in the previous chapter. If we thus restrict the term 'social structure' to mean those more permanent and important relationships and groups, we perhaps need another term to refer to the other activities which go on in society, and which frequently represent variations from the structural forms. Firth (1951, ch. 2) has proposed the term 'social organization', which he defines as 'the systematic ordering of social relations by acts of choice and decision'. 'In the aspect of social structure is to be found the continuity principle of society; in the aspect of organization is to be found the variation or change principle – by allowing evaluation of situations and entry of individual choice' (Firth, 1951, ch. 1, p. 40).[1]

A third approach, which defines social structure in a still more restricted way is that which makes use of the notion of *social role*; it is exemplified by Nadel (1957), and by Gerth and Mills (1954). Nadel argues that, 'We arrive at the structure of a society through abstracting from the concrete population and its behaviour the pattern or network (or "system") of relationships obtaining between actors in their capacity of playing roles relative to one another' (1957, p. 12). Similarly, Gerth and Mills say that the concept of role is 'the key term in our definition of institution', and 'just as role is the unit with which we build our conception of institution, so institution is the unit with which we build the conception of social structure' (1954, pp. 22–3). This latter account makes clear, as is implied by Nadel, that the analysis of social structure in terms of social roles is not fundamentally different from an analysis in terms of social institutions; for an institution is a complex or cluster of roles. Nevertheless, there is, I think, some difference of emphasis. There is some advantage in introducing the concept of role since, as Gerth and Mills observe, it forms a major link between character and social structure and thus facilitates the necessary co-operation between psychology and sociology in the study of social behaviour. Yet the emphasis upon individual actors enacting roles also has disadvantages. It tends to produce an excessively individualistic conception of social behaviour, in which society is viewed as an aggregate of individuals related only through the complex role system of the society as a whole, while the social groups within society are neglected. We shall see later how this occurs in some theories of social stratification in terms of role and status, where the existence of distinctive social groups (e.g. social classes) and the relations of competition or conflict between them receive little attention. It is perhaps worthy of note that the concept of role seems to have been accepted most readily by psychologists interested mainly in individual behaviour, and by social anthropologists who study societies in which there is little diversity of social groups.

Of the different conceptions we have considered the most useful seems to me that which regards social structure as the complex of the major institutions and groups in society. But the analysis in the following chapters of these institutions and groups should be read with two other considerations in mind. First, a distinction has sometimes been made between social structure as the system of 'ideal' relations between persons (as expressed in legal codes and cultural norms), and social structure as the system of 'actual' relations. This corresponds broadly with Firth's distinction between 'structure' and 'organization', and it is related to those conceptions of social life which emphasize the contrast between 'system' and 'action' (see Chapter 3 above) and the extent to which structure itself is a product of human agency. Secondly, and in an antithetical sense, modern structuralists and realists (also discussed in Chapter 3 above) make a distinction between structure as the 'apparent' order of social relationships, and a more significant underlying structure (to be discovered by scientific investigation) which explains the visible, directly observable order.

It is not difficult to identify, in a preliminary and descriptive way, the major social institutions and groups. The existence of a human society requires certain arrangements and processes; or, as it has been expressed, there are 'functional prerequisites of society' (Aberle *et al.*, 1950).[2] The minimum requirements seem to be: (1) a system of communication; (2) an economic system, dealing with the production and allocation of goods; (3) arrangements (including the family and education) for the socialization of new generations; (4) a system of authority and of distribution of power; and perhaps (5) a system of ritual, serving to maintain or increase social cohesion, and to give social recognition to significant personal events such as birth, puberty, courtship, marriage and death. The major institutions and groups are those concerned with such basic requirements. From them, others may emerge, such as social stratification, which then influence them in turn. There is little disagreement among sociologists about which are the major institutions, and in the following chapters I shall examine these elements of social structure in detail.

We still have one other difficulty to face. Every society has a social structure, although several societies may have similar structures. But how are we to determine what is a society; or in other words, the extent of a particular social structure? Was ancient Greece a society, or were the city-states distinct societies? Was India, until recently, a single society, or was it an aggregate of societies brought into some kind of unity by a cultural, and

especially a religious tradition? It is difficult, in many cases, to
determine the boundaries of a society. Firth (1951) has argued
that unless there is stark physical isolation, no society can be
given a definite limit. But political independence has often been
taken as the criterion of a separate society. Schapera (1956), for
example, writes:

> By a 'political community' I mean a group of people organized into a
> single unit managing its affairs independently of external control . . .
> No community is completely isolated . . . But so long as it alone
> decides on matters of local concern, so long as there is no dictation
> from outside, and so long as its decisions and actions cannot be
> overruled by any higher authority, it may be said to have political
> independence. (p. 8)

Even so, difficulties arise, since 'political independence' is relative
(there *are* satellites and client states), and we have to decide what
degree of independence shall qualify any group as being a
separate society. Moreover, we have to deal with many instances
of the absorption of societies into larger units through conquest
and imperialist expansion; or conversely, with the emergence or
re-emergence of separate societies within such larger units. The
latter is the case with the feudal societies resulting from the
dissolution of the Roman Empire, and with the new nations that
emerged from colonial empires in the twentieth century. And we
have already seen how observers at certain periods characterized
Indian villages as 'little republics'. In spite of these difficulties, the
criterion of political independence in a defined territory is valuable, and where we find political independence along with
distinct economic, cultural and familial institutions we can safely
regard the group as constituting a separate society.

So far we have been concerned with the spatial separation of
societies, but what of their separation in time? Britain is a society,
but is Britain in the late twentieth century the same society as in
the eighteenth century or the sixteenth century? Is India the same
society as a hundred or two hundred years ago? Here we readily
find a criterion, though its practical application may not always
be easy. Wherever there is an important change in social structure
we should regard the society after this change as a new and
distinct society. We have to decide what constitutes an *important*
change; and this is not easy. We might say provisionally that it is a
change which transforms all or most of the institutions in the
society. Thus capitalist Britain or France are different societies
from feudal Britain or France; the USSR is a different society
from Tsarist Russia. But our judgement will be influenced to

some extent by more general considerations about the classification of societies which we have now to discuss.

Types of Society

One of the first steps in sociology, as in any science, is a systematic classification of the phenomena with which it deals. I have discussed in earlier chapters the classification of social relations and social groups. Here I shall be concerned with the classification of inclusive societies, or social structures.

We may begin by considering the numerous dichotomous classifications which have already been mentioned on several occasions: Tönnies's '*Gemeinschaft*' and '*Gesellschaft*', Durkheim's 'mechanical solidarity' and 'organic solidarity', Maine's 'status' and 'contract', Spencer's 'militant' and 'industrial' societies. The first thing to remark is that such classifications appear very inadequate to encompass all the varieties of human society which exist or have existed. If we now look more closely at the classifications we shall find that they resemble each other in important ways. All four writers contrast a type of society in which the group dominates the individual and determines for him a more or less unalterable situation, with a type of society in which the individual is properly speaking an 'individual', whose situation in society is at least partially the outcome of rational choices and contractual relations with other individuals. There are important differences between these writers on points of detail, in the accounts which they provide of how the change has come about, and in their valuations of the change. But the essential similarity of the classifications is unmistakable. It results from the fact that all four writers were profoundly impressed by the characteristics of the new industrial societies in which they lived. Thus they were led to contrast modern industrial societies with all other human societies; this was, in their eyes, the supreme distinction.

This can be seen best in the work of Tönnies and some later German sociologists. Tönnies's distinction between *Gemeinschaft* and *Gesellschaft* is entirely a distinction between modern capitalist, rationalistic, contractual societies, and all pre-capitalist societies. The theme reappears in Simmel's (1907) study of the cultural characteristics of a society based upon a fully developed money economy, and it underlies all Max Weber's work, in his fundamental concern with the increasing rationalization of social life (Brubaker, 1984). More recently, many sociologists have reiterated the distinction between industrial and non-industrial societies in the context of studies of 'developing countries' in the present-day world (Aron, 1961, and Chapter 17 below). But while the significance of the emergence of industrial societies is evident we may still question the adequacy of a classification which places all other societies in a single class and neglects the differences between the industrial societies themselves (for example, whether they are capitalist or socialist in form).

Spencer and Durkheim, of course, were aware that societies might be classified in other ways. Spencer (1876–96, Vol. 1, pt 2, ch. 10) proposed to distinguish four types of society: (1) *simple societies*, (2) *compound societies*, (3) *doubly compound societies*, and (4) *trebly compound societies*. The types are distinguished primarily in terms of scale (or size), but also in terms of associated phenomena such as the more extensive division of labour, more elaborate political organization, developed ecclesiastical hierarchy and social stratification. But the utility of the classification appears less when it is realized that the first three social types comprise only primitive societies, while all civilized societies are grouped together in the fourth class, which includes, according to Spencer, ancient Mexico, the Assyrian Empire, the Roman Empire, Great Britain, France, Germany, Italy and Russia. Spencer recognized that this classification cut across the distinction between militant and industrial societies, and he outlined, in effect, a composite classification of eight types of society (although industrial societies are mainly to be found among the trebly compound societies). Moreover, Spencer warned that 'pure' types are difficult to find for many reasons, including survivals and a kind of societal miscegenation.

Durkheim (1895, ch. 4) also outlined, in similar terms to those of Spencer while criticizing the latter's scheme, a classification of societies. He distinguished: (1) *simple societies* (the horde); (2) *simple polysegmentary societies* (e.g. Iroquois tribes); (3) *simple compounded polysegmentary societies* (e.g. the Iroquois confederation, the three tribes which founded Rome); (4) *doubly compounded polysegmentary societies* (e.g. the ancient tribes, the Germanic tribes). Durkheim did not go beyond these examples, but Moret and Davy (1926) later attempted a more elaborate classification in terms of scale and internal differentiation.

Most of these classifications implied an evolutionary scheme. Other evolutionists proposed classifications in terms of intellectual development. Thus Comte, having formulated his 'law of three stages', according to which human thought developed from the theological through the metaphysical to the positive stage, attempted to correlate material life, types of social unit, types of order, and prevailing sentiments with these intellectual phases. Hobhouse (1906) in a similar way distinguished five phases in intellectual development: (1) formation of the elements of articulate thought in primitive societies; (2) proto-science in the ancient East (Babylonia, Egypt and ancient China); (3) the stage of reflection in the later East (China, Palestine and India); (4) the stage of critical and systematic thought in Greece; (5) the stage of 'experiential reconstruction', represented by modern science. He then attempted to correlate types of social institution (forms of political organization, family, property and social stratification) with these intellectual stages. In the same work, however, he proposed two other classifications: a classification of primitive societies in terms of their economic level, and a general classification of societies in terms of the nature of the social bond. Using the latter criterion Hobhouse distinguished three types of society, based upon kinship, authority and citizenship respectively. In a later work (1924) he introduced other criteria – scale, efficiency, mutuality and freedom – which should also enter into the classification of societies. Nowhere did Hobhouse attempt to bring the different criteria together in an ordered scheme of classification. Indeed, neither Comte nor Hobhouse can be regarded as having formulated a classification of actual societies. They were both primarily concerned with levels of civilization, and much of their work is an intellectual history of mankind. In this respect their schemes are less useful than those of Spencer and Durkheim, who attempted to define types of society as intelligible units of study.

The best-known, and probably the most influential, classification of societies that has yet been proposed is that of Marx, who distinguished the principal historical types of society in terms of their mode of production and class structure. In a famous passage Marx (1859, Preface) wrote that, 'In broad outline we can designate the Asiatic, the ancient, the feudal and the modern bourgeois modes of production as progressive epochs in the economic formation of society', while elsewhere he also referred to primitive communism as the earliest form of human society. The profound influence of Marx's classificatory scheme comes, I think, from two elements in it: first, that the types of society which are distinguished correspond with actual, recognizable societies in different historical periods, and the criteria for distinguishing them – the organization of the economy and the nature and interrelations of the principal social groups – refer to definite, empirical phenomena which are amenable to historical and sociological investigation; secondly (as will be discussed more fully in Chapter 17 below), that the historical framework of the classification makes possible an explanation of the transition from one form of society to another.

Nevertheless, Marx's classification poses a number of problems and needs to be elaborated in certain respects. It is clear, for example, that the major types of society may include subtypes. Thus Hobhouse, Wheeler and Ginsberg (1915) classified more than 400 tribal societies in terms of their levels of economic development, and showed that the forms of other social institutions were correlated with the type of economy. Marx himself, in his most substantial analysis of pre-capitalist economic formations (1857–8, pp. 471–514), noted the different forms that tribal and early societies might assume, and a Marxist anthropologist has explored in detail the difficulty of defining a single form of 'tribal society' (Godelier, 1973, ch. 3). Similarly, it may be necessary to distinguish subtypes of feudal society (within European feudalism, in Japan, etc.), and of capitalist society (early liberal, competitive capitalism and the 'organized capitalism' of the twentieth century).

The category of 'ancient society' presents many problems (Finley, 1983), but the most intense debates, among Marxists particularly, have concerned the 'Asiatic' type of society, to a large extent with reference to its place in a periodization of history (Turner, 1978, 1983a). Marx defined the Asiatic type of society as one which had an agricultural economy with small units of production, and at the same time a centralized state and bureaucracy, whose power rested upon its regulation of water supplies. He examined particularly the case of India:

> Climate and territorial conditions, especially the vast tracts of desert, extending from the Sahara through Arabia, Persia, India, and Tartary, to the most elevated Asiatic highlands, made artificial irrigation by canals and waterworks the basis of Oriental agriculture . . . This prime necessity of an economical and common use of water, which, in the Occident, drove private enterprise to voluntary association, as in Flanders and Italy, necessitated, in the Orient where civilization was too low and the territorial extent too vast to call into life voluntary association, the interference of the centralizing power of Government. Hence an economical function devolved upon all Asiatic Governments, the function of providing public works . . . These two circumstances – the Hindoo, on the one hand, leaving, like all Oriental peoples, to the central government the care of the great public works, the prime conditions of his agriculture and commerce, dispersed, on the other hand, over the surface of the country, and agglomerated in small centres by the domestic union of agricultural

and manufacturing pursuits – these two circumstances had brought about, since the remotest times, a social system of particular features – the so-called *village system*, which gave to each of these small unions their independent organization and distinct life. (Marx, 1853, pp. 85–6)

Later (1867, ch. 14) he observed that 'One of the material foundations of the powers exercised by the State over the small and disconnected productive organisms of India was the regulation of the water supply'.

Max Weber (1923) later used the same idea in his account of the differences between East and West in respect of the growth of towns and the emergence of a *bourgeoisie*:

> The distinction is based on the fact that in the cultural evolution of Egypt, western Asia, India and China, the question of irrigation was crucial. The water question conditioned the existence of bureaucracy, the compulsory service of the dependent classes upon the functioning of the bureaucracy of the King. That the King also expressed his power in the form of military monopoly is the basis of the distinction between the military organization of Asia and that of the West. In the first case the royal official and the army are from the beginning the central figures of the process, while in the West both were originally absent. (p. 237)

More recently there have been several studies of what are variously called *irrigation civilizations* or *hydraulic societies* (Steward, 1955; Wittfogel, 1957). These studies have been related to the general study of bureaucracy, though little has yet been done in the way of large-scale comparative work on bureaucratically organized societies (but see Eisenstadt, 1963). The concept of 'irrigation civilization' has been used by Karim (1956) in explaining the absence in India of Western-type towns and of a *bourgeoisie* able to acquire social and political influence. He writes, 'The primary function of the State was to look after the water supply . . . Its power was built upon the control of water works. And to control, regulate and supervise public works, and collect land tax, the State stationed its agents at various local centres, which became the towns' (pp. 45–6). These did not resemble the European medieval towns, with their commercial middle class, communal organization, and relative independence of the feudal state (Pirenne, 1925). The greatest changes in Indian social structure, during the period of British rule, were the decline of public works and thus of the paternalistic state, the development of capitalist enterprise, and the growth of towns (not so much in relative size, as in social and political importance). One sign of the

emergence of a self-conscious urban middle class was the nationalist movement, which was created, organized and supported by
the new professional groups and the commercial and industrial
bourgeoisie (Desai, 1948, ch. 11).

It is not enough, however, to characterize pre-British India as
an 'irrigation civilization', with a centralized bureaucracy and a
village system of production. The unity and stability of Indian
society depended also upon two other factors, caste and religion.
Here, the aspect of caste to be emphasized is not so much its rigid
hierarchical character and the way in which it divided groups
from each other, as its integrating function, closely connected
with religion. Srinivas (1952, ch. 2), in a discussion of Indian
social structure, observes that:

> caste guarantees autonomy to a community, and at the same time it
> brings that community into relation with numerous other communi-
> ties all going to form a hierarchy. The importance of such an
> institution is obvious in a vast country like India which has been the
> meeting place of many different cultures in the past and which has
> always had considerable regional diversity. While the autonomy of a
> sub-caste was preserved it was also brought into relation with others,
> and the hierarchy was also a scale of generally agreed values. Every
> caste tended to imitate the customs and ritual of the topmost caste, and
> this was responsible for the spread of Sanskritization ... Caste
> enabled Hinduism to proselytize without the aid of a church.

Thus the separate village communities were integrated and
maintained in a larger social and political system not only by the
central bureaucracy which controlled water supplies, but also by
a religious system of values expounded and interpreted by a
priestly caste. How far there was anything similar in other
'irrigation civilizations' is a matter for more detailed comparative
study. The work of Wittfogel suggests that many important
similarities can be found, in ancient Egypt, in Byzantium, and
elsewhere, especially in the social functions of the priests and in
the elements of caste revealed in detailed regulation of the
division of labour.

The foregoing account indicates some features of traditional
Indian society which may enable us to classify it, however
tentatively, as belonging to a particular social type. A similar
account might be given of other societies which are now often
grouped together as 'developing countries'. China, like India, has
been studied as a hydraulic society, in which a highly developed
bureaucracy ruled over village communities (Wittfogel, 1957;
Weber, 1915). In quite a different category are many of the new
African societies, which are emerging from a tribal form of

society overlaid by colonial rule; or again, the countries of Latin America in which there are elements of a feudal structure, along with an exceptional degree of military intervention in political life. It is evident that any classification of types of society which took account of this diversity would be much more complex than the schemes proposed by the early sociologists, who derived their ideas largely from the experience of European history. There has been relatively little effort, however, to work out any more complex classifications; on the contrary, sociologists seem to have reverted to one of the simplest distinctions made by early writers – that between industrial and non-industrial societies. Of course, there is a good deal of justification for the revival of this distinction. The developing countries, regardless of their past, are all attempting to bring about economic growth, generally on the basis of industrialization; and they are profoundly affected, in a great variety of ways, by their relationships with the industrial societies. Nevertheless, the distinction is scarcely adequate by itself, however much it may correspond with important economic and political concerns of the present time. The course of development in the non-industrial countries will be strongly influenced by their traditional social structures as well as by the aims which they now set themselves, and we shall not understand the new developments properly unless we grasp the different conditions from which they begin.

On the other side, in the case of the industrial societies, we have to recognize at least the existence of two different types: those societies with a collectivist economy and those with a capitalist economy. Over the past two decades much has been done to elaborate and refine the conception of an industrial society (Aron, 1962, 1967; Galbraith, 1971), and more recently there have been some interesting discussions of the advent of a 'post-industrial society' (Touraine, 1969; Bell, 1973). But in spite of the fact that there are obviously some very general features of industrialism, it is not clearly established that the different types of industrial society are fundamentally alike in their social structures or that they are tending to become more alike, as was suggested at one time by proponents of the 'convergence thesis' (Kerr et al., 1962). One of the difficulties in making comparisons between the types of industrial society[3] is the dearth of comprehensive sociological studies of capitalism and socialism that have the scope and profundity, for example, of Bloch's (1939–40) historical study of feudal society; though there is a magnificent analysis of the emergence of capitalism as a distinct civilization by Braudel (1979). The major sociological accounts of capitalism that deal to some extent with the social structure as a whole rather than with the purely economic aspects, are those of Weber (1923, pt 4), Sombart (1902, 1930) and Schumpeter (1942). The study by Neumann (1942) of Nazi Germany as a distinctive form of capitalist industrial society is important in the context of the rise of fascist states during the period of economic and political crisis between the two world wars. Comprehensive sociological studies of socialism as a type of society are also rare, though there is a good analysis of the state-socialist societies by Lane (1976); for the most part, however, attention has been largely concentrated on socialist economies (Horvat, 1982; Bottomore, 1987), and on individual countries or specific aspects of the social structure such as the emergence of new classes and elites (see Chapter 11 below).

Sociological studies of particular modern societies are somewhat more plentiful, although many of them are mainly descriptive and statistical, and do not go on to analyse the basic structural or cultural elements. Among the studies of the USSR and its development those by Kassof (1968) and Lane (1970) are especially useful to sociologists. There is a good collection of readings on Chinese society and politics from 1949 to the Cultural Revolution in the book edited by Schurmann and Schell (1967). Since the death of Mao Tse-Tung in 1976, however, there has been a marked change of direction in China's development (in economic organization, population policy and the cultural sphere) with a particular emphasis on 'socialist modernization',[4] and it is impossible to foresee at present what kind of society will eventually emerge from these transformations. Other socialist societies have also been studied in some detail; especially Yugoslavia, which introduced at an early stage a distinctive system of workers' self-management that has been emulated to some extent elsewhere in the socialist world (Horvat, 1969; Broekmeyer, 1970).

Individual capitalist countries have also been studied, with more or less thoroughness. The American social structure has been analysed by Williams (1965), and there is an interesting study of the USA as the 'first new nation' by Lipset (1963). A particularly good analysis of a distinctive society within a larger political entity, inspired by a growing national self-consciousness in the 1960s, is Rioux and Martin's *French-Canadian Society* (1964). There are a number of studies of West European nations. One outstanding work, by a historian, is that of modern France from 1848 to 1945, which ranges widely over the class structure, marriage and morals, everyday life, the cultural and intellectual sphere and politics (Zeldin, 1979–81). An illuminating study of

Germany (Dahrendorf, 1965) analyses the 'long road into modernity' from Imperial Germany, through the Weimar Republic and the Nazi dictatorship, to the 'two Germanies' of the present day. There is, I think, no such notable single work on Britain, with the rather surprising exception of an early study, very sociological in its approach, of 'the condition of England' (Masterman, 1909). The most interesting recent studies, understandably enough, are those which concentrate on Britain's long-term economic decline in relation to the peculiarities of the class structure and of the traditional culture (Wiener, 1981; Pollard, 1984; Gamble, 1985).

Clearly, it is extremely difficult to analyse the structure of a large and complex society in the context of its historical development, and the difficulties are compounded when we try to define and classify the 'types of society'. Nevertheless, this is the kind of analysis, involving comparative and historical studies, which sociologists must attempt if they are to set their investigations of any aspect of social life, no matter how small-scale it may be, in a systematic framework. What should be recognized, however, is that 'pure' instances of the different types of society are not to be expected, and it is better to regard them as 'ideal types' in Max Weber's sense; that is, as intellectual constructs which do not describe any actual society, but are useful in directing the analysis and investigation of actual societies.[5]

Civilization and Culture

The terms 'civilization' and 'culture' are widely used, with a variety of meanings, in ordinary discourse and in sociological writing. The *Oxford English Dictionary* defines 'to civilize' as 'to bring out of a state of barbarism, to instruct in the arts of life; to enlighten and refine', and quotes in illustration Addison's line, 'to civilize the rude unpolish'd world'. 'Civilization' is then 'the civilized condition or state'. 'Culture' is defined as 'the training and refinement of mind, tastes and manners; the condition of being thus trained and refined: the intellectual side of civilization'. The terms have often been used in this way in general writing on the intellectual and artistic aspects of human society. Clive Bell (1928), however, employs them in a narrower way to refer to the condition of refinement or enlightenment of a small elite in society, and this is one of the modern usages examined in an illuminating study by Raymond Williams (1958).

Many of the early social scientists used the terms to distinguish between 'savage' and 'civilized' societies, or between 'nature peoples' and 'culture peoples'; the point of division being the invention of writing. There are many examples of this usage in the works of the eighteenth-century Scottish historians mentioned earlier, in L. H. Morgan's *Ancient Society* (1877) which distinguishes between 'savagery', 'barbarism' and 'civilization', and in the early anthropological literature. The usage persists in a customary differentiation between 'primitive' and 'civilized' societies, though the terminology here is largely a matter of convenience.

Later, a different distinction was introduced; not between 'civilization' or 'culture' on one side, and 'savagery' on the other, but between 'civilization' and 'culture' as applicable to all human societies. The distinction was made most clearly and elaborately by Alfred Weber (1935), who differentiated between three processes in human history: social process, civilization and culture. I shall discuss his general scheme later, in examining the problems of social change. By civilization he meant primarily scientific and technical knowledge and the command which they give over natural resources; by culture, the artistic, religious, philosophical and similar products of a society. A similar usage is the common distinction in anthropological and archaeological writing between 'material culture' and 'non-material culture'.

More recently, 'culture' has become a central concept in social anthropology, and has been given a very wide meaning. The major contribution here was that of Malinowski (1930), who defined culture as comprising 'inherited artefacts, goods, technical processes, ideas, habits and values'.[6] He also included social structure within the notion of culture, since 'it cannot be really understood except as part of culture'. In a later essay, Malinowski reiterated these views: culture 'obviously is the integral whole consisting of implements and consumers' goods, of constitutional charters for the various social groupings, of human ideas and crafts, beliefs and customs'. Further, 'the essential fact of culture as we live it and experience it, as we can observe it scientifically, is the organization of human beings into permanent groups' (1944, pp. 36, 43). The most important feature in Malinowski's use of the term was his conception of culture as an integral whole, within which the functions of the various parts (institutions) could be studied.[7]

In other discussions the term 'culture' has been used in the same broad way (for example, by Kluckhohn, 1953, and Hallowell, 1953), but there has been a tendency to distinguish more strictly between culture and social structure, especially among British social anthropologists. Thus Firth (1951, p. 27) says that these terms represent two ways of looking at the same phenomenon: 'social structure' refers to the relations between individuals and the form of those relations, while 'culture' refers to 'the component of accumulated resources, immaterial as well as material, which the people inherit, employ, transmute, add to, and transmit'; it is 'all learned behaviour which has been socially acquired'.[8] This seems a valid and useful distinction, which corresponds broadly with a distinction often made in sociology between the study of social structure (or the comparative study of social institutions) and the *sociologie de l'esprit*, that is, the sociology of mind or culture, which includes as one important part the sociology of knowledge. In studying culture we are concerned with ideas and values such as are found in religious and moral codes, in literature, science, philosophy, art and music.

The term 'civilization' has not acquired the same central importance as 'culture' in either sociology or social anthropology, and it is used in a very general and imprecise way.[9] Alfred Weber's distinction between civilization and culture does not seem to have been widely adopted, although MacIver advanced it independently and emphasized its significance.[10] Civilization has remained largely a historian's term, and is often used to describe what anthropologists would refer to as a culture; for example, in Burckhardt's *The Civilization of the Renaissance in Italy* (1860). But in the work of Arnold Toynbee (1934–56) the term 'civilization' is given a different meaning, which may contribute to a more precise sociological conception. Toynbee distinguishes twenty-one independent civilizations (which he then confusingly calls 'societies') as 'intelligible fields of historical study'. These 'civilizations' are distinguished from 'primitive societies', along lines which I mentioned earlier (Vol. 1, pp. 147–9). We need not be concerned here with Toynbee's view that only civilizations and not societies (which he refers to as nation-states, city-states, and the like) are 'intelligible fields' of study. From the sociologist's point of view the contrary is true: actual societies are the most intelligible fields of study. But Toynbee's discussion is of great interest in drawing attention to the fact that distinct societies are related to each other by sharing a common culture and cultural tradition. The number of societies thus related may be a significant feature of social development. It should be noted that a similar conception of civilization was briefly formulated by Durkheim and Mauss, in their 'Note sur la notion de civilisation' (1913), where they observed that although social phenomena could ordinarily be most usefully studied within well-defined units such as particular societies, there were some phenomena which transcended these limits and which they proposed to call 'phenomena of civilization'.

We can now suggest a consistent, though still broad and general, usage for the terms *culture* and *civilization*. By *culture* we mean the ideational aspects of social life, as distinct from the actual relations and forms of relationship between individuals; and by *a culture* the ideational aspects of a particular society. The distinction which Alfred Weber made between 'culture' and 'civilization' can be recognized by distinguishing between material and non-material culture. This terminology has certain advantages, since it differentiates two elements within culture as a whole, and does not lend itself to a rigorous and overemphatic distinction between two fundamentally different types of phenomena. Weber made the distinction because he wished to contrast the growth and diffusion of science and technology with the uniqueness and independence of cultural products in each epoch and place. But it is not demonstrated that there is no development in the cultural sphere, or that cultural products cannot be diffused; and at the same time it is evident that within a particular society the material and non-material elements of culture are closely interconnected.

Finally, by *a civilization* we mean a cultural complex formed by the identical major cultural features of a number of particular societies. We might, for example, describe Western capitalism as a civilization, in which specific forms of science, technology, religion, art and so on are to be found in a number of distinct societies. I shall not attempt here to classify civilizations, but only remark that a sociological classification would probably differ in many respects from that of Toynbee, though the latter is a valuable guide.[11]

The concepts of 'culture' and 'civilization' are obviously important in studying India and other developing countries today, for one of the outstanding questions concerns the relationship between the traditional culture and the values and beliefs which have been introduced from the West. Here we can study empirically the question of the material and non-material elements in culture. The developing countries have imported modern science, technology, and forms of economic organization, but is it the case that the non-material culture has been unaffected and has remained unchanged? According to Alfred Weber's conception material culture is transmissible from one society to another, while non-material culture is unique, incommunicable, and bound to time and place. The developing countries may acquire science and technique from the West, but they will retain their own systems of religion and philosophy, their own forms of art, which, so far as they change at all, will change unpredictably through the influence of outstanding individuals working within the traditional culture. This view, as I have already said, exaggerates the independence of these two elements in culture. The existence of socialist, communist and other political parties demonstrates the absorption of Western political philosophies and values. Parliamentary government in India and other countries shows the acquisition not merely of a system of government machinery, but also of political ideas and conceptions of how a political community should be organized. Elsewhere, in China and Cuba, the whole social structure is being refashioned under the influence of Marxist thought which, though it has been modified to take account of different structural and cultural conditions, is still manifestly a Western doctrine. It may be said that some of the new values can be related to particular elements in the traditional culture, but that is only because (contrary to Weber's view) there are many similarities in the doctrines of the major world religions, philosophies and ethical systems. The importance given to particular aspects of these doctrines may well vary with changes in material culture and in social structure.

This is not to deny that particular cultures and areas of civilization – in India, China, Africa, the Arab world, Latin America – have distinctive features, but simply to propose that these should be considered in relation to other features which are more universalistic in character, and to the impact which present social changes are having on cultural life. There is now much intermingling of cultures throughout the world,[12] one aspect of which is the growing assertion of the universal elements in human culture, and another the recognition of the value of many diverse variations on the common theme (and a gradual abandonment of a Eurocentric view of the world).

These general observations provide a starting point for sociological inquiry. How are the various elements of culture, 'traditional' and 'Western', perceived and grasped by individuals and by different social groups? How do they appear in popular literature and other media (science fiction against the *Ramayana*)? A book published in the late 1950s (Hoggart, 1957) depicted, in a striking fashion, the changes in the culture of the English working class, and there is great scope for similar investigation of changes in popular culture in the developing countries. In a more formal way, changes in education and in law bring about a modification of cultural values, and their influence will be discussed in later chapters. Sociological research in these various fields should be able to show how culture changes or persists, how new elements are incorporated or rejected, and how traditional elements are conserved, modified or abandoned.

But the formulation of a contrast or opposition between 'traditional' culture and 'modern' culture in the developing countries should not lead us into the error of treating these types of culture (and especially the latter) in an unhistorical way, as if they were uniform, harmonious and unchanging. During the 1940s and 1950s many sociologists, under the influence of functionalist ideas, assumed too easily that the Western capitalist countries were 'stable' societies, in which a 'modern' culture (to be emulated elsewhere) existed in a more or less settled form. They virtually ignored the existence of an alternative socialist culture in diverse forms throughout Europe, as well as the cultural divisions in their own societies. But since the 1960s the functionalist assumptions have been upset by the growth of vigorous and widespread movements directed against the established culture (as has also happened in the socialist industrial countries of Eastern Europe), while the meaning and value of 'modernity' itself has been questioned by the post-modernist movement, which harks back in some respects to the idea of community expressed by Tönnies. Such problems of cultural conflict and transformation in both industrial and developing countries will be examined more fully in later chapters dealing with the forms of social control and theories of social and cultural change.

Notes to Chapter 7

1   This is also a way of conceiving the interaction between structure and agency, which has become, as I noted in Chapter 3 above, a central issue in recent sociological controversies. However, it may be questioned whether 'social organization' provides *the* change principle, for there are large-scale structural changes which could not be brought about by the kinds of evaluation and choice which Firth gives as examples. For further discussion of such structural changes, see Chapter 18 below.

2   This classification of necessary elements of social structure need not, of course, be expressed in functionalist terminology; one can refer simply to 'prerequisites' or 'necessary conditions' of society.

3   One important work (Moore, 1966) does, however, illuminate the differences between the principal types of twentieth-century industrial society through a historical study of the alternative routes to modernization.

4   See, for an account of the economic reforms, White *et al.*, 1983.

5   Weber, 1923, himself provided an ideal type definition of capitalism, and some of Marx's observations on method justify regarding his definitions of various types of society in the same way. Marc Bloch (1939–40, Vol. 2, pt 8) provides such an ideal type definition of feudalism.

6   A similar definition had in fact been proposed much earlier by Tylor, 1871, p. 1, where culture is regarded as 'that complex whole which includes knowledge, belief, art, law, morals, customs, and all other capabilities and habits acquired by man as a member of society'.

7   For an appraisal of Malinowski's views, see Richards, 1957.

8   There is, however, still much variation in the use of the term 'culture', as may be seen from a survey of definitions and usages by Kroeber, and Kluckhohn, 1952.

9   There is a good discussion of the usages in Centre International de Synthèse, 1930, with a contribution from a social anthropologist, Marcel Mauss.

10 MacIver (1926, p. 325): 'Our culture is what we are, our civilization is what we use.' See also MacIver and Page, 1952, ch. 21.

11 For example, it would hardly be possible (or indeed useful) to regard 'Western civilization' throughout its history as a single type.

12 In the political culture of the developing countries this mingling of indigenous and foreign elements can be seen very well, for example, in the social doctrines of Gandhism, and in the ideas of 'African socialism'.

8 Economic Institutions

Modern economic theories have not, on the whole, shown much interest in the study of economic structure, although many economics textbooks contain brief accounts of the organization of industry, the division of labour, the structure of enterprises, and so on. Economic sociology, on the other hand, is almost entirely concerned with problems of structure; its major fields of interest, which we shall examine in turn, have been the division of labour and occupational specialization, the property system, types of economy and structural changes (especially the process of industrialization), the structure of the industrial enterprise or factory, and industrial relations.

The Division of Labour

One of the best known of Durkheim's works is his study of the division of labour (1893) in which he analysed the social functions of the division of labour and sought to show how in modern societies, by contrast with primitive societies, it is the principal source of social cohesion or social solidarity. In the course of his inquiry, Durkheim distinguished two types of solidarity, mechanical and organic, which he associated with two types of law that he called repressive and restitutive. In a later part of the book Durkheim discussed 'abnormal forms' of the division of labour in modern industrial societies, which diminish rather than promote social cohesion, and distinguished two principal forms: the 'anomic' and the 'forced' division of labour. By the first he meant a condition of extreme specialization of labour in which the individual became isolated in his specialism; and particularly a condition in which there was a permanent division between capital and labour. Durkheim proposed as remedies the fostering of regular and prolonged contacts through professional associations and corporations, and through institutional arrangements for discussion and negotiation between capital and labour. By the second form Durkheim meant a condition in which individuals did not freely choose their occupations but were forced into them. He regarded this discrepancy between the abilities of individuals and the functions imposed upon them as a principal source of class conflict.

Durkheim thought that modern societies could and would get rid of these abnormal forms of the division of labour, and it is interesting to consider the extent to which his expectations have been realized. In capitalist societies the relations between capital and labour have been institutionalized in elaborate procedures for consultation, negotiation and arbitration; and the choice of occupations has become wider for many people as a result of educational expansion and changes in the occupational structure. The effects may have been to reduce, in some measure, the intensity of class conflict, especially during the period of expansion of 'welfare capitalism' in the 1950s and 1960s. Some writers have referred to a 'class compromise' which was established at that time, and to the emergence of a 'corporatist' form of society dominated by large corporations and organized labour with which the interventionist state negotiates in order to maintain social stability (Offe, 1980; Panitch, 1980). The situation is different in socialist societies where both the managers of collectively owned enterprises and the trade unions are subject to the control of a single dominant party, and the development of independent trade unions is strongly resisted (as in the case of Solidarity in Poland), but there is nevertheless a large area of consultation and negotiation; and the distinctive Yugoslav system of self-management enables the division of labour to be overcome, at least in some degree, through widespread participation in the management of economic enterprises and other associations.

Many sociologists have discussed the relation between the division of labour and social stratification. Marx's theory connected the existence of classes with the division of labour, and especially with what he called 'the first great distinction between manual and intellectual labour', and envisaged a future 'classless society' in which the division of labour would be overcome (at least in that sense which Durkheim referred to as a 'forced division') by being brought under the conscious control of the producers (Mohun, 1983).[1] A quite different early theory is that of Schmoller (1890), who defined classes as occupational groups created by the division of labour and maintained by heredity; a conception which finds an echo in some more recent studies of the ranking of occupations in terms of prestige as a basis for investigations of the extent of social mobility, where particular attention has been given to the recruitment of the more prestigious and influential professions.

The traditional Indian caste system displays a particularly close and formal relationship between occupations and social status. In the past, new castes were often formed when changes in technique occurred or entirely new occupations came into existence. Hutton (1951) quotes an observation by Enthoven in 1932 concerning the formation of a new caste of chauffeurs: 'Modern India, having created a caste of chauffeurs from the menials who tend motor cars, is almost ripe for a Rolls Royce caste rejecting food or marriage with the Fords' (p. 117). In the more recent development of new industrial occupations the formation of new castes does not seem to be an important feature, and more significance attaches to the growth of trade unions and of class differences; but it is still of interest to study the influence of established castes on recruitment to high status occupations and the persistence of traditional caste distinctions in new forms (Bottomore, 1975b, ch. 10).

These questions will be discussed more fully in Chapter 11 below; meanwhile we should note another important field of research, which concerns the social and psychological effects of the detailed division of labour in modern production. Friedmann (1956) examined the modern division of labour as it affects both work and leisure, provided an excellent review of research up to that date, and in a statistical appendix presented data on the extent and character of specialization and the subdivision of tasks in a number of industrial societies. He also examined critically Durkheim's view of the social functions of the division of labour:

> if highly subdivided jobs are to have meaning restored to them, certain conditions must play a part which Durkheim has failed to take into account: in particular, economic and social equality must be accorded to the worker, making him a full member, with equal rights, of the community to which he belongs . . . But even this is insufficient . . . A sense of solidarity is quite incapable of transforming the microscopic nature of tiny work units, if they are the only jobs allotted to the worker and he is chained to them for weeks, for months or even years . . . The present reaction against job simplification, the multiplication of experiments with transfer, work rotation, and even job enlargement, show that the division of labour is not necessarily a good thing in itself; also that it would be too easy a solution to our problem to treat as 'abnormal' the vast majority of its effects upon our technical civilization.[2] (pp. 75–6)

Friedmann went on to note that two different kinds of solidarity might be engendered by capitalist production – either the solidarity of all those engaged in production in an enterprise or branch of industry, or the solidarity of workers as a class – and that it is the latter which has developed most strongly up to the present time.

There is another aspect of the social division of labour which has acquired increasing importance. Marx argued that capitalist production always required a 'reserve army of labour' (i.e. unemployed workers), which would expand in periods of economic depression, as at the present time in the capitalist industrial countries. But this phenomenon has also to be seen in the context of the international division of labour, determined in part by the activities of multinational corporations and governments, which effectively transfers some of the costs of economic crisis to the poorer countries. Moreover, a new order of problems has emerged in the capitalist countries themselves with the surge of technological innovation (and specifically, the increasing automation of production, distribution and a variety of services) which steadily diminishes the quantity of human labour required and poses the question whether, and in what kind of society, the reduction of necessary working time will be accomplished through permanent large-scale unemployment or through some collective reorganization of the whole labour process.[3]

Property

Property, according to Hobhouse (1913a, p. 6), 'is to be conceived in terms of the control of man over things', a control which is recognized by society, more or less permanent, and exclusive. Property may be private (individual or collective) or common. In his account of the development of property Hobhouse observed that there is some personal private property in all societies, but that in many primitive societies the principal economic resources are communally owned (e.g. hunting land, grazing land, pasture). In more developed agricultural societies private ownership comes to predominate, but Hobhouse pointed out that although tribal common ownership disappears, common ownership may be maintained for the joint family. Lowie (1950, ch. 6), in an excellent short account of property which uses comparative material from primitive and civilized societies, presents much the same view. There is personal private property among all primitive peoples, including names, dances, songs, myths, ceremonial regalia, gifts, weapons, household implements. So far as the 'instruments of production' are concerned there are differences between hunters and food-gatherers, where the land is tribal property (not always well defined), and agriculturalists and pastoralists. Among agriculturalists individual private property in land is frequently found, though the clan or tribe may still exercise some control over its use or alienation. In the case of pastoralists, land may be communally owned but not the livestock: 'the ownership of livestock strongly develops the sense of individual property'.

Common ownership by a joint family occurs in many societies. In Europe, the Yugoslav *Zadruga* was a well-known example, but there were similar forms of property in other peasant societies. Most of these had given place to individual ownership by the early twentieth century. The nature of property rights in the Hindu joint family in the Vedic period is not entirely clear. Macdonell and Keith (1912, Vol. 1, p. 351) argued that 'The [Vedic] passages all negative the idea that the property of the family was family property: it is clear that it was the property of the head of the house, usually the father, and that the other members of the family only had moral claims upon it which the father could ignore . . .' But Kapadia (1958, p. 194) has concluded that there is no clear indication in the Vedic literature that the patriarchal family was the only type of family organization. Later, according to the same writer, there were tendencies towards the disintegration of the joint family, and the scope of individual property was broadened, but the old patriarchal tradition was utilized to strengthen the joint family. Thus, at no period was there common family property, but in later periods there were restraints upon the powers of the family head to alienate property (pp. 200 ff).

In general, with the development of agriculture, manufacture, and commerce, individual or collective ownership of productive resources was extended, but some common ownership continued in most societies, for example, in the manorial system of feudal Europe where the community retained a general control of cultivation and certain rights in the settlement of disputes. In Russia such community control lasted until the present century. The characteristic feature of all these property systems, as Hobhouse emphasized, was that they were concerned with property for use, and even where private ownership was highly developed there remained some community control and responsibility for ensuring that no member became entirely destitute. Property for power, and unlimited individual acquisition of wealth, reached a peak in nineteenth-century capitalist Europe and North America, but was relatively quickly subjected to some community restraints. The recent history of property is very largely a history of the imposition or reimposition of such restraints upon the private owners of economic resources, and in a later phase the deliberate redistribution or appropriation of such resources by the community.

A number of writers have attempted to distinguish the principal types of property system, or stages in the development of property. I have already mentioned Hobhouse's scheme, which has three phases: the first, in which there is little social differentiation, little inequality, and economic resources are owned in common or are strictly controlled by the community; the second in which wealth increases, great inequalities appear, and private ownership escapes from community control; and a third in which a conscious attempt is made to diminish inequality, and to restore community control. This scheme has some resemblances to the Marxist distinction into three stages: that of the primitive classless society, followed by class differentiation and the growth of inequality, and the final stage of a classless society at a higher level. Vinogradoff (1920) distinguished four principal stages: the establishment of property rights in a tribal and communal context, the application of the notion of tenure to land, the development of individual appropriation, and finally the imposition of restrictions under the influence of modern collectivist ideas.

More recent writers have emphasized the complexity of property systems and have rejected the notion of a unilinear evolution. There have been a number of comparative studies of property in primitive societies, which illustrate the difficulty of determining the character and extent of property rights (Lowie, 1950, ch. 6; Herskovits, 1952, chs. 14–17). Nevertheless, the evolution of property in Western Europe is fairly clear; it has been well documented by economic historians, and its recent phases are reflected in property ideologies from John Locke's natural right theory to the modern socialist doctrines (Schlatter, 1951).

The history of property rights in India is less clear. The principal form of productive property was, until recently, land, and the tenure of land was regulated by Hindu customary law, later supplemented by Muslim law. Land tenure only became precisely determined during the period of British rule, after the Bengal Permanent Settlement Regulation of 1793. It is doubtful whether under Hindu law, as recorded in the Code of Manu, there were any proprietary rights in land. The king had a right to a share of the produce, and the cultivator had the right to be protected in the occupation of his land and to transmit this to his heirs. The version of Muslim law which was generally followed in India after the twelfth century seems to have created some

proprietary rights (Lindsay, 1941, pp. 115–27). But the Permanent Settlement of 1793 created in Bengal, and later in other
parts of India, definite proprietary rights for the *zamindars*, who
were originally revenue collectors employed by the Muslim
conquerors and who thus became landed gentry (Gopal, 1949).
Elsewhere, in Bombay and Madras, a different settlement (the
ryotwari system) created a class of peasant proprietors. The
general results of British legislation were, therefore, to establish
clear proprietary rights in land, to make land an alienable saleable
commodity and thus to bring it within the general property
system of a capitalist economy.

Recent sociological studies of property in the capitalist industrial societies have been mainly concerned with two aspects; first,
the distribution of personal property and its social implications,
and secondly, the concentration of productive property in large
corporations and the related question of the separation between
ownership and control. There have been numerous studies of the
distribution of wealth and income. In Britain, Tawney (1952)
examined in detail the inequalities of wealth and income, and
their connection with the class system. More recent studies, some
of which use data from the reports of the Royal Commission on
the Distribution of Income and Wealth (established in 1974 and
disbanded in 1979), include Atkinson (1974), Routh (1980), Scott
(1982) and Field (1983). They show that both wealth and income
are very unequally distributed (wealth more than income), but
that there has been a trend towards greater equality over the long
term; thus the share of the top 1 per cent of wealth holders
declined from about 69 per cent in 1911–13 to 23 per cent in 1975,
and the share of the top 5 per cent from some 85 per cent to
around 50 per cent, while the share of the bottom 80 per cent of
the population increased from about 5 per cent to 18 per cent.
Income inequalities have diminished somewhat more rapidly,
largely as a result of progressive taxation and the expansion of
social services; but it should be noted that one major inequality –
between the earnings of men and women – though it diminished
in particular occupational categories, changed only slightly
overall between 1913–14 and 1978 (Routh, 1980, p. 123).

Britain is an exceptionally unequal society, and as Atkinson
observed (1974, p. 21), 'It seems quite possible that, as far as the
distribution of wealth is concerned, Britain has the doubtful
distinction of leading the international inequality league.' Moreover, since 1979 inequality has been increasing again as a result of
changes in taxation and in the provision of public services, and
the massive growth of unemployment. But there are clearly very

great inequalities in other capitalist societies, as is shown in the case of the USA by Mills (1956, chs. 5 and 7), Harrington (1962), and Kolko (1962). Elsewhere, in Europe (and notably in Sweden and Austria), inequality has been mitigated by more strongly redistributive fiscal and social policies, and the stark poverty which characterizes some areas of other Western societies is largely absent. In the socialist countries of Eastern Europe the accumulation of large amounts of personal wealth is impossible, but considerable inequalities of income, status and power exist (Lane, 1982) which will be examined in Chapter 11 below.

The rise of large corporations, including multinational corporations, is a distinctive feature of the development of capitalism in the twentieth century. The industrial capitalists of the early nineteenth century were both owners and managers of their enterprises, but as the enterprises grew larger more and more capital had to be drawn from outside, and this was made possible by joint-stock legislation. At present, the large companies which dominate the major branches of industry are managed and directed by individuals who do not own them. The owners of much of the capital are the thousands of small and medium shareholders who have little interest except in the profitability of the company and may not even know what it manufactures. In a well-known study, Berle and Means (1934) examined in detail the large corporations of the USA, and their conclusions were the basis for later theorizing about the 'managerial revolution' and the transformation of capitalism (Burnham, 1941; Berle, 1955).

These changes have been exaggerated by some writers. Although the managers of modern industry do not own the enterprises outright, they usually have an important shareholding and they are wealthy men in their own right; there is no fundamental divorce between ownership of property and management of industry. Sargant Florence (1953) showed that 'on average in large companies, twenty shareholders out of some ten to twenty thousand hold, in Britain and America, nearly a third of voting shares', and this is quite enough to give them control of the company. He argued that 'there is certainly evidence for believing that the managerial revolution has not proceeded as far as is sometimes thought (or stated without thought) and that leadership and the ultimate decision on top policy may remain in many companies or corporations with the largest capital shareholders'. Mills (1956) indicated how ownership and control are interwoven in American industry and observed that 'the chief executives and the very rich are *not* two distinct and clearly segregated groups'. A more recent study (Scott, 1979) which examines in detail the structure of large corporations, in the context of two alternative theories – of 'industrial society' and of 'capitalist society' – also concludes that

> the developmental trends in industrial capitalism have not been associated with the demise of the capitalist class . . . a propertied class still exists and . . . derives its advantages from ownership of company shares and participation in strategic control. The 'impersonal' structure of possession has not resulted in a loss of power by wealthy persons. (p. 175)

This study also draws attention to the increasing 'effective possession' of industrial companies by financial institutions (insurance companies, pension funds, banks), a phenomenon which is investigated thoroughly, in the case of Britain, in Coakley and Harris (1983). The changes in conceptions of property which the emergence of large corporations and state-owned enterprises has brought about will be discussed further in the following section.

Types of Economy

It was shown in an earlier chapter that the classification of societies has often been based upon a preliminary classification of economic systems. Such was the case with Marx's distinction of five major types of society: primitive society, ancient society, Asiatic society, feudal society, and capitalist society. In accordance with Marx's basic assumptions the distinction is made not only in terms of the level of technology and the mode of production, but also in terms of property and class relations. Rather similar classifications have been proposed by other writers, especially by the German historical economists and sociologists, such as Bücher and Sombart. This broad classification of types of economy seems to have been generally accepted, and there have also been a number of attempts to distinguish subgroups within the principal types. Thus Hobhouse, Wheeler and Ginsberg (1915), as I noted earlier, correlated different types of economic organization among primitive societies with differences in other social institutions (stratification, government, etc.). The distinction between food-gatherers, hunters, pastoralists and agriculturalists, in the case of primitive societies, has become a commonplace, though some anthropologists (e.g. Forde, 1941) have cast doubt upon the correlations between the type of economy and the forms of other social institutions by showing that there is very considerable variation in institutions within the same economic type. The same is true, no doubt, of feudal societies and modern capitalist or socialist societies, but this does not exclude fundamental similarities between societies which have the same type of economy and fundamental differences where the economy differs.

In the case of modern capitalism, Pirenne (1914) distinguished several stages in the 'social history of capitalism', in terms of the principal directions of economic activity and the social groups which took the leading role at each stage. Sociologists, from Marx onwards, have devoted much of their effort to the analysis of capitalism as an economic and social system (Bottomore, 1985). Aside from the debate about the origins of modern capitalism, initiated by Weber (1904–5) and critically reviewed by Marshall (1982), most attention has been given to the changes in capitalism during the twentieth century, and particularly to the growth of large-scale enterprise and of state intervention in the economy. Marxist writers have distinguished in various ways between nineteenth-century capitalism and the 'monopoly capitalism' (Baran and Sweezy, 1966), 'state monopoly capitalism' (Harris, 1983), 'organized capitalism' (Hilferding, 1927; Habermas, 1973, pt 2, ch. 1), or 'late capitalism' (Mandel, 1975) of the twentieth century, which they also connect with imperialism or with the 'neo-imperialism' of the post-colonial period (Brewer, 1980, pt 3).

But the rapid growth of large enterprise, and the concentration of economic power, is to be found in all the industrial countries, whether their economic regime is one of predominantly private ownership of the means of production, mixed public and private ownership, or mainly collective ownership. In the USSR, as in Britain or the USA, a relatively small number of individuals manage the giant enterprises on which material well-being depends and decide major economic issues as to the use of resources. This situation has led to a reconsideration of the notion of property, and in particular the elaboration of a distinction between juridical 'ownership' and effective 'possession' (Hegedüs, 1976, pp. 93–105); and to critical studies of bureaucratic domination in 'state-socialist societies' (i.e. the USSR and other East European countries).

In those capitalist countries in which some basic industries have been nationalized problems have arisen in the control of the public corporations which manage them. From the point of view of the employee and the ordinary citizen public bureaucracies may be no easier to deal with, and offer no greater opportunities

for participation in decision-making, than do private managements. And in many socialist countries the absence of independent organizations outside the sphere of state control (e.g.
independent trade unions, professional and cultural associations,
political groups) makes the control of bureaucracy still more
difficult. These developments confirm the importance of Max
Weber's analysis of bureaucracy, and of the whole process of
'rationalization', as formulated particularly in his essay on politics
(1919) where he suggested a parallel between the concentration of
productive powers and the concentration of administrative
powers. In discussing the development of the modern state he
observed that the prince, in his conflict with the nobility, opened
the way for the expropriation of the autonomous, private owners
of executive power, those who possess in their own right the
means of administration, welfare, and so on. 'The whole process
is an exact parallel to the development of the capitalist enterprise
through the gradual expropriation of the independent producers.' In the future development of industrial society Weber
saw (but in my view also exaggerated) the danger that socialism
might result, not in the liberation of human beings, but in their
enslavement to an all-powerful bureaucracy.

Sociological studies of types of economic system have thus
contributed notably to recent political controversies. Strachey
(1956) saw a conflict between political democracy and the oligarchic tendencies of modern capitalism, while Mills (1956)
noted the emergence of a 'mass society' in the USA, in which
power becomes increasingly concentrated in the hands of the
leaders of large-scale organizations, in the economic field and
elsewhere. In the state-socialist societies during the Stalinist
period the process of concentration of power in a small elite
reached its zenith, but more recent changes seem to be gradually
reversing this trend. These social changes have re-awakened
interest in problems of the control of economic power through
decentralization and 'industrial democracy' (which I shall discuss
in the following section), and in the analysis of oligarchic
tendencies in political organizations (which will be considered in
the next chapter), as well as in the general characteristics of
bureaucratic organization.

The study of types of economy shows well the value of a
sociological approach, which attempts to view synoptically and
to elucidate the complex interrelations between the property
system, the organization of industry, social stratification and
political organization. This is also apparent in the study of change
from one type of economy to another. An early controversy,

initiated as I have noted by Weber's study (1904–5), but arising ultimately from Marx's theory, concerned the origins of capitalism. In Weber's view the development of capitalism required a generalization of attitudes towards work and wealth which had previously been exceptional in human societies (see also the concise discussion in Heilbroner, 1952, ch. 2). The social ethic of Protestantism aided the diffusion of such attitudes; thus it helped to accelerate the development of capitalism in Western Europe and North America, and may also have contributed certain specific characteristics. The importance of values and ideologies in the functioning of economic systems is brought out in later writing on the 'decline of capitalism'; for example in Schumpeter's (1942) study, where it is argued that the decay of capitalism will be largely the consequence of the rejection of 'bourgeois' values, not of economic breakdown. The argument recalls Max Weber's dictum: 'The Puritan wanted work to be his vocation; we are forced to want it', which expresses disillusion and suggests eventual hostility to the culture of capitalism.

Perhaps more significant is the recent development of a theory of industrial societies and industrialization which takes account of many social factors, including ideologies, and represents at present one of the main points of convergence of economics and sociology. The writing in this field emphasizes the distinction between two types of economy, industrial and non-industrial, and is concerned with industrialism rather than capitalism since it is evident that industrialization can occur in a variety of ways in different social and political contexts. Lewis (1955) deals comprehensively with the economic and other factors involved in economic growth: the desire for goods, attitudes to work, the influence of property systems, social mobility, religion and family structure, the effects of population growth, and the role of government. A more specific problem of industrialization, the recruitment and training of labour for industrial employment in agricultural countries, has been exhaustively studied by Moore (1951). This is an outstanding problem in all non-industrial countries, for the agricultural worker who is brought into industrial work also moves from the village to the town, and the process of adjustment to the new conditions may be long and difficult. In Europe, the problem of 'peasant workers' and their families has called forth much useful research in two countries of collectivist industrialization, Poland and Yugoslavia.

In the previous chapter I made some critical comments on the distinction between non-industrial and industrial societies. This question will be considered further in a later chapter on social change, in the context of a discussion of economic development in the Third World, as will the more recent analyses of the development of both capitalist and socialist societies.

The Industrial Enterprise and Industrial Relations

Within the general field of study of industrial societies there has emerged a more limited branch of study, now called industrial sociology, which is concerned with two main aspects of industrial life: the internal organization of the enterprise and the social relationships existing there, and industrial relations in the wider sense of the relations between the different groups in industry, principally between owners and managers, supervisors and white collar workers, and manual workers. Two major books by Moore (1946) and Friedmann (1946) survey a large part of the field of industrial sociology in the immediate postwar period, and give some indication of how sociological studies of industry developed. In the first place, there were practical problems of fatigue, boredom, absenteeism and other factors which adversely affected output. The study of such problems became particularly urgent during the First World War with the growing demands upon industry, and it was then, for instance, that the first systematic inquiries (by psychologists) were undertaken in Britain. The next phase was the rise of the 'scientific organization of work' movement sponsored by the American engineer, Taylor, and enthusiastically received by manufacturers like Ford. A third phase was reached with the work of the 'human relations movement' inspired by Elton Mayo, the first which had a distinctively sociological character (Mayo, 1933; Roethlisberger and Dickson, 1939). All these studies were basically concerned with productivity, and with the psychological and social factors affecting it. From another direction, the trade unions and the labour movement brought pressure to improve working conditions, to create a more humanly satisfying working environment, and to provide opportunities both for individual advancement and promotion, and for greater participation by employees in determining the organization of work processes. These interests converged to favour sociological studies of social relations in the enterprise, particularly as the problems became more acute with the development of mass-production, conveyor belt production, and more recently, automation.

The major themes of study, over the past ten years, have been the interpersonal relations in working groups and their influence upon productivity, the role of supervisors, problems of management and bureaucracy, the effects of specialized work and possible compensations in leisure time, and the problems created by technological change. Special attention has been given to particular groups of workers, such as young people and women workers. The volume of research and writing is now vast, but the major issues and findings are well summarized in the books by Friedmann and Moore mentioned above, and in a more recent survey by Parker *et al.* (1967).

Research in industry has covered publicly owned industries as well as private enterprise, and has been conducted in both capitalist and socialist industrial countries, as well as in the Third World. It was mentioned earlier that the concentration of economic power had revived interest in the problems of 'industrial democracy'. This interest has been stimulated also by the discovery that the public ownership of industry did not resolve all the problems of the enterprise, or eliminate conflict (although authoritarian governments might suppress overt conflict); and by concern over the 'meaninglessness' of specialized industrial work, and its effects on the individual and on output. In fact, there have been numerous experiments, in recent years, in workers' participation in management or workers' self-management, and these experiments have been closely studied by sociologists. There is an account of some of this research in Friedmann (1956) and in several more recent studies of the Yugoslav system (Broekmeyer, 1970). There have also been interesting new policies for a gradual 'socialization' of industry and wider participation in management, notably the Swedish 'wage-earners investment funds', which are critically examined in Himmelstrand *et al.* (1981, pt 4).

The other aspect of industrial sociology, industrial relations in the broad sense, was for a time overshadowed by the studies within the enterprise. There was even some inclination, especially among American sociologists, to explain the wider industrial relations in terms of relationships within the factory, and to reduce the latter to problems of individual personality, familial relationships, and so on, while entirely ignoring the broader institutional framework of property, the class system, and political institutions. But this phase has now passed. There have been numerous studies of the different groups involved in industrial conflict and negotiation, though these have tended to concentrate upon trade unions and to leave in some obscurity the structure and policies of the organizations of technicians, managers and owners. This is partly because the immediate postwar growth of trade unions, and the more favourable social climate of the welfare state, gave them greater power, while the extension of public ownership created difficult problems of relationships between trade unions and the managements of nationalized industries. At all events there have been many investigations of trade union leadership and organization, though the character of these studies has tended to change in recent years as trade union power has diminished, with rising unemployment and the implementation of government policies, especially in Britain, which are specifically designed to curb that power. One aspect of postwar trade unionism which is especially significant is the rapid growth of white collar unions (Sturmthal, 1967), and in many countries their increasing militancy and radicalism.

The processes of negotiation, arbitration and conflict have also been widely studied, though for the most part in a national context. One comprehensive analysis of industrial conflict in Britain from 1911 to 1945 (Knowles, 1952) correlates strike activity with other social phenomena, and there are other more limited studies along the same lines; but there have been few major attempts to undertake systematic comparisons between countries or between historical periods, though two books (Kornhauser, Dubin and Ross, 1954: Ross and Hartman, 1960) make some contribution in this direction, and there is a brief comparison of Britain and Scandinavia in Ingham (1974). It is evident that industrial conflict is closely associated with questions of class and politics; and the trade union movement, industrial relations and conflict have been analysed in very different ways in the context of alternative conceptions of the structure of capitalist (and also socialist) societies. Durkheim, as we saw, thought that class conflict would diminish as the different interest groups in the economic sphere, and in particular capital and labour, were brought into a closer relationship and regulated by an interventionist state which represents the interests of society as a whole. Much subsequent writing on industrial relations has explicitly or implicitly adopted this conception. Marxist writers, on the other hand, conceive trade unions as class organizations, and regard industrial conflict as a major element in the class struggle, which may assume exceptional importance in some circumstances, through the 'mass strike' (Hyman, 1975, 1984). One significant issue which has not been fully explored, though it has become prominent recently with the rise of the Solidarity movement in Poland, is the role of trade unions, and the significance of industrial conflict, in the socialist countries.

In this brief survey I have tried to illustrate the distinctiveness of a sociological approach, which consists in studying economic phenomena in the context of the social structure as a whole. The division of labour, property ownership, the type of economic system and the character of the industrial enterprise and industrial relations, as well as social stratification and the political order – viewed in the light of the historical changes which they undergo – may all be involved when we try to describe and explain a particular set of economic conditions or events in one society at a particular moment of time.

Notes to Chapter 8

1　It is important to note here that Marx distinguished between a *technical* division of labour which necessitates functions of co-ordination (i.e. management), and a *social* division of labour which separates workers from the means of production and requires supervision, or domination, only because of that separation. For a brief discussion of this question see Hirst, 1976, pp. 120–1, and also Bottomore, 1984a, ch. 10.

2　For some detailed accounts of the nature of work in industrial societies, see Fraser, 1968–9; Terkel, 1974; Beynon, 1984.

3　On the issues raised by what has been called 'the scientific and technological revolution', see Friedmann, 1966; Richta, 1969; Mukherjee *et al.*, 1977.

9 Political Institutions

Political institutions are concerned with the distribution of power in society. Max Weber defined the state as 'a human community which successfully claims the monopoly of the legitimate use of physical force within a given territory'. Thus the state is one of the important agencies of social control, whose functions are carried out by means of law, backed ultimately by physical force. It is *one* association within society, and not society as a whole. I discussed earlier the distinction established between 'civil society' and the state, which was an important step in the formation of sociology as a science. The early sociologists, having established this distinction, proceeded to examine the relationship between civil society and the state, and to attempt a classification of political systems based upon the different forms of civil society. Their approach was evolutionary and they were interested especially in the *origins* and *development* of the state. Regarding the state as one association within society, and as characterized by definite territorial limits, and being acquainted through the growing literature of ethnography with societies which seemed to have no formal political organization, they were naturally led to consider the question of origins; and some of them went on to speculate, under the influence of the philosophy of history, about the future of the state. This same philosophical view (and the political revolutions of the age) determined their interest in the different historical forms of the state, especially in Western civilization.

I shall consider first, therefore, the theories of the state which provide the framework of sociological analysis, then the classifications of political systems, and finally discuss in greater detail political organization and political behaviour in present-day societies, which can be directly studied by social scientists and to which most of the literature is devoted.

Theories of the State

The early sociologists made a distinction between those societies which had, and those which had not, a formal political system, but they made it in different ways and they diverged in their accounts of how the state originated. Spencer distinguished in his category of 'simple societies' some which had no headship and others which had only occasional or unstable headship. It was only at the stage of 'doubly compound societies' that any elaborate political organization was to be found. Hobhouse distinguished between three types of society characterized by different fundamental social bonds: kinship, authority and citizenship; and in a study of primitive societies demonstrated a correlation between the level of economic development, increasing social differentiation, and the emergence and consolidation of a regular political authority. Marx and Engels, having elaborated a classification of societies in which the state came into existence only at a stage of economic development where antagonistic social classes appeared, found confirmation of their views in the anthropological researches of L. H. Morgan. Engels's (1884) systematic formulation of the Marxist view was based upon Morgan's work and Marx's manuscript notes thereon.

The explanations of the emergence of the state were broadly of two kinds. Spencer and Comte regarded it as a consequence of the increasing size and complexity of societies, in which warfare was a major factor. According to Spencer, war consolidated the 'compound society' and still more the 'doubly compound society'. Comte attributed to warfare the 'first great mission' of bringing about the expansion of human societies and the establishment of settled political authority. These views agree in some respects with the theory of Oppenheimer (1907) who, criticizing Marxism, discovered the origin of the state *and* of social classes in the conquest of one tribe by another: 'the state is a juridical institution unilaterally imposed upon a conquered people by the conquerors, originally with the sole object of subjecting them to a tribute'. In contrast, the Marxist theory accounts for the emergence of the state by differentiation into social classes within the community following the growth of productive forces and of wealth, though Marx himself, in discussing early societies, emphasized the importance of war in their expansion and in the establishment of slavery and serfdom.

Recent sociological and anthropological study has confirmed some of these distinctions and modified others. It is generally agreed that some primitive societies lack a political authority, and Lowie (1950, ch. 14) writes: 'The earliest communities must have been tiny, egalitarian groups corresponding to a Semang or Eskimo camp. Such a community was in the main a body of kindred . . . ' At the same time, the role of kinship in maintaining social unity should not be exaggerated, as it probably was by Hobhouse, Morgan and others. Maine (1861, p. 76) argued that in early societies kinship was 'the sole possible ground of community in political functions', but Lowie (1950, p. 317) remarks that this 'exaggerates the correct view that kinship has played an enormous part in the social life of aboriginal and archaic peoples', and goes on to say: 'That the territorial tie is never wholly negligible is proved a fortiori by two extreme instances of kinship–dominated tribes, the Ifugao and the Yurok.' One distinctive feature, in primitive and early societies, is that where a separate political authority exists it is closely bound up with kinship, religion and other institutions.[1]

From an analysis of the origins of the state the early sociologists went on to consider its development, in the framework of a general evolutionary scheme. Thus they discussed the question of how small communities developed into larger, politically organized societies. Some, like Spencer or Comte, emphasized military conquest, while others stressed the integration brought about by economic or religious developments. Fustel de Coulanges (1864) attributed the formation of the Greek and Roman cities to the elaboration of a more inclusive religion (and his ideas profoundly influenced Durkheim's theory of religion), while Marx saw the mainspring of development in the emergence, and transformations, of an economically dominant class, its pursuit of specific interests, and its conflict with subordinate classes.

The nineteenth–century evolutionists also agreed broadly in tracing a course of development, in the more recent history of Western civilization, from authoritarian states to less coercive types of political system, variously termed 'industrial society' or 'citizenship'; and Marxists foresaw an eventual culmination of this process in a liberated 'classless society'. What most of these writers neglected, however, was the rise of the most significant political form in the modern world – the nation–state – and the immense power of nationalism. There was some analysis of the phenomenon, particularly by Marxist thinkers in relation to imperialism (Bauer, 1907; Brewer, 1980), but it is only in the last few decades that sociologists have begun to give it the attention it merits (Smith, 1971; Tilly, 1975; Bottomore, 1979, ch. 5).

Besides these questions concerning the origins and development of the state we have also to consider how sociologists have conceived the nature of the state. Here there are two broad alternative conceptions: one which treats the state as essentially a *coercive* agency, another which regards it as a *moral* agency embodying some kind of social consensus. Clearly, for Marxists the state, in class society, is an instrument of coercion, an essential means by which a dominant class maintains its dominance. But the relatively simple view which Engels (1884) expounded has attracted much criticism, and has certainly been modified in later Marxist writing concerned with the specific characteristics of the modern democratic state (as contrasted, for example, with the absolutist state, fascism, or military dictatorships), with the 'relative autonomy' of the state in relation to class interests, and with the problem of the state and its role in the present-day socialist societies.[2] More attention has also been given to Gramsci's (1929–35) distinction between state coercion and 'hegemony', which emphasizes the element of consent (brought about by persuasion or 'ideology') in the maintenance of domination.[3]

The coercive nature of the state is also emphasized by Oppenheimer (1907) and by Max Weber (1921). Weber's position is close to that of Marx in some respects, in recognizing that state power may be in the hands of a particular class. But there is a considerable divergence in Weber's actual analysis of political power. First, Weber assumes, like the elite theorists,[4] that there is always and necessarily a dominant group in society. Secondly, his analysis is concerned above all with the ways in which domination is legitimated, and he makes a distinction between three types of legitimate domination: traditional, charismatic and legal-rational (Mommsen, 1974, ch. 4; Parkin, 1982, ch. 3).

What is central in these conceptions of the state is the idea of domination and of an ultimate coercive power. On the other side stand those theories which emphasize the nature of the state as the expression of some kind of moral unity of a society. Hobhouse (1912, p. 133) also defined the state as an association 'distinguished by its coercive power, by its supremacy, and by its claim to control all who dwell within its geographical limits', but in discussing the modern democratic state based upon the principle of citizenship he qualified this definition substantially in arguing that 'the people or at any rate the citizens, are the state . . . Law is no longer a command imposed by a superior, but an expression of those who obey it' (Hobhouse, 1911, p. 133). The most forceful statement of this view of the state is to be found in Durkheim's (1950) brief discussion, which omits any reference to the state as a repressive organ associated with particular social interests: 'The state is a special organ responsible for elaborating certain representations which are valid for the collectivity . . . Strictly speaking, the state is the very organ of social thought' (p. 62).

Types of Political System

The early and classical sociologists, for the most part, conceived the different types of state or political system in terms of an evolutionary scheme, though Weber, who rejected the idea of a universal history, is something of an exception (Mommsen, 1974, ch. 4). As Aron (1967, Introduction) argued, 'a sociology which tends towards the interpretation of society as a whole is almost irresistibly led to define social types; and the definition of social types leads to the hypothesis of an evolution from one type to another'. But the types of political system which the nine-teenth-century sociologists distinguished were relatively few, and their evolutionary schemes were mainly relevant to Western civilization: tribal and archaic societies, city-states, feudal states and modern democracies were the principal forms considered. Thus the Asiatic type of society and government was little discussed; but at the same time the rise and expansion of nation-states in the West was also neglected. At the present time it seems possible to outline a more comprehensive classification, which is set out schematically below:

Tribal and archaic societies

(1) without a distinct and permanent political structure
(2) with a distinct and permanent political structure, but strongly influenced by kinship and religion

City states
Empires based upon city states
Feudal states
Asiatic states with a centralized bureaucracy
Nation states

(1) absolutist states
(2) modern democratic states (capitalist or socialist)
(3) modern totalitarian/authoritarian states

Empires based upon nation states

This classification is largely descriptive, but it takes into account the scale of societies, the economic system, social stratification, religion, and other factors which have been seen to be important in determining political structure. It does not imply a universal evolutionary scheme, or any unilinear process of political devel-opment, but it does provide a framework for analysing particular historical transitions (e.g. from feudalism to capitalism and the emergence of nation–states, or from absolutism to democracy) and specific types of political regime (in socialist and capitalist societies, totalitarian or imperialist systems). Clearly, the classification has many other complexities and poses a number of problems (e.g. that some of the categories may overlap) which cannot be fully explored here,[5] and I shall confine myself to considering some examples of the major historical types of political system before turning in the following sections to a discussion of the political institutions of present-day societies.

Earlier, I discussed the application to India of the concept of 'Asiatic society'. This implied a political classification, since an essential feature of the Asiatic type of society is the existence of an authoritarian government ruling through a centralized bureaucracy. At the same time, however, we have to consider that this type of government is superimposed upon a large number of small, and to some extent self-governing, communities. Thus there are two levels of political organization and action. The centralized state may be little more than a tax collecting and public works agency; there is no fundamental political integration, but, on the contrary, a strong tendency for the separate units within the state to break away. In the actual development of political unity in India we can see at work the forces of conquest and co-operation discussed above. India was unified at various times by conquest, by the Maurya and Gupta Empires, the Muslim conquest, and most completely by the British conquest. Yet in all these periods, and still more in the periods of breakdown of the central authority, the unity of the society was maintained largely by the caste system and religion. Secular and religious authority were closely related, and the influence of the Brahmins seems to have gradually increased. Moreover, the law books were written and interpreted by Brahmins, and law in India retained until recently a strongly religious character (see Chapter 15 below). The situation resembled that in other 'Asiatic societies' discussed by Wittfogel (1957): Byzantium, the Inca Empire, ancient Egypt. The important political role of priests seems to have been connected in part with the rigid stratification system, which required religious justification. In later Indian history this political structure was complicated by the introduction of feudal type relations, after the Muslim conquest, and it was finally dissolved by the development of capitalism and the growth of towns as industrial and commercial centres, under British rule, and by the emergence of a democratic political system after independence.

The political system of the European feudal societies was

characterized by Bloch (1931, 1939–40) as the rule of a warrior class, which had securely in its hands the ownership of land, military force, and political authority, in a decentralized political system where the power of the central state was often weak and precarious. The emergence from this system of the absolute monarchies was a long and complex process, in which the early development of capitalism and the growth of towns played an important part; it involved the substitution of hired soldiers for vassals and the constitution of a corps of salaried officials (both requiring enhanced financial resources), and marked the first stage in the formation of modern nation-states (Bloch, 1931; Anderson, 1974b; Tilly, 1975).

The transformations of the political system in Europe form a distinct historical sequence in which the main factor is the rise of capitalism and, at a later stage, of socialism as an alternative to it. Elsewhere in the world the course of development has been different; starting out from diverse forms of society, profoundly affected by the expansion of capitalism and colonial conquest, new independent nations have emerged which are inextricably involved in the world economy and global politics. In the following sections I shall examine in particular the main features of politics in the modern industrial societies and in the societies of the Third World.

Political Institutions and Behaviour in Industrial Societies

We must begin by reiterating the distinction made earlier between capitalist and socialist industrial societies, while recognizing that there are considerable variations within each of these categories; and on the other hand, that some general characteristics of political systems in all the industrial societies can be identified: (1) the political community as a nation-state, (2) the existence of political movements, parties and pressure groups, (3) the election of the political executive by universal adult suffrage, and (4) the administration of public affairs by a large centralized bureaucracy.

The first of these characteristics, as noted earlier, received relatively little attention from sociologists until recent decades, and the significance of the nation-state has been altogether underestimated, especially in its bearing upon the development of capitalism. Similarly, nationalism as an ideology, and its connections with religion or class interests, have been much less closely investigated than have other political ideologies. Yet the force of nationalism in the modern world is very great, and creates problems in relation to international order. Some of the major problems of the present day arise from the contradictions between the need for an international political authority and the forces of new nationalisms and old and new imperialisms.

The study of political parties and elections in the capitalist societies has developed rapidly in the past few decades, along several different lines. The connection between political parties and social classes, which is the central conception of the Marxist theory of politics and the state, has been thoroughly investigated. The general relationship between class interest, party affiliation and electoral choice is unmistakable (Rose, 1968). Numerous inquiries have shown that the main political parties in most societies are perceived by the electors as representing class interests, and that most electors vote in accordance with what they take to be their own class interests. Nevertheless, the relationship is by no means simple or unchanging. Political parties are also seen as representing diverse elements in a national tradition, and as being concerned in some degree with general, rather than class or sectional, interests. Moreover, not all individuals vote in accordance with their social class position as an external observer might define it. In British General Elections between 1951 and 1974, approximately one-third of those in the working class voted for the Conservative Party, although this party is regarded by a large majority of electors as the party of the 'upper class'.[6] Over the same period some 20 per cent of those in the middle class voted for the Labour Party. At the same time there was a general loss of support for the two 'class-based' parties, and it has been argued that 'only half of the electorate held an enduring allegiance to the party of their occupational class' by the election of 1974 (Crewe et al., 1977). In the more recent elections of 1979 and 1983 there was a further loss of working-class support for the Labour Party. In the USA, although the class system differs in important ways from that in European countries, and class ideologies are less influential, a similar correlation between socio-economic status and electoral choice has been demonstrated, but with the same or greater divergences. There are in particular important regional and religious influences upon party affiliation and electoral choice (Heberle, 1951, ch. 12; Lipset, 1960). In some countries, however, class alignment appears to be stronger; thus in Sweden in the 1960s working-class support for the Social Democratic Party was around 80 per cent (Scase, 1975), and more generally in Western Europe, in contrast with the British experience, membership of working-class parties, and electoral support for them, has increased since 1945 (Bottomore, 1984a, ch. 11).

One important element in the changing relation between class and party is the continued growth of the middle classes in all the industrial societies (see Chapter 11 below); but the political consequences of this process have been interpreted in diverse ways. Some analyses envisage the gradual consolidation of predominantly middle-class, post-industrial societies, characterized by a broad political consensus and in a certain sense 'classless'; others, a more conservative middle-class orientation, hostile to socialism and tending towards the revival of a more *laissez-faire* type of economy and society; and yet others, the emergence of a new kind of dichotomous class structure, constituted by the controllers and managers of the institutions of economic and political decision-making on one side, and the rest of the population, reduced to a condition of restricted and dependent participation in public affairs, on the other, with the middle classes divided between the two categories on the basis of educational levels and the possession or non-possession of relevant technical knowledge (Touraine, 1969; Bottomore, 1979, ch. 1; Abercrombie and Urry, 1983).

Another interest in the study of political parties stems from the classical work by Michels (1911), who concluded that modern mass parties were not, and could not be, democratically organized, in so far as they were engaged in a struggle for power; on the contrary, they were ruled by a small oligarchy which controlled the bureaucratic apparatus. Michels was led, like his mentor and friend Max Weber, to question the possibility of any broad democratic participation, in the sense of 'government *by* the people', in a modern industrial society,[7] and (again like Weber) he came to emphasize strongly the role of the 'leader' and in due course was converted to the cause of Mussolini and Italian fascism. His study of political parties (especially in its second edition, 1925), a critic has argued, 'is to be understood as the work of someone who has passed over from revolutionary Marxism into the camp of elite theory' (Beetham, 1981). The oligarchic and bureaucratic tendencies in political parties (and in political life generally) can, of course, be seen as creating problems for democratic participation rather than making any extension of democracy impossible (Brym, 1980, ch. 3), but the tendencies themselves are real and important. A thorough study of British political parties (McKenzie, 1963) broadly confirmed Michel's analysis, and a comparative study by Duverger (1951) also brings out the oligarchic character of party leadership, especially in those societies which have a single-party system.

The critical attitude towards democracy expressed by the elite theorists bears upon one of the main features of the development of political regimes in the modern world, namely the transition from absolutist and authoritarian states to democratic systems of government. The growth of modern democracy has been a very slow and halting process; universal and equal suffrage has only been achieved during the twentieth century, in many cases since 1945, and democratic regimes have quite frequently been destroyed again by fascist movements and military dictatorships. Thus, even in the narrow sense of the right of all adult citizens to choose their leaders by means of free elections, democracy is a recent and somewhat delicate growth. Furthermore, the development of the oligarchic and bureaucratic tendencies that I have mentioned, the cult of leaders (exemplified by Weber's advocacy of what he called a 'plebiscitarian leader-democracy'), and the strong resistance by dominant groups to those extensions of democracy which would encourage the regular participation of citizens in decision-making at all levels of social life are all serious impediments to 'government *by* the people'.

Weber's preoccupation with the growth of bureaucratic power has been echoed in many more recent studies of bureaucracy in various spheres: in public administration, industry, trade unions and political parties. There are many divergent lines of inquiry (Mouzelis, 1967; Albrow, 1970), but one major emphasis has been on the separation between leaders and masses in large-scale organizations of all kinds, and a second on the possible emergence of a bureaucratic or managerial ruling class.

The latter question has been discussed especially in relation to the socialist countries, which demonstrate, according to some scholars, the truth of Weber's proposition that socialism would bring, not the 'dictatorship of the proletariat' but the 'dictatorship of the official'. At all events there is now considerable criticism of 'bureaucratism' in socialist societies (Hegedüs, 1976) as well as more extensive discussion of the emergence of a new dominant class in such societies (see Chapter 11 below). But the most salient feature of these societies is the existence of a single party which monopolizes political power. This situation is justified in terms of Marxist theory as the expression of social unity resulting from the elimination of antagonistic social classes. The dictatorship of the party is equated with the dictatorship of the proletariat in a transitional period during which the foundations of the ultimate classless society are being laid. According to the orthodox Marxist theory, after the achievement of the classless society the state, and presumably *all* political parties, will 'wither away'. Critics, however, have pointed out that the coercive apparatus of the state has vastly increased in many socialist societies, to the detriment of individual liberty, and that the social distinctions between the leaders and officials on one side, and the mass of people on the other, are very great. The major sociological criticism of orthodox or 'official' Marxism is that it asserts that political power is always based upon, and can only be based upon, economic power, and at the same time fails to analyse in a scientific and exact way the notion of 'economic power'. The latter point was briefly discussed in the previous chapter, where I drew attention to the ambiguities in the notion of 'ownership of the means of production'. The assertion of a one-to-one causal relationship between economic power and political power goes back to the eighteenth-century distinction between 'civil society' and the state, and to the impression made upon social theorists by the rapid emancipation of economic life from political regulation in the early stages of industrial capitalism. But in a broader historical perspective, while recognizing the important influence of economic structure upon other social institutions, we must also admit the relative autonomy of politics, as has been done increasingly in recent Marxist theory, and as Hilferding (1941) asserted forcefully at an earlier time. The major question is then the nature and degree of the state's autonomy, in specific historical conditions, and this has been vigorously debated in recent decades (Giddens, 1981, ch. 9; Miliband, 1983b, pt 1; Offe, 1984). It is clear, at least, that we can no longer ignore the issues of bureaucratic or managerial power, the formation and influence of various elites, or the activities of pressure groups in the political process.

Political sociology has dealt with a far greater range of subjects than can be discussed here. The detailed study of administrative behaviour and organization has resulted in much useful knowledge which can be, and is, applied to improve the efficiency of administration. The conflict of ideologies, within and between societies, has promoted studies of the social influences upon political beliefs, and of the influence which those beliefs may in turn have upon political power (Larrain, 1979; Abercrombie, Hill and Turner, 1980). Mannheim contributed greatly to this branch of the sociology of knowledge, notably in his classical essay on 'conservative thought' (1927a). Socialist ideologies have been less studied, but Bouglé (1925) analysed the influence of social structure upon the emergence and spread of egalitarian ideas, and

Raymond Aron (1955) examined the social factors which affect the acceptance of Marxism. More recently sociologists have studied the extent to which science and technology have become ideologies in the advanced industrial societies (Habermas, 1968; Leiss, 1972). These diverse studies have led to an increasing interest in the political role of intellectuals (Brym, 1980), especially in the particular situation of developing countries where intellectuals frequently represent modern Western culture and find themselves separated from, and in conflict with, the traditional cultural values of the mass of their fellow countrymen.

One aspect of political behaviour, however, was relatively neglected by sociologists until the 1960s; namely, the development of social movements. As I have indicated, parties and pressure groups have been quite thoroughly studied, but the more diffuse movements out of which they arise received much less attention. One major reason for this neglect was the preoccupation during the 1950s with 'stable democracy' – that is, with the political systems of Western capitalist societies, regarded as having attained a more or less definitive form with their existing array of parties and interest groups – and on the other side with the 'totalitarian' socialist societies, similarly regarded as having a permanent character.[8] Only with the emergence, during the 1960s, of new radical movements in the industrial countries, and the continuing growth of revolutionary movements in the Third World, did sociologists begin to devote themselves seriously to the study of such phenomena. Since then a large literature has appeared, beginning with the accounts of the early stages of the movements in the USA (Jacobs and Landau, 1966) and the student movement in France (Touraine, 1968), and continuing with comprehensive accounts of all the various movements (students, ethnic and regional movements, the women's movement, the peace movement, the ecology movement, the civil rights movements in Eastern Europe, the Polish Solidarity movement, and national liberation movements in many parts of the world), notably in the studies carried out by Touraine and his co-researchers. The political significance of these movements is very great, in two respects. First, they are, in the main, non-class movements (quite different from the early labour movement) and their development poses new questions about the social bases of political action, especially in relation to Marxist theory. Secondly, they are major forces for change in the present-day world, which have already profoundly influenced the established political parties and have engendered new parties; for example, the Green Party in the German Federal Republic and similar, though less prominent, ecology parties elsewhere.

Politics in the Developing Countries

There are some political conditions which are common to most, if not all, developing countries; in particular, the problems of establishing a new political system, and of making government and administration effective in bringing about rapid economic growth and a general improvement in levels of living, which is a major aspiration of the mass of the people. Many developing countries have one-party rule, arising out of the pre-eminence of a national liberation or revolutionary movement at the time when the new nation was formed. In many countries military officers have taken power, either because of the failure of other political forces, or because the military have already acquired a political role and see themselves as more 'modern' and efficient than other groups (Janowitz, 1964).

But the circumstances in which these problems have to be faced are extremely diverse. If we disregard for the moment the enormous differences in size and natural resources, and also the unique characteristics of each country, arising from its history, its geographical situation, or its particular relationships with other nations, we may distinguish, as I have argued elsewhere:

> four main categories of underdeveloped countries, within each of which there are important similarities of social structure and culture: (i) the African states; (ii) the Arab states of the Middle East and North Africa; (iii) the Asian states; and (iv) the Latin American states. The countries belonging to the first group have established themselves by means of anti-colonial struggles which have affected profoundly their political regimes. They have to face, in addition to the problems of economic development, those of consolidating a national community formed out of tribal groups whose existence within their frontiers is in some measure the result of the arbitrary division of Africa among the colonial powers. Among the countries of the second group, a number have been formed by independence struggles against direct colonial rule, but many others have enjoyed political independence for some time and have had chiefly to resist the indirect control of their economic resources by foreign powers. Their political problems are mainly those of breaking down feudal and autocratic systems of government, which are linked with highly inegalitarian and rigid class systems. The third group, that of the Asian countries, is characterized especially by the fact that these are, for the most part, countries of ancient civilization in which traditional social institutions are very strongly established. They are also countries which have liberated

themselves very recently from colonial rule, and although they do not confront major problems of integrating tribal groups into a national community, as is the case with the African countries, they face some similar problems of national integration in so far as they are divided into castes or linguistic regions (as in India), or into ethnically and linguistically separate groups (e.g. Tamils and Sinhalese in Ceylon, Malays and Chinese in Malaya). The fourth group, that of the Latin American countries, differs in important respects from all the others. These countries are, for the most part, more advanced economically, and they are already urban rather than agrarian societies, although they have only recently begun to industrialize on a large scale; and they have been politically independent for a relatively long time. Thus, their political problems are not to the same extent those of national integration, although in some of them, such as Peru, the large Indian population has still to acquire full citizenship; nor has recent political activity been directly inspired by nationalism, although it has been directed increasingly against North American economic influence in the region. The main problems are those created by industrialization, the rapid increase of population, and the rise of a labour movement within a political system in which the large landowners have long been dominant, and have often ruled through military dictatorships. (Bottomore, 1964, ch. 5)

There are, however, other differences which traverse this classification, one of them being that between capitalist and socialist developing countries. The latter, according to some recent studies (Jameson and Wilber, 1981; White et al., 1983), have done reasonably well in promoting economic growth, and better than other countries in terms of economic equality, provision of health and education services, and tackling unemployment; moreover, there have been signal achievements which 'are hard to measure ... enhanced national identity and pride, greater cultural self-confidence, abolition or reduction of previously exploitative or oppressive social relationships, the spread of "modern" or secular attitudes towards nature and society, and the political mobilisation of previously inert strata', though these benefits 'often entail serious costs' (White et al., 1983, p. 10), among them the emergence of a powerful state apparatus in which there are strongly authoritarian tendencies.

However, authoritarian states – dominated by landowners, indigenous and foreign capitalists, the military, or a combination of these groups – are also common in the capitalist developing countries, which are characterized further by extreme economic inequality and the absence of civil and political rights for large sections of the population. India is a rather exceptional case of a developing country which has maintained a democratic system since independence (except for the brief period of emergency rule in the mid-1970s), in the framework of a capitalist welfare society that embodies elements of socialism, both in the existing degree of central planning and in the long-term commitment, in principle, of most Indian political parties to the creation of a socialist society. The problem of political unity has not arisen mainly from differences of caste or religion, or from factional conflicts, though all of these play some part,[9] but from the diversity of regional cultures and the danger (which was much discussed, and in my view greatly exaggerated, in the 1960s) of a 'balkanisation' of India (Bottomore, 1975b, ch. 10). The need for a strong central state is determined above all, however, by the extent of the economic and social problems that emerge in the process of development; as Somjee (1979, ch. 6) observes, India has

> a rich legacy of contradictions which are not going to be overcome in the near future. For while there is a widespread commitment to liberal values, and . . . people have been stirred into political action in defence of such values, there is also a realisation that, given the immensity of India's problems, an administrative firmness, similar to that which was seen in the days of the emergency rule, is sorely needed.

Finally, it should be recognized that the politics of the developing countries are embedded in world politics and profoundly affected by the conflict between the two main power blocs; and it is in this context that another distinction between countries, in terms of their size and resources, becomes important. Manifestly, it is very much easier for a country such as China or India, or perhaps some of the larger Latin American countries (though here the hostility of the USA to any kind of socialist regime, and its readiness to intervene in their domestic politics, constitute a formidable obstacle), to pursue an independent course of development than it is for small, extremely poor African states to do so. The political development of Third World nations (and also, of course, in a somewhat different sense and degree, that of the industrial countries) has always to be examined in this world context, and political sociology will need to be concerned more closely in future with the study of international relations and of global and regional political institutions (Bottomore, 1979, ch. 6).

Notes to Chapter 9

1   On the subject of 'stateless societies', the significance of kinship and other bonds, and territoriality, see also Schapera, 1956; Middleton and Tait, 1958; Southall, 1968.

2   For a general discussion of these issues and the controversies sur-
    rounding them see Miliband (1983a; 1983b, pt 1).
3   On Gramsci's concept of 'hegemony' see Showstack Sassoon, 1983,
    and more generally on what is now often referred to as the 'dominant
    ideology thesis', Abercrombie, Hill and Turner, 1980.
4   And in particular Mosca, 1896, p. 50, who argued that 'In all societies
    – from societies that are very meagrely developed and have barely
    attained the dawnings of civilization, down to the most advanced and
    powerful societies – two classes of people appear – a class that rules
    and a class that is ruled.' For further discussion of the elite theorists
    see Bottomore, 1964, and on the affinity between their ideas and
    those of Weber, Bottomore, 1984a, ch. 7.
5   I have discussed some of them elsewhere (Bottomore, 1979, ch. 3).
6   Two interesting studies of Conservative working-class voters are
    McKenzie and Silver, 1968, and Nordlinger, 1967.
7   In a letter to Michels (in 1908) Weber asserted that 'any idea which
    proposes to eliminate the domination of man by man through an
    extension of "democracy" is utopian' (see Bottomore, 1984a, ch. 7).
8   The ideas about 'stable democracy' are critically examined in Barry,
    1970, chs. 3 and 4. The differences between the democracies and the
    totalitarian countries are formulated, in a more subtle and qualified
    way than by some other writers on the subject, in Raymond Aron,
    1965.
9   There is a good account of the influence of factions, caste, and other
    forces upon state politics in the study of the Congress Party in Uttar
    Pradesh by Brass, 1965.

10 The Family and Kinship

The Nuclear Family

The individual nuclear family is a universal social phenomenon.[1] As Lowie (1920, pp. 66–7) writes:

> It does not matter whether marital relations are permanent or temporary; whether there is polygyny or polyandry or sexual licence; whether conditions are complicated by the addition of members not included in *our* family circle; the one fact stands out beyond all others that everywhere the husband, wife, and immature children constitute a unit apart from the remainder of the community.

The universality of the nuclear family can be accounted for by the indispensable functions it performs and the difficulty of ensuring the performance of these functions by any other social group. 'In the nuclear family or its constituent relationships we thus see assembled four functions fundamental to human social life – the sexual, the economic, the reproductive, and the educational' (Murdock, 1949, p. 10). We may distinguish between the social and the psychological functions of the nuclear family. Kingsley Davis (1948, p. 395) has distinguished four major social functions; reproduction, maintenance (of immature children), placement, and socialization. Of these the first two, and the fourth, are most important, since placement in the sense of allocation to a position in the occupational system or the status hierarchy is not a universal function; it occurs in rigidly stratified societies (e.g. in a caste society) but not invariably, or even predominantly, in modern industrial societies. The psychological functions are primarily the satisfaction of the sexual needs of the marital partners, and of the need for affection and security, both for parents and for children. The family has often had other functions in addition to those we have mentioned. Murdock observes that:

> As a firm social constellation it frequently, but not universally, draws to itself various other functions. Thus, it is often the centre of religious worship, with the father as family priest. It may be the primary unit in

landholding, vengeance, or recreation. Social status may depend more upon family position than upon individual achievement. And so on. (1949, p. 11)

Anthropologists have consistently emphasized the economic functions of the family in primitive societies. The bond between the father and mother is not only, or even predominantly, the sexual privileges accorded to married spouses, since many primitive societies allow unrestricted pre-marital sexual relations, and a number of societies allow extra-marital relations either unrestricted or more frequently with prescribed relatives. A major factor in maintaining the nuclear family is economic co-operation based upon division of labour between the sexes. Lévi-Strauss (1949, p. 49) has given a graphic account of the miserable situation of unmarried individuals in the most primitive societies; he writes of the spectacle of a young man in a village of central Brazil,

> crouching for hours on end in the corner of a hut, gloomy, ill-cared for, terribly thin and, it seemed, in the most complete dejection . . . he seldom went out except to hunt alone, and at the family meals round the fire he would usually have fasted if a relative had not from time to time placed a small portion of food beside him which he ate in silence. When I asked what was the matter with him, believing that he had some serious illness, my suppositions were laughed at and I was told, 'He is a bachelor'.

Economic co-operation also strengthens the ties between parents and children, and between siblings. The loss of these productive functions involving co-operative labour by the family members is a significant feature of the nuclear family in modern industrial societies, which I shall consider later.

The basic structure of the nuclear family, it has been held, depends upon incest taboos; from these it follows that the nuclear family is discontinuous over time and confined to two generations. A third generation can only result from the formation of new families by an exchange of males and females between existing nuclear families.

> In consequence . . . every normal adult in every human society belongs to at least two nuclear families – *a family of orientation* in which he was born and reared, and which includes his father, mother, brothers and sisters, and *a family of procreation* which he establishes by his marriage and which includes his husband or wife, his sons, and his daughters. (Murdock, 1949, p. 13)[2]

The incest taboos, and their extensions outside the nuclear family, in rules of exogamy, together with rules of descent, are the source of all the complexities of kinship usages and terminology which I shall briefly consider later. Here we need simply note that the extended incest taboos establish interdependence between families, sibs, and clans, and thus play an important part in the integration of primitive societies.

Types of Family Structure

The universality of the nuclear family does not mean that family structure is everywhere the same. On the contrary, it is extremely variable. Kingsley Davis (1948, pp. 414–16) has listed some of the major items of variation in the marital relation (number of spouses, authority, strength of bond, choice of spouse, residence, etc.), in the parent–child relation, and in sibling relations. We may, however, make a broad distinction between family systems in which the nuclear family is relatively independent, and systems in which the nuclear family is incorporated in, or subordinated to, a larger group, the polygamous or the extended family.[3]

The independent nuclear family is characteristic of modern industrial societies. Its predominance seems to be due to the growth of individualism, reflected in property ownership, law, and general social ideals of individual happiness and self-fulfilment, and to geographical and social mobility. It has also been affected by the increasing public provision for individual misfortune; the individual is no longer so dependent upon his family in times of distress. The marked predominance of the relatively autonomous nuclear family is a recent phenomenon, which has appeared most fully in the most advanced industrial societies. The solidarity of this type of family depends largely upon sexual attraction and companionship between husband and wife, and companionship between parents and children. This does not seem to be such a firm basis as the wider complex of rights and obligations (economic, sexual and so on) which exist in the extended family. Divorce is frequent and has been increasing in most industrial countries. The solidarity of the independent nuclear family is greater where it includes young children, but as the children grow up the bonds tend to weaken again, first through the influence of peer groups, and later as a result of social and geographical mobility.

Recent studies of the Western family have raised new questions about the development of the nuclear family. The studies have been usefully surveyed by Anderson (1980) who examines three principal approaches to family history: (1) the demographic, exemplified by the work of the Cambridge Group for the History of Population and Social Structure (Laslett, 1977), which concludes that large and complex households were never common, at least in England, and more generally that 'a nuclear familial form may have been one of the enduring and fundamental characteristics of the Western family system'; (2) the 'sentiments' approach, in the work of Ariès (1960), Shorter (1975) and others, who argue that an understanding of family history requires attention not so much to stability or change in structure, but to changes in meaning, and that the modern nuclear family is to be seen as the product of ideas such as 'home', 'domesticity' and 'privacy';[4] (3) the household economics approach, which interprets households and families in terms of the economic behaviour of their members, looking at such things as inheritance practices (Goody *et al.*, 1976), peasant production (Arensberg and Kimball, 1940; and see also the further references given by Anderson, 1980, pp. 91–2), and the proletarianization of labour (Medick, 1976; Thomas and Znaniecki, 1918–20; and other studies cited by Anderson, 1980, pp. 92–3).

It has also been argued, notably by Shorter (1975, ch. 8), that the Western nuclear family has been undergoing major changes in the past few decades – which could be characterized as the 'destruction of the nest' – and that a new 'post-modern' family is emerging in which the individual members increasingly find their attachments and cultural identities outside the family circle, one major aspect of this process being 'women's liberation'.

The composite forms of the family are to be found frequently in primitive societies, but also in many non-industrial societies. In Europe, the Yugoslav form of the extended family, the *zadruga*, survived until the beginning of the present century. Different types of extended family are still common in Asia, even in an industrialized country such as Japan. Ariga (1956b), discussing the role of the Japanese *dozoku* (familial aggregates) in economic life, writes:

> the managing bodies which operated business were commonly familial ... A *dozoku* was composed of a main family and families which were dependent upon it and affiliated through consanguinity or some other kind of relationship with the main family. When the scale of an enterprise grew too large for such a *dozoku* to manage the entire business, the enterprise was organized into a joint stock company with *dozoku* members constituting the governing body of the whole organization. Thus the *Zaitbatsu* (financial cliques) of pre-World War II came into existence. (Vol. 8, p. 238)

In the nineteenth century, until the land-tax reforms of 1873–6, family property (land, houses, etc.) was owned by the family as a unit, and there was little individual property. More recently Morishima (1982), in an interesting study of the influence of religion in the economic development of Japan, has also emphasized the role of the family, observing that 'the Japanese are strong believers in the importance of the family and of kinship' (p. 197, footnote 2).

In India, the joint family has existed since the earliest times. It was, in the past, a corporate body with property held in common, common worship of a tutelary deity, and authority exercised by the head of the family (usually the eldest male in the eldest male line). According to Hindu law the family property was not strictly impartible, but partition was infrequent and it was quite usual for families to comprise three or four generations living, working and eating together (Maine, 1861). Besides property and work, religion was an important force uniting the joint family, for its members included the dead and unborn as well as the living. There is an obvious parallel here between the Hindu family and the family in ancient Greece and Rome; Fustel de Coulanges (1864, p. 42) wrote that 'The members of the ancient family were united by something more powerful than birth, affection, or physical stength; this was the religion of the sacred fire and of dead ancestors.'

These general characteristics are well illustrated in the study by Srinivas (1952, ch. 5) of the joint family among the Coorgs of south India, who consider themselves to be Kshatriyas, that is, to belong to the second highest rank in the traditional caste hierarchy.

> The *okka* or the patrilineal and patrilocal joint family is the basic group among Coorgs. It is impossible to imagine a Coorg apart from the *okka* of which he is a member. It affects his life at every point and colours all his relations with the outside world. People who do not belong to an *okka* have no social existence at all, and the elders always bring pressure on the parties concerned to see that children born out of wedlock obtain membership in their father's or mother's *okka*.
>
> Membership of an *okka* is acquired by birth, and the outside world always identified a man with his *okka*. His association with his *okka* does not cease even after death, because he then becomes one of a body of apotheosized ancestors (karanava) who are believed to look after the *okka* of which they were members when alive. The ancestors are worshipped, and offerings of food and drink (bharani) are occasionally made to them.
>
> Formerly, the boys in an *okka*, all sons of agnatically related males, grazed the *okka*'s cattle together, hunted birds, and played games.

When they grew up all of them jointly looked after the ancestral estate under the guidance of the head of the *okka*.

Membership of an *okka* determines to a very large extent the choice of a spouse. First of all, marital relations are forbidden between members of the same *okka*. Where agnation overflows the *okka*, the taboo extends to agnatic relatives who are not members of the *okka*. Again, children of sisters may not intermarry.

The ancestral, immovable property of an *okka* was formerly regarded as impartible. It usually descended from one generation of agnatically related males to another without being split up in the process. Partition did, however, occur when every adult member of the *okka* wanted it. But such cases were unusual – at least that is what one is told. Both the difficulty of partition and the preference for leviratic unions added to the strength of the *okka*. The members of an *okka* have to live together from birth till death. They are bound together by numerous strong ties, and they cooperate in performing common tasks. After death, they become ancestors who continue to show an interest in their *okka* and demand propitiation from their descendants. The *okka* is something very much more than the group of living members in it at any given moment. It is a continuum through time, and the body of living members at any particular moment form only points on it. Coorgs themselves clearly state that the *okka* has a longer life than its members. They are also aware that an individual lives, in a social sense, as long as his *okka*. There is a great desire for the continuance of the *okka*, and there is no greater calamity than its extinction. When an *okka* is threatened with extinction certain traditional devices are resorted to perpetuate it.

In recent times the importance of the joint family has gradually declined, largely under the influence of economic changes, especially in the diversification of employment and the fostering of an individualistic, acquisitive spirit.[5] The latter is reflected in changes in the law of property. After the establishment of British rule in India there was increasing resort by Hindus to the power of testamentary disposition of property, and an Act of 1870 recognized will-making along the lines of English law. Later legislation further modified the legal position of the joint family; the Gains of Learning Act 1930 recognized an individual right to property acquired through an education paid for out of family funds, while the Hindu Law of Inheritance (Amendment) Act of 1929 allowed matrilineal as well as patrilineal inheritance. The Hindu Succession Act 1956 is a further step in the direction of establishing individual property rights.

In the Report on the 1951 Census of India (Vol. 1, p. 50) it is argued, on the basis of a classification of households by number of members, that families 'do not continue to be joint according to the traditional custom of the country and the habit of breaking away from the joint family and setting up separate households is quite strong', and although this conclusion has been criticized (Desai, 1955, pp. 97–117) the critics concede that co-residence, commensality, worship and even property have become less important as criteria of jointness, and what they emphasize is the persistence of joint family sentiment. In this attenuated form the joint family may still have some importance, like tribal affiliations elsewhere, in providing a degree of economic and social security for the individual.

In the past few decades a major change in family systems of all types, but especially in the nuclear family (Shorter, 1975, ch. 8), has resulted from the changing position of women in society and the rise of the women's movement. At the same time, the study of the family has been transformed by the work of feminist scholars. Much of the theoretical debate, particularly on the question of domestic labour, has taken place between feminists and Marxists, and there has been sustained criticism of traditional Marxist views, as well as of the social practice of present-day socialist societies (Hamilton, 1978; Barrett, 1980; Himmelweit, 1983).

Marriage

The forms of marriage are as diverse as the types of family system. The basic structure of the nuclear family is little affected by the diversity of marriage customs; it is rather the differences between the independent nuclear family and the composite forms of the family which influence marriage. Where the extended family predominates plural marriage is likely to occur (since it is economically advantageous), the choice of a spouse will probably be made by the head of the family, economic transactions will accompany marriage, and divorce will probably be infrequent.[6] Where the nuclear family is relatively independent marriage will be monogamous, individuals will choose their own spouses, there will be few economic transactions connected with marriage, and divorce may be frequent.

There are, however, certain uniformities in marriage customs. Monogamy is the prevalent form of marriage in all societies, for the good reason that the sex ratio is approximately 1:1 in most times and places. As Samuel Johnson said, 'No man can have two wives, but by preventing somebody else from having one'. Polyandry (the marriage of one woman to two or more men) is so rare as to be, as Murdock says, 'an ethnographic curiosity'. It occurs sporadically in several societies but where it has any permanence it may be accompanied by female infanticide, as among the Toda of South India. Polygyny (the marriage of one man to two or more women) occurs more widely, and is made possible by a surplus of females due to higher mortality among males. Even where polygyny is allowed, however, monogamy is the prevalent form of marriage and usually only the wealthier and more powerful males have more than one wife. Divorce is controlled and limited in some fashion in all societies, since a very high rate of divorce would endanger the functions of the family in maintaining and socializing children. The regulation of divorce, and its prevalence, are affected by numerous factors. The influence of religion has been very strong in the sphere of marital relations, and some of the major religions, for example, Hinduism and Roman Catholicism, have not allowed divorce. The actual prevalence of divorce is influenced, as was noted earlier, by the extent to which wider family and kin groups are involved, and by the existence of economic obligations. It is also influenced by the presence of alternative means of sexual and emotional satisfaction, through plural marriage, or permitted extra-marital relationships. According to Hindu law marriage is a sacrament, not a contract, and it was formerly indissoluble (except in the case of some lower castes which had a custom of divorce, and in the case of conversion of one spouse to Christianity). But at the same time, polygyny was legal, and there existed legal forms of concubinage. These arrangements, of course, met the needs only of the male population. The law was first changed by the Bombay Prevention of Hindu Bigamous Marriages Act 1946, which enforced monogamy in Bombay State, and this had soon to be followed by legal provision for divorce (in the Bombay Hindu Divorce Act 1947). Since then monogamy and provision for divorce have been extended to the whole of India by the Hindu Marriage Act 1955.

In the Western industrial societies divorce has increased rapidly since the beginning of the twentieth century, and particularly since the mid-1960s (Shorter, 1975, pp. 277–9); and much sociological research has been devoted to the problems of family 'instability'[7] and of predicting marital harmony.[8] The causes of the increase in divorce are not entirely clear, but a comparison with primitive societies and many non-industrial societies is suggestive. In these societies, marriage is entered into as an economic arrangement and in order to have children (for economic and religious reasons), and not simply for the satisfaction of sexual needs; moreover, it has the support of a wider kinship group, and the personal satisfactions of the two individuals who marry are not unduly emphasized. In some Western societies a combination of monogamous marriage, a rigid Puritan ethic which strongly condemned pre-marital and extra-marital sexual relations, and an ideal of romantic love established a model of the marital relation which is difficult, perhaps impossible, to realize. Marriage is no longer an economic partnership, and is no longer sustained by wider kinship groups. Finally, the desire for a numerous progeny is replaced by the deliberate aim of limiting family size. Thus the marriage bond is reduced to a simple relation of mutual attraction, and this is less strong than the network of economic, ritual and kinship interests which unite the family in other societies. We may regard a relatively high divorce rate, therefore, as a concomitant of modern individualism, the pursuit of happiness and strict control of sexual relations outside marriage. In practice, however, Western societies have greatly relaxed their control of sexual behaviour in the last few decades, and these changes may affect the divorce rate by diminishing the exclusive concern with sexual felicity in marriage.

Kinship

As I noted earlier, it is family exogamy, and the resulting fact that every normal individual is a member of two nuclear families (family of orientation and family of procreation), which gives rise to kinship systems. The ramifications of kinship are considerable. Each individual has primary relatives in the nuclear families to which he belongs; outside these families he can have 33 types of secondary relatives, 151 types of tertiary relatives, and so on in increasing numbers. No society, even among the Australian tribes where kinship had a very prominent role, has taken account of all the degrees of relationship in its kinship system. But societies may usefully be classified in accordance with the types of relationship which are emphasized, both in terminology and in behaviour. Lowie and Kirchhoff (Lowie, 1950, p. 63) distinguish four major types of kinship terminology, based on the treatment of the parental generation. Murdock (1949, ch. 8) has a more elaborate classification of eleven 'types of social organization', in which six types are differentiated by kinship terminology, and the other five (characterized by kinship terms similar to the foregoing) are differentiated by descent.

Social anthropologists have devoted much of their effort to

analysing kinship systems of particular societies, and to the comparative study of kinship. This interest reflects the fact that kinship is supremely important in primitive societies. It is a chief factor in maintaining social unity, even where there is a political system and a conception of territoriality, and it constitutes the framework within which the individual is assigned economic and political functions, acquires rights and obligations, receives community aid and so on. Usually, therefore, the most effective way to study the social structure of a primitive society is to begin with an analysis of kinship. The comparative study of kinship systems, which bulked large in the work of the early evolutionary anthropologists and sociologists, has received much less attention since that time, and as Lowie says (1950, p. 86), 'nearly everything remains to be done in this field'. Kinship systems have been classified in various ways (as by Lowie and Murdock), but it has proved extremely difficult to find any general framework of explanation which would account for the occurrence of particular types of kinship system. Murdock has emphasized the importance of the rule of residence, and has shown how this is itself influenced by economic, political and religious factors. With such partial explanations we must for the present be satisfied. In recent years, however, there has been a renewal of theoretical discussion through the work of Lévi-Strauss and the structural anthropologists, who attempt to show the basic structure of kinship as a logical schema, in terms of the exchange of women between social groups (Lévi-Strauss, 1949; and for critical comments Leach, 1970, ch. 6).

Modern sociologists have shown relatively little interest in kinship, since it plays a smaller part in the life of the industrial societies which they have mainly studied. It may be that they have unduly neglected the phenomenon, due to their preoccupation (especially in the USA) with the urban middle-class family, which exhibits most plainly the characteristics of the independent nuclear family. In the industrial working class, as a number of studies have shown, kinship is still important in controlling individual behaviour and as a system of mutual aid.[9] Moreover, kinship has played, and continues to play, a significant part in consolidating the unity of upper classes and of various types of elites, especially through the transmission of property. But it remains true that kinship and family structure do not have the same fundamental importance in modern societies as they have in tribal or non-industrial societies.

The Family and Society

In the study of kinship and the family, as in other fields, the early sociologists and anthropologists were largely concerned with the construction of evolutionary schemes. Marriage and the family were supposed to have evolved from primitive promiscuity through various forms of plural marriage to monogamy. Kinship was regarded as having developed from matrilineal descent through patrilineal descent and patriarchy to a system of bilateral descent associated with the independent nuclear family. The hypothesis concerning the priority of matrilinear descent, and its connection with the lowest levels of primitive culture, was first put forward by Bachofen (1861). This was widely accepted, and broadly similar evolutionary schemes were proposed by many scholars up to the beginning of this century.[10]

In more recent work the evolutionist approach has been abandoned. Anthropologists have concentrated upon the study of particular kinship systems and forms of the family, or on the analysis of the 'elementary structures' of kinship, while sociologists have for the most part limited their interest to the problems of the family in modern industrial societies. The belief in a single line of development has had to be given up in the face of anthropological evidence (Murdock, 1949, ch. 8), and it has even proved difficult to find any general framework of explanation to account for the varieties of kinship usages and family structure, or for changes in kinship and the family. Nevertheless, as we have shown, it is possible to establish broad classifications of kinship systems and types of family, although kinship usages appear to vary in a more random and arbitrary way than do marriage and the family. In respect of the types of family, and changes therein, it seems possible to formulate a number of useful generalizations which relate them to other elements of social structure.

The first generalization concerns the nature of the relation between the family and society. The nuclear family, I said earlier, is a universal phenomenon because it performs indispensable social functions. It is a group of major importance in any society; but its importance is of a very specific kind. Human young remain immature for a period which is long in relation to the span of human life, and during this time they must be maintained and socialized. This is the principal function of the nuclear family. Its performance is independent of the form of the family, of wider kinship arrangements, of marriage customs, of the type of control of sexual behaviour, or of the performance of additional functions by the family. All these vary with the variations in other social institutions. Moreover, the ways in which the nuclear family performs its major function are also determined by other elements in society. The family first socializes the child, but it does not originate the values which it imparts; these come from religion, nation, caste or class. Thus the specific character of the nuclear family in any society is determined by other institutions; it does not determine them. Similarly, social change originates in other institutions, not in the family; the family changes in response. I shall consider this point more fully below, in connection with the effects of industrialization. Here it may be noted that the point I have made about the nuclear family has a wider application to *primary groups* as such. In an earlier chapter I examined the view of Cooley that such groups as the family and neighbourhood are primary above all in that they are 'fundamental in forming the social nature and ideals of the individual'. A study of the nuclear family shows that the proposition is false. The family transmits values which are determined elsewhere; it is an agent, not a principal. In primary groups we may perhaps more easily study the effects of major 'social forces', but we cannot, in this way, investigate the forces themselves or explain their action.

Another characteristic of the relation between the family and society has very often been neglected by modern sociologists. No other group in society is so much influenced by religious and moral codes. The fact is surprising. Cupidity and lust for power would seem to be as powerful individual impulses as sexual desire, and as potentially disruptive of the human community. At the present time human society appears to be more gravely threatened by nuclear warfare than by the increase in divorce or the spread of pre-marital sexual intercourse. Yet religious and moral codes have rarely given as much attention to economic and political arrangements as to sexual behaviour and the family.[11] This connection between the family and religion can be seen in the preoccupation (though this is perhaps now diminishing) in Western societies with sexual 'promiscuity' and divorce, and in India in the concern about the future of the joint family. The connection has had two important consequences: first, that scientific research into sexual behaviour and family life has been difficult or impossible until recent years, and secondly, that it has been more difficult here than in other areas of social life to bring about rational changes.

While the influence of religions has usually been to preserve established forms of the family, changes in economic institutions have been a major factor in bringing about changes in the family.

Durkheim (1898) once observed that the inadequacy of the 'economic materialist' conception of history was most evident in the study of the family. But this is doubtful. While the early evolutionist schemes, including that of Engels, have to be rejected, it is undeniable that more limited sequences of change can be discovered and that economic factors are prominent in these. The anthropologists (especially Lowie and Murdock) who have undertaken comparative studies of kinship and the family have emphasized this point.[12] The influence of modern industrialism upon the family is universally recognized. The specific characteristics of the modern Western family are very generally attributed to the development of industrial society in its specific capitalist form (Ogburn and Nimkoff, 1955; Shorter, 1975). In India, the changes in the joint family are, as I have shown, closely connected with the emergence and growth of an industrial economy. Kapadia (1958, ch. 12), in discussing recent trends affecting the Hindu family, notes that British rule introduced a new economic order, ideology and administrative system, which began to transform Indian culture. Capitalism and liberalism alike emphasized individual effort and rationality, and the spread of these ideologies challenged the sentiments maintaining the joint family. Economic development was accompanied by the growth of cities and the breakdown of village isolation; these changes also stimulated individualism, and brought about a revolt against the inferior position of women in the joint family. Kapadia also shows how, in recent years, the development of social insurance has begun to diminish the importance of the joint family as an organization for social security.

In the long run, as economic development continues, there is no reason to suppose that the family system in India or in other Third World countries will differ radically from that which exists today in the industrial countries (although cultural tradition, as I noted in the case of Japan, may produce some variations). This family structure implies low rates of fertility and mortality, a short childbearing period which, together with other factors, brings about large-scale employment of married women outside the home, and the public provision of education and other services with a consequent restriction of family functions. And in the Third World, as in the industrial countries, the family will continue to change under the impact of economic, political and cultural transformations.

Notes to Chapter 10

1   There are a few possible exceptions to this generalization, the most frequently cited case being that of the Nayar of South India (Gough, 1960).

2   I cannot discuss here the various explanations of the incest taboos; the problem has been examined by Lévi-Strauss, 1949, ch. 2, and most comprehensively by Murdock, 1949, ch. 10. But see the criticism in Leach, 1970, of Lévi-Strauss's equation of exogamy with the converse of the incest taboo; and the discussion of the problem in Fox, 1967.

3   Murdock, 1949, p. 2, makes this distinction between the independent nuclear family and composite forms of the family. A *polygamous family* 'consists of two or more nuclear families affiliated by plural marriages, i.e. by having one parent in common'. An *extended family* 'consists of two or more nuclear families affiliated through an extension of the parent–child relationship ... i.e. by joining the nuclear family of a married adult to that of his parents'. Murdock found, in the 192 societies of his sample for which information was adequate, that 47 had normally only nuclear families, 53 had polygamous but not extended families, and 92 had some form of the extended family.

4   Thus Shorter (1975, p. 205) writes:

> The nuclear family is a state of mind rather than a particular kind of structure or set of household arrangements ... What really distinguishes the nuclear family ... from other patterns of family life in Western society is a special sense of solidarity that separates the domestic unit from the surrounding community.

But the change in states of mind or sentiments may itself be the outcome of structural changes, and Shorter indeed regards capitalism as the driving force behind it (ch. 7).

5   O'Malley (1941, p. 384) wrote that:

> The joint-family is an institution which had its origin in an earlier order of society, when the country was thinly peopled, the population was mainly agrarian, and cultivation was capable of expansion to meet the needs of growing families. Each family depended on its own labour and the larger it was, the greater was the number of hands available for work ... The conditions favourable to it were those of a stable society, in which the members of a family lived in the same place and followed the same pursuits from generation to generation. The economic complex has been transformed during the last hundred years. A largely increased population has caused pressure on the soil ... There is no longer the same community of interests owing to the small size of holdings and the pressure of circumstances necessitating the adoption of different callings ... The extension of communications has facilitated migration, which may be periodic or permanent.

6   Among primitive peoples divorce is relatively easy, but as Lowie, 1950, p. 112, observes:

Considering the difficulty of getting a mate in many societies and the widespread notion of wedlock as a group covenant, there would be powerful deterrents to hasty rupture of relations caused by individual disillusionment or caprice. Intimately linked with these factors are the heavy economic obligations that attach to matrimonial arrangements.

7   The term 'unstable family' was first used by Le Play (in his study of European working-class families) to refer to the type of family in which children left home on reaching maturity, and often lost contact with their family of origin, so that each family regularly broke up into smaller units and there was no such solidarity as existed in the patriarchal family. The term has come to be used more widely to include also the break-up of families through the separation of the marital couple (Goode, 1966), but it should be noted that a very high proportion of divorced persons remarry and thus establish new families. The modern situation has been aptly described by Margaret Mead as 'serial monogamy.'

8   A survey of family research in the USA (Hill, 1958) showed that almost 30 per cent of it was concerned with mate selection and marital adjustment.

9   In a study of working-class districts of Paris, Chombart de Lauwe, 1952, showed that kinsfolk usually live close together and that social relationships in leisure time are very largely between kinsfolk. A study in London by Young and Willmott, 1957, also demonstrated the fact of residential propinquity, and showed the important social role of the wife's mother. Katz and Kemnitzer, 1983, have emphasized the importance of kin-based networks among the urban poor in capitalist societies and have contrasted this phenomenon with the contractual, privatized nuclear family of the middle class.

10 The best known are McLennan, 1876; Morgan, 1877; Spencer, 1876–96, Vol. 1. Hobhouse, 1906, who was greatly influenced by Spencer, presented the same kind of evolutionary scheme. Morgan's work, as is well known, was the basis of Engels's 1884 study, which provided the framework for all later Marxist writing on the family, at least until recent times.

11 There are, of course, differences between the major religions in this respect. The emphasis upon the regulation of sexual behaviour is strongest in Judaism and Christianity. Hinduism and Buddhism pay relatively more attention to the problems of violence and self-assertion. Thus, for example, in the writings of Radhakrishnan (especially 1947) on Hindu religion and philosophy there is much discussion of social problems, and particularly of violence and non-violence.

12 Murdock (1949, p. 137) in discussing the determinants of kinship terminology specifies one of his assumptions as being

that the forms of social structure are not determined by kinship patterns or terminology, or influenced in any major degree by them, but are created by forces external to social organization, especially by economic factors. It is assumed herewith, for example, that the available sources of food and the techniques of procuring it affect the sex division of labour and the relative statuses of the sexes, predisposing peoples to particular rules of residence, which can eventuate in the formation of extended families, clans, and sibs. It is further assumed that the prevailing types and distribution of property favour particular rules of inheritance, that wealth or its lack affects marriage (e.g. encouraging or inhibiting polygyny), and that these and other facts external to social structure can strongly influence rules of residence and marriage and through them the forms of social organization and kinship structure.

11 *Social Stratification*

The division of society into classes and strata, which form a hierarchy of prestige and power, is an almost universal feature of social structure which has, throughout history, attracted the attention of philosophers and social theorists. But it is only with the growth of the modern social sciences that it has been subjected to critical study and analysis. Sociologists have commonly distinguished four main systems of stratification – slavery, estates, caste and social class – and within these systems a variety of status groups and elites. I shall briefly examine the first three systems, then consider at greater length the phenomena of social class, and finally discuss some general theories of social stratification.

Slavery

Hobhouse (1906, ch. 7) defined a slave as 'a man whom law and custom regard as the property of another. In extreme cases he is wholly without rights, a pure chattel; in other cases, he may be protected in certain respects, but so may an ox or an ass.' He continued, 'if [the slave] has by his position certain countervailing rights, e.g. to inherited property, from which he cannot (except for some default) be dislodged, he becomes . . . no longer a slave but a serf'. Slavery thus represents an extreme form of inequality, in which certain groups of individuals are entirely or almost entirely without rights. It has existed sporadically at many times and places[1] but there are two major examples of a system of slavery: the societies of the ancient world based upon slavery (especially Greece and Rome), and the southern states of the USA in the eighteenth and nineteenth centuries. Nieboer (1900) gave an excellent account of the social condition of the slave in such a system.

> First, every slave has his master to whom he is subjected. And this subjection is of a peculiar kind. Unlike the authority one freeman sometimes has over another, the master's power over his slave is unlimited, at least in principle; any restriction put upon the master's free exercise of his power is a mitigation of slavery, not belonging to

its nature, just as in Roman law the proprietor may do with his property whatever he is not by special laws forbidden to do. The relation between master and slave is therefore properly expressed by the slave being called the master's 'possession' or 'property', expressions we frequently meet with. Secondly, slaves are in a lower condition as compared with freemen. The slave has no political rights; he does not choose his government, he does not attend the public councils. Socially he is despised. In the third place, we always connect with slavery the idea of compulsory labour. The slave is compelled to work; the free labourer may leave off working if he likes, be it at the cost of starving. All compulsory labour, however, is not slave labour; the latter requires that peculiar kind of compulsion, that is expressed by the word 'possession' or 'property' as has been said before.[2]

The basis of slavery is always economic; it is, as Nieboer argued, an industrial system. Along with the emergence of slavery there also appears an aristocracy of some kind, which lives upon slave labour. But it is, also, in the opinion of most writers, the inefficiency of slave labour which is largely responsible for the decline of slavery.

Along with this, however, there is another influence tending to the decline of slavery, which can best be traced in the ancient world. There is always a certain conflict between the conception of the slave as an *object* of property rights, and the conception of him as a human being *possessing* rights. We find, in both Greece and Rome, that with the development of debt-slavery a distinction is made between foreign slaves and slaves originating within the group. In Athens debt-slavery was prohibited by Solon, and ultimately it was abolished in Rome under the influence of the Stoics. Hobhouse (1906, p. 277) pointed out that

> the formation of debtor-slaves has a certain softening influence upon the institution of slavery itself, for while the captive slave remains an enemy in the sight of law and morals and is therefore rightless, the debtor or the criminal was originally a member of the community and in relation to him there is apt to arise some limitation of the power of the master.

In the ancient world, slavery was gradually modified by progressive limitation of the master's right of punishment, the securing of personal rights to the slave (marriage, acquisition and inheritance of property) and the provision for manumission. The latter was supported and encouraged by the Christian church in the Roman Empire and later in feudal Europe, at least so far as Christians were involved.

Some writers (e.g. Nieboer) have characterized slavery as an industrial system rather than a system of stratification, on the grounds that in a society divided between slaves and those who are (relatively) free, there is usually a system of ranks within the latter group. Hence slavery by itself does not constitute a system of stratification. But this argument raises some fundamental issues which will be more fully explored in discussing the theories of stratification; and in particular the distinction that has to be made between 'class' and 'stratification'. In Marxist theory slaves, serfs and wage earners are all categorized as the 'direct producers' upon whose labour the whole social edifice, including distinctive dominant classes, rests; but this does not exclude the existence, in feudal societies and capitalist societies as well as in slave societies, of numerous 'intermediate strata'. There are, however, various problems in defining a distinctive slave 'mode of production', as Finley (1983) has observed.

Estates

The feudal estates of medieval Europe had three important characteristics. In the first place, they were legally defined; each estate had a *status*, in the precise sense of a legal complex of rights and duties, of privileges and obligations. Thus, as has been said, 'to know a person's real position it was first of all necessary to know "the law by which he lived"'. In the twelfth century, when serfdom was increasing and a legal theory of the feudal state was emerging, the English lawyer, Glanville, listed the disabilities of serfs as being: inability to appeal to the king for justice, absence of rights over their chattels and holdings, liability to pay the fines of *merchet* and *heriot*. The differences between estates can be seen also in the different penalties imposed for similar offences.

Secondly, the estates represented a broad division of labour, and were regarded in the contemporary literature as having definite functions. 'The nobility were ordained to defend all, the clergy to pray for all, and the commons to provide food for all.'

Thirdly, the feudal estates were *political groups*. Stubbs, in his *Constitutional History of England* (1874–8), wrote: 'An assembly of estates is an organized collection . . . of the several orders, estates or conditions of man who are recognized as possessing political power.' In this sense the serfs did not constitute an estate. Classical feudalism knew only two estates, the nobility and the clergy. The decline of European feudalism after the twelfth century is associated with the rise of a third estate, not of the serfs or villeins, but of the burghers, who behaved for a long period as

a distinctive group *within* the feudal system before they transformed or overthrew it (Pirenne, 1925, especially pp. 112–19,
122 ff).

The system of feudal estates was more complex and varied, as
well as less rigid, than this summary account can show. The
distinctions within estates, and the political aspect of feudalism,
are excellently portrayed in Bloch (1939–40, Vol. 2). The opportunities for individuals to change their position in society are
considered in Southern (1953, ch. 2) and in Poole (1946). There is
a useful short account of Marxist views of feudal society by
Hilton (1983).

Some modern historians and sociologists have been much
concerned with the similarities between the European feudal
societies and other societies which might be considered as
belonging to the same type. The social system of Japan from the
twelfth century has often been described as feudal, for instance
by Marc Bloch (1939–40) and by Coulborn (1956). The existence of feudalism in India is more controversial. It must be
recognized, first, that even if feudal relationships existed during
some periods of Indian history they certainly existed alongside,
and were interwoven with, caste relationships and this implies
that the *social system* cannot be described, without important
qualifications, as feudal. Secondly, the 'feudalism' of the
Maurya, Gupta and Mogul empires, and of their periods of
decline, obviously lacked some characteristics of European
feudalism. All scholars agree that Indian 'feudalism' had as its
basis independent village agriculture, not the manorial system:
in the words of Shelvankar (1940), 'Indian feudalism remained
fiscal and military in character. It was not manorial.' Many
scholars hold also that the conception of royal power in India
was so different from that in the West that it could not establish
a feudal system. 'In India, the king did not, in theory, create
subordinate owners of land, because he himself was not, in
theory, the supreme owner of land. What he delegated to his
intermediaries was only the specific and individual right of
zamin, i.e. the revenue-collecting power' (Karim, 1956, ch. 2).
This view is not universally accepted (Kosambi, 1956, chs. 9
and 10), but there is, at least, agreement on the fact that feudal
relationships often developed more strongly when the empires
were in decline, since in such periods revenue collectors could
more easily establish proprietary rights in land and usurp political and judicial functions. In a different form the decline of
empire was also a factor in the emergence of European
feudalism.

Caste

The Indian caste system is unique among systems of social stratification. This is not to say either that it is wholly incomparable with other types of stratification, or that no elements of caste are to be found elsewhere. In the first place, caste possesses the common characteristic of being evidently connected with economic differentiation. This is apparent whether we consider the effective caste groups (*jatis*) or the four traditional *varnas* of Brahmins, Kshatriyas, Vaisyas and Sudras. The *varnas*, as Senart (1894) observed in a classical study, originally resembled feudal estates in certain respects. They were like estates both in the character and, to a great extent, in the hierarchical ordering of the groups (priests, warriors and nobles, traders, serfs), and also in the fact that they were not totally closed groups; individuals could move from one *varna* to another and intermarriage was possible.

The *jatis*, which developed later and which continued to grow in number through the extending division of labour, the incorporation of tribes and, to a lesser extent, the operation of factors such as religious innovation, are the basic units of the traditional caste system. In modern India there are some 2,500 *jatis* in each major region. The *jati* is the endogamous group, and the principal reference group of the individual, embodying a distinctive way of life and maintaining it by the exercise of customary and, in earlier times, juridical sanctions. The economic significance of the *jatis* is plain; they are for the most part occupational groups and in the traditional village economy the caste system largely provides the machinery for the exchange of goods and services.[3]

On the other hand, elements of caste can be observed in other societies where more or less strict segregation of particular groups occurs; for instance, segregation of those engaged in 'unclean' occupations, or of those belonging to a particular ethnic group. But such individual features do not constitute a caste system. The only cases in which a caste system has been established outside Hindu India are those of non-Hindu groups in India (e.g. Muslims) or of Hindu settlement outside India, notably in Sri Lanka.

The sociological problem of caste is, therefore, to account for the existence and persistence of this unique type of social stratification. An explanation may be sought in two ways, either in terms of historical events or in terms of some factor or factors which are present in Indian society and not elsewhere. One of the most plausible historical accounts so far offered seems to be that

given by Hutton (1951, ch. 11), who suggests that the original
Aryan invaders of India, with their distinct ranks, introduced the
principle of social stratification into a society already divided into
exclusive tribal groups by taboos connected with food, and that
they took over and consolidated these taboos as a means of
maintaining social distance between themselves and the subject
population.[4] In this manner the principle of stratified exclusive
groups was reinforced, and provided with a powerful sanction in
the shape of a religious and magical doctrine of pollution through
food, and later, pollution through contact.

The second way of explaining caste, in terms of some specific
feature of Indian society, involves a brief consideration of the
relationship between *jati* and *varna*. Modern students of caste
have emphasized the role of the magical and religious ideas of the
varna system, as expounded in the ancient religious literature.
Srinivas (1952, ch. 2) observes that the notions of *karma*, which
'teaches a Hindu that he is born in a particular sub-caste, because
he deserved to be born there', and *dharma*, the code of duties (or
rules of the caste), 'have contributed very greatly to the strengthening of the idea of hierarchy which is inherent in the caste
system'. The concept of pollution, he says, is 'fundamental to the
caste system and every type of caste relation is governed by it'.
Dumont (1966) also emphasizes this feature and argues that the
basis of caste is to be found in the religious distinction between
'pure' and 'impure'. The notions of *karma*, *dharma* and pollution
have figured prominently in Hindu religious and legal thought,
and together they constitute a doctrine which is undoubtedly one
of the principal sustaining forces of the caste system.

We may conclude, then, that an explanation of the caste system
would involve reference to some general theory of social stratification, to the specific features of the Hindu religion, and possibly
to other factors such as the fragmentation of Indian society and
the maintenance of a traditional economy. Such an explanation
might be tested, albeit with difficulty, by studies of the effects
upon the caste system of the far-reaching economic and political
changes in recent times. In fact, studies in this field are still quite
limited, and empirical studies have mainly contributed a more
precise knowledge of the traditional caste system (Srinivas *et al.*,
1959; Srinivas, 1965). Almost all of them have been carried out in
rural areas, where the impact of economic and political changes is
weakest; even so, a number of studies reveal significant changes.
Wealth and education have become accessible to members of
lower as well as higher castes although not perhaps on equal
terms, and Dube (1955) has shown how this affects a village

community; wealth, education, or personal qualities may bring an individual prestige and power despite membership of a low caste. Similarly, Bailey (1957) shows how the 'extending frontiers' of the economy and the polity bring about changes. With the development of trade, and of a money economy, land ceases to be the main source of wealth; the lower castes enrich themselves through trade and then use their wealth to buy land and so acquire prestige and power. The extension of government and administration also changes the balance of power; the lower castes in the village are no longer defenceless, for they can appeal, outside the village, to public officials and administrative bodies.

We should expect changes in caste to be greater in urban areas than in the villages, for economic change is greater there, the anonymity of town life facilitates social mobility, and the intellectual life of the town is more favourable to change. As yet, however, there are relatively few urban studies, and this no doubt accounts in part for the uncertainties and disagreements about whether caste is being strengthened or weakened in Indian society as a whole. Many sociologists have observed that caste associations have developed rapidly, especially in the towns, and Srinivas (1960) writes: 'There is a good case for arguing that caste-consciousness and organization have increased in modern India. Witness for instance the proliferation of caste banks, hostels, cooperative societies, charities, marriage halls, conferences and journals in Indian towns.' The influence of caste in politics is disputed, and it certainly varies from one region to another; there is no doubt that castes play an important part as electoral organizations and as vote collecting agencies, but empirical studies show that local castes are frequently divided on political issues, and that many other considerations influence political allegiance (see Chapter 9 above). In the sphere of education and opportunities for occupational mobility it is clear that caste retains its importance; in particular, higher education is still mainly open to the higher castes.

We have seen that the strength of caste, and the tendencies to change, have been variously estimated, while the evidence is neither abundant nor clear. But whatever may be said about the strength of castes themselves, and of the individual's attachment to his own caste, it may be claimed that the traditional *caste system* has been profoundly altered (Bailey, 1963, pp. 122–35; Béteille, 1965). In that system each individual caste had its ascribed place and co-operated with other castes in a traditional economy and in ritual. No doubt there was always some competition between castes and there were changes of position in the hierarchy of prestige; but there was no generalized competition. It is quite otherwise with the modern caste associations, which exist in order to compete for wealth, educational opportunities, and social prestige in a much more open society. These associations are, in fact, interest groups of a modern type; in Tönnies's sense, they are 'associations', while the traditional caste groups were 'communities'. It is easy to understand that they should have grown up on the basis of traditional castes, but equally that they contradict the caste system and may well give rise to, or be absorbed into, the secular groups of a modern society – trade unions, professional associations and social classes.

Social Class and Social Status

A social class system differs radically from those systems which we have so far considered. Social classes are *de facto* (not legally or religiously defined and sanctioned) groups; they are relatively open, not closed. Their basis is indisputably economic, but they are more than economic groups. They are characteristic groups of the capitalist industrial societies which have developed since the seventeenth century.[5] Considerable difficulties arise when the attempt is made to specify the number of social classes, or to define their membership precisely. However, most sociologists would probably agree in recognizing the existence of an upper class (comprising the owners of the major part of the economic resources of a society), a working class (chiefly the industrial wage earners), and a middle class, or middle classes (a more amorphous group, but including most white collar workers and most members of the liberal professions). In some industrial societies until recently, and in most of the developing countries, the peasantry has been an important class.

Disagreement among sociologists begins generally on the issues of the cohesiveness of the different classes, their role in society and their future. These problems will be discussed later in considering some theories of social stratification. The different classes, and especially the middle class, have been extensively studied. On the working class, an early work by Briefs (1926) begins from a Marxist definition and expands it to differentiate more clearly between the working class and the white collar middle class. Subsequently, there was relatively little research in this area until the 1960s when controversies about the effects of 'affluence' upon the working class stimulated a number of studies on 'embourgeoisement' and the emergence of a 'new working class' (Mallet, 1963; Touraine, 1966; Hamilton, 1967; Goldthorpe *et al.*, 1968–9; and for a general review of the literature Mann, 1973). General studies of the middle class include those by Mills (1951) and Lockwood (1958), but there have also been many accounts of specific groups within the middle classes, especially of the liberal professions, and a recent work (Abercrombie and Urry, 1983) has critically reviewed many of the major studies and interpretations. In the nature of things it has been less easy to study the upper class, and sociological writing here extends from theoretical and historical studies of elites to studies based upon statistical information about property ownership, income, educational privilege, and so on (Mills, 1956; Bottomore, 1964; Domhoff, 1970; Stanworth and Giddens, 1974).

The picture of social stratification in capitalist societies is complicated by the existence of *status groups* as well as social classes. Max Weber (1921 pt 1, ch. 4) was the first to distinguish rigorously between the two, and to examine their interrelation: 'With some over-simplification one might thus say that "classes" are stratified according to their relation to the production and acquisition of goods; whereas "status groups" are stratified according to the principles of their *consumption* of goods as represented by special "styles of life".' The notion of social status has been analysed by a number of recent writers; thus Marshall (1953) examined the factors which produce differences in status as well as different types of status – personal, positional, and so on – and in a later essay (1956) discussed the changes in social stratification in capitalist societies, arguing that there has been a shift from class organization to status organization or, as he terms it, from multibonded but unidimensional groups to multidimensional and unbonded groups. There have been many empirical studies of status groups, especially in terms of occupational differentiation; indeed, recent investigations of social stratification and social mobility have been carried out largely in terms of occupational prestige scales. A pioneer study in Britain (Glass, 1954) gave rise to broadly comparable studies elsewhere, for example in Japan (Research Committee of the Japan Sociological Society, 1958) and in the USA (Blau and Duncan, 1967); and the British inquiry has been repeated more recently, making possible a comparison of social mobility in 1949 and 1972 (Goldthorpe, 1980, and for a more general discussion Heath, 1981).

The emphasis, in much recent sociology, upon studies of social status and mobility reflects a variety of influences. The needs of research have favoured the use of occupational scales, since these facilitate the design and implementation of research projects. The predominance of American sociology in the immediate postwar decades was an important influence; in the USA, which is unique among Western industrial societies in having no strong tradition of class organization or ideological conflict, sociologists have naturally been concerned with social stratification in those aspects which, on the surface, do characterize American society – status and mobility. But the singularity of American society was not always recognized, so that some writers simply confused status with class, while others attempted to analyse social stratification in all societies in terms of the American model.

A third influence has been the actual changes in Western societies, resulting in a real abatement, though by no means a disappearance, of class differences and class conflicts. This process of change can only be clearly grasped, however, if the phenomena of class and status are first carefully distinguished and their interrelations then examined. I have discussed this problem briefly elsewhere, and have suggested that:

> Stratification by prestige affects the class system, as Marx conceived it, in two important ways: first, by interposing between the two major classes a range of status groups which bridge the gulf between the extreme positions in the class structure; and secondly, by suggesting an entirely different conception of the social hierarchy as a whole, according to which it appears as a continuum of more or less clearly defined status positions, determined by a variety of factors and not simply by property ownership, which is incompatible with the formation of massive social classes and with the existence of a fundamental conflict between classes. The relations between status groups at different levels are relations of competition and emulation, not of conflict. With the growth in numbers of the middle classes, which form an increasing proportion of the whole population, this view of the social hierarchy as a continuum of prestige ranks (or statuses), without any sharp breaks, and thus without any clear lines of conflict between major social groups, has acquired a much greater influence upon social thought and its diffusion has served to check the growth of class consciousness. (Bottomore, 1965, and for more recent discussions Giddens, 1973; Bottomore, 1975b, pt 2; 1984a, chs. 10 and 11)

The analysis of social stratification in the present-day capitalist societies is complex and difficult. Equal, and perhaps greater, difficulties appear in the study of socialist industrial societies in Eastern Europe. An initial obstacle has been the relative paucity of data on income distribution, educational opportunities and social mobility generally, attitudes and group sentiments in these societies, although the situation has improved in recent years with the extension of sociological research. An 'orthodox'

Marxist view would be that in the socialist countries social classes, or at least a hierarchical class system, have ceased to exist as a result of the abolition of private ownership of the major means of production. But critics of this view point to the existence of considerable economic inequalities, educational and other privileges, the monopolization of political power by a small elite, and other characteristics, which together amount to a system of social stratification (Lane, 1982). Much of the debate about this system has turned on the question of whether a new ruling class has been formed, as Djilas (1957) and more recently Konrád and Szelényi (1979) have argued, or whether the socialist societies are dominated by various elite groups, and in particular by a political elite. On the other side, a study by Weselowski (1979) of the changing class structure in Poland rejects the idea of a new dominant class while recognizing that status differences persist, as well as conflicts of interest between various social groups and strata.

The classical notion of social class, in both Marxist and non-Marxist writing, is closely connected with the notion of political power and especially with the concept of a 'ruling class' (see Chapter 9 above). This connection, however, may give rise to two different lines of thought: one of which – the Marxist – makes political power dependent upon economic power; while the other treats the economy and the polity as interrelated systems, each of which may at different times be either 'base' or 'superstructure', and in the case of the elite theories gives pre-eminence to political power. The characterization of Soviet society as 'state socialism' (as well as some characterizations of present-day capitalism as 'state capitalism') implicitly or explicitly adopts a view of the independent influence, if not the pre-eminence, of the political system.

These questions have provoked fresh thought, as well as empirical research, on the ways in which various social groups – classes, elites, ethnic groups, and so on – develop and become involved in political conflict (see Chapter 9 above). In the context of social stratification, particular importance attaches to the study of elites and the elite theories. Pareto's theory, at least in its major concern with the 'governing elite', treated the terms 'class' and 'elite' as practically synonymous, and it was in the framework of his own conception of the 'circulation of elites' that Pareto regarded the notion of class conflict as the most important of Marx's contributions to sociology. More recent social theorists have generally used the term 'elite' to refer to small and more cohesive social groups, which may be more or less closely connected with social classes as traditionally conceived. Thus Cole (1955, p. 106) observed that:

> Not all elites rest on a class basis, or are to be regarded as class representatives; but some do and are, and a special importance attaches, in modern societies and especially in the older societies which have been developing from aristocracy towards some form of democracy, to the relations between classes and elites and to the differences that emerge with the increasing complexities of class structure.

Aron (1950, 1960) provided some of the best studies of the relationship between elites and social classes, formulating the problem as that of the relation between social differentiation and political hierarchy in modern societies, and arguing that the 'abolition of classes' in the classical sense of abolishing private ownership of the means of production would not resolve the problems of social differentiation, formation of elites, and inequalities of political power. It might be added that the conflicts of elites and other differentiated social groups have some importance in themselves as checks upon the power of the rulers of society at any particular time, and that the question of social and political 'pluralism' is a crucial issue in the existing socialist societies.[6]

Theories of Social Stratification

There have been two major attempts to formulate a general theory of social stratification, that of Marx and that of the functionalists. The main outlines of the Marxist theory are well known, although neither Marx himself nor any later Marxist thinker formulated it in a comprehensive and systematic way. In this theory social classes are defined by their relation to the means of production (ownership or non-ownership) and this becomes the basis of the view that there are in every society, beyond the early tribal societies, two principal contending classes. The nature of the classes depends upon the mode of production, and this in turn upon the level of technology, in different societies. Marx, as Schumpeter observed, was primarily interested in the *development* of classes and, we may add, in their role in bringing about social and political changes. His own empirical studies were concerned with the origins of the bourgeoisie and the establishment of capitalism, and still more with the formation and growth of the proletariat as a class within capitalist society.

Marx first distinguishes the proletariat as a 'class in itself', an aggregate of individuals who are in the same economic situation, and then attempts to show how it becomes a 'class for itself', that is, how its members become aware of their common interests and political aims. In the *Poverty of Philosophy* and in *Capital*, Marx describes the circumstances favourable to this growth of class consciousness: the concentration of industry, the development of communications, the increasing economic and social distance between the bourgeoisie and the working class, the increasing homogeneity of the latter as a result of the decline of skilled trades, and so on.

Marx was well aware that social differentiation produced many other groups with conflicting interests in addition to the two principal classes. Thus, in the unfinished chapter on classes in Vol. 3 of *Capital*, he describes capitalists, landowners and wage earners as 'the three great classes of modern society', and also refers to 'intermediate and transitional strata [which] obscure the class boundaries'. Elsewhere, in his political writings (e.g. 1850, 1852), Marx distinguishes as many as ten major groups that are involved in political struggles, and on two occasions in the manuscript of *Theories of Surplus Value* he recognizes the growing importance of the middle classes (including the 'new' middle classes); for example, in discussing Ricardo:

> What [Ricardo] forgets to emphasize is the continual increase in numbers of the middle classes ... situated midway between the workers on one side and the capitalists and landowners on the other ... [who] rest with all their weight upon the working basis and at the same time increase the social security and power of the upper ten thousand. (ch. 18, B1d)

These complexities of Marx's theory have been much discussed by sociologists in recent times (Ossowski, 1957, ch. 5; Poulantzas, 1968; Bottomore, 1983), but the Marxist theory has still not been fully elaborated in a way which would take account of the whole range of situations to which it may be applied.

One particular problem concerns the development of class consciousness. In the *Poverty of Philosophy* Marx sketched a process which seemed to imply a more or less ineluctable development of working-class consciousness, but some later Marxists — and notably Lenin and Lukács — argued that this consciousness could only be introduced into the working class from outside, through the actions of a revolutionary party. Subsequent events have shown, however, that in the advanced capitalist countries revolutionary parties have themselves been largely unsuccessful, and the problem remains, as Hilferding (1941) indicated in his preliminary analysis of working–class consciousness, that 'nowhere has *socialist* consciousness taken hold of the entire working class'. On the other side it may be noted that the consciousness of dominant social groups and classes is generally much more highly developed and securely based, in part no doubt because these are more compact and closely knit groups which enjoy the advantages that Mosca (1896) attributed to all 'organized minorities'.

Other problems with the Marxist theory of class arise in applying it to specific types of social stratification, to particular classes other than the two major classes, or to various groups that may be deeply involved in social conflicts (for example, as I noted in Chapter 9 above, ethnic movements or the women's movement). Thus, it has proved difficult to analyse the Indian caste system in Marxist terms, even though most scholars have recognized that it embodies important elements of class (Béteille, 1965). Equally, the peasantry has been an 'awkward class' for Marxist analysis (Shanin, 1971). Marx (1852) described the peasantry in France as a class which could not become a politically conscious and effective force, but later in life he was led to reflect on the Russian peasant commune as a possible basis for a transition to socialism (Shanin, 1983); and in the twentieth century the largely peasant revolutions which have established socialist societies have revived debate about Marxism and the agrarian question (Hussain and Tribe, 1981).

The second major theory of social stratification, which begins from the general presuppositions of functionalism that I discussed in Part I above, has been clearly and succinctly stated by Davis and Moore (1945):

> Starting from the proposition that no society is 'classless', or unstratified, an effort is made to explain, in functional terms, the universal necessity which calls forth stratification in any social system . . . the main functional necessity explaining the universal presence of stratification is . . . the requirement faced by any society of placing and motivating individuals in the social structure . . . Social inequality is thus an unconsciously evolved device by which societies ensure that the most important positions are conscientiously filled by the most qualified persons.

If we disregard here the difficulties of functionalist explanation as such, the theory is still open to many specific criticisms. In the first place it assumes that stratification is universal, and this, so far as it implies the existence of a definite system of ranks in every society, is untrue. It also assumes that the 'most important positions' and 'most qualified persons' are unambiguously defined, independently of the influence of interested groups, in all societies. Next, it will be observed that the theory is conceived in terms of the ranking of individuals, and that it does not explain the existence of well-defined social groups: status groups, elites and classes. Moreover, the theory does not account for, but merely recognizes, the existence of different types of social stratification and processes of change from one type to another. Finally, it entirely neglects the role of force in establishing and maintaining systems of stratification, and thus has little to say about the relationship between social stratification and political conflict.

The functionalist theory had its principal adherents in the USA, where it corresponded broadly with a distinctive social situation in which neither an independent working-class party nor a working-class ideology ever became established, and the social hierarchy has popularly been conceived as a system of loosely organized status groups, membership of which is closely related to individual abilities. But this view of American society was increasingly contested by social scientists who drew attention to the existence of well-established elites (Mills, 1956) or of a dominant class (Domhoff, 1970), and it is doubtful whether the functionalist theory now has any important influence on studies of stratification.

On the other hand, the Marxist theory, for all its imperfections, has demonstrated its explanatory power in relation to social and political conflict in Europe since the nineteenth century, and to some extent (since 1945) in other regions of the world. Even its imperfections have been a fruitful source of sociological thought and research, notably in studies of the changing character of property ownership, the expansion of the middle classes, the situation of the working class in 'organized' welfare capitalism, and the nature of social stratification in the socialist countries. Today, therefore, it may be claimed that the dominant paradigm in studies of social stratification is one inspired by Marxism and complemented or amended in diverse ways by the ideas of Weber and the elite theorists (with a varying balance between the Marxian, Weberian and Paretian elements in different analytical schemes).

Notes to Chapter 11

1   See the entry on 'Slavery' in the *Encyclopaedia of the Social Sciences* (1934) which distinguishes between primitive, ancient, medieval and modern slavery.

2 See also the discussion of diverse forms of unfree or dependent labour in the ancient world by Finley, 1980.

3 The *jajmani* system; see Wiser, 1936.

4 The resemblance between *jati* and tribe has been emphasized by Rosas, 1943, who also cites historical examples of the easy transition from tribe to caste.

5 Marx recognized that class was a uniquely prominent feature of capitalist society even though he also used the term in a wider sense to refer to the 'owners of the conditions of production' and the 'direct producers' in other types of society as well. This question will be discussed further in relation to the theories of stratification.

6 On the question of elites see also the writings of Mosca, the study of Mosca's work by Albertoni, 1987, and the discussion in Bottomore, 1964.

Notes on Reading for Part III

I Social Structure

1 The Concept of Social Structure

Blau, Peter M. (ed.), *Approaches to the Study of Social Structure* (1975).
Gurvitch, Georges (ed.), *Traité de sociologie* (1958), Vol. 1, sect. 2, ch. 4, 'Structures sociales'.
Lévi-Strauss, Claude, *Structural Anthropology* (1958), chs. 15 and 16.
Nadel, S. F., *The Theory of Social Structure* (1957).
Radcliffe-Brown, A. R., *Structure and Function in Primitive Society* (1952), ch. 10, 'On social structure'.

2 Types of Society

In the work of the earlier sociologists the classification of societies had an important place, and the student should be familiar with such classifications as those of Spencer, Marx, Durkheim, Tönnies, Maine and Hobhouse, which are discussed in the text. In recent work there has been less interest in the problems of morphology, but some important contributions are referred to in the text. For some early surveys of the attempts to classify societies see:

Rumney, J., *Herbert Spencer's Sociology* (1934), ch. 3, 'Types of society'.
Steinmetz, S. R., 'Classification des types sociaux et catalogue des peuples' (1898–9).
   A very thorough and comprehensive survey of the schemes of classification proposed up to that time, with a critical discussion of the uses and principles of classification.

On particular types of society the following works will be useful:

Anderson, Perry, *Passages from Antiquity to Feudalism* (1974a).
Aron, Raymond, *18 Lectures on Industrial Society* (1961).
Bloch, Marc, *Feudal Society* (1939–40), especially Vol. 2, pt 8.
Finley, M. I., *The Ancient Economy* (1973).
Finley, M. I., 'The Ancient City: from Fustel de Coulanges to Max Weber and beyond' (1977).
Fried, Morton, 'On the concepts of "tribe" and "tribal society" ' (1966).
Fustel de Coulanges, N. D., *The Ancient City* (1864).
Galbraith, J. K., *The New Industrial State* (1971).
George, Vic and Manning, Nick, *Socialism, Social Welfare and the Soviet Union* (1980).
Godelier, Maurice, *Perspectives in Marxist Anthropology* (1973), ch. 3, 'The

concept of the "Tribe"', and ch. 4, 'An attempt at a critical evaluation'.
Krader, Lawrence, *The Asiatic Mode of Production* (1975).
Lane, David, *The Socialist Industrial State* (1976).
Schumpeter, J. A., *Capitalism, Socialism and Democracy* (1942).
Sombart, Werner, 'Capitalism' (1930).
Turner, B. S., 'Asiatic society' (1983a).
Weber, Max, *General Economic History* (1923), pt 4.

3 Culture and Civilization

For a discussion of the concept of culture see:

Bauman, Zygmunt, *Culture as Praxis* (1973).
Goldmann, Lucien, *Cultural Creation in Modern Society* (1971).
Kroeber, A. L. and Kluckhohn, C., *Culture* (1952).
Malinowski, B., 'Culture', in *Encyclopaedia of the Social Sciences* (1930).
Malinowski, B., *A Scientific Theory of Culture* (1944).
Outhwaite, William, 'Culture' (1983b).

On the notion of civilization, see:

Centre International de Synthèse, *Civilisation, le mot et l'idée* (1930).
Durkheim, Émile and Mauss, Marcel, 'Note sur la notion de civilisation' (1913).
Toynbee, Arnold J., *A Study of History* (1934–56), Vol. 1, Introduction, C. 'The comparative study of civilizations'.

II Economic Institutions

1 General Works

Seddon, David (ed.), *Relations of Production* (1978).
Weber, Max, *Economy and Society* (1921), pt 1, ch. 2.

See also the works by Aron, Galbraith, Schumpeter, and Weber mentioned in the previous section.

2 The Division of Labour

Bottomore, Tom, *Sociology and Socialism,* (1984a), ch. 9, 'Socialism and the division of labour'.
Bouglé, C., 'Théories sur la division du travail' (1903).
Durkheim, Émile, *The Division of Labour in Society* (1893).
Friedmann, Georges, *The Anatomy of Work* (1956).

3 Property

For general conceptions and theories of property see:

Gore, Charles (Bishop of Oxford) (ed.), *Property: Its Duties and Rights* (1913).

Hegedüs, András, *Socialism and Bureaucracy* (1976), ch. 7.
Lowie, R. H., *Social Organization* (1950), ch. 6.
Macpherson, C. B. (ed.), *Property: Mainstream and Critical Positions* (1978).
Schlatter, R., *Private Property: The History of an Idea* (1951).

On the distribution of property in modern capitalist societies see, for example:

Kolko, Gabriel, *Wealth and Power in America* (1962).
Mills, C. Wright, *The Power Elite* (1956).
Scott, John, *The Upper Classes: Property and Privilege in Britain* (1982).
Tawney, R. H., *Equality* (1952).

There has been much study of industrial property, and especially its concentration, in capitalist societies. A pioneer study of the business corporation is A. A. Berle and G. C. Means, *The Modern Corporation and Private Property* (1934), and a more recent account, John Scott, *Corporations, Classes and Capitalism* (1979). A classical Marxist study is Karl Renner, *The Institutions of Private Law and their Social Functions* (1904), the English translation of which (1949) has a valuable introduction and notes by O. Kahn-Freund, who discusses the changes in property and property law since Renner's work was first published.

4   The Industrial Enterprise and Industrial Relations

Friedmann, Georges, *Industrial Society* (1946).
Hyman, Richard, *Strikes* (1984).
Mayo, Elton, *The Human Problems of an Industrial Civilization* (1933).
Moore, Wilbert E., *Industrial Relations and the Social Order* (1946).

On a distinctive form of socialist organization of enterprises see:

Broekmeyer, M. J. (ed.), *Yugoslav Workers' Self-Management* (1970).

III   Political Institutions

1   Types of Political System

On tribal societies see:

Balandier, Georges, *Political Anthropology* (1967).
Schapera, I., *Government and Politics in Tribal Societies* (1956).

and also the works on 'stateless societies' referred to in the text.
On other pre-modern societies see:

Bloch, Marc, *Feudal Society* (1939–40), pt 2.
Glotz, G., *The Greek City* (1928).
Wittfogel, K. A., *Oriental Despotism* (1957).

For general accounts of European and North American political systems, the rise of nation states, modern democracies and totalitarianism, and socialist regimes, see:

Anderson, Perry, *Lineages of the Absolutist State* (1974b).
Aron, Raymond, *Democracy and Totalitarianism* (1965).
Lane, David, *The Socialist Industrial State* (1976).
Lindsay, A. D., *The Modern Democratic State* (1943).
MacIver, R. M., *The Modern State* (1926).
Macpherson, C. B., *The Real World of Democracy* (1965).
Neumann, Franz, *Behemoth: The Structure and Practice of National Socialism* (1942).
Tilly, Charles (ed.), *The Formation of National States in Western Europe* (1975).
Tocqueville, Alexis de, *Democracy in America* (1835–40).

2 Theories of the State

Engels, Friedrich, *The Origin of the Family, Private Property and the State* (1884).
Gramsci, Antonio, *Selections from the Prison Notebooks* (1929–35), pt 2, ch. 2, 'State and civil society'.
Lowie, R. H., *The Origin of the State* (1927).
Miliband, Ralph, *Class Power and State Power* (1983b), pt 1, 'The capitalist state'.
Oppenheimer, Franz, *The State* (1907).
Poulantzas, Nicos, *Political Power and Social Classes* (1968).
Weber, Max, *Economy and Society* (1921), pt 1, ch. 3 and pt 3, chs. 1–3.

3 Parties, Pressure Groups and Social Movements

General studies of political parties include:

Duverger, M., *Political Parties* (1951).
Michels, R., *Political Parties* (1911).
Ostrogorski, M. I., *Democracy and the Organization of Political Parties* (1902).

On parties in particular countries or regions see, for example:

Hodgkin, Thomas, *African Political Parties: An Introductory Guide* (1962).
Lane, David, *Politics and Society in the USSR* (1970), ch. 5.
McKenzie, R. T., *British Political Parties* (1963).
Nettl, J. P., 'The German Social Democratic Party 1890–1914 as a political model' (1965).
Schurmann, Franz, *Ideology and Organization in Communist China* (1970), ch. 2.
Weiner, M., *Party Politics in India: The Development of a Multi-Party System* (1957).

On pressure groups see:

Finer, S. E., *Anonymous Empire* (1958).

Key, V. O., *Politics, Parties and Pressure Groups* (1950).
Stewart, J. D., *British Pressure Groups* (1958).

For studies of social movements, both general and relating to particular movements, see:

Aberle, David F., *The Peyote Religion Among the Navaho* (1966), ch. 19, 'A classification of social movements'.
Banks, Olive, *Faces of Feminism* (1981).
Habermas, Jürgen, *Toward a Rational Society* (1968–9), chs. 2 and 3.
Heberle, Rudolf, *Social Movements* (1951).
Lanternari, Vittorio, *The Religions of the Oppressed* (1960).
Piven, Frances F. and Cloward, Richard A., *Poor People's Movements* (1977).
Rudé, George, *The Crowd in History* (1964).

4 Political Action

Most of the extensive literature is devoted to elections and electoral behaviour, but there are, of course, many other forms of political action ranging from the activities of social movements and pressure groups to riots, revolutions and war; and a guide to reading on these kinds of action is provided in various places (e.g. with reference to Chapters 12 and 17 below). On elections see, in addition to the studies of elections which are regularly conducted in particular countries, the following general works:

Dupeux, G., 'Electoral behaviour' (1954–5).
Lipset, S. M., and Rokkan, S. (eds.), *Party Systems and Voter Alignments* (1967).
Rokkan, S., 'Mass suffrage, secret voting and political participation' (1961).

For further reading see the entry on 'Elections' in *International Encyclopaedia of Social Sciences* (1968).

5 Political Ideologies

The general concept of 'ideology', as well as Mosca's 'political formula', Gramsci's 'hegemony' and the idea of a 'dominant ideology' will be discussed in Part IV below. Two outstanding early sociological studies of political ideologies are:

Bouglé, C., *Les Idées égalitaires* (1925).
Mannheim, Karl, 'Conservative thought' (1927a).

Among more recent studies, including discussions of the role of intellectuals in politics, see:

Aron, Raymond, *The Opium of the Intellectuals* (1955).
Bell, Daniel, (ed.), *The Radical Right* (1963).
Brym, Robert, *Intellectuals and Politics* (1980).

Friedrich, Carl J., Curtis, Michael and Barber, Benjamin R. (eds.),
  Totalitarianism in Perspective: Three Views (1969).
Weiss, John, *The Fascist Tradition* (1967), esp. ch. 2.

As I noted earlier, the study of nationalism as an ideology has been
relatively neglected, though Bauer (1907) analysed it in the context of the
multinational Habsburg Empire. See, for a general account:

Kohn, Hans, *The Idea of Nationalism* (1944).
Smith, Anthony D., *Theories of Nationalism* (1971).

6 *Bureaucracy*

The origin of modern studies of bureaucracy is the analysis by Max
Weber, *Economy and Society* (1921), pt 3, ch. 6.
For more recent general accounts see:

Blau, Peter M., *Bureaucracy in Modern Society* (1956).
Mouzelis, Nicos P., *Organisation and Bureaucracy* (1967).

IV The Family and Kinship

1 *Kinship*

Fox, Robin, *Kinship and Marriage* (1967).
Lowie, R. H., *Social Organization* (1950), ch. 4.
Murdock, G. P., *Social Structure* (1949). A comparative study based
  upon the files of the Yale Cross-Cultural Survey, which discusses the
  major problems of kinship analysis. Also has chapters on the types of
  family and on the social regulation of sexual behaviour.
Radcliffe-Brown, A. R., 'Introduction' to Radcliffe-Brown and Forde
  (1950), pp. 1–85. An outstanding short survey of kinship and marriage. The rest of the volume contains valuable studies of the kinship
  systems and marriage customs of particular African tribes, by leading
  social anthropologists.

2 *Marriage and the Family*

On the history of marriage and the family see:

Goodsell, W., *A History of Marriage and the Family* (1934).
Rabb, T. K. and Rotberg, R. I. (eds.), *The Family in History* (1973).
Westermarck, E., *A Short History of Marriage* (1926).

and more specifically on the Western family:

Anderson, Michael, *Approaches to the History of the Western Family* (1980).
Shorter, Edward, *The Making of the Modern Family* (1975).

As examples of studies of the family in civilizations other than that of
Europe or North America see:

Kapadia, K. M., *Marriage and Family in India* (1958).
Lang, Olga, *Chinese Family and Society* (1946).

Marxist analysis of the family, as was noted in the text, began with Engels's book (1884), and more recently has become involved with feminist criticism of the traditional mainstream sociology of the family; see, for example, the literature discussed in:

Barrett, Michèle, *Women's Oppression Today* (1980).
Poster, Mark, *Critical Theory of the Family* (1978).

V   Social Stratification

1   General

Bottomore, Tom, 'Social differentiation and stratification', in *Encyclopaedia Britannica* (1974), Macropaedia Vol. 16.
Cox, O. C., *Caste, Class and Race* (1948).
Davis, K. and Moore, W. E., 'Some principles of stratification' (1945).
Mayer, Kurt B. and Buckley, Walter, *Class and Society* (1969).
Tumin, Melvin M., *Social Stratification: The Forms and Functions of Inequality* (1967).

2   Slavery

Entry on 'Slavery' in *Encyclopaedia of the Social Sciences* (1934).
Finley, M. I. (ed.), *Slavery in Classical Antiquity* (1968).
Finley, M. I., *Ancient Slavery and Modern Ideology* (1980).
Nieboer, H. J., *Slavery as an Industial System* (1900).

3   Feudal Estates and Serfdom

Bloch, Marc, *Feudal Society* (1939–40), Vol. 2, pt 6, 'Social classes'.
Bloch, Marc, *Slavery and Serfdom in the Middle Ages* (1975).
Dobb, Maurice, *Studies in the Development of Capitalism* (1946), ch. 2.
Hilton, R. H., *The Decline of Serfdom in Medieval England* (1969).
Southern, R. W., *The Making of the Middle Ages* (1953), ch. 2.

4   Caste

Béteille, André, *Caste, Class and Power: Changing Patterns of Stratification in a Tanjore Village* (1965).
Bouglé, C., *Essays on the Caste System* (1908).
Dumont, Louis, *Homo Hierarchicus: The Caste System and its Implications* (1966).
Hutton, J. H., *Caste in India* (1951). The most systematic account of the caste system. In pt 3 there is a most useful discussion of theories of the origins of caste. Has a good bibliography.
Srinivas, M. N., *et al.*, 'Caste' (1959). An excellent review and evalu-

ation of recent studies of caste, with an annotated bibliography. The introduction brings out very clearly the complexity of the caste system.

Srinivas, M. N., *Caste in Modern India and Other Essays* (1965).

5 Class and Status

There is a vast literature on classes and status groups in modern societies. The following works deal with some of the major issues, from diverse points of view:

Bottomore, Tom, *Classes in Modern Society* (1965).
Dahrendorf, Ralf, *Class and Class Conflict in an Industrial Society* (1959).
Giddens, Anthony, *The Class Structure of the Advanced Societies* (1973).
Halbwachs, M., *The Psychology of Social Classes* (1938).
Marshall, T. H., *Citizenship and Social Class and Other Essays* (1950).
Schumpeter, J. A., 'Social classes in an ethnically homogeneous environment' (1927).
Weber, Max, *Economy and Society* (1921), pt 1, ch. 4, 'Status groups and classes'; pt 3, ch. 4, 'Classes, status, parties'.

There have been many studies of individual countries or regions, and of particular classes and status groups, among which the following are especially useful:

Abercrombie, Nicholas and Urry, John, *Capital, Labour and the Middle Classes* (1983).
Archer, Margaret and Giner, Salvador (eds.), *Contemporary Europe: Class, Status and Power* (1971).
Goldthorpe, John H. *et al.*, *The Affluent Worker in the Class Structure* (1968–9).
Mann, Michael, *Consciousness and Action among the Western Working Class* (1973).
Mills, C. Wright, *White Collar: The American Middle Classes* (1951).

6 Elites

Albertoni, Ettore A., *Gaetano Mosca and the Theory of Elites* (1987).
Aron, Raymond, 'Social structure and the ruling class' (1950).
Bottomore, Tom, *Elites and Society* (1964).
Mills, C. Wright, *The Power Elite* (1956).
Mosca, Gaetano, *The Ruling Class* (1896).
Pareto, Vilfredo, *A Treatise on General Sociology* (1916), pp. 1421–32.

7 Social mobility

Sorokin, P. A., *Social Mobility* (1927). Reprinted, together with a chapter from the author's *Social and Cultural Dynamics* (1937), under the title *Social and Cultural Mobility* (1959).

This pioneer study provides a very comprehensive survey on the basis of data available at that time. More recent data are used for comparative purposes in:

Heath, Anthony, *Social Mobility* (1981), ch. 7.
Lipset, S. M. and Bendix, R., *Social Mobility in Industrial Society* (1959).
Miller, S. M., 'Comparative social mobility' (1960).

Studies of particular countries include:

Blau, Peter M. and Duncan, Otis D., *The American Occupational Structure* (1967).
Carlsson, Gösta, *Social Mobility and Class Structure* (1958).
Girard, Alain, *La Réussite sociale en France* (1961).
Glass, D. V. (ed.), *Social Mobility in Britain* (1954). This study was repeated, with some modifications, a quarter of a century later by the Oxford Social Mobility Group; see Goldthorpe, J. H., *Social Mobility and Class Structure in Modern Britain* (1980).

PART IV

The Regulation of Behaviour

12   Force in Social Life

The regulation of behaviour in society, whether of individuals or of groups, is undertaken in two ways: by the use of force, and by the establishment of values and norms which may be more or less fully accepted by the members of a society as binding 'rules of conduct'. The term 'social control' is generally used by sociologists to refer to this second kind of regulation, in which the appeal to values and norms resolves or mitigates tensions and conflicts between individuals and between groups in order to maintain the solidarity of some more inclusive group. The term is also used to refer to the arrangements by means of which the values and norms are communicated and instilled (Gurvitch, 1945). We may distinguish, therefore, between the *types* of social control, and the *agencies* and *means* which are the vehicles of social control. The principal types of control are those which will be discussed in subsequent chapters: custom and opinion, law, religion, morals and education (knowledge, science). The educational system also figures as an agency of social control, along with the political system, churches and other religious bodies, the family (in which the initial socialization of new generations takes place), and many other specialized organizations. Every social group, indeed, can be studied from the aspect of the social control which it exercises over its own members,[1] and the contribution which it makes to the regulation of behaviour in society at large.

From another standpoint social control can be analysed in terms of Marx's concept of 'ideology' or Mosca's notion of a 'political formula', as one of the means by which a dominant class or elite maintains its dominance. The Marxist conception was elaborated in a distinctive way by Gramsci (1929–35) in his discussion of the state and civil society:

> What we can do, for the moment, is to fix two major superstructural 'levels': the one that can be called 'civil society', that is the ensemble of organisms commonly called 'private', and that of 'political society' or the 'State'. These two levels correspond on the one hand to the function of 'hegemony' which the dominant group exercises throughout society and on the other hand to that of 'direct domination' or command exercised through the State and 'juridical' government. (p. 12)

In some recent writing the importance of a 'dominant ideology' in maintaining class rule has been questioned (Abercrombie, Hill and Turner, 1980), but in a wider sense social control is obviously important in the life of any organized and complex society. Moreover, the Marxist notion of the 'withering away of the State' in a classless society can best be understood as implying that in such a society the use of force would greatly diminish, its place being taken by a more profound influence of moral and cultural norms.

In most societies up to the present time, however, behaviour has been regulated both by social control as defined above, and by frequent and often large-scale use of force. These two modes are not, of course, entirely separable in actual social life. The ultimate sanction of law is physical coercion, and physical force may enter more or less prominently into all the types of social control; public opinion may transform itself into witch-hunts and lynchings or into riots and rebellions, religious sentiment may turn to religious persecution, the burning of heretics and wars of religion. On the other hand, physical coercion itself is usually most effective where it can be justified in terms of widely accepted values; and even in the most extreme case of rule by force (for example, in a military dictatorship) the ruling group itself must be bound together by other means. Nevertheless, the distinction is clear and important. In political philosophy it has long been represented in the opposition between those thinkers who conceive the state as based upon force and those who regard it as based upon consent. Social analysis is here connected with conceptions of what *ought* to be the basis of political obligation. Sociological researches have thrown new light upon the actual processes by which social order is maintained, and perhaps because these studies have concentrated upon primitive societies on one side, and upon modern democratic societies on the other, there has been a strong emphasis upon the normative aspects of the regulation of behaviour. In some modern sociological theories, such as that of Talcott Parsons, the element of physical coercion in social relationships is almost entirely neglected (Lockwood, 1956). Yet it is contrary to our experience even of present-day societies to underestimate the role of force; in the modern world there are police states and colonial regimes (in a variety of forms) as well as democracies. And in the history of human societies the significance of violence, conquest and oppression is all too evident.

The sociological theories which emphasize the regulation of behaviour by values and norms also tend to be preoccupied with such regulation at the level of an inclusive society and to depict social control as a relatively harmonious, unified and stable system, while they treat conflicts between values as secondary phenomena under the heading of 'deviations'. Such a framework seems applicable only to very small and simple societies. I have already noted that every social group regulates the behaviour of its members, and in complex societies different social groups may be in conflict with each other, each seeking to extend its own values and norms over the whole society. Examples of such situations are to be found in the conflicts between social classes, between different religious groups, and between ethnic groups and nationalities.

In this chapter I shall be concerned with those conflicts between social groups which involve the use of force. I shall not discuss social conflict in a more general sense (see Bottomore, 1975b, ch. 11). Nor shall I deal here with individual violence, although the degree and trend of violence in a society may be an indicator of social problems.[2] Violent conflict between social groups has obviously had a very great influence upon the form of human societies by extending, destroying or modifying particular ways of life, and its causes and consequences deserve the most serious study. We may usefully begin by distinguishing two main types – violent conflict between whole societies (war), and violent conflict within a society (revolution and counter-revolution, civil war) – which I shall consider separately before looking at any more general features.

War

Modern sociologists have shown comparatively little interest in the study of war. As one writer has noted: 'until very recently . . . the study of war and peace attracted nothing like the degree of intellectual attention that has been devoted for three or four generations to economic analysis . . . and, whatever the reasons, there is no generally acknowledged corpus of theory' (Buchan, 1966). The case was different with the early sociologists, and with a number of later thinkers up to the beginning of this century. Both Comte and Spencer assigned to war a very important role in the development of society. According to Comte (1830–42, Lecture 57): 'There was no other means, in the early stages, to bring about the indispensable expansion of human society, and to restrain within society a sterile warlike ardour incompatible with an adequate growth of productive work, except the gradual incorporation of civilized populations into one conquering nation.' Similarly, Spencer (1876–96, Vol. 2) argued that in the early stages of development those societies were most likely to survive which were most effectively organized for war: 'The social type produced by survival of the fittest will be one in which the fighting part includes all who can bear arms and be trusted with arms, while the remaining part serves simply as a permanent commissariat.'

Both Comte and Spencer could take this realistic view of the historical importance of warfare partly because they believed the age of international war was ending. They made a distinction between a military and an industrial type of society; in the former work was subordinate to war, while in the latter, represented by the modern Western nations, war is subordinate to work. As Comte rashly declared: 'At last the time has come when serious and lasting war must disappear completely among the human elite'; a view which was critically assessed by Aron (1958) in his study of war and industrial society. Later writers such as Gumplowicz and Oppenheimer took a similar view of the importance of war in social development, without sharing the belief of Comte and Spencer that it was about to disappear from human affairs; and at the beginning of the twentieth century studies of war were stimulated again by the threat of renewed warfare among the advanced nations, for example, in the essays by William James (1910) and Sumner (1911). This was also the period in which a theory of imperialist war was developed from the writings of J. A. Hobson, Hilferding and Lenin on imperialism.

Subsequently, as I have noted, the interest of sociologists in this field of study declined, though there were some exceptions. Ginsberg (1939) published an essay on the causes of war, but Sorokin (1937) was the only sociologist who dealt at length with war, as an integral aspect of his general social theory, in his major work on social and cultural dynamics. In part, this neglect may have been due to a belief that the subject was too vast and complex to be treated adequately in a more or less scientific manner; but this view is no longer plausible now that sociologists have embarked upon studies of equal scope and difficulty concerned with the nature of industrial societies or the processes of economic development. Much more important, probably, was the abandonment of historical and comparative inquiries, and the adoption of a functionalist approach which diverted attention from problems of conflict to problems of the integration of particular societies. Whatever the reasons, the systematic study of war, and of conflict generally, languished for several decades; but it has revived strongly in recent years. This is due not only to changes in the whole theoretical orientation of sociology, but also to the recognition that war, in the nuclear age, is one of the most dangerous problems confronting humanity, and that a social science which ignores it can hardly claim to be comprehensive or fully relevant to the practical problems of human welfare.

Among recent works the most wide-ranging and profound is the study of peace and war by Aron (1962), who discusses first the concepts and schemes of classification that are required for systematic inquiry in this field – power, force, the international system of states, different types of war and of peace – and then considers some of the possible determinants of war, and the theories which have been offered about them, before turning, in the third part of the book, to a historical examination of the global system of states in the nuclear age. In the last section of the book he discusses some moral evaluations of war, and their political and strategic implications, and raises the question of the possible alternatives to war as a means of regulating the relations between sovereign states, each of which is pursuing its own national interest. Two possibilities are peace through law, and peace through empire – either of which would involve, in different ways, a greater or lesser sacrifice of national sovereignty. A third possibility is peace through the balance of power as it now exists, but this may be difficult to maintain in conditions of rapid technological advance and of the spread of nuclear weapons. In a final note Aron criticizes the indiscriminate use of game-theory models in some recent studies (the limitations of which are also pointed out by Rapoport, 1960), and advocates paying more attention to 'reasonable policy' than to 'rational strategy'.

Another interesting kind of inquiry is that which was undertaken by Richardson (1960a) in an attempt to discover the correlates of war by means of a careful quantitative study; and in a second book (Richardson, 1960b) to determine the influence of an arms race upon the probability of war.

The recent studies of war and peace, some of which have brought together sociology and other social sciences under the general title of 'strategic studies', differ in important respects from the earlier sociological theories. They are no longer very much concerned with long-term evolutionary trends but devote their attention rather to modern war, and to the specific practical issue of avoiding a major war, through an analysis of the conditions and situations which may provoke it (for example, what Richardson called a 'runaway arms race').[3] Such studies draw upon historical and comparative investigations, but they do not aim at the construction of an ambitious general theory of war. What they have contributed so far is a clarification of ideas about the complex phenomenon of war and an indication of some of its proximate causes. Like sociology in general, sociological studies of war and peace do not provide the grounds for a single correct course of action, but help to enlarge the area of rational choice and control.

It is understandable that most of the recent studies should have concentrated upon the dangers of a nuclear war between the super-powers, but this does not exhaust the subject matter of the use of force in international affairs. Indeed, from the point of view of the regulation of behaviour by force, the occurrence of limited wars fought with conventional weapons, and various kinds of military intervention by the super-powers (the USA in the Dominican Republic, Vietnam, Grenada, the USSR in Czechoslovakia, Afghanistan), are more immediately significant. The problems which these examples indicate are not likely to be easily solved. They arise in part out of the general confrontation between power blocs, but they also reflect the permanent inequality in the international order between large and small nations; and we are still far from having a clear conception of how the rights of small nations can be guaranteed, let alone an effective practical policy.

Revolution and Counter-Revolution

The study of revolution was never neglected to the same extent as the study of war, largely because one important sociological theory – Marxism – treated revolution as a basic phenomenon of social life. In recent years the interest of sociologists in the study of revolutions has become much more widespread, and at the same time the implementation of such studies has encountered great difficulties. The interest is not difficult to explain: the twentieth century is, more than any other, a century of revolutions. The Russian and Chinese Revolutions have at least as great a historical and political significance as had the French Revolution, marking in a similar way the beginning of a new course of social development; while many revolutions in smaller countries (in Yugoslavia, Algeria, Cuba) have contributed new political ideas and models of new social institutions. The cumulative effect of these events and the revival of radical and revolutionary ideas in the Western industrial countries themselves during the 1960s have obliged sociologists to pay more attention to such phenomena.

The difficulties arise in two ways. In the first place, while sociologists, like most other people, condemn war and are apprehensive about the possibility of a conflict involving nuclear weapons – and thus agree broadly upon the aim of their studies as being the eventual control or elimination of international warfare – there is no such agreement in respect of the use of force in revolutionary struggles. Sociologists may, and do, approach the study of revolutions with sympathy or aversion; they may become advisers to revolutionary leaders, or more frequently, it seems, to counter-insurgency agencies.[4] For various reasons, including the predominance of a conservative style of social thought during much of the postwar period, there has grown up an idea that a sympathy with movements of rebellion is somehow more ideological, and a greater threat to sociological objectivity, than is an attachment to the *status quo*. This is obviously not the case. Nor is it self-evidently true that violence and the use of force are more prevalent in revolutionary movements than in counter-revolutions or in the defence of an established order. It would be difficult, no doubt, to draw up a balance sheet of violence, but there are numerous historical examples of the savage repression of radical or even reforming movements in modern societies, from the suppression of the Paris Commune to the armed attacks on the early trade unions (especially in the USA) and the overthrow of the Allende government in Chile, and on quite a different scale the Nazi movement, and the massacre of Indonesian communists in 1965–6; and it appears quite probable that the *status quo* is generally defended much more violently than it is attacked. Questions of moral attitude and political commitment thus become exceptionally intrusive in this field of inquiry, with the result that many sociologists have been deterred from entering it.

The second kind of difficulty is theoretical. The major theory of revolution – that of Marx – was concerned principally with the transition from feudalism to capitalism in Western Europe, and with the development of a revolutionary working class within capitalist society. But the twentieth-century revolutions have taken place in peasant societies, while the revolutionary movement in the advanced capitalist countries seems (or seemed) to many sociologists to have subsided. As yet these events have not been fully incorporated into a revised Marxist theory, even though the peasant revolutions have often been led by parties which profess Marxism as their doctrine; nor has any alternative theory of social change dealt adequately with the new circumstances. However, a recent major study (Skocpol, 1979) of the French, Russian and Chinese Revolutions, which is strongly influenced by the Marxist conceptions of structural change and class conflict, sets out three valuable principles of analysis involving the notions of structure, the international context, and the potential autonomy of the state. Skocpol concludes her book by arguing, with reference to Lenin's view of the state and revolution, that: 'Questions of state power *have* been basic in social-revolutionary transformations, but state power cannot be understood only as an instrument of class domination, nor can changes in state structures be explained primarily in terms of class conflicts' (p. 284).

A revolution, in the words of Schurmann and Schell (1967, Introduction), 'is the sweeping away of an old order – an ancient political system, a traditional culture, an uncreative economy, a ruling class which only exploits, and a system of social organization which no longer satisfies men'. It does not necessarily involve the use of force and armed conflict; but most modern revolutions have occurred through such conflict, either because the established rulers have used force to resist change or because the leaders of the revolutionary movement have encountered a situation in which their aims could be achieved very rapidly by force. The underlying causes of revolutionary movements and revolutions are conflicts of interest, principally between social classes as Marx's theory maintains; although many other elements may enter into the process – ethnic and religious differences, or nationalist sentiments. The success of a revolutionary movement depends upon diverse factors; Crane Brinton (1957), elaborating upon ideas which were expressed at various times by Marx, particularly in his early writings, has suggested that the favourable conditions include economic progress in a society, bitter class antagonisms, desertion of the ruling class by the intellectuals, inefficient governmental machinery, and a politically inept ruling class.

These notions enable us to understand, in some measure, the absence or failure of revolutionary movements in the Western industrial countries since the end of the nineteenth century. In particular, it is the fact that class antagonisms have not become more acute – but on the contrary have been limited by the growth of the middle classes, by the achievement of reforms through the activities of the labour movement, and in the postwar period by increasing prosperity – which explains these conditions. At the same time, the ruling classes in these societies have experienced few crises in which they have been wholly deserted by the intellectuals or have become demoralized to such an extent that they have lost control of events. Only on rare occasions – for example, following a military defeat in which the rulers were discredited, as in Germany in 1918 – could a revolutionary movement develop. Or to take an example from a different sphere, the attempted revolution in Hungary in 1956 was only possible because the political leaders had been thrown into confusion by the revelations concerning the nature of Communist rule during the Stalinist period. The absence of any large-scale revolutionary movements in most of the Western countries in this century does not mean that the opposition between classes – economic, cultural and ideological – has ceased to exist. At times, as in the 1950s, it has been muted, but it has always reappeared; and in the late 1960s there was a revival of revolutionary ideas, not in the working class, but in the student movements. However, in spite of the example of the student-inspired revolt of May 1968 in France, it seems unlikely that there will be any serious revolutionary movements in the Western industrial countries.[5] On the other hand, it is probable that there will be accelerated social and political change, broadly along the lines which the labour movement has followed, and this may be accompanied by sporadic violent conflicts in some societies.

In the predominantly peasant societies where revolutions have occurred the conditions which I mentioned earlier have generally prevailed: bitter class antagonisms resulting from the gross disparities of wealth, and from the autocratic rule of a small minority; the defection of Westernized intellectuals, often influenced by Marxism; the ineptitude of traditional ruling groups in dealing with economic problems and with the impact of more advanced societies. These revolutions, while inspired by Marxism and socialism, have also been intricately involved with anti-colonial, national liberation movements, and with the effort to modernize and industrialize which now characterizes all the countries of the Third World. Thus their achievement is not necessarily the creation of a socialist society as this was conceived in the West during the nineteenth century, but rather the successful implementation (at least in some cases) of a policy for rapid economic growth. At the same time they have had a great influence upon world politics, by reanimating revolutionary ideas elsewhere and to some extent giving them a new form, in which the violent conflicts which will bring about profound changes in the structure of society are seen not so much as conflicts between classes within capitalist society but as conflicts between the 'bourgeois' and the 'proletarian' nations. Clearly, these ideas involve a substantial revision of Marxist theory, such as has been attempted in diverse ways by Marcuse (1964), Frank (1969), and a number of other social scientists more or less closely associated with the radical movements of the 1960s. There is quite a different interpretation, which remains closer to the original Marxist scheme, in so far as it rests upon an analysis of the nature of internal class relations, in Barrington Moore (1966), where 'three routes to the modern world' are distinguished and compared: the bourgeois revolution (England, France, USA); the revolution from above (Germany, Japan); and the communist revolution (Russia, China).

In recent years the growing preoccupation with the violent character of this century has led to a revival of interest in the notion of an aggressive instinct or propensity in human nature. This was, of course, discussed at a much earlier time. Simmel (1908b, p. 29), in studying conflict, wrote that 'it seems impossible to deny an *a priori* fighting instinct', and Freud (1933), in an exchange of letters with Einstein on the prevention of war, asserted the existence of a destructive or aggressive instinct in human beings. A study by Durbin and Bowlby (1938, p. 15) concluded that 'the willingness to fight is so widely distributed in space and time that it must be regarded as a basic pattern of human behaviour'. Recent biological and anthropological studies have generally supported the view that there is an aggressive instinct, resulting from natural selection, which is widely distributed among the vertebrates and is to be found among the primates, including man (Lorenz, 1966; Washburn, 1966); but most writers recognize that to posit such an instinct is far from providing a complete explanation of the occurrence of violent conflict. An aggressive instinct, like other instincts, can be regulated and controlled, as indeed must be the case, since men are not fighting all the time. As Durbin and Bowlby observe: 'Peaceful cooperation predominates – there is much more peace than war.'

What has to be explained is the occurrence of violent conflict at particular times, and this can only be done by investigating the social conditions which lead to a situation in which groups of men determine (or have determined for them by their leaders) that they will fight to defend or promote their interests. In whatever way the causes of such conflicts are explained – and I have outlined above some of the theories of war and revolution –

there can be no question about the significance which the use of force, in these different forms, has had in sustaining or destroying a particular social order, and in creating new types of society. Pareto (1902, Vol. 1, p. 17) took an extreme view when he argued that 'it is by force that social institutions are established, and it is by force that they are maintained', but his argument, derived from Marx's theory, is still nearer to the truth than the conception which prevailed in sociology for some time, according to which human social behaviour is regulated only by values.

In the following chapters I shall be concerned with this second kind of regulation, but instead of taking the values and norms for granted, as is so often done in studies of social control, I shall also be concerned to examine the ways in which they emerge, change and are diffused or checked; or in other words, to look at the same phenomena from the standpoint of the sociology of mind.[6] In each particular study it is necessary to be aware of both aspects; to observe how the real situation and interests of a group influence its values (its doctrine or ideology), and how these values in turn influence its situation and the actual behaviour of its members. The case of social groups in conflict, and especially class conflict, brings out very clearly this double aspect of the phenomena. Social classes are the source of important ideologies, which then contribute to the cohesion of the classes in their struggles with each other. Further, each class seeks to make its own norms and values prevail in the society as a whole, and at certain periods in the history of a particular society we may be able to discern plainly the predominance of the values of specific classes. In other cases it may be the ideologies of particular religious or ethnic groups which become predominant.

The phenomena of social control are thus more complex and more difficult to analyse than many accounts of the matter would suggest. We have to take account, first, of the relation between force and social control in the regulation of behaviour and the maintenance of group cohesion. Secondly, we have to consider the relation between the different types of social control: custom, opinion, law, religion, morals, education, and so on. Next, we must remember that social control refers to systems of values and norms which undergo change, which are challenged and criticized by other systems, which are always in process of being built up or reconstructed, or are declining and succumbing to criticism. This is true of social control both in total societies and in the social groups within a society. At the level of an inclusive society social control is a more or less precarious and temporary balance between conflicting groups and ideologies; at the same time it is subject to external influences, receiving support from the civilization to which it belongs and being challenged by other civilizations. These broader aspects of the question should be borne in mind throughout the following discussion of particular types of social control.

Notes to Chapter 12

1 Simmel's studies of social groups, discussed in an earlier chapter, were very largely concerned with variations in the nature of social control in groups of different size.

2 This aspect will be referred to in a later chapter. There is evidently much concern about the apparent growth of violence in the industrial countries, and in the USA it was the subject of a large-scale official inquiry in the 1960s; see the Report of the National Commission on the Causes and Prevention of Violence, 1969, and the associated Task Force reports. See also the symposium on 'Collective violence', *Annals of the American Academy of Political and Social Science* (September 1970).

3 The literature on nuclear weapons, the arms race, and the consequences of nuclear war is now immense. Useful sources of information are the publications of the Stockholm International Peace Research Institute (SIPRI) and in particular *The Arms Race and Arms Control* (1982), and the regularly published *World Military and Social Expenditures* edited by R. L. Sivard.

4 Some of the issues involved are well illustrated by the notorious 'Project Camelot'; they are discussed in Horowitz, 1967, and Dahrendorf, 1968, ch. 10.

5 There is a good discussion of this subject in Barrington Moore, 1966.

6 I use the term 'sociology of mind' as the English equivalent of the French *sociologie de l'esprit* which includes besides the sociology of knowledge, the sociology of art, religion, morals, and so on.

13 *Custom and Public Opinion*

Custom and public opinion may be considered together, since they have certain features in common and there are important connections between them. In the first place, they are to be counted among the less formal types of social control. They do not have the kind of systematic elaboration which we find in the case of law, morality or religion. There is a certain vagueness, and sometimes ambiguity, in regard to infractions of the code of behaviour which they prescribe, and in regard to punishments.

Custom has frequently been contrasted with law, and a distinction made between societies which possess law, in the sense of rules promulgated by a single recognized authority and sanctioned by definite punishments, and societies in which behaviour is regulated by traditional norms which are simply 'accepted' rather than sanctioned or enforced. I shall examine later the problems raised by this conception of law. Custom, as thus conceived, presents other difficulties. Conformity with custom is made to appear almost automatic, and indeed some early anthropologists, in their accounts of primitive societies, gave the impression that individual deviation from the customary rules was hardly conceivable. For example, Marett (1912) wrote that: 'one reason why it is hard to find any law in primitive society is because, in a general way of speaking, no one dreams of breaking the social rules'. Such views underlay the emphasis upon the conservative, unchanging nature of custom, and the contrast between the 'cake of custom' which immobilizes primitive societies and critical, reflective thought which enables civilized societies to progress. This total and automatic submission to custom was explained largely by the force of habit; although some writers (e.g. Hobhouse, 1924) also referred to public opinion and supernatural beliefs as additional supports for conformity.

This distinction between types of society in which behaviour is regulated by custom and law respectively is too simple and clear cut, and the explanations of the submission to custom are inadequate. It is one of the major contributions of Malinowski

(1926) to have shown the complexity of social control in primitive societies, and to have provided a more satisfactory account of the influence of custom.[1] He argued, first, that 'besides the rules of law, there are several other types of norm and traditional commandment', such as morals, manners, rules of craftsmanship and ceremonial, and religious precepts. In discussing custom, he showed that neither the force of habit, nor respect for tradition, nor public opinion, nor the fear of supernatural beings, could entirely account for conformity, and emphasized the role of 'binding obligations' and 'reciprocity' as positive inducements to customary behaviour. As Schapera (1957) comments,

> life in a primitive community involves every individual in specific obligations to others, who in turn are similarly duty-bound to him. Those obligations he fulfils partly because of early training, and partly because of public opinion and self-interest; it pays him in various ways to do as he should, and if he does not he suffers loss of material benefit and of social esteem. (p. 149)

Further, Malinowski combated the notion that in primitive societies submission to custom is automatic, by showing that contraventions of the social rules are frequent and motivated by considerations of personal advantage similar to those found in more complex societies.

Taken as a whole Malinowski's work made untenable the earlier conceptions of the 'tyranny of custom' and of the irresistible force of habit and early training. It implied also a greater degree of comparability between different types of society in respect of social control. While in primitive societies custom has a large influence, in civilized societies custom, habit, public opinion and reciprocity still play a part, but some of the major forms of behaviour are more strictly and precisely regulated by law, religion and morality. There are important differences, also, between civilized societies in which social change is taking place rapidly and those in which change is slow. The social life of the medieval European societies, feudal and absolutist, was regulated not only by an armed aristocracy, by the religious and moral doctrines of an organized church, and by law, but also by custom and tradition. At the very end of the *ancien régime* the power of custom was recognized by conservative political philosophers, such as Burke, who argued that political wisdom consisted in following the traditions of one's society as embodied in its existing social institutions. The social structure of India, until the last two centuries, underwent few and gradual changes; and the importance of custom was correspondingly great. Mayne (1950), in his classical work on Hindu law, argued that 'the great body of existing law consists of ancient usages, more or less modified by Aryan or Brahmanical influence', and observed that the greatest effect was given to custom by the courts and by legislation under British rule.

Even in modern industrial societies the importance of custom is far from negligible, for much religion and morality is customary rather than reflective, and ordinary social intercourse is largely regulated by custom and public opinion. But in most of these societies we should rather speak of 'customs' and 'opinions', for they are characterized by a diversity which springs from the existence of numerous competing and conflicting groups, and from the rapidity of social change. Some present-day socialist societies constitute an exception, in so far as they aim by a variety of means at the inculcation and enforcement of a uniform pattern of attitudes and behaviour; and a number of writers have seen in such societies an extreme form of the regulation of opinion and conduct towards which all industrial societies are tending, because of the concentration of power and the massive growth of effective media of mass persuasion. Thus Mills (1956, p. 304) observed that the USA has 'moved a considerable distance along the road to the mass society. At the end of that road there is totalitarianism, as in Nazi Germany or Communist Russia.' He distinguishes a mass society from a 'society of publics' by four characteristics: (1) far fewer people express opinions than receive them, (2) the communications are so organized that it is difficult or impossible for the individual to answer back immediately or with any effect, (3) the realization of opinion in action is controlled by authorities, (4) the mass has no autonomy from the official institutions of society, but is permeated by agents of these institutions. In Britain, Hoggart (1957) studied the influence of 'mass culture' upon working-class attitudes and opinions, and emphasized the increase in 'passive acceptance'.

But it remains true that in many modern societies there is a greater diversity of opinion, more rapid variation in opinion, and a larger number of voluntary groups engaged in formulating and influencing opinion, than in other types of society. The phenomena of public opinion have been increasingly studied by social scientists and historians. Among the earlier works should be noted Dicey's (1905) work on law and opinion in England in the nineteenth century, which examined the influence upon legislation of the highly articulate opinion represented in social and political doctrines;[2] and Lippmann's *Public Opinion* (1922), which set out the problems of democracy that arise from the absence of, and the immense difficulty – or impossibility – of creating, over the whole society, an informed and rational public opinion. Lippmann's account had affinities with the still earlier work of Graham Wallas (1908) on human nature in politics, which emphasized the significance of propaganda and the facility with which the irrationality of public opinion could be manipulated. More generally, the attention given to the moulding of attitudes and opinions has brought the studies in this field closer, in some respects, to the ideas of Pareto (1916), who made a fundamental distinction between 'logical' and 'non-logical' action, and implicitly presented the view that by far the greater part of human behaviour is 'non-logical' in his sense, that is, that it is the result of impulses or sentiments which he calls 'residues'. These residues are the driving forces of human action, but they are often camouflaged in doctrines and theoretical systems which Pareto terms 'derivations' and Marxists might call 'ideologies'. Thus, for Pareto, even those opinions which Dicey and others treated as more or less rational constructions are merely rationalizations of the basic residues, and genuine rationality is strictly confined to the domains of science and economic calculation.[3]

Many later studies, like the earlier writings, concentrated largely upon political attitudes and opinions. The rise of fascism in Europe in the 1920s and 1930s incited a good deal of research, much of it guided by Marxist and psychoanalytic theory, as in the works of Fromm (1942), Reich (1942) and Adorno et al. (1950).[4] Since 1945 the study of political opinion has developed rapidly, but in a largely descriptive way. Opinion polls, which are now regularly and frequently conducted in the Western industrial countries, can deal only with relatively simple opinions on very clearly defined issues, do not explore the ways in which opinions are supported or connected with other opinions and beliefs,[5] and cannot distinguish between identical opinions in terms of the degree of rational conviction with which they are held. Moreover, as I have indicated, they can do little or nothing to explain, as against describing, the fluctuations of opinion, or to trace the connections between opinions and behaviour.

Another field of inquiry which has attracted considerable research is that of 'prejudice', especially race prejudice, which is related to what Lippmann first called 'stereotypes'. Aside from the general studies, in textbooks of social psychology and in such works as Rose (1952) and Allport (1954), there are more specific inquiries, like that of Myrdal (1944) into the situation of black Americans, which brought out the discordance between a widely held 'egalitarian ideology' and the concurrently held opinions concerning the 'inferiority' of negroes. National stereotypes play a part in international affairs, and especially in periods of war or preparation for war, when they are a major element in political propaganda. Much recent research has also drawn attention to the importance of gender stereotypes in sanctioning and maintaining unequal relations between men and women.

In order to explain the formation of attitudes and opinions, their fluctuation over time, and their variation between countries and regions, it is necessary to examine the agencies and means by which opinion is influenced. Clearly, political parties and social movements play an important part in this process. Marx's theory provides an explanation of the development of the labour movement and the diffusion of socialist attitudes and opinions in the nineteenth century, and as I have noted, Marxist writers offered various explanations – both sociological and psychological – of the rise of fascism in Europe. But it is far from easy to discover the causes of the ebb and flow of opinion, or of any general trends of opinion, in many twentieth-century societies: for example, of those changes which gave rise to and then were sustained by new radical movements – the youth movement (including students), the women's movement, the ecology movement – in the 1960s, or which have led to greater sexual permissiveness. There may also be more specific changes in public opinion brought about by pressure groups of various kinds. One classic study in this field (Odegard, 1928) describes and analyses the ways in which the Anti-Saloon League succeeded in imposing prohibition in the USA.

The means by which opinion is influenced are diverse, but the mass media (film, radio and television, the press) and advertising play a major part. The media, and especially the press and television, have been increasingly studied in recent decades, but the precise extent of their influence is not clear. In all societies, at most times, the media tend to support the *status quo*. This support is most overt and complete where the dominant group in society imposes, through strict regulation and censorship, some kind of official doctrine or world view, but in the capitalist democracies too, despite their relative 'openness', there is much 'hidden persuasion', and most of the media present information in a way which favours the established order of society (Glasgow University Media Group, 1976, 1980; Qualter, 1985), and more generally encourages passive and conformist attitudes (MacNeil, 1970). Nevertheless, the potency of the media, or of a 'dominant ideology' as such (Abercrombie, Hill and Turner, 1980), should not be exaggerated, for even in those societies where public opinion is most strictly controlled critical opinions emerge and are diffused (and rebellions occur), while in the capitalist democracies the socialist movement and more recently the peace movement have succeeded in changing public opinion on many issues despite the hostility of most of the media.

Public opinion and its changes have therefore to be seen in a very broad context, which includes the structural changes in society, the interests of particular social groups and their expression in parties, movements and pressure groups, the influence of other types of social control – law, religion, moral codes, or custom – upon attitudes and opinions, and psychological dispositions to respond, in one way or another, to propaganda and advertising. In modern societies, and especially in those which are most 'open', there is not just one 'public' but several, and hence diverse 'public opinions'. Consequently, what is referred to as 'public opinion' in a general sense is inherently mutable; divergent and sometimes contradictory customs and traditions are invoked, and competing interest groups endeavour to spread their distinctive ideologies. It is difficult, without field research of the intensive kind which social anthropologists practise, to discover the nature and strength of the different pressures upon the individual, and opinion surveys can do little more than provide a framework for further inquiry. There is a need to examine on one side the formal symbolic systems of law, religion, scientific knowledge, and their influence; and on the other side to study the attitudes and opinions manifested in the everyday life of social groups which can conveniently be directly observed. The relevance of many small group studies is evident here (see Chapter 6 above), but much could also be learned from studies of neighbourhoods, economic enterprises, cultural groups and local occupational groups, if they were undertaken from this point of view.

All studies of social control lead eventually to the issue of the relation between the individual and society, and the problem of freedom and coercion. This concern is unmistakably the central reference point in the work of the classical sociologists – in the quite different but related analyses of the preconditions for individual freedom and autonomy by Marx and Weber (Löwith, 1932), and in Durkheim's (1950) study of professional associations and the state in relation to the individual, as well as in the later work of Mannheim (1940, pt 5; 1950). The early writers on public opinion, as we have seen, raised as a particular problem of modern democracy whether the individual is sufficiently autonomous, well-informed, critical and rational to resist the stream of persuasion and propaganda in forming, and acting in accordance with, his/her attitudes and opinions. I shall return to some of these fundamental issues in a discussion of sociology and social practice in the concluding section of this book.

Notes to Chapter 13

1   Malinowski's own views on social control varied at different periods in his career; they are usefully discussed and evaluated in Schapera, 1957.
2   A more recent work (Ginsberg, 1959) attempts to extend his study by tracing the changes that have occurred in the twentieth century, but as a collection of essays it lacks the unity and critical power of Dicey's book, though the introductory chapter by Ginsberg, on 'the growth of social responsibility', makes some interesting comparisons between the various currents of opinion in the nineteenth and twentieth centuries.
3   For criticism of Pareto's conception of 'residues' and 'derivations' see Ginsberg, 1947, ch. 4, and for a general analysis of reason and impulse in social attitudes and behaviour Ginsberg, 1921.
4   The larger part of the Marxist writing on fascism, however, was concerned with economic changes and class relations, not with the psychological aspects; see Beetham, 1983.
5   That is, they do not deal with 'attitudes', which may be regarded as more general and enduring dispositions to respond in a distinctive way in the expression of particular opinions (see Qualter, 1985, pp. 38–45). In the present chapter I use the term 'attitude' in this sense, and also relate both attitudes and opinions to the still wider body of beliefs which constitutes an individual's 'world view' (however vague and inchoate it may be), into which evidently many social elements enter.

14   *Religion and Morality*

The early sociological studies of religion had three distinctive characteristics: they were evolutionist, positivist and psychologistic. These features may be illustrated from the work of Comte, Tylor and Spencer. In Comte's sociology one of the fundamental conceptions is the so-called 'law of three stages' according to which human thought has passed, historically and necessarily, from the theological stage (primitive and early society), through the metaphysical stage (medieval society), to the positive stage (modern society, beginning in the nineteenth century). Comte treats theological thinking as intellectual error which is dispersed by the rise of modern science; he traces, within the theological stage, a development from animism to monotheism; and he explains religious belief in psychological terms by reference to the perceptions and thought processes of early man. It is true that Comte later propounded his own 'religion of humanity' and thus recognized, in some sense, a universal need for religion, but he did not succeed in bringing these later ideas into harmony with his fundamental conceptions.

The work of Tylor and Spencer was much more rigorous, and it shows more clearly the features I have mentioned. Both thinkers were concerned to explain, in the first place, the origin of religion. They believed that the idea of the soul was the principal feature in religious belief and set out to give an account, in rationalist terms, of how such an idea might have originated in the mind of primitive man. According to this, men obtained their idea of the soul from a misinterpretation of dreams and death; Spencer (1876–96, Vol. 3) refers to 'that original theory of things in which, from the supposed reality of dreams, there resulted the supposed reality of ghosts; whence developed all kinds of supposed supernatural beings'. From this point, Spencer goes on to describe the development of religious institutions in the different stages of society. As with Comte, the explanation of religious phenomena is in terms of psychological dispositions, intellectual error, and the evolution of social life.

Other social theorists of the nineteenth century approached the study of religion in a similar way. Marx held that religion originated in the fear and anxiety provoked by natural phenomena, and that it was an illusion which would ultimately disappear. But he also made a new departure in considering the role of religious doctrines as ideologies in different types of society; that is, the part played by religion in social control. Frazer (1890) also approached the problem from the point of view of evolutionary theory and positivist or rationalist philosophy. He made a distinction between magic and religion; the former involves an assertion of man's power over natural processes ('a spurious system of natural law as well as a fallacious guide of conduct'), and the latter 'a belief in powers higher than man and an attempt to propitiate or please them'. He conceived the intellectual progress of mankind as a passage from the age of magic to the age of religion, and then to the age of science; but he recognized that magic and religion were frequently intermingled even in civilized societies, and that in modern societies a substratum of magical beliefs persisted.

An alternative approach to the study of religion was first formulated by Durkheim (1912), although it had been propounded earlier in a less systematic form by Fustel de Coulanges (who was at one time Durkheim's teacher).[1] Durkheim argued that in all societies a distinction is made between 'sacred' and 'profane' things. Religion is 'a unified system of beliefs and practices relative to sacred things, that is things set apart and forbidden – beliefs and practices which unite into one single moral community called a Church all those who adhere to them'. In Durkheim's theory the collective aspects of religion are emphasized; the function of religious rituals is to affirm the moral superiority of the society over its individual members and thus to maintain the solidarity of the society. 'The god of the clan can be nothing but the clan itself.' Durkheim, in the first part of his book, criticized the work of the earlier anthropologists and sociologists on the grounds that their explanations of religion were psychological (in terms of individual sentiments), not sociological, and that they made religion an illusion whereas in his view nothing so universal and important in human society could be illusory. Nevertheless, his own theory makes religion equally an illusion, for as Lowie (1936) asked : in what sense are natural phenomena less real than society?

If, however, we eliminate from Durkheim's theory any philosophical claim to explain the 'essence' of religion, and its rejection of any psychological contribution to the understanding of religious phenomena, we are in possession of a functionalist account of religion which has a definite, though limited, usefulness. Later anthropologists, among them Malinowski (1948) and Radcliffe-

Brown (1922), have shown in field studies how religion works in primitive societies to maintain social cohesion and to control individual conduct. Durkheim's emphasis upon ritual as against belief was salutary in turning the attention of anthropologists away from exegesis of exotic religious ideas to the observation and description of religious behaviour (Radcliffe-Brown, 1952, ch. 8).

In the study of civilized societies, Durkheim's theory has proved less helpful, for here religion is as frequently a divisive as a unifying force. That is to say, while it unites particular groups it may provoke conflict between these groups within the larger society. There are, of course, many instances of inclusive societies which are unified, to some extent at least, by religion – the states of medieval Christendom, some Islamic states and Hindu India; but in modern industrial societies particularly there is considerable religious diversity and some religious conflict, as well as widespread rejection of religious belief and ritual, and in various forms and degrees a process of 'secularization'.

These features have meant that the sociological study of religion has diverged from that of social anthropology; and it has been characterized especially by a concern with the ethical doctrines of the world religions. This approach is illustrated, in different ways, by the work of Hobhouse and Max Weber. Hobhouse's sociology as a whole is concerned with the influence of intellectual development upon social institutions, and within this general intellectual development he gives particular attention to the development of moral ideas; thus, in discussing religion in his major work *Morals in Evolution* (1906) he is entirely concerned with the moral codes of the major religions and especially of Christianity. These moral codes are examined as doctrines and are analysed in a largely philosophical way; their relation to social behaviour is then considered in very general terms. Max Weber's (1920) treatment of religious beliefs differs in important respects. In the first place, it is not based upon any evolutionary scheme. Secondly, it is largely concerned with a single major aspect of religious ethics, namely their connections with the economic order. Weber examines these connections from two points of view; the influence of particular religious doctrines upon economic behaviour, and the relation between the position of groups in the economic system and types of religious belief. Thirdly, he is less concerned with ethical doctrines as expounded by theologians than with these doctrines in their popular form as they guide everyday behaviour. Weber's best-known work (1904–5), which was the starting point for his studies of religion, aims to show the part played in the origin and development of modern capitalism by Calvinist ethics. The thesis has been well summarized by Aron (1936, pp. 94–5):

> The Calvinist, never certain that he is one of the elect, looks for signs of his election in his earthly life, and he finds them in the prosperity of his enterprise. But he is not permitted to enjoy leisure as a result of his success, or to use his money in the pursuit of luxury or pleasure. Thus he is obliged to re-employ his money in his business, and the formation of capital takes place as a result of this ascetic obligation to save. Moreover, only regular and rationalized work, exact accounting which makes possible a knowledge of the state of the business at every moment, and pacific commerce are consistent with the spirit of his morality. For the Calvinist is master of himself, distrusts instinct and passions, is independent and has confidence only in himself, and studies and reflects upon his actions as the capitalist must do . . . [But] Weber did not believe that 'ideas rule the world'; he presents the case of Protestantism as a favourable example which enabled one to understand the way in which ideas act in history. The theological and ethical conceptions of the Protestants were influenced in their for-mation by various social and political circumstances, and further, they had no direct influence upon economic affairs. But ideas have their own logic, and they give rise to consequences which may have a practical influence; thus the dogmas of Calvinism, established in the consciousness of individuals belonging to particular groups, brought about a particular attitude to life and a specific form of behaviour.

In his later studies of religion (Judaism, China, India) Weber followed the same line of inquiry, examining the religious doctrines of particular social groups, and the social (especially economic) consequences of particular attitudes to life derived from religious systems. Thus in analysing religion in India, he examines first the relation between modern, rational business activity and religious beliefs, showing the appeal to traders and businessmen of such religious cults as Jainism, Parsiism, and Vallabhacharya. Orthodox Hinduism, on the other hand, which makes contemplation the supreme religious value accessible to man, restrains rather than stimulates business activity. Secondly, Weber emphasizes the importance of caste as the institutional framework of Hinduism. 'Caste, that is the ritual rights and duties it gives and imposes and the position of the Brahmans, is the fundamental institution of Hinduism', (p. 396). The intercon-nections of caste and Hinduism are now generally recognized, and as Srinivas (1952, p. 212) writes: 'The structural basis of Hinduism is the caste system which occasionally even survives conversion to Christianity or Islam.' He also observes that the spread of Hinduism in India has proceeded by 'Sanskritization' of the ritual and belief of tribes or other non-Hindu groups and at the same time by the incorporation of these groups as castes within the caste system. 'The complete absorption of any group of people into the Hindu fold is indicated by their becoming a caste.'

At the same time Hinduism was willing to leave much in the original beliefs and rituals untouched, allowing them, so to speak, to wither away as the newly incorporated group sought to improve its status in the caste hierarchy by purifying its customs and ideas. This tolerance, however, was an additional reason for the failure of Hinduism to spread elsewhere; though tenaciously defended as a way of life Hinduism lacks missionary fervour as a system of beliefs. It could not be expected, either, that it would give rise to a sect so convinced and ruthless as the Puritans in Western Europe. On the contrary, with the exception of Buddhism, which spread outside India, all the sects and reforming movements in Hinduism have been assimilated again into the main tradition, often as new caste groups.

Since the work of Durkheim and Max Weber, few theoretical contributions have been made to the sociological study of religion, and until recently the Marxist influence in this field was slight (Kiernan, 1983). Social anthropologists, as I mentioned earlier, have based their studies largely upon Durkheim's theory. In sociology, Weber's influence has been predominant, and has stimulated two principal, and related, lines of inquiry: one concerned with the characteristics, doctrines and social significance of religious sects, and the other with the connection between religious doctrines and social classes. An important early contribution came from his friend, Ernst Troeltsch, whose book on *The Social Teaching of the Christian Churches* (1912) complemented Weber's writings by giving a more detailed account of the social ethics of different Christian churches and sects. In the same field of concern with sectarian movements is the work of Niebuhr (1929) on denominationalism. More recently there have been detailed empirical studies of particular sects, in terms of their relations with and responses to the social milieu in which they exist (e.g. Wilson, 1961), and also, especially in the work of Desroche (1955), as precursors of socialist political groups.

The second line of inquiry has also dealt with issues which Weber formulated. First, there has been a continuing debate on the significance of the Protestant ethic in the origin and growth of modern capitalism.[2] Secondly, there has been more intensive and exact study of the differences between social classes in religious belief and observance. Thus, there has gradually emerged a very useful *sociography of religion*, which was particularly advanced in France, where Le Bras inspired many descriptive and quantitative studies.[3] This kind of study has been pursued in a wider context, that of the process of secularization which, it is generally agreed, has been taking place in most of the industrial societies over the past century. In this process an early stage was the decline in working-class allegiance to the established religion. Thus, in Britain the 1851 Census (the only one in which a question about religious affiliation has been included) showed that the official church, the Church of England, had already lost many adherents to the Non-conformist churches and sects, and many of these were working-class or lower-middle-class people.

Throughout the latter half of the nineteenth century and during the twentieth century church attendance, and to a lesser extent religious belief, has steadily declined, and it has declined most in the working class. One survey (Cauter and Downham, 1954) has shown that whereas one-fifth of middle-class informants say they never attend church, almost one-third of working-class informants say this; and at the other end of the scale the proportion of those in the middle class who say they attend church frequently is two and a half times as great as that in the working class. The same phenomenon has been observed, in a more extreme form, in France, where the Catholicism of the upper and middle classes contrasted, in the 1950s, with Marxism as the dominant creed of the working class. In both Britain and France the recognition of this decay of religion in the working class led to the organization of working-class missions, in Britain especially at the end of the nineteenth century (e.g. the Salvation Army), and in France at various times, most recently in the form of the *prêtres ouvriers*.

It is interesting to observe here that the USA constitutes an exception to the account we have given of secularization. In American society religious belief and observance have tended to increase rather than decline, and church attendance is high; at the same time class differences in the extent of religious practice are slight. Here also, sociological explanation is for the most part lacking, although one important study by Herberg (1955) proposes an explanation along Durkheimian lines in terms of the needs of immigrants' descendants for a community to which they can refer for moral rules and purposes. On the other hand, in the socialist countries of Eastern Europe, and in China, where religious belief and observance are discouraged, the decline of religion has been very rapid in most cases, though there are important exceptions, such as the continuing strength and influence of the Roman Catholic Church in Poland. India, after independence, was established as a secular or multi-religious state (Sharma, 1966; Smith, 1963) although it is predominantly Hindu; and notwithstanding the fact that there has been intermittent religious conflict between Hindus and Muslims and between Sikhs and Hindus (in the latter case, however, mainly political in character with the aim of creating a distinct Punjabi-speaking state, in the same way as other linguistic regions have become constituted as states within the Indian federation), and the emergence of some Hindu traditionalist parties and movements, secularism seems to prevail and to become stronger, at least in the political sphere, facilitated by the spread of new social doctrines.

In considering the secularization of modern societies we should note that this process does not necessarily conflict with Durkheim's theory of religion, which defines religion not in terms of supernatural beings but in terms of a distinction between 'sacred' and 'profane' things in social life and the rituals connected with the former. From this standpoint, bodies of belief and practice other than those of the traditional religions may still be regarded as religious phenomena – for example, nationalism, socialism or Marxism[4] – and Durkheim himself (1912, Conclusion) observes:

> What essential difference is there between an assembly of Christians celebrating the principal dates in the life of Christ, or of Jews celebrating the flight from Egypt or the promulgation of the decalogue, and a meeting of citizens commemorating the establishment of a new moral code or some great event in the nation's history?

He goes on to say that Comte's attempt to create a new religion was a failure because it was based upon an artificial revival of old historical memories, whereas a vital new religion has to grow out of social life itself, as occurred in the French Revolution.

This idea of the functional equivalence of traditional religions and the doctrines of modern social movements, which also establish norms of behaviour and through a variety of rituals impress them upon individuals and reinforce their effects, is well illustrated in a field of study which has received increasing attention in recent decades; namely, the 'religions of the oppressed' (Lanternari, 1960), which have been seen as 'pre-political' movements of subordinate groups and classes, especially among colonial peoples and peasants (Worsley, 1957; Hobsbawm, 1959). At the same time traditional religion has been linked more explicitly with social movements in what has come to be called 'liberation theology' (Davis, 1980; Turner, 1983), which has some evident and acknowledged affinities with the 'emancipatory' critical theory of the Frankfurt School, and more particularly of Habermas.

In Max Weber's sociology of religion, and still more prominently in the work of Troeltsch, the significance of religious sects is strongly emphasized, and we should note as a particular feature of religion in some modern societies the proliferation of sectarian groups and movements. Thus, in Britain and the USA, over the past century, innumerable sects have been founded, and many of them have flourished;[5] and the process seems even to have intensified in recent times. This may reflect an 'individualization' of religious belief, which should perhaps be considered, along with secularization, as a major characteristic of the religious situation in modern industrial societies.

In other types of society religion was always a major factor in social control, largely determining the moral norms which regulate behaviour, and in Durkheim's theory religion and morality are equated: 'Religious forces, therefore, are human, moral forces' (Durkheim, 1912, Conclusion). But this already expresses a modern view in which morality no longer depends upon traditional religious conceptions, and becomes open not only to philosophical rather than theological discussion, but also to sociological analysis. The early sociological studies of morality were largely guided by evolutionist and positivist ideas. Two classical works of an evolutionist character are those by Hobhouse (1906) and Westermarck (1906). Although differing in their conceptions of the source and basis of moral ideas, these two thinkers largely agreed in their accounts of the development of morals and especially in the conclusion that the history of mankind was marked by moral progress. Hobhouse claimed to show that moral ideas had developed towards the ideal of a rational ethic, and to establish a broad correspondence between this evolution of morals and general social development. Westermarck, although giving more emphasis to the similarity in the moral rules of different societies (primitive and civilized), also considered that in the course of social evolution moral ideas have become more enlightened and that the influence of reason upon morality is likely to increase in the future. This approach to the study of moral rules was first criticized, and then largely abandoned, by later sociologists. Various influences contributed to this change; a general rejection of the evolutionist approach, scepticism about social progress, new philosophical views on the character of moral judgements, and doubts about the value of associating sociology and social philosophy as closely as Hobhouse, in particular, had done.

The last of these issues was also important in French sociology, where the influence of Comte led to attempts to construct a normative 'science of morals'. This was an important aspect of Durkheim's sociology, the whole of which was quite evidently dominated by a concern with the moral and social problems of France at the end of the nineteenth century; but the most influential expression of this positivist endeavour was probably the book by Lucien Lévy-Bruhl (1903). Both Durkheim and Lévy-Bruhl argued that moral rules could be derived from a science of morals; Lévy-Bruhl in the work just cited, and Durkheim principally in the preface to *The Division of Labour in Society* (1893), and in his essay on 'La détermination du fait moral' (1906).

Recent sociologists have given up the attempt to formulate a sociological moral theory. For the most part, they have also ceased to concern themselves with the general direction of moral development or progress. A notable exception is Ginsberg, who in an essay on the diversity of morals (1953), after criticizing those social scientists who have assumed a necessary connection between the diversity of moral codes and ethical relativity, and philosophers who have regarded moral judgements as emotive and consequently neither true nor false, goes on to propose an examination of moral variations in terms of 'differences of level'. He argues persuasively that different levels can be distinguished in terms of such characteristics as the universality of rules, the range of experience embodied in the rules, the rationality of underlying principles, and the extent of self-criticism, and that development from lower to higher levels can be traced; although, as he concedes, it is 'the higher that decide that they are the higher'. Ginsberg recognizes that the comparison of moral codes can only be made in terms of very general and abstract moral ideas, and that the actual 'moral life' or 'way of life' of a particular society may be extremely complex and comprise divergent elements. In fact, when we examine moral codes in this way as the effective complexes of values which regulate behaviour, it becomes extremely difficult to make any classification in terms of levels of development. Moreover, the existence of divergent elements in the moral systems of complex societies renders more doubtful the identification of the dominant moral ideas. It might be argued, indeed, that one characteristic of the development of morality, at least in some modern societies, is the increasing diversity of moral beliefs within each society; a phenomenon which is perhaps recognized in the references to the 'permissiveness' of such societies.

Most recent sociologists and anthropologists who have made any study of moral codes have confined their attention to particular societies. Anthropologists seem to have been relatively successful in describing comprehensively, and with some impartiality, the system of social control, including morality, in the societies which they study, and there are, in particular, illuminating studies of peasant societies (Banfield, 1958; Foster, 1965); though it should be noted that few anthropological studies are tested by other independent observations. Sociologists, because of the diversity and conflict of moral codes in more complex societies, have had a more difficult task, and their interpretations are notoriously controversial. What is presented as the 'central value system' of a society often turns out to be little more than the individual sociologist's own prejudiced view of the society in which he lives, strongly influenced, in many cases, by the ideology of a dominant group. It should be added that many sociological and psychological accounts of moral values fail to distinguish between the values which are asserted in a formal way and the values which actually guide behaviour in everyday situations of moral choice.

However, a number of sociological studies, avowedly 'interpretative' in their approach, do illuminate some aspects of morality in advanced industrial societies. A prominent theme in these studies, mainly in the USA, is the decline of the Protestant ethic. Riesman (1950) and Whyte (1956) have described and analysed the change from social behaviour directed by individual self-reliance and self-assertiveness to behaviour ruled by the wish to conform and to be fully accepted by the social group. According to Whyte, whereas the Protestant ethic in America emphasized the 'pursuit of individual salvation through hard work, thrift, and competitive struggle', the new Social Ethic 'makes morally legitimate the pressures of society against the individual'. It involves 'a belief in the group as the source of creativity; a belief in "belongingness" as the ultimate need of the individual; and a belief in the application of science to achieve the belongingness' (p. 7). In the 1960s another 'new morality', associated with the radical movements of that time, made its appearance, propounding the ideas of 'participatory democracy' and a different quality of life in opposition to a technocratic culture (Roszak, 1970); and although the radical wave subsided again some of the ideas have remained influential, notably in the ecology movements, and particularly in Europe. More recently, in the USA, moral conceptions seem to have been most strongly affected by the rise of various forms of fundamentalist Christianity, and the American outlook differs increasingly from that in other industrial societies.

But the historical changes in moral notions and social values, and the differences between countries, have attracted relatively little systematic investigation, and this remains an area in which sociological inquiry is still woefully underdeveloped. One interesting study (Ossowska, 1971), however, does set out a view of the social determinants of moral ideals, and illustrates the relation between class and morality by a comparison between aristocratic and bourgeois ethics, in the course of which there is a brief analysis of the 'gentleman ideal' that has played a significant part in English culture and politics, appearing most notably in Trollope's novels and discussed subsequently by literary historians and others, sometimes in a sociological vein (Gilmour, 1981; Wiener, 1981).

What may be argued in general terms is that in the industrial countries (with the USA constituting something of an exception) the cultural changes of the past century have established a separation between morality and religion, both in the sense that a clear distinction has been made between ritual and moral rules, and in the sense that, with the decline of religious belief, it has been necessary to find a new basis and content for the moral rules. To some extent this separation has shown itself in the fact that religion has become more an individual and private matter (as is indicated by the multiplication of sects and the spread of personal religion not involving church membership), while morality has become more social, in that it is increasingly concerned with social justice rather than individual virtue. This change of emphasis is apparent even in the moral doctrines of religious organizations, which are much more concerned with social relations and social problems than ever in the past. Whyte (1956), in discussing the religion of the 'organization man', observes that there is a disposition to tone down the doctrinal and ritual aspects of religion, and to emphasize above all the utility of religion in solving social problems and creating fellowship.

This increasing concern with social morality has had two consequences, which are more evident in European societies than in the USA. The first is a greater tolerance of diversity in such individual behaviour as is not connected with major social controversies. The social sciences have also played a part in this, by disclosing some of the external factors influencing conduct, and thus diminishing the scope of moral praise and blame. The second consequence is that moral codes have become closely associated with political doctrines. Moral disagreements are now very frequently political disagreements, and moral beliefs are largely incorporated in political ideologies. In all these respects there is great scope for sociological studies of morality which have hardly yet been attempted. Such studies would have to take account of the influence upon moral codes of the development of modern science (including social science) and its popularization (Douglas, 1970a), and to relate the diversity of moral codes to the conflict of political doctrines, tracing in particular the influence of nationalism, socialism and other modern ideologies.

In the Third World these changes in morality are still in their early stages. Morality is still closely associated with religious belief, and moral and ritual rules are interfused. Tribe, caste and extended family have to some extent curbed the growth of individualism and a traditional social ethic still largely prevails; but some significant precursors of change can be seen in the rise of modern political doctrines such as nationalism and socialism which expound new conceptions of morality, and in re-interpretations of traditional ethics. A good example of the latter is to be found in the writings of Radhakrishnan, especially in his *Hindu View of Life* (1927), which expounds the moral teaching of Hinduism in relation to issues which have become particularly significant in the modern world: violence and war, social equality, and the position of women in society.

In the development and transformation of moral codes, as of culture generally, intellectuals play an important role, by their critical appraisal of tradition and their formulation of new ideals in the context of new economic and social interests. Mannheim (1956, pt 2), in a fascinating essay dating from the early 1930s on the European intelligentsia, examined the secularization of learning and its social consequences in a way which is highly relevant to the activities of 'modernizing' intellectuals in the Third World. In the industrial societies intellectuals contribute to the revision and renewal of moral norms mainly through the elaboration of social and political ideologies, as I have noted; and it is in this political rather than religious sense that we should now understand Durkheim's (1912, Conclusion) expression of the hope that 'a day will come when our societies will again experience a period of creative effervescence, in the course of which new ideals will arise, new principles will emerge, that will serve for a time to guide humanity'.

Notes to Chapter 14

1 Fustel de Coulanges, in *The Ancient City* (1864), showed the influence of religion in creating larger social groupings and maintaining them in existence. A similar approach is to be found in the work of W. Robertson Smith, 1894.

2 There is now an extensive literature on this subject, but the debate has been usefully reviewed in a recent work by Marshall, 1982. An interesting study of Japan's economic development by Morishima, 1982, argues that the Japanese form of Confucianism played a role similar to that of the Protestant ethic in Western Europe.

3 See Boulard, 1954. Le Bras's own work has ranged very widely, from historical studies of Catholicism in France to studies of religious belief and observance in contemporary France and then to studies of other world religions. His major writings are collected in *Études de sociologie religieuse* (1955–8). The exact description and measurement of religious practice has made some progress in other countries more recently. There is now published an *International Yearbook for the Sociology of Religion* (1965 on), and a *Sociological Yearbook of Religion in Britain* (3rd volume 1970), which bring together surveys of religious affiliation and practice, and more general studies.

4 Thus Kolakowski, 1978, Vol. 3, Epilogue, concludes his comprehensive study of Marxism by arguing, in a rather sweeping and exaggerated way, I think, that it 'performs the functions of a religion', but is 'a caricature and a bogus form of religion'.

5 For example, in England and Wales between 1851 and 1952 the number of places of worship of 'other denominations' (i.e. denominations considered too small for listing separately by the Registrar-General) increased ninefold; a much greater proportionate increase than occurred in any of the larger denominations.

15   *Law*

The Sociology of Law

The study of law has always involved some consideration of the general character of social institutions and societies. Traditionally, however, legal theory in Europe was based upon a philosophical conception of natural law, and was thus closely associated with moral philosophy and theology. The beginnings of a sociology of law can be traced to Montesquieu's *De l'esprit des lois* (1748). Montesquieu still discussed law partly in terms of 'natural law', but he also described and compared the laws of different societies, and related the differences to the diversity of conditions, both geographical and social, of these societies.

From the middle of the nineteenth century, with the emergence of sociology as a distinct discipline, the sociological study of law progressed rapidly, although it assumed diverse forms. Marx and the later Marxists undertook their critique of law as an ideology which conceals class divisions at the same time as it promotes the interests of the dominant class. A major work of Marxist scholarship, by Karl Renner (1904), examines how the functions of the legal norms which regulate property, contract, succession and inheritance change with changes in the economic structure of capitalist society, yet without necessarily altering the formulation of the legal norms themselves, which thus come to obscure the significant social relationships of developed capitalism.

Other sociologists, and jurists receptive to sociological ideas, began to study legal rules in the context of the theories of social evolution which dominated European social thought in the latter part of the nineteenth century, many of them influenced particularly by the German historical school of jurisprudence founded by Savigny. Maine (1861) made a distinction between 'static' and 'progressive' societies, and argued that 'the movement of progressive societies has hitherto been a movement from status to contract'. He meant by this, as he explained elsewhere, that 'the individual is steadily substituted for the family, as the unit of which civil laws take account'. Maine considered that these changes were brought about by non-legal

factors, since 'social necessities and social opinion are always
more or less in advance of Law', and he examined under three
headings, 'Legal Fictions', 'Equity', and 'Legislation', the agencies by which, in progressive societies, law is brought into
harmony with society. Durkheim's conception of the development of law is similar in important respects to that of Maine, for
his distinction between 'repressive' and 'restitutive' law resembles that between 'status' and 'contract'. Repressive law is
characteristic of societies in which the individual is scarcely
distinguished from the group to which he belongs; while restitutive law is typical of modern societies in which the individual
has become a distinct legal person able to enter freely into
contractual relationships with other individuals. Hobhouse
(1906, ch. 3), in conformity with his general evolutionist
approach, dealt systematically with the development of law and
justice, from private redress and the blood feud, through the
stage of composition for offences, to the stage of civilized justice.
In discussing the latter he records not only the establishment of
the notion of individual responsibility (following Maine), but
also the influence of increasing class differentiation until recent
times. He also discusses changes in the character of punishment,
and examines the relations between law, religion and morals.
Another study, by an outstanding jurist (Vinogradoff, 1920), is
similar in its approach. Max Weber's studies of law showed, in
the view of Roscoe Pound (1945), a much clearer understanding
of the nature of law than those of earlier sociologists, and they
have had a greater influence in the growth of a sociological
jurisprudence, since Weber's conception of law as being concerned with the adjustment of conflicting values is close to the
jurist's conception of law in terms of the adjustment of conflicting interests. Weber, although not an evolutionist, was also
interested in the classification of types of law and in the development of law in Western societies; a development which he
conceived as an increasing rationalization of law, accompanying
the general rationalization of life in industrial societies through
the growth of capitalist economic enterprise and of bureaucracy
(Rheinstein, 1966, Introduction).

A particular problem which emerged from the evolutionist
studies concerned the existence of law in primitive societies.
Some of the earlier sociologists and anthropologists made a sharp
distinction between primitive societies governed entirely by
custom, and civilized societies ruled primarily by law. It was a
major contribution of Malinowski, as I noted in Chapter 13
above, to emphasize the study of social control as a whole, and to

distinguish the different types of rules which regulate behaviour in primitive (as in civilized) societies. Malinowski's definitions of law and his account of primitive law are no longer generally accepted (Schapera, 1957), but they greatly influenced the study of law as a type of social control in primitive societies and did much to clarify the whole sociological discussion of social control. At the present time a widely accepted definition of law is that proposed by Roscoe Pound (1945): 'social control through the systematic application of the force of politically organized society', and in similar terms by Hoebel (1954, p. 28): 'A social norm is legal if its neglect or infraction is regularly met, in threat or fact, by the application of physical force by an individual or group possessing the socially recognized privilege of so acting.' In this sense law exists in many primitive societies. Lowie (1950, ch. 7) gives examples of developed systems of administration of justice, particularly in Africa, and Gluckman (1955) studies in detail the judicial process among one African people, the Lozi of Barotseland, showing how closely it corresponds with the judicial process in Western societies, in the modes of reasoning and in the underlying concepts. However, in the case of more primitive peoples, law may be entirely lacking; for example, the Eskimo, as Lowie observes, 'closely approach anarchy'.

The anthropological studies have brought out clearly an aspect of the sociology of law which is emphasized by Roscoe Pound in his survey of the subject. The earlier writers largely identified law with 'laws' or legislation, and their distinction between primitive and civilized societies was based upon the absence of legislation in the former. But jurisprudence and the sociology of law, as Pound says, have to be concerned with three things: (1) the legal order, that is, a regime of adjusting relations and ordering conduct by the systematic application of the force of a politically organized society; (2) the authoritative principles and guides to the determination of disputes in a society, a code of precepts based upon accepted ideals; and (3) the judicial process (see Cardozo, 1941) and the administrative process. The scope of the sociology of law is thus very wide and it overlaps with other fields of sociological study. It is not concerned only with types of legal system and their development but with the character of legislation (and thus with some problems of political sociology and social philosophy), with the judicial process and the social influences upon it, and with the administration of justice involving problems of punishment which are also the concern of criminology and moral philosophy. I shall consider some aspects of these problems later in this chapter.

Law in India

Indian law has a number of features which are of interest to the general sociology of law. A pre-eminent characteristic is the historically close connection between law and religion. Maine (1861, p. 14) observed that 'India has not passed beyond . . . the stage at which a rule of law is not yet discriminated from a rule of religion'. Max Weber discussed the same feature, but gave a somewhat different emphasis by referring to a dominant 'priest-hood' which 'was able to regulate the whole range of life ritualistically, and thus to a considerable extent to control the entire legal system', and by maintaining that 'according to prevailing *Hindu* theory, all law is contained in the Dharma-Sutras' (Rheinstein, 1966, p. 234). Maine considered that all early law was characterized by lack of differentiation between legal and religious rules and he made explicit comparisons in this respect between Hindu and early Roman law. In *Ancient Law* he argued that the absolute predominance of religion in Hindu law only gradually emerged (1861, p. 113, and see also Derrett, 1968). In later works he illustrated this development in the case of the property rights of married women, which were slowly restricted under religious influence (Maine, 1875), and attributed the general development to the important place of ancestor worship in the Hindu religion, which invested almost all legal rules and relationships with a religious significance as family rituals. J. D. Mayne (1950) takes a similar view, arguing that 'Hindu law is based upon immemorial customs, which existed prior to, and independent of, Brahminism', but that as Hinduism spread and the influence of the Brahmin caste grew, law was increasingly dominated by religious conceptions. He adds that while the great codes, such as that of Manu, and the outstanding commentaries such as the Mitakshara were addressed primarily to Brahmins and acquired increasing authority for all Hindus with the spread of Brahminism (now often referred to as 'Sanskritization'), nevertheless many local usages remained distinct and retained their authority. In addition, there grew up particular systems of law for certain occupational groups, especially in trade and commerce, and also, as Weber observes, the castes came to establish their own laws and to acquire autonomy in the admin-istration of justice through their possession of a highly effective means of compulsion, namely expulsion (Rheinstein, 1966, p. 327).

The influence of British rule upon Indian law was complex. In the administration of justice it established a centralized system, by the creation of British courts and by the removal of judicial functions from the caste *panchayats*. But the law administered was still customary and largely Hindu law, and until 1864 the British judges were obliged to consult the pundits attached to their courts on all disputed points of law. Subsequently, with the growth of knowledge of the Hindu codes and texts, the British judges themselves decided points of law, and it has been argued that in their determination to administer Hindu law without introducing any changes they imparted to it a rigid character which it had not previously had, by their exclusive reliance upon ancient authorities.[1] At the same time, some legal changes were deliberately brought about where Hindu customs directly conflicted with the moral ideas of the rulers, as in the cases of child marriage and the immolation of widows.

Beyond this, British rule necessarily introduced into India new cultural values and ways of life and, especially, new forms of economic activity. The development of industry, trade, urban centres and Western education brought about changes in opinion, which ultimately affected law through the growing body of legislation. One general tendency of legislation has been to extend the legal rights of the individual; for example, the right to retain personal earnings by the Gains of Learning Act 1930, and the right of women to a share in the property of the joint family, by the Hindu Law of Inheritance (Amendment) Act 1929 and the Hindu Woman's Right to Property Act 1937. Since independence the process has continued and fundamental changes in the law of inheritance have been brought about by the Hindu Succession Act 1956. In this respect, Indian law shows a development from 'status' to 'contract', similar to that which Maine traced in Western societies. This has been accompanied by an increasing rationalization of law, both in the administration of justice and in the body of legal rules themselves. The rationalization of the legal rules was promoted first by the endeavours of British judges to reconcile conflicting texts, and later by the growth of systematic legislation, especially since the attainment of independence, to deal with the social problems of a developing industrial society. This recent development exemplifies the process which Max Weber termed 'substantive rationalization'; that is, the elaboration of a type of law appropriate to the expediential and ethical goals of the political authority concerned. And since this political authority is no longer predominantly influenced by a priestly caste, the rationalization is taking place, as it did in Western Europe, by the separation of religious commands from legal precepts for the settlement of those human conflicts which have no religious relevance (Rheinstein, 1966; Derrett, 1968).

Law and Social Change

Many writers, among them Maine, Hobhouse, Vinogradoff and Max Weber, whose writings we have briefly considered, have distinguished between types of legal order, and have discussed aspects of the development of law over longer or shorter periods. Their work constitutes the basis for modern sociological studies of particular systems of law, and of specific changes in legal systems. A particular interest attaches to the changes which have occurred in the modern world, with the transformation of Western capitalist societies, the emergence of socialist societies, and the establishment of new independent nations.

The first of these changes has been brilliantly analysed by W. G. Friedmann (1951, 1959). He begins from the observations made by Dicey in his classical study of law and opinion in nineteenth-century Britain, that Benthamite reforming legislation which had been intended merely to do away with inequalities which interfered with free competition could be extended, and was being extended, to deal with the new inequalities arising out of that competition. The increase in social legislation and the rise of the labour movement tended to halt or reverse the process which Maine had referred to as the movement from status to contract. Friedmann has summarized the outcome of these changes in the mid-twentieth century (with reference to Britain, but with a wider bearing) in the observation that: 'Freedom of contract, in so far as it survives today, no longer pertains to the individual' (1951, p. 19). He shows how the role of property in bargaining has been modified, first, by changes in the relations between employer and worker through the abolition of the crime of conspiracy, the recognition of collective bargaining, social security legislation and changing legal interpretations by the courts of the employment contract, and secondly, by direct limitations on the use of private property (stricter interpretation of abuse of rights, limitation of patent rights, statutory obligations imposed upon owners of industrial property, and public ownership). The functions of contract itself have changed with the development of the 'standard contract', resulting from economic concentration, the substitution of collective for individual bargaining, and the expansion of the welfare, social service, and industrial management functions of the state.

These changes in law are evidently connected with the more general change, in Western societies, from *laissez-faire* and individualism towards some form of collectivism. In an essay published in 1930 and significantly entitled 'The new feudal system', Roscoe Pound observed that: 'Today the typical man (i.e. the wage earner or salaried employee) finds his greatness not in himself and in what he does but in the corporation he serves.' More recently, this aspect of modern Western societies has been discussed and analysed at length, especially by American sociologists and social commentators, who have introduced into the social sciences such expressions as 'the other-directed man', 'the organization man', to refer to the typical individual of mass society (see Chapter 13 above). The contrast is great with those nineteenth-century figures, the independent capitalist entrepreneur, or the anomic individual, who attracted the attention of Weber and Durkheim.

The socialist societies present many similar features. Here too the legal situation of the individual is largely determined by his status in a particular group; and in these societies the groups themselves are organized in more inflexible official hierarchy. Such societies have, in addition, experienced difficulties in maintaining a rule of law, because of the extreme concentration of political power. It is interesting that the reaction against Stalinism in the USSR has given rise to doctrines of legal positivism, which are critical of any sociological interpretation of judicial decisions.[2] Such doctrines are no doubt intended to establish and support a rule of law, but in the absence of any sociological studies of the administration of justice they also conceal important social pressures upon the judiciary which, in the USSR as elsewhere, frequently arise from conceptions of 'public policy' formulated by political organizations.

In the Third World countries which have experienced nationalist revolutions, in some cases against colonial rule, other features are apparent. There is a continuous rationalization of law, by codification or the introduction of foreign codes (e.g. at an earlier stage, the adoption of the Swiss Code in Turkey), and by the growing proportion of systematic legislation in relation to customary and traditional law. In some societies, as for example India, there is an increasing separation of law from religion and morality. Associated with this is the emergence and growth of a legal profession (whose members have in many cases been educated in the West) distinct from the priestly caste which formerly had a monopoly in interpreting the law. Finally, in those societies where kinship groups were an exceptionally important element in the social structure (and this is so in such countries as India and China, as well as in tribal societies), there is apparent the kind of development, which Maine traced historically, from 'status' to 'contract', in which the individual rather than the family or other kin group comes to be treated as the basic legal entity. This development, however, takes a different form from that in the nineteenth-century European societies, since in most cases the growth of contractual relationships is limited by the extent of economic planning and the provision of social welfare services.[3]

In Western societies the changes in law which we have considered came about partly as a result of economic concentration, partly as a result of changes in class relations and in the character of the state. During the nineteenth century law could be studied, by Marx and later Marxists, as an element in the ideological superstructure of society and an instrument of class domination (see the discussion in the next section); and class influences upon law could easily be discerned in the character of legislation and of judicial decisions, and in the nature of the penalties inflicted for offences against private property. But this situation has changed in some degree during the twentieth century, with the development of 'mixed economies' and 'welfare capitalism'. The rise of the labour movement, the extension of the franchise, and the spread of social reform and egalitarian doctrines have all brought about changes in legislation, in the social climate which influences judicial decisions, and in the class structure of the Western capitalist societies. In consequence, law now functions somewhat more impartially, in some periods at least, in the regulation of conflicts between individuals and groups where class interests are concerned, and it also manifestly regulates many important relationships which are unconnected with class, including those between the individual and large organizations, whether private or public.

One of the most significant changes over the past century in almost all societies has been the growing mildness of punishment. Hobhouse (1906) referred to the barbarity of the criminal law in Europe down to the nineteenth century, but observed that from the end of the eighteenth century many individual reformers and reform movements (among the latter especially 'the Society of Friends, French Rationalists, English Utilitarians and the Evangelicals') began to have an effect in disseminating more humane views. The changes have been most rapid in the present century, both in the reform of the criminal law and in penal reform. They have been brought about by the combined action of diverse influences. In the first place, as Hobhouse noted:

> As society becomes more confident in its power to maintain order, the cruelty and callousness that are born of fear are seen in a new light. More humane influences make themselves felt, and from that moment excessive severity begins to militate against the proper execution of the law ... (p. 124)

Secondly, the generally greater stability of modern societies, resulting from the extension of rights, the growth of citizenship and a real, if limited, diminution of class differences, and rising material standards has been a favourable condition for the spread of humanitarian ideals, which received powerful support from the labour movement. There have been many setbacks even in the recent progress of humanitarian ideals – the fascist regimes, the Stalinist period in the USSR, some colonial regimes, some political regimes established by nationalist revolutions, military dictatorships, and above all the mounting horror of modern warfare – yet on balance the ideals are more firmly and widely held and are more clearly expressed in legal systems. Finally, the social sciences themselves, and especially sociology and psychology, have played an important part in bringing about reforms, by, their direct influence upon policy-makers and their more diffuse influence upon public opinion. A new discipline, criminology, which is to a large extent a specialized and applied branch of sociology (see Chapter 20 below), has grown rapidly during the present century, and has begun to affect legal thought and the general public discussion of punishment and penal institutions.

Law in the System of Social Control

At various points in this chapter I have referred briefly to the relations between law and other means of social control, and between law and social structure. These relations have been the subject of much controversy and deserve a fuller examination.

It is well established that early law, and primitive law, are not clearly distinguished from religious and moral precepts and doctrines. Maine refers to an early state of society in which a rule of law is not yet discriminated from a rule of religion. Firth (1956, p. 137), in discussing the regulation of conduct in tribal societies, observes:

> If a system of European law is intelligible only by reference to the changing practices of the people, their system of ethics, their institutional structure, their judges' ideas of what is 'reasonable', and

non-legal factors which lead them to keep it or break it, how much more must this be so in the case of a primitive people without such a clear-cut scheme?

Even in some more advanced societies law, religion and morals are still largely fused; for example, classical Hindu society represents an extreme form of the permeation of law by religion. It is very largely, indeed, among the European societies that we can trace the growth in thought and social practice of a clear distinction between religion, morals and law which is now taken for granted. This distinction does not, however, imply a complete autonomy of the three forms of control. In many societies moral rules are still strongly influenced by religious conceptions, and in all societies law is based upon moral notions. This is evident in the sphere of legislation, which always derives from social doctrines and ideals; but equally, in the administration of justice and in judicial decisions there has almost always been reference to the fundamental moral ideals of the society, in terms of 'reason', 'natural law', 'equity', or in recent times 'public policy', as well as to the written or traditional law.

The dependence of law upon morals, sometimes religiously interpreted,[4] does not make the distinction between them any less important. The domains of law and morals are not co-extensive. There are many legal rules which concern matters of expediency rather than morality; on the other hand, there are many things which might generally be regarded as morally desirable but either cannot be brought about by law or would lose their moral character if they were so brought about. But where the two domains overlap law seems to be determined rather than determining; it serves to consolidate a social order and way of life which has been brought into existence by moral and political doctrines or by unwilled changes in social structure. Thus the changes in law in European societies since the nineteenth century can be attributed, as we have seen, to changes in economic structure and class relations, to the rise of the labour movement, and to the spread of democratic, socialist and humanitarian doctrines. In modern India, again, changes in law are resulting from economic development, and from the spread of modern social and political doctrines. In a more general way, the maintenance of a legal order depends upon the moral climate of a society. The effectiveness of legal regulation never rests solely upon the threat of physical sanctions, but upon a general attitude of respect for law, and for a particular legal order; and this attitude itself is determined by moral approval of law as embodying social justice. From this standpoint – to take one example – it may be doubted whether the recent wave of inner-city riots in Britain can effectively be tackled by strengthening the apparatus of what is called 'law and order', rather than by measures of public policy designed to restore participation in the benefits of society, and a sense of belonging to a community of equal citizens, among those social groups which have been involved.

The major influence of sociological and anthropological studies of law and social control has been, indeed, to show that social life is regulated in many different ways. Kamenka and Ehr-Soon Tay (1980, ch. 1, pp. 3–4), observe that:

> Anarchic and violent self-help, or utter lawlessness, are not the only alternatives to a centralized, state-sanctioned codified legal system . . . Societies have rules, and quite sophisticated rules and procedures, without having a sovereign, codes, courts and constables. It may be, indeed, that the elevation of state-centred law, of the will of the sovereign and of a complex machinery devoted to producing stability and justice, is in inverse proportion to the authority of other norms: religion, custom and sheer fellow-feeling and neighbourliness.

And Willock (1974), writing in the first issue of the *British Journal of Law and Society*, argues that 'the most salutary functions of sociology for the lawyer and jurist' are that it 'emphasizes the involved, interconnected character of human relationships' and links legal studies with other control systems, thus correcting the tendency to isolationism.

These sociological studies approach, in some respects, Marxist conceptions of law, which have been much more widely discussed in recent years (Collins, 1982). An early Marxist view sketched by Engels and Lenin held that law, as an integral part of the state, is simply an instrument of class oppression, and like the state will wither away in a classless, fully developed socialist society, its place being taken by what Lenin called 'elementary rules of social life'. This idea has been criticized in some recent studies, and Collins (1982, ch. 5) has argued that 'Many laws govern disputes which appear far removed from the class struggle, as for example in the case of the enforcement of moral standards' (and, one might add, driving offences, contracts dealing with personal property, and so on), and that Lenin's concession 'that some social rules would remain in a Communist society . . . in effect . . . acknowledges the continuation of laws but under another name because they will no longer be connected to a repressive state apparatus'. Much Marxist writing, however, is concerned with analysing law in relation to the development of capitalism, in a more profound and systematic way (Fine *et al.*, 1979), and does not discuss at any length the more speculative

question of the role of law in a socialist society, or the phenomenon, to which I referred earlier, of the rehabilitation of the 'rule
of law' in the socialist countries of Eastern Europe. What can be
derived at least from Marxist conceptions is the idea that law is
only one element in a complex body of rules and norms which
maintain an orderly social life and resolve disputes, and that it
need not necessarily be the dominant element in a 'classless', or at
any rate more equal and more democratic, society; and this has a
close affinity with the conclusions of more general sociological
studies of law.

From another aspect, however, we must recognize the specific
character of the legal regulation of conduct. In general, legal rules
are more precise than moral or customary rules and legal sanctions are more definite and frequently more effective.[5] As Bert-
rand Russell remarked, the good behaviour of even the most
exemplary citizen owes much to the existence of a police force. It
is hardly possible, and in my view not at all useful, to conceive a
society of any degree of complexity in which social behaviour
would be regulated entirely by the moral sanctions of praise and
blame. Present-day international relations provide an illustration
of the importance of law in social control. It may well be true that
the moral unity of mankind is now greater than ever in the past,
at least in the sense that a moral duty towards all human beings,
irrespective of their nationality, race, religion, and so on, is more
or less clearly recognized by many people in all countries. But
these moral sentiments are largely ineffective in regulating the
relations between societies when clashes of interest or doctrine
occur, because they have not been precisely stated in legal rules,
and above all because they are not supported by any legal
sanctions. During the twentieth century, there have been
attempts through international political organizations to lay the
foundations of an international legal order, but they have made
little progress in face of national sovereignty. Sanctions are easily
imposed when the interests of powerful nations coincide, but
then justice is not always done; and when justice needs to be done
there is lacking any international authority with power to constrain.

The preceding discussion has indicated the importance of law,
which, though it rests in varying degrees upon custom, moral
sentiments and the institutional arrangements of a society,
especially its economic and class structure, brings about by the
precision of its rules and sanctions a degree of certainty in human
behaviour which is difficult to attain through other types of social
control. At the same time, however, it is apparent that law has

only a relative autonomy, and that it does not and need not enjoy, in every type of society, an absolute pre-eminence in the system of social control. But it may still have an independent influence upon social behaviour, in the sense of establishing generally in a society attitudes and norms of behaviour which were initially those of minority groups of social critics, reformers and revolutionaries.

Notes to Chapter 15

1 J. D. Mayne, 1950, p. 44. 'The consequence was a state of arrested progress, in which no voices were heard unless they came from the tomb.' Kapadia, 1958, pp. 247–51, illustrates this with reference to the Hindu joint family, observing that the British courts were accepting, for nineteenth-century conditions, the law as it had been expounded in the eleventh and twelfth centuries.
2 See S. F. Kechekyan, 1956:

> Soviet juridical science refutes such propositions [i.e. of the 'sociological' school of jurists] aimed at justifying the arbitrary actions of the judge and administrative discretion . . . Socialist law proceeds from the precept that it is the duty of the judge and administrative bodies to follow exactly and implicitly the directives comprised in law and in the normative acts issued on the basis of the laws.

3 For a discussion of some of these issues see Anderson, 1968.
4 For example, in European countries where Roman Catholicism is the predominant religion, and the law relating to marriage and divorce has been strongly influenced, or even determined, by religious rules; or in some Islamic countries, and in parts of Hindu India, where there is a legal prohibition of alcohol, as at an earlier date in the USA. There is also a very powerful religious influence in many countries on the law relating to abortion.
5 Durkheim, and later Radcliffe-Brown, distinguished between 'diffuse' and 'organized' sanctions, the latter being those of law. Llewellyn and Hoebel, 1941, have carefully examined the distinction between legal and moral sanctions in a tribal society; and in this and other writing Llewellyn argues that law is more imperative than normative – 'Law has teeth'.

16 *Education*

Durkheim (1922, p. 71) defined education as

> the action exercised by the older generations upon those who are not
> yet ready for social life. Its object is to awaken and develop in the child
> those physical, intellectual and moral states which are required of him
> both by his society as a whole and by the milieu for which he is
> specially destined.

This action, the socialization of new generations, necessarily
takes place in all societies, but it assumes many different forms in
respect of the social groups and institutions involved, and in
respect of its own diversity and complexity.

We may consider, first, the extent to which education is a
specialized social activity. In the simplest societies, where there is
in any case little specialization of function, education is not
organized as a separate activity; it is provided by the family, the
kin group and the society as a whole through participation in
their everyday routines of living. But in many primitive societies
above the simplest level formal instruction is given at puberty,
before initiation as an adult member of the society. Lowie (1950,
pp. 195–6) gives as an example the educational scheme of the
Yaghan (Tierra del Fuego):

> Each Yaghan novice gets two sponsors, who supervise his conduct
> throughout the several months' seclusion. Physically, each boy or girl
> has to learn rigorous self-control ... For moral instruction the
> neophytes jointly listen to some venerable tribesman's lectures. In
> addition to mass instruction, each boy or girl is tutored by some close
> relative who has noted defects in the pupil's character and now takes
> pains to correct them ... Finally, there is true vocational preparation.
> The girls' training, to be sure, amounts to little more than rounding
> out previously acquired skills ... The boys, however, are relatively
> backward at corresponding tasks of adult life, and hence require
> schooling.

In more developed societies, formal education acquires greater
importance, the period of systematic instruction increases, and a
specialized occupational group of teachers is formed. Thus, in
ancient India, formal instruction was provided by the Brahmins:

> The pupil's first introduction was at the age of 5. He commenced by
> learning the alphabets for the first time, and this was open to the

children of all ages. Then followed the ceremony of tonsure, which was followed by the student initiation ceremony at the normal age of 8 for a Brahmin, 11 for a Kshatriya, and 12 for a Vaisya . . . The entire educational system was based upon this ancient system of studentship which laid more emphasis on life than on learning or instruction. It was based upon constant personal contact between teacher and pupil, bound together by a spiritual tie, living in a common home . . . The student, after his initiation, entered into a new life whereby he was re-created by his teacher and had to undergo a twofold course of discipline – physical and spiritual. (Basu, 1957)

This educational system, however, extended to only a small minority of the population; and it was conducted by a hereditary priesthood chiefly concerned with the transmission of religious doctrines and largely excluding secular instruction. Technical skills were imparted mainly through the family and the occupational group, in informal and practical ways. This was very largely the case in all societies before the rise of modern science and industry, but the predominance of religious education was greater in India than in Western or Islamic societies, or in China.

British rule in India, as in other colonial territories, brought about considerable changes in education. At first the British rulers supported traditional Hindu schools, but in 1835 it was decided to promote European literature and science in India, with English as the medium of instruction. This policy received the support of many Indian reformers, and generally of the new commercial middle class; but as D. P. Mukerji (1948, ch. 4) observed, it tended to reinforce the separation of the upper classes from the rest of society. In principle, it is true, the object was 'to extend European knowledge throughout all classes of the people', but in practice resources were concentrated upon the education of the upper and middle classes, and very little progress was made in establishing an adequate system of primary education. In 1939, 90 per cent of the Indian population were still illiterate. One of the first priorities of newly independent nations has been to eradicate illiteracy, and with notable assistance from UNESCO mass literacy campaigns have been very successful, especially in the socialist developing countries (e.g. Cuba).

But distinctions within the educational system exist in almost all societies, corresponding with the differentiation between classes. This is the case even in some primitive societies; the Maori, for example, had commoners' schools during the winter, but also 'sacred colleges' which were open only to the nobility, especially the elder sons of chiefs. In most literate societies, until recent times literacy has been largely confined to the upper social strata. Modern industrial societies, which established mass literacy for the first time, did not by this means remove the educational distinctions between different social classes. These were maintained by the existence of different types of schools for the various social groups, such as the English 'public schools', reserved for children of the upper class, and by the unequal distribution of opportunities for higher education.

Higher education in most Western countries traditionally involved the languages and culture of classical Greece and Rome, and this reinforced the distinction between the educated gentleman and the rest of society. Such cultural differences have persisted, in an attenuated form, into the twentieth century; they underly the conflict between the 'two cultures', literary and scientific, and in some societies have constituted an obstacle to the development of technical education. As Lowie (1950, p. 208) says: 'Historical accident had lent distinction to verbal felicity, while manual dexterity and whatever savoured of the utilitarian had long ranked low in the social scale.' Besides this broad division between elites and masses, between education for intellectual and for manual occupations, there has existed a more refined graduation of educational facilities. Thus, in England before 1944, the educational system can be broadly characterized as having provided elementary education for working-class children, secondary (grammar school) education for middle-class children, and public school (fee-paying) education for children of the upper and upper middle classes. The Education Act of 1944 modified without destroying this differentiation; it is still largely the case that upper- and upper-middle-class children go mainly to public schools while those of the lower middle class and working class attend comprehensive schools.[1]

It should be observed that this kind of educational differentiation exists in some degree in all modern societies, however much they may be committed to egalitarian and welfare policies. The socialist countries have made large claims for their success in establishing social equality, but, for example, while the progress of education in the USSR since 1917 has been extremely rapid, it has not resulted in the elimination of educational privilege. During 1958 a number of speeches and memoranda in connection with the reform of the Soviet educational system provided data which had hitherto not been available, and which showed that only 55 per cent of children actually completed the ten-year educational course by reaching the eighth grade in schools, and that in the institutions of higher education in Moscow only one-third of the students were of working-class or peasant origin, the other two-thirds coming from families in a relatively small social stratum, the intelligentsia.[2] This seems to correspond with the class structure as depicted by Konrád and Szelényi (1979), who conceive the social structure of 'early socialism' as dichotomous, with an evolving intellectual class at one pole, and a working class at the other. In India, since the achievement of independence, there has been considerable progress in the expansion of educational facilities, and with the development of village schools and of educational opportunities for children of lower castes there is substantially more equality of access to education. Yet there are still notable inequalities; basic education which incorporates Gandhi's ideas on the combination of intellectual and manual work is provided for most children (and most do not go beyond the primary stage of education), but the upper classes of Indian society still send their children to English type grammar and public schools.

These data, taken from different modern societies, show that educational differences are closely related to social stratification, and educational reforms have been less successful than their advocates hoped in bringing about greater social equality. As Ferge (1977, p. 24) observes: 'Society proves to be the stronger factor.' Other types of social differentiation – between the sexes, ethnic groups or religious groups – have also frequently been associated with differences in kind or quality or education. In most societies until recently women had very much less chance than men of obtaining higher education, and this is still the case in many Third World countries. Africans, in the Union of South Africa, have very limited opportunities even for secondary education; and in the USA black Americans, although their situation has improved, are still educationally handicapped. In many societies, at different times, religious minorities have been discriminated against in education as in other respects.

Thus the function of education in preparing the child for a particular milieu in society (as Durkheim defined it) has traditionally meant preparing him or her for membership of a particular group in the social hierarchy. The experience of modern egalitarian policies indicates that it is very difficult to eliminate this feature, not least because the intellectual and social criteria frequently overlap; the children of high status families are in general better qualified for higher education, because of a variety of advantages which they enjoy. It may be that if more egalitarian societies come into existence in the future, and social equality comes to be taken for granted, these difficulties will cease; but it seems more likely that so long as there is educational selection privileged groups will always be emerging within society and that only deliberate policy and contrivance will succeed in maintaining a rough equality.

So far I have been largely concerned with educational differentiation; that is, with the transmission to younger generations of different codes of behaviour, largely influenced by social class. But as Durkheim observed, education also prepares the child for life in society as a whole, by transmitting common social traditions through the language, religion, morals and customs of the society. The inculcation of national values has been especially apparent in modern societies, and was for long reflected in the social prestige of teachers. The French *instituteur* who was given his title in the Revolution of 1789 ('celui qui institue la Nation') acquired under the Third Republic a remarkable prestige and importance (Thabault, 1945, pt 3, ch. 5). In the USA the school-ma'am played a similar role from the end of the nineteenth century in transforming the children of immigrants into 100 per cent Americans. The way of life which is taught may derive from different sources. In France, under the Third Republic, an attempt (to which Durkheim contributed by his writings) was made to teach a secular morality, but its principal result was to establish a deep division, and conflict, between the state schools and the Catholic schools and eventually between the adult generations which they produced. In Britain the 1944 Education Act imposed as a statutory obligation that in every school the day shall begin with collective worship and religious instruction shall be given, and official circulars and pamphlets have emphasized the Christian tradition as a foundation of the British way of life; but this religious emphasis has been attenuated in the past two decades. The schools in some socialist societies instil into their pupils the social and political doctrines of Marxism. In India, the whole conception of basic education is founded upon the social philosophy of Gandhi, itself inspired by Hinduism, and almost all public discussions of education link the present with the traditional Hindu system of education.

The emergence of new nation-states and the growth of nationalism in nineteenth-century Europe were concurrent with the spread of literacy, and in most societies they resulted in an increasing emphasis upon indoctrination in the educational process.[3] The same phenomenon has reappeared in the twentieth century, in those societies which have attained independence from colonial rule or have constituted themselves as modern nation-states, but it has been countered by other influences. The diffusion and acceptance of the ideal of the underlying unity of mankind, despite international conflict, has brought greater tolerance of cultural diversity and genuine efforts to conceive and present each specific cultural tradition as a single element in a larger and richer whole. At the same time, while educational differentiation within societies has remained, increasing social mobility through the educational system has tended to break up the dominant national culture, and to create some diversity. The growth of science and the rapidity of social change have also affected the codes of behaviour taught in educational institutions, imparting to them, in some modern societies, a tolerant or tentative character which may have as one result adolescent and adult aimlessness. A balance between firm traditions and standards of behaviour, tolerance, adaptability to change, and the spirit of free inquiry is difficult to attain; and some of the failures of modern education (exacerbated by other social influences) in its prime function of socialization can be seen in the youth problems which are prevalent in all industrial societies.

These problems raise a larger question about the effectiveness of formal education as a means of social control. In earlier societies, where literacy was highly valued as a basis of prestige and power, teachers were also highly regarded; moreover, the teachers themselves usually came from high status families. Formal education imparted to a minority destined to rule and administer society a definite code of morals and behaviour. In China, the examinations 'tested whether or not the candidate's mind was thoroughly steeped in literature and whether or not he possessed the *ways of thought* suitable to a cultured man', and in the eyes of the Chinese masses 'a successfully examined candidate and official was by no means a mere applicant for office qualified by knowledge ... He was a proved holder of magical qualities' (Weber, 1915, p. 433). In this respect, although not a priest, he resembled the Hindu *guru* who was a spiritual counsellor as well as teacher and official. With the achievement of mass literacy in modern industrial societies the social prestige of the teacher tended to decline, for he was no longer set apart as the literate individual; moreover, teachers for the primary levels of education were themselves recruited from the lower social strata. In addition, the development of capitalism, and more generally the emphasis upon economic growth and rising material standards, have established the pre-eminence of wealth in conferring prestige and power. As an Indian educationalist writes of present-day India, 'In sharp contrast to the past when teachers were honoured however poor or powerless they may have been, contemporary India places a disproportionate emphasis on monetary standards'

(Kabir, 1956). The values professed by the teacher are no longer authoritative; they have to compete with the values presented to the child by his family, peer group, and the media of mass communication. Neither sociologists nor social psychologists have yet given enough attention to the conflicts between different codes of behaviour and different agencies of social control in contemporary societies. Yet there are manifest conflicts between family and school,[4] arising from social mobility (e.g. in many Western societies the conflict between the working-class standards of the family and the middle-class standards of school and university), from the secular character of state education as contrasted with the religious values of the family (or vice versa), or from inter-generational differences in outlook; and there are equally serious conflicts between school and peer group, and between school and mass media.

Education as a Type of Social Control

Helvétius, referring to education in eighteenth-century France, observed that men 'are born ignorant, not stupid; they are made stupid by education'. This has not been, on the whole, the modern view. From the end of the eighteenth century, in the Western world, formal education came to be seen as a principal instrument of enlightenment and civilization, but also of national power, concerned not so much (ostensibly at least) with transmitting a 'way of life' as with communicating the growing mass of empirical knowledge, above all in the sphere of science and technology, and diffusing, as many reformers hoped, the capacity for critical thought that is needed in a rapidly changing world.

It is from this aspect that we can regard formal education in modern industrial societies as a relatively independent source of ideas and values which play a part in regulating behaviour. Malinowski rightly mentioned this feature in its rudimentary form in primitive societies when he included the 'rules of craftsmanship' as an element in social control. Modern science and technology are not only the basis of infinitely more complex rules of craftsmanship but also of a general rational approach to nature and social life, which has an increasingly important role in establishing and maintaining social co-operation. More than this, scientific thought has, over the past three centuries, implicitly or explicitly criticized the ideas propounded in religious and moral doctrines and has been largely responsible for the changes which the latter have undergone. The whole rationalization of the modern world with which Max Weber was preoccupied is connected with the development of science, and since the chief vehicle of this development, at least during the past century, has been the educational system, we can legitimately speak of formal education as a type of social control.

There is another way in which education has contributed independently to the regulation of conduct, and that is in the early socialization of the child. The work of educational reformers such as Montessori and Froebel brought about significant changes in the education of young children. Certainly these reforms in part reflect moral notions external to the education system, but in part they have been influential in changing moral ideas in society at large. So far as they were connected with scientific studies of the development of children, such as those of Piaget, they arose from the development of the social sciences. Moreover, being based upon this observation and analysis of the actual development of children's activities, needs and problems, they can be regarded as having arisen very largely within the educational sphere itself, as independent discoveries. We should observe, also, that the changes in the formal education system have themselves brought about changes in family socialization, aided by the spread of social science knowledge. In this sense, the formal education of children has genuinely originated new forms of regulation of behaviour.

But this account of the role of education in the system of social control needs serious qualification. As I have noted, education has also been conceived as a means to national power, and every modern educational system (increasingly organized and financed by the state) purveys elements of a national culture which is pre-eminently the culture of a dominant class or elite; or in other words, a 'dominant ideology'. In some societies this ideology is overtly and dogmatically expounded, and critical reflection on the views and policies of political or religious authorities is, so far as possible, suppressed. Elsewhere, the dominant ideology may be more subtly conveyed, as Bourdieu and Passeron (1970) have argued in their analysis of cultural reproduction in capitalist society, in terms of 'pedagogic action' (education in the broadest sense) which they define as 'the imposition of a cultural arbitrary by an arbitrary power'. Critical reflections upon the nature and role of education proliferated in the 1960s, from Goodman's *Growing Up Absurd* (1960) to the literature attacking the prevailing conceptions of the university as a 'knowledge factory' (Miller and Gilmore, 1965; Jacobs and Landau, 1966; Bottomore, 1967, ch. 6).[5]

Education, therefore, like other types of social control, is profoundly affected by external political and economic forces. Through the educational system new generations learn the dominant social norms and the penalties for infringing them; as well as being instructed in their 'station and its duties' within the prevailing system of social differentiation and stratification (not only with respect to class membership but, as recent studies have demonstrated more and more fully, also with regard to gender roles). Nevertheless, in modern societies where formal education has a pre-eminent place, and a large professional group of teachers comes into existence, the educational system itself has an important independent influence on the social norms and it has always proved difficult, if not impossible, to suppress critical thought altogether, or even to diminish substantially its long-term effects. The experiences of the late 1960s in the sphere of higher education – which will no doubt recur in the future in new contexts – showed the potential of the educational system as a major source of change and innovation in the social norms.

Notes to Chapter 16

1   See Floud, Halsey and Martin, 1956, on school entrants. The authors also discuss the reasons for the continuing inequalities, and the problems of differences in educational performance between middle-class and working-class children. On the universities, see Kelsall, 1957, and for a general discussion of these aspects of education in Britain, Glass, 1959. A number of studies of educational selection in different societies are brought together in Halsey, Floud, and Anderson, 1961.
2   See also some more recent data in Lane, 1982, ch. 4.
3   The connection between universal literacy, education and nationalism has been forcefully argued by Gellner, 1983.
4   These were discussed in an illuminating study by Waller, 1932, which has been rather neglected in later work.
5   In the 1980s, with the relative decline of radical movements, and the deepening economic crisis, the 'knowledge factory' view seems to have regained its pre-eminence.

Notes on Reading for Part IV

1 War

See especially the following general studies:

Aron, Raymond, *Peace and War: A Theory of International Relations* (1962).
Bramson, Leon and Goethals, George W. (eds.), *War: Studies from Psychology, Sociology, Anthropology* (1964).
Buchan, Alastair, *War in Modern Society: An Introduction* (1966).
Richardson, L. F., *Statistics of Deadly Quarrels* (1960a).
Wright, Quincy, *A Study of War* (1942).

There is a useful collection of papers dealing with war in primitive as well as modern society, with aggression, and with alternatives to war, in Morton Fried, Marvin Harris, and Robert Murphy (eds.), *War: The Anthropology of Armed Conflict* (1968).

Useful data on present-day weapons and the arms race can be found in the reports of the Stockholm International Peace Research Institute (SIPRI), and in the annual reports edited by Ruth L. Sivard, *World Military and Social Expenditures*.

2 Revolution and Counter-Revolution

The following general studies deal with the subject from various aspects:

Brinton, Crane, *The Anatomy of Revolution* (1957).
Eckstein, Harry (ed.), *Internal War* (1964).
Friedrich, Carl J. (ed.), *Revolution* (1966).
Meisel, James H., *Counter-Revolution: How Revolutions Die* (1970).
Meusel, Alfred, 'Revolution and counter-revolution' (1934).
Skocpol, Theda, *States and Social Revolutions* (1979).
Wolf, Eric R., *Peasant Wars of the Twentieth Century* (1970).

There is a large literature on particular revolts, revolutions and counter-revolutions; the following works illuminate diverse aspects of these phenomena:

Carr, E. H., *The Bolshevik Revolution, 1917–1923*, Vol. 1 (1950).
Fitzgerald, C. P., *The Birth of Communist China* (1952).
Guevara, Che, *Guerrilla Warfare* (1960).
Hobsbawm, E. J., *Primitive Rebels* (1959).
Lefebvre, Georges, *The Coming of the French Revolution* (1939).
Luxemburg, Rosa, *The Russian Revolution* (1922).
Rudé, George, *The Crowd in the French Revolution* (1959).
Trotsky, Leon, *The History of the Russian Revolution* (1932–3).

3   *Social Control*

A pioneer study, which established the general use of the term, is E. A. Ross, *Social Control* (1901). Among other earlier studies the most useful and interesting is W. G. Sumner, *Folkways: A Study of the Sociological Importance of Usage, Manners, Customs and Morals* (1906).

G. Gurvitch, 'Social control' (1945), provides a short review of studies in this field and an analysis of the major problems; and a good introduction to the subject, with particular reference to tribal societies, is R. Firth, *Human Types* (1956), ch. 5, 'The regulation of conduct'.

Some of the outstanding contributions to the study of social control are to be found in the writings of B. Malinowski; especially his *Crime and Custom in Savage Society* (1926), and his Introduction to H. I. Hogbin, *Law and Order in Polynesia* (1934), pp. xvii–lxxii. The conception of social control through a 'dominant ideology' is critically examined in Nicholas Abercrombie, Stephen Hill and Bryan Turner, *The Dominant Ideology Thesis* (1980).

4   *Custom, Public Opinion*

On custom see particularly the works of Malinowski and Sumner cited above.

Two valuable early discussions of public opinion are:

Ginsberg, M., *The Psychology of Society* (1921), chs. 9, 10.
Lippmann, W., *Public Opinion* (1922).

More recent accounts will be found in D. Katz *et al.*, *Public Opinion and Propaganda* (1954) and W. Albig, *Modern Public Opinion* (1956). A very useful recent work by Terence H. Qualter, *Opinion Control in the Democracies* (1985) reviews some of the earlier contributions and goes on to examine problems of opinion formation and control in democratic societies.

5   *Religion*

Useful general studies are:

Lowie, R. H., *Primitive Religion* (1936).
Malinowski, B., *Magic, Science and Religion, and Other Essays* (1948).
Radcliffe-Brown, A. R., *Structure and Function in Primitive Society* (1952), ch. 8, 'Religion and society'.
Robertson, R., *The Sociological Interpretation of Religion* (1970).
Turner, Bryan S., *Religion and Social Theory* (1983b).
Wach, Joachim, *Sociology of Religion* (1944).
Wilson, Bryan, *Religion in Sociological Perspective* (1982).

Among the classical studies of religion from a sociological, anthropological or psychological perspective, see:

Durkheim, Émile, *Elementary Forms of the Religious Life* (1912).
Frazer, J. G., *The Golden Bough* (1890). The abridged version of chs. 1–7

published under the title *Magic and Religion* (1944) provides a succinct account of Frazer's views.

Freud, Sigmund, *The Future of an Illusion* (1927).
James, William, *The Varieties of Religious Experience* (1902).
Tawney, R. H., *Religion and the Rise of Capitalism* (1937).
Troeltsch, E., *The Social Teaching of the Christian Churches* (1912).
Weber, Max, *Gesammelte Aufsätze zur Religionssoziologie* (1920). Most of these are now available in English as follows:

> *The Protestant Ethic and the Spirit of Capitalism* (1904–5).
> *The Religion of China: Confucianism and Taoism* (1952).
> *Ancient Judaism* (1953).
> *The Religion of India: The Sociology of Hinduism and Buddhism* (1958).

6 Morality

Two well-known evolutionist works are:

Hobhouse, L. T., *Morals in Evolution* (1906).
Westermarck, E., *The Origin and Development of Moral Ideas* (1906).

Durkheim was particularly concerned with the role of moral ideas and codes in social life, and discussed the subject in essays and lectures which have been collected and published in the following works: *Sociology and Philosophy* (1924), *Moral Education* (1925), *Professional Ethics and Civic Morals* (1950). See also the discussion in Steven Lukes, *Émile Durkheim: His Life and Work* (1973), ch. 21, 'The sociology of morality'.

The writings of Max Weber on religion (cited above) were largely concerned, as I have indicated in the text, with the moral codes of the world religions.

Other useful general works are:

Ginsberg, M., *On the Diversity of Morals* (1956), ch. 7.
Ossowska, Maria, *Social Determinants of Moral Ideas* (1971).

Marxist conceptions of morality are examined in Steven Lukes, *Marxism and Morality* (1985).

7 Law

There are several useful general studies:

Friedmann, W. G., 'Sociology of law' (1961–2). A trend report with bibliography.
Hunt, Alan, *The Sociological Movement in Law* (1978). A good account of some of the major contributions: Roscoe Pound, American legal realism, Durkheim, Max Weber.
Kamenka, Eugene and Erh-Soon Tay, Alice (eds.), *Law and Social Control* (1980). Includes chapters on anthropological and sociological approaches.

Pound, Roscoe, 'Sociology of law' (1945). An excellent short survey of the principal contributions, and an analysis of problems.
Rheinstein, M. (ed.), *Max Weber on Law in Economy and Society* (1966).

On primitive law see the writings of Malinowski cited earlier, and E. A. Hoebel, *The Law of Primitive Man* (1954).

A well-known Marxist study of law in capitalist society is Karl Renner, *The Institutions of Private Law and their Social Functions* (1904), and Marxist conceptions of law are examined more generally in Hugh Collins, *Marxism and Law* (1982).

On law and social change see particularly:

Dicey, A. V., *Lectures on the Relation Between Law and Public Opinion in England During the Nineteenth Century* (1905).
Friedmann, W. G., *Law in a Changing Society* (1959).
Maine, H. S., *Ancient Law* (1861).
Vinogradoff, P., *Historical Jurisprudence* (1920).

There is a good account of changes in law and society in India in J. Duncan M. Derrett, *Religion, Law and the State in India* (1968).

8   *Education*

A major work on the sociology of education is still Durkheim's *Education and Sociology* (1922). N. Hans, *Comparative Education* (1958) is a useful study of different types of educational system, and more recently Margaret Archer, *Social Origins of Educational Systems* (1979) has examined in detail the development of education in England, Denmark, France and Russia. Many aspects of the relation between education and society are studied, on a comparative basis, in A. H. Halsey, J. Floud and C. A. Anderson (eds.), *Education, Economy and Society* (1961), and more recently in J. Karabel and A. H. Halsey (eds.), *Power and Ideology in Education* (1977).

Much sociological study of the educational system has been devoted to its connection with social stratification and social mobility. A comprehensive early work dealing with Britain is Jean Floud, A. H. Halsey and F. M. Martin, *Social Class and Educational Opportunity* (1956), and a more recent study, A. H. Halsey, A. F. Heath and J. M. Ridge, *Origins and Destinations: Family, Class and Education in Modern Britain* (1980). On particular aspects of the problem, see Brian Jackson and Dennis Marsden, *Education and the Working Class* (1963), and the study by J. W. B. Douglas reported in *The Home and the School* (1964) and *All Our Future* (1969). On the USA see S. Bowles and H. Gintis, *Schooling in Capitalist America* (1976), and C. Jencks et al., *Inequality: A Reassessment of the Effect of Family and Schooling in America* (1972).

The social role of teachers and intellectuals was discussed in two stimulating earlier works:

Veblen, Thorstein, *The Higher Learning in America* (1918).
Znaniecki, F., *The Social Role of the Man of Knowledge* (1940).

More recently there has been widespread discussion and analysis of the role of intellectuals in politics and in the 'scientific and technological revolution'; see the study by Robert Brym, *Intellectuals and Politics* (1980), and the highly critical account by Eva Etzioni-Halevy, *The Knowledge Elite and the Failure of Prophecy* (1985), both of which provide substantial bibliographies.

PART V

Social Change

17 Change, Development, Progress

From its beginnings sociology was closely connected with the philosophy of history and the interpretations of the rapid and violent changes in European societies in the eighteenth and nineteenth centuries. The Scottish historians and philosophers (in particular, Ferguson, Millar and Robertson), the French *philosophes* (Voltaire, Turgot, Condorcet), and the German historians and philosophers (Herder, Hegel) were all concerned to explain or interpret the social and political revolutions of their age, within the framework of a general theory of history. Their influence was profound and can be seen plainly in later writers such as Saint-Simon and Buckle, and in the work of the first sociologists, Comte, Marx and Spencer. Even later in the nineteenth century a historical or evolutionary approach was dominant in sociology and anthropology. Max Weber presented no theory of universal history, but it is evident that all his sociological work was inspired by a historical concern with the origins and significance of modern Western capitalism and more widely by his preoccupation with the increasing rationalization of social life and its implications for human freedom (Löwith, 1932). Durkheim rejected Comte's evolutionary sociology, but his own outline of a classification of societies is conceived in terms of an evolutionary scheme, and his *Division of Labour in Society* (1893) is concerned with a process of development from primitive to modern societies. Hobhouse was more immediately indebted to Comte and Spencer, and the whole of his sociological work is clearly directed by a philosophical conception of social progress.

In these earlier sociological theories, the notions of 'change', 'evolution', 'development' and 'progress' are sometimes confused, or combined in a single concept; in other cases, a distinction is made between them but they are treated as logically related terms. Subsequent criticism has been largely concerned with the fittingness of the terms in their application to social phenomena, and with the character of the relations between them. The notion of social evolution was taken directly from the theories of biological evolution which, in the nineteenth century, powerfully reinforced the influence of the philosophy of history upon sociology. Spencer in his *Social Statics* (1850) and at greater length in his *Principles of Sociology* (1876–96) propounded an analogy between society and an organism and between social and organic growth, but in his account of social evolution he paid little attention to the more specific features of the biological theory: its definition of evolution as 'descent with modifications' and its explanation, in the Darwinian theory, of the mechanism by which evolution takes place. Similarly, Tylor (1871) used the term 'evolution' in a very imprecise way:

> On the one hand the uniformity which so largely pervades civilization may be ascribed, in great measure, to the uniform action of uniform causes; while on the other its various grades may be regarded as states of development or evolution, each the outcome of previous history and about to do its proper part in shaping the history of the future.

Modern writers have indicated the differences between the biological theory and the various theories of social evolution. Ogburn (1922, p. 57), while not entirely rejecting the concept of social evolution, observes: 'The attempts to find laws of heredity, variation and selection in the evolution of social institutions have produced few results either vital or significant.' Similarly, Gordon Childe (1956, pp. 16–17) writes that

> it is essential not to lose sight of the significant distinctions between historical progress and organic evolution, between human culture and the animal's bodily equipment, between the social heritage and the biological inheritance. Figurative language, based on the admitted analogy, is liable to mislead the unwary ... Man's equipment and defences are external to his body; he can lay them aside and don them at will. Their use is not inherited, but learned, rather slowly, from the social group to which each individual belongs. Man's social heritage is not transmitted in the germ-cells from which he springs, but in a tradition which he begins to acquire only after he has emerged from his mother's womb. Changes in culture and tradition can be initiated, controlled, or delayed by the conscious and deliberate choice of their human authors and executors. An invention is not an accidental mutation of the germ-plasma, but a new synthesis of the accumulated experience to which the inventor is heir by tradition only. It is well to be as clear as possible as to the sort of differences subsisting between the processes here compared.

The weaknesses of the analogy between biological and social evolution, had, of course, been realized earlier, and some sociologists preferred to use the term 'social development' to refer to the process of historical change. Even so, the distinction was not rigorously maintained. Hobhouse, for example, seems to have used the terms as synonyms in most of his writings, although he criticized certain aspects of Spencer's evolutionary theory (Hobhouse, 1913b, Introduction). Moreover, in *Social Development* (1924) he proposed four criteria of development, namely, increases in scale, efficiency, mutuality and freedom, which he then explicitly related to criteria of biological evolution and in the case of the last two criteria also to his conception of progress. Many other sociologists have used the criterion of scale in their account of social development; as we saw earlier both Spencer and Durkheim did so in their classification of societies, within an evolutionary framework. More recently, Gordon Childe has suggested that 'the continuity between natural history and human history may allow numerical concepts to be introduced into the latter. Historical changes can be judged by the extent to which they have helped our species to survive and multiply' (1956, p. 12). This is close to the idea of changes in the scale of a society, although as Durkheim pointed out the latter involves more than growth of population. Another frequently used criterion of development is that of the extent of social differentiation, which is discussed by Spencer and Durkheim, as well as by Hobhouse in his account of efficiency and mutuality, and is treated as the principal criterion by MacIver and Page (1952, ch. 27).

The term 'development' is, however, no more precise than the term 'evolution' in its application to social phenomena. In ordinary usage development means 'a gradual unfolding; a fuller working out, of the details of anything; the growth of what is in the germ' (*Oxford English Dictionary*). It is in this sense that we can speak of the development of a child, or of a disease. But it is difficult to speak in the same way of social development, for we cannot always, with any certainty, refer a particular phenomenon to its germ, or clearly distinguish in a particular process between development and decay. There are only two (related) social processes to which it seems possible to apply the term 'development' with any accuracy, namely the growth of knowledge and the growth of human control over the natural environment as shown by technological and economic efficiency. It is, indeed, these two processes which have figured most prominently in developmental or evolutionary accounts of human society.[1]

In much recent sociological writing the term 'development' has been used in quite a different way: first, to differentiate two broad types of society – on one side the prosperous industrial societies and on the other side all those societies (very diverse in other respects) which are predominantly rural, agricultural and poor – and secondly, to describe the process of industrialization or modernization (Bernstein, 1973; Alavi and Shanin, 1982). This current notion of development has several distinctive features. It is not dependent upon a general theory of social evolution or development covering the whole span of human history, but deals with a specific kind of change, occurring at the present time or in the recent past, which can be represented in a simple historical model as a movement through three stages: traditional society, transitional society, modern society. Furthermore, studies of development in this sense have concentrated particularly upon economic growth, and in so doing they have brought out what was implicit in many of the early theories; namely, that the growth of knowledge and of control over nature – or in other words, the development of human powers of production – is the most significant element in the transformation of society. In some forms, however, this idea has given rise to a technological determinism which ignores many important aspects of social structure.

The fact that recent studies do not appeal to a general theory of development does not mean that they neglect entirely comparative and historical inquiry. On the contrary, many contributors to this field of research make explicit comparisons between the present industrialization of developing countries and the earlier industrialization of Western societies. This approach may sometimes lead to the error of supposing that the developing countries will follow exactly the same path as did the present industrial countries, but a number of writers have pointed out that there are substantial differences. Thus Parsons, in an essay 'Some reflections on the institutional framework of economic development' (1958), begins from Weber's analysis of capitalism in order to emphasize the *different* circumstances of present-day industrialization, and he concludes his argument by saying that today 'governments, within the framework of the ideological symbols of nationalism and "socialism", are likely to be by far the most important agencies'. This question is also very thoroughly discussed in Hunter, *Modernizing Peasant Societies* (1969). I shall consider later the Marxist studies which, in the past two decades, have introduced quite new elements into the analysis of development in the Third World.

There is also a more general problem which arises from the idea of a transition from traditional to modern society, for this suggests that 'modern industrial society' is in some way the terminal point of development. This has two important consequences: first, that the changes going on in industrial societies tend to be neglected, as was certainly the case until the 1960s; and secondly, in a more specific way, that the contrast between capitalism and socialism as stages of development, or alternative forms, *within* modern industrial society is either obscured or deliberately excluded.

The conception of development as a single great transformation, bound up with the advance of science and technology (Gellner, 1964, Aron, 1966), owes much to the methodology of Max Weber; it concentrates upon particular processes of change and the emergence of a particular type of society, and leads to the formulation of explanations and interpretations in terms of specific historical circumstances and general concepts about human action rather than in terms of comprehensive 'laws of development'. But it may be questioned whether industrial society or modern society can be treated in exactly the same way as Weber treated capitalism; namely, as a single, highly specific form of society. Indeed, one of the most illuminating studies of modernization – Barrington Moore's *Social Origins of Dictatorship and Democracy* (1966) – argues convincingly that there are three main routes to the modern world: by a bourgeois revolution, by a fascist revolution from above, and by a peasant revolution. Moore also considers a possible fourth route, represented by the development of India since independence. The importance of these distinctions is that they show not merely the different origins (influenced by the relations between classes in a given society), but also the different structures and possibilities of further development of the various types of industrial society.

In recent years there has been a burgeoning of Marxist studies of development (Taylor, 1983), though these have taken several different directions. One influential school of thought has been that which emphasizes the dependence of Third World countries, and 'peripheral' countries generally, upon the 'metropolitan' centres of capitalism. This 'dependency theory' was expounded particularly by Baran (1957), Frank (1969) and Amin (1976), but it has been widely criticized by other writers for concentrating too exclusively on exchange relationships between countries while largely ignoring the mode of production and class structure in the developing countries themselves (Taylor, 1979, 1983; Dore, 1983). Hence an alternative approach has emerged which attempts to analyse directly the nature of 'post-colonial' societies (Alavi and Shanin, 1982; Alavi, 1983). It is relevant to this kind of study to consider the process of development in socialist developing countries, some of which are examined and discussed in a general context in White *et al.* (1983).

The earlier conceptions of social evolution and social development which I have discussed were all intimately connected with the idea of progress.[2] In the case of Comte and Spencer this is so obvious as to need no illustration. Hobhouse proposed a distinction between social evolution and social progress,[3] but his work was clearly dominated by a concern with progress.

> To form by a philosophic analysis a just conception of human progress, to trace this progress to its manifold complexity in the course of history, to test its reality by careful classification and searching comparisons, to ascertain its conditions, and if possible to forecast the future – this is the comprehensive problem towards which all sociological science converges and on the solution of which reasoned sociological effort must finally depend. (Hobhouse, 1908, p. 11)

It is not clear whether a precise distinction can be made between the notions of development and progress in their application to social changes. In Hobhouse's account the two processes coincide, and no example is given of general social development which is not progressive, although of course he does show that growth in a *particular* sphere of social life may have undesirable consequences elsewhere.

Since the end of the nineteenth century the idea of progress has fallen into disfavour or neglect, not only in sociology but more generally in the *Weltanschauung* of intellectuals in Western societies. This is a phenomenon which itself deserves sociological study. Both intellectual and social influences have been important. Intellectually, there has been the persistent effort to make sociology a 'value-free' science, and during the same period the growth in philosophical thought of 'ethical relativism'; together they have produced a widespread belief that the sociologist can and should avoid value judgements, and that this self-restraint is made all the easier by the fact that values are in any case not matters of judgement. But the social influences may have had a greater effect. Here we should take into account not only the widespread pessimism about the human prospect which arises from the nature and extent of modern war and from the experience of recent totalitarian regimes and dictatorships, but also a quite different phenomenon; namely, the uncertainty about what ends are worthwhile in societies which already enjoy high standards of living. When many of the aims of the nineteenth-century disciples of progress have been achieved, yet without giving all the satisfaction which was anticipated, a doubt arises whether any state of society likely to result from human effort would be ultimately satisfying. At the least, there is a recognition that if the major social evils of ignorance, poverty, and oppression can be overcome, the ends and means of progress become more complex and less easy to determine.

In this respect, there is an immense difference between the Western industrial countries and the low income countries in much of the rest of the world. In the latter the evils of poverty, ill-health, ignorance, and sometimes oppression are still almost untouched, and it is absurd for Western intellectuals to expound their own scepticism concerning progress to the people or political leaders of such countries. There, at least, the line of progress is unmistakable, and sociologists in particular would be well occupied in studying the pre-conditions for overcoming the present great (and increasing) disparity in levels of living between rich and poor countries.

But in any event the idea of progress is still far from being extinct in modern social thought. It has inspired, for the past forty years, the fervent commitment to economic growth in the industrial countries, and subsequently in the Third World. More recently, it has provided the impetus for critical reappraisals of unlimited and uncontrolled economic growth, and has animated powerful ecology movements in most of the industrial countries, as well as stimulating renewed debates about the nature of a 'good society' in relation to the rapid advance of science and technology, and to unrestrained 'consumerism' (Habermas, 1968–9). And this persistence of the idea should occasion no surprise, for it is inescapable that sociology, and other social sciences, should justify their studies in part – even in large part – by the contribution which they can make to human progress.

Nevertheless, the difficulties encountered in the theories of evolution, development or progress, as well as changes in the climate of opinion, led to a general adoption of the term 'social change' to refer to all the historical variations in human societies. The diffusion of this more neutral term was aided by the publication of the book by Ogburn (1922) in which, after discussing conceptions of social evolution, and examining in detail the role of biological and cultural factors in social change, he made a distinction between material and non-material culture and advanced the hypothesis of 'cultural lag', according to which changes in the adaptive culture (i.e. a part of the non-material culture) do not synchronize exactly with the changes in material culture and thus become a source of stresses and conflicts. Ogburn's analysis has some affinity with earlier studies; in particular, with Alfred Weber's distinction between culture and civilization, and with the distinction made by Marx between 'basis' and 'superstructure'. Ogburn's treatment of the problems is different, especially in the attention which he pays to the process of invention, but he has in common with the writers mentioned that he concentrates upon the changes which have originated in the sphere of material production since the advent of modern industrialism. It is indeed within such a context that most recent studies of social change have been made. Thus, we have numerous studies of the demographic trends in industrial societies, of changes in the family, in the class structure, in law and religion. But there has been lacking, for the most part, any systematic consideration of the interrelations between the various changes, or any comparative study of changes occurring in different times and places, or finally any general view of the main directions of change such as was formulated in earlier theories by Hobhouse, Marx or, in a more tentative way, Max Weber. Only in the recent discussions of 'developing countries', and the still more recent revival of interest in the prospects for radical change in the industrial societies, is it possible to discern a new attempt to formulate or reformulate a more general theory of social change.

Theories of Social Change

The major theories of social change which have so far been propounded have been closely associated with a philosophy of history or a 'philosophical anthropology' (Löwith, 1932). They can be classified in various ways, but it is convenient to make a preliminary distinction between linear and cyclical theories. Among the former the most significant are those of Comte, Spencer, Hobhouse and Marx. Comte's theory, which derives from Saint-Simon, and more remotely from Condorcet, explains social change as the outcome of intellectual development, which is formulated in the 'law of three stages' as a progress from theological modes of thought, through the metaphysical mode to the positive mode of thought represented by modern science. This intellectual progress is accompanied by moral development, especially the growing predominance of altruism over egoism, and by changes in social institutions.

> Human activity, as I have long since shown, passes successively through the stages of Offensive warfare, Defensive warfare, and Industry. The connection of these stages with the preponderance of

the theological, the metaphysical or the positive spirit respectively, leads at once to a complete explanation of history. (Vol. 3, ch. 1)

Recent criticisms of Comte have been largely concerned with the deterministic character of his theory (Berlin, 1954), or with its 'totalitarian implications' (Hayek, 1952). It is open to objection on other counts: its claim to have discovered the laws of social evolution, its assumption concerning the influence of intellectual development upon moral ideas, and its assertions, unsupported by any detailed evidence, of a close correspondence between the state of knowledge and the type of social structure. But Comte's analysis of the influence of modern scientific knowledge retains some value, as does his discussion of the characteristics of industrial society and their bearing upon the prevalence of war (Aron, 1958).

Spencer's theory of social change was in some respects more comprehensive, and was based upon more adequate empirical data, than that of Comte. Spencer recognized more fully the variety of factors involved in social change, but also the difficulties of demonstrating evolution in each particular society. On the latter question he observed that 'though taking the entire assemblage of societies, evolution is inevitable, it cannot be held inevitable in each particular society or indeed probable' (Spencer, 1876–96, Vol. 1, p. 107). In discussing the actual course of social evolution he regarded as important features the increasing differentiation of function within societies, and the increasing size of societies (the latter brought about largely by warfare). But his analysis of social change ultimately depended upon a theory (long since rejected) of cosmic evolution, according to which there is a universal movement from 'an indefinite unstable homogeneity' to a 'definite stable heterogeneity'. Spencer did not in fact show how the societies he studied might be systematically arranged in an evolutionary sequence.[4]

Hobhouse was strongly influenced by both Comte and Spencer, but his theory of social change was worked out in a more rigorous way and his use of historical and anthropological data was more scholarly and critical. From Comte he took the idea that the development of the human mind was the crucial factor in social development, but he did not accept Comte's dogmatic positivism, and he was able to support his account of mental development with a much sounder psychological theory (to which he made independent contributions). Thus he distinguished five stages in the intellectual history of mankind,[5] and set out to demonstrate the growth of rationality in all spheres of thought rather than accepting Comte's too simple contrast between theology, metaphysics and science. He was also indebted to Comte for a method which involves studying the development of particular spheres of social activity through the whole history of mankind, and not the development of particular societies or types of society. Except in the case of primitive societies Hobhouse does not attempt a systematic classification of societies, nor does he examine in detail any specific process of social change. The principal criticism of his sociological approach is that which Durkheim brought against Comte; namely, that he deals with an abstraction, humanity, and not with actual societies as intelligible objects of study. From Spencer, Hobhouse adopted the notion of social evolution or development as a process of increase in scale, complexity and internal differentiation. Thus his conception of social change is that the development of mind brings about social development (estimated by the criteria mentioned); and further that since this mental development includes a development of moral ideas towards the ideal of a rational ethic, which transforms the major social institutions, it can be regarded as progressive.

Marx's theory of history – generally referred to as 'historical materialism' – has had a far broader and more profound influence than any alternative view, not only in sociology but in the other social sciences, and particularly in economic and social history. As Isaiah Berlin (1963, p. 158) wrote of it:

> In the sharpness and clarity with which this theory formulates its questions, in the rigour of the method by which it proposes to search for the answers, in the combination of attention to detail and power of wide comprehensive generalization, it is without parallel. Even if all its specific conclusions were proved false, its importance in creating a wholly new attitude to social and historical questions, and so opening new avenues of human knowledge, would be unimpaired.

In Marx's theory two elements in social life have a pre-eminent place: the development of technology (productive forces) and the relations between social classes. Briefly, the theory states that there corresponds to a particular stage in the development of productive forces a definite mode of production and system of class relations, which is stabilized and maintained by the dominant class. But the continuing development of productive forces changes the relations between classes, and the conditions of their conflict, and in due course the hitherto dominated class is able to overthrow the existing mode of production and system of social relationships and to establish a new social order.[6] Marx himself only sketched his theory of historical change; he used it as a 'guiding thread' (or as we should now say, a hypothesis) for research, and devoted his powers to the analysis of one complex historical phenomenon, the emergence and growth of modern capitalism. Later Marxists have had to grapple with an array of problems that arise from this theory in its most general form: the precise relation between economic 'base' and political/cultural 'superstructure', the extent to which class conflict has played a determining part in all major historical transformations, the nature of capitalist development in the twentieth century, the origins and character of the existing socialist societies. The revival of Marxist thought in the past few decades has produced not only reassessments of the general theory of historical materialism (Habermas, 1976; Larrain, 1986), but also diverse reconsiderations of the stages of development (Kiernan, 1983) and particular transitions (Holton, 1985), and of the fundamental characteristics of 'advanced' or 'late' capitalism in relation to a transition to socialism (Habermas, 1973, pt 2; Mandel, 1975; Bottomore, 1985).

The linear theories which I have discussed had the great merit that they delineated, in one form or another, a number of significant cumulative changes in human social history: the growth of knowledge, the development of human productive powers, the increasing scale and complexity of societies, and in modern times the growing movement towards social and political equality. They all recognized the particular significance of the changes which occurred in Europe from the seventeenth century – the development of modern science and industry – which subsequently transformed human social life throughout the world. The cyclical theories of social change depict other aspects of human history, but they ignore these fundamental facts. Pareto (1916) presented in his theory of the circulation of elites an interpretation of history according to which social change is brought about by the struggle between groups for political power, and there are alternating periods of harsh rule by a vigorous and newly triumphant elite, and of mild, humanitarian rule by a declining elite. The theory rests upon the assertion of biological differences between groups within society (derived from the racist theories of Ammon and others), and is supported by little historical evidence. Pareto only seriously investigates one instance of the circulation of elites, namely in ancient Rome, and his conception of political change wholly ignores the growth of democratic government in modern times (which he particularly detested).[7] More recently, Sorokin and Toynbee have presented theories which have some cyclical features. Sorokin (1937), while recognizing the occurrence of linear processes, draws attention to other cyclical processes which occur within human societies. He also makes a distinction between three broad types of culture – ideational, idealist and sensate – which he conceives as succeeding each other in cycles in the history of societies. Toynbee's theory is expounded in his massive ten–volume study (1934–56). Its cyclical character is expressed in the conception of the growth, arrest and decay of civilizations; but the theory is, perhaps, in a more fundamental sense, linear, for according to Toynbee the different civilizations, 'though they are certainly separate individuals, are also representatives of a single species and are also engaged upon an identical enterprise . . . The differentiating Yang-movement of growth is leading towards a goal which is a Yin-state of integration' (Vol. 3, p. 390). The process of growth and decay of civilizations is a vehicle of progressive religious revelation, and its consummation a 'communion with God'. In the work of both Sorokin and Toynbee the mass of historical analogies, and the oracular style, obscure the analysis of historical change, despite the many illuminating comments upon particular social transformations. They represent a return to philosophy of history in the grand manner.

In the theories I have considered, whether linear or cyclical, relatively little attention was given to the analysis of particular processes of social change or to the discrimination of the factors involved in social change. The major exceptions are Marx and Sorokin: the former studied in great detail one historical transformation, and the latter discussed at length the different factors which produce change. In the next chapter I shall turn to this more detailed analysis.

Notes to Chapter 17

1   There are other difficulties which are indicated in the brief discussion of the term 'development' by Ernest Nagel, 'Determinism and development' (1957). Nagel points out that the term has not only a backward reference in the suggestion that something latent or hidden is progressively made manifest, but also a prospective one: 'it possesses a strong teleological flavour'. This is apparent in the examples we have given; for instance, the development of a child is related to some known characteristics of the adult human being. In the case of social phenomena we can relate the development of knowledge to a condition of more extensive and exact knowledge, and the development of control over nature to such things as survival

and population size. But the development of society as such can hardly be related to any prospective condition of society except in terms of a moral ideal, and development then becomes synonymous with progress.

2 For the history of the idea see Bury, 1920; Ginsberg, 1953; Nisbet, 1980.

3 'By evolution I mean any sort of growth; by social progress, the growth of social life in respect of those qualities to which human beings attach, or can rationally attach, value' (*Social Evolution and Political Theory*, 1911, p. 8). In this book, which is infrequently mentioned, Hobhouse gives an admirably clear account of his sociological approach and principal conclusions.

4 For a general account of Spencer's theory see Rumney, 1934. Spencer's major influence was in America rather than England, and there is a good critical account of the theory of social evolution in Hofstadter, 1955. Some of Spencer's ideas were more recently revived by Talcott Parsons in *Societies: Evolutionary and Comparative Perspectives* (1966).

5 These were: (1) the beginnings of articulate thought in pre-literate societies, (2) proto-science in the ancient East (Babylon, Egypt and ancient China), (3) the stage of reflection in the later East (from the eighth to the fifth centuries BC in China, Palestine and India), (4) the stage of critical and systematic thought in Greece, and (5) the development of modern scientific thought from about the sixteenth century.

6 'At a certain stage of their development, the material forces of production in society come in conflict with the existing relations of production, or – what is but a legal expression for the same thing – with the property relations within which they had been at work before. From forms of development of the forces of production these relations turn into their fetters. Then occurs a period of social revolution.' (Karl Marx, 1859, Preface)

7 Pareto's theory is outlined, more or less sympathetically, in Burnham, 1943, and is cogently criticized in Borkenau, 1936. See also Bottomore, 1964.

18 Factors in Social Change

General Considerations

A sociological analysis of social change requires models which are more specific than most of the general theories I discussed in the last chapter, although conceived within a broader theory or conceptual scheme. Gerth and Mills (1954) outlined one such model, in terms of six major questions which can be asked about social changes: (1) what is it that changes? (2) how does it change? (3) what is the direction of change? (4) what is the rate of change? (5) why did change occur or why was it possible? (6) what are the principal factors in social change?

In dealing with the first of these questions it is useful, I think, to define social change as a change in social structure (including here changes in the size of a society), or in particular social institutions, or in the relationships between institutions. Following the distinction proposed earlier between social structure and culture, we might then employ the term 'cultural change' to refer to variations in cultural phenomena such as knowledge and ideas, art, religious and moral doctrines, and so on. Obviously, social and cultural changes are closely linked in many cases; for example, the growth of modern science has been closely associated with changes in economic structure. In other cases, however, the relations may be less close, as in changes of fashion, or changes in the forms of artistic creation.

The questions concerning the manner, direction and rate of change require for their answer historical description and interpretation, such as have been provided, for example, in the various accounts of population changes, of the increasing division of labour in industrial societies, of the changes in the character of the modern Western family and so on. Discussion of the direction of change need not involve any value judgements; the diminishing size of the family, and the increasing size of economic units, are matters of historical fact. But in other cases, the direction of change may be less obvious and may become the subject of divergent interpretations. Moreover, the change itself may be one which is difficult to observe in a detached way, for example, increase in the divorce rate, or the extension of 'bureaucracy'; and discussions of the direction of change are then likely to become closely involved with moral evaluations. Finally, when it is a matter of analysing changes in the total structure of a society, whether it be a historical or present-day society, the line of demarcation between critical analysis and the expression of a social philosophy becomes obscure and uncertain, and can perhaps never be rigorously established. This is apparent if we consider the widely divergent account of the changes taking place in the British welfare state, or in the USSR since the death of Stalin, or in India since the attainment of independence; or, on a larger scale, the contradictory accounts proffered by Marx and Max Weber of the dominant trends of change in capitalist societies.

The rate of change has always interested sociologists, and it is a commonplace to refer to the acceleration of social and cultural change in modern times. Ogburn (1922, pt 2) was one of the first to examine the phenomenon systematically and to undertake quantitative studies of the rate of change, especially in the sphere of technological inventions. He also focused attention upon the discrepancies between the rates of change in different sectors of social life; the hypothesis of 'cultural lag' is concerned with a major disharmony between the rapid growth of technology, and the slower transformation of familial, political and other institutions and of traditional beliefs and attitudes (religious, moral, etc.). In recent decades these problems have acquired greater importance, with the emergence of economic development in the Third World as a major issue in world politics (Hoselitz, 1960). Research has followed two principal lines: sociological studies of the changes in social structure and culture induced by industrialization and the structural disharmonies of the transition period, and psychological studies of the adaptation of individuals to rapid social changes (Mead, 1953, esp. pt 5). The problems have also been studied in the industrial societies, both in the context of changes in the family, in social stratification, in religious and moral ideas, and in law, and from the aspect of *attitudes*, the reactions of the individual to social change, and the implications and consequences in education, crime and delinquency, and mental health. On the other hand, there has been relatively little study of the differences between societies in which change has been rapid but continuous, and societies in which revolutionary and abrupt changes have occurred.

The problem of why change occurred, or why it was possible,

is closely linked with the general problem of the factors in social change and raises very complex issues concerning social causation. Gerth and Mills briefly discuss some of these issues, as for example, the role of individuals in bringing about social change, and the relative influence of material factors and of ideas. Ginsberg (1958) undertook a systematic analysis of the factors which have been invoked by different writers to explain social change: (1) the conscious desires and decisions of individuals (exemplified by the development of the small family system in Western countries); (2) individual acts influenced by changing conditions (e.g. the decline of villeinage in England between 1300 and 1500); (3) structural changes and structural strains (including as one instance the contradictions between forces of production and relations of production emphasized by Marxists); (4) external influences (culture contact, or conquest); (5) outstanding individuals or groups of individuals; (6) a confluence or collocation of elements from different sources converging at a given point (e.g. in revolutions); (7) fortuitous occurrences (e.g. the Norman conquest of England, the Black Death in the fourteenth century, the British conquest of India); and (8) the emergence of a common purpose. The final section of the essay contains an illuminating discussion of the concept of cause in social science, and its connection with teleology. What remains difficult is to determine the weight that should be assigned to different factors, whether in general theories or in studies of particular historical transformations; and in particular, as I shall discuss further below, what importance should be attributed to impersonal 'social forces' as against individual choices and decisions, or how these two elements are related.

In the 1950s, under the influence of the functionalist theory, many sociologists were inclined to disregard problems of change, or to present them in such a way as to suggest that social change is something exceptional. The emphasis was placed upon the stability of social systems and of systems of values and beliefs, and upon consensus rather than diversity and conflict within each society. It is clear, however, that all societies are characterized by both continuity and change, and that a major task of sociological analysis is to discover how the two processes are related to each other. Continuity is maintained by force and by the social controls which I discussed earlier, and especially by education, both formal and informal, which imparts to new generations what may be seen either as an accumulated 'common culture' or as a 'dominant ideology'. On the other hand, there are also certain general conditions which make for social change; the most important being the growth of knowledge, above all in its effects on economic production, and the occurrence of social conflict. The growth of knowledge has not been continuous, nor has it occurred at the same rate in all societies; but since the seventeenth century there has been a more or less steady growth which has now affected all societies. This has become a major condition of recent social change. Conflict, as a condition of social change, may be regarded from different aspects. In the first place, conflict between societies has played an important part historically in bringing about larger social units (as Comte and Spencer recognized), in establishing or reinforcing social stratification (as Oppenheimer, 1907, argued), and in diffusing social and cultural innovations. In modern times international conflict has profoundly influenced the economic and political structure of societies, social policies, and norms of behaviour but these phenomena have hardly received the attention they deserve (see Chapter 12 above). Secondly, conflicts between groups within society have been, and are, a major source of innovation and change. Among these conflicts, that between social classes, although it may not have had the universal and decisive influence attributed to it by Marxists, has been an important agent of change, particularly in modern times. The establishment of political democracy in Western Europe has been very largely the outcome of class struggles.

Finally, we should consider the conflict between generations, which has received much less than its due attention from sociologists.[1] Continuity in society, I have noted, is maintained by imparting the social tradition to new generations through processes of socialization; but socialization is never complete in the sense that new generations exactly re-enact the social life of their predecessors. Always there is criticism, rejection of some aspects of tradition, and innovation. In modern times these features become more prominent because of the general changes which are taking place in the environment, and because of the diversity of norms and values, which allows the new generation to choose, in some degree, between different 'ways of life' or to re-combine diverse elements in the culture in new patterns. It is a significant feature of the industrial societies that a distinctive youth culture and organized youth movements appear, which oppose in various ways the cultural values of the older generations; but the phenomena of inter-generational conflict are also apparent in societies such as India which are undergoing extremely rapid change from one type of society to another.

The early theories of social change, which I examined in the previous chapter, tended to emphasize a single factor in the causation of change. For the most part, however, they were not mono-causal theories (as they are sometimes classified), nor were they deterministic in any strict sense, as has been alleged by some critics (Berlin, 1954). Comte and Spencer both conceived of some ultimate law of social evolution (the development of mind for Comte, and a cosmic process of differentiation for Spencer), but in examining actual social change they took into account many factors, not least the conscious and deliberate acts of individuals. Spencer, for example, did not confine his studies to differentiation within societies, but considered the effects of knowledge, warfare, and other factors in bringing about social change. Marx's theory has often been condemned as mono-causal and deterministic, but his account of social causation is in fact extremely complex, involving several related but distinct phenomena – the forces of production, relations of production, class relations and ideologies – and his doctrine of political action is the very opposite of a deterministic theory.

Nevertheless, these theories raise a number of broad problems which need to be considered. The first (which I mentioned earlier in this chapter, and discussed in relation to the theories of 'social action' in Chapters 2 and 3) is that concerning the part played respectively by individuals and 'social forces' in inducing social change. It should be remarked that the term 'social forces', as I employ it here, does not refer to any forces which are entirely distinct from the actions of individuals, but to values and tendencies which are resultants of the interaction of individuals yet confront any single individual as something external and relatively impervious to his or her individual criticism or influence. As Marx (1852, Section I) expressed it, in a manner still unsurpassed: 'Men make their own history, but they do not make it just as they please; they do not make it under circumstances chosen by themselves, but under circumstances directly encountered, given, and transmitted from the past.'[2] Thus the voluntary acts of individuals enter as constituents into 'social forces', while being constrained and shaped by them; in this sense any individual may contribute to social change, although the effects may only be perceptible when a number of individuals, in the particular circumstances confronting them, begin to act in a new way (for example, by limiting the size of their families, creating trade unions, joining revolutionary movements).

A more specific problem concerns the influence of outstanding individuals. At one extreme, it may be held that all important social and cultural changes are brought about by men of genius; at the other, that men of genius owe all their influence to the fact that they incarnate or represent the dominant social forces or tendencies of their time, as Plekhanov (1898) argued. Neither of these extreme views is acceptable. For one thing, the influence of outstanding individuals may be greater in the field of artistic creation than in that of technology.[3] It would be arbitrary, however, to deny the personal influence of 'great men' in the sphere of morals, religion, politics or economics. In the modern world, Lenin, Gandhi, Hitler and Mao Tse-tung have had a profound influence and it would be difficult to demonstrate that our world would have been just the same had they not lived and acted as they did. Of course, they too confronted a given set of circumstances, and their influence arose in part from their ability to formulate persuasively the latent aspirations, or fears and anxieties, of large numbers of people; but they were also 'charismatic leaders' in Max Weber's value-neutral sense, owing their positions of leadership to personal qualities and imposing upon events, for good or ill, the imprint of their own convictions.

A second major controversy has concerned the role of material factors and ideas in social change. Marxists, it is claimed, attribute a primary influence to material, economic factors, while others (e.g. Comte, Hobhouse) give pre-eminence to the development of thought. One of the principal disputes in sociology is that between Marx and Weber concerning the origins of modern capitalism, in which Weber argued, not that 'ideas rule the world', but that in some historical situations ideas or doctrines may independently affect the direction of social change. It would be a mistake, in any case, to establish a simple opposition between material factors and ideas, for material factors as such do not enter into social behaviour. In Marx's own theory of change the 'forces of production' are a determining element, but they are no more than the applications of science and technology; and the development of the productive forces can only mean the growth of scientific and technical knowledge and ideas. The fundamental problem is to determine the ways in which the growth or arrest of knowledge and thought affect society, in given circumstances of economic development, social structure and political conflict; whether through the influence of science and technology upon economic relationships and class structure, or through the emergence of new religions, moral or philosophical doctrines; and how these diverse strands are connected in particular sequences of change.

Social Change in the Third World

The most common approach in much recent work has been to
treat the developing countries as a present-day instance of a
particular kind of change from traditional society to modern
industrial society. But even if we accept this framework for
understanding the changes which are going on in these societies
there are still many distinctions to be made and alternative
interpretations to consider. The traditional structure and culture
of a society will obviously influence the nature of the changes
which take place, and here we can distinguish broadly between
developing countries in four main regions: Asia, Africa, the
Middle East and Latin America (see Chapter 7 above). Again, the
origins of the process of development – whether it has begun
from a social revolution or in a more gradual way – will
profoundly affect its course. So too will the nature of the relations
– economic, political and cultural – between a developing
country and one or more of the industrial countries. The recognition or neglect of these factors colours the diverse interpretations
of development, and it is not too difficult, as I showed in the
previous chapter, to criticize those economic and sociological
theories of the last few decades which ignored the colonial past,
the economic dominance and political influence of the advanced
industrial countries, and the differences between revolutionary
and non-revolutionary change, in their accounts of the development process. In addition to these factors of a traditional civilization, historical experiences affecting whole regions of the Third
World, and present-day international relations, it is essential
finally to take account of particular elements in each individual
country, so that any account framed in general sociological terms
needs to be complemented by historical and anthropological
studies.

    The case of India will illustrate some of these points. Two
elements have played a decisive part in bringing about social
change in India: first, Western science and technology, and
secondly, social planning. The influence of technology has been
apparent in diverse areas of social life. By the improvement of
living conditions and medical care it has affected the mortality
rate, and is thus largely responsible for the rapid growth of India's
population. The introduction of capitalist industry brought
about changes in the property system[4] and in the division of
labour, and gave rise to new social strata and classes which played
an important part in the political development of India (Desai,
1948). In earlier chapters I have traced some of the effects of

industrialization upon the joint family, property, law and the caste system. But technology did not only bring about change indirectly through the gradual transformation of economic relationships; technology and the scientific thought which was its basis constituted a new view of the world which came into conflict with the traditional culture. Moreover, British rule introduced into India social as well as technological inventions (a new system of government and administration, judicial procedures, forms of education), and new cultural values such as rationalism and, later on, egalitarianism and socialism.

The concept of 'cultural lag' is very relevant to India (as to other developing countries). The development of a modern capitalist economy brought into existence some social movements which rejected traditional Indian culture and others which set out to reform and modernize it; but it is by no means the case that the social institutions and cultural values of present-day India are fully adapted to the way of life of an industrial society, whether capitalist or socialist. The large joint family is not a useful or necessary institution in a modern society where individual mobility is considerable and the provision of welfare services a public responsibility. A caste system is incompatible with the rationality, mobility, and egalitarianism of a democratic society; in India, the principle of caste is unmistakably in conflict with the assumptions of the political regime, with the educational system, and with the needs of industry. The strains involved in this transition are, and have been for some time, apparent in the situation of Indian intellectuals who have to reconcile the divergent claims of two cultures, and in the conflict between generations. There are other conflicts similar to those which occur in industrial societies, notably conflicts between social strata and classes. Caste, like every system of social stratification, involves economic differentiation and economic interest groups, although in the past these features have been partly obscured by the ritual significance of the institution. In conditions of economic change the privileged groups are led to resist innovations which would diminish their own prestige and economic advantage. These various conflicts are, in one sense, sources of change, but they may also retard change over a longer or shorter period, or even produce stagnation or regress.

Social planning, in India as elsewhere, overrides to some extent the conflicts I have mentioned. It represents the factor in social change which has sometimes been described as the emergence of a common purpose, or more often as a movement towards socialism. There is now, in almost all societies, whether industrial or developing, central economic and social planning intended to promote social well-being. The extent and forms of planning vary widely from one society to another but the objectives and implications are similar. For the first time in human history, the mass of the people are drawn into a process of rational and deliberate transformation of their social life; and social change has been brought, to some extent, under purposeful human control. The Indian Constitution of 1950 defined the purposes of the new political system as being to establish social, economic and political justice, liberty of thought, expression, belief and worship, equality of status and opportunity, and fraternity. The Government Planning Commission, established in the same year, was conceived as a major agency for achieving these purposes, although its work has been somewhat narrowly restricted to economic problems.

In recent years the assessments of the Indian way of development have become much more critical than they were during the 1950s in the heyday of Nehru's leadership. Thus Barrington Moore (1966), while he singles out India as the example of a fourth alternative route to the modern world – contrasted with the bourgeois and fascist revolutions of the past, and with the communist revolutions of recent times – deals not only with the factors which made this kind of industrialization possible, but also with what he calls 'the price of peaceful change': the very slow rate of economic development which makes the success of the venture doubtful. In similar fashion Gunnar Myrdal, in his massive study of South Asian countries (1968), arrived at the conclusion that 'much of the momentum in Indian planning has been lost', while fundamental problems of land reform, modernizing village structure, raising levels of agricultural output, and controlling population growth remain unsolved.

On the other side, however, we should take account of some of the benefits of peaceful change. India, unlike many other developing countries, has not succumbed to authoritarian rule, whether it is that of a military elite or of a revolutionary party. In India the hundred flowers, which soon withered in China, can still bloom. Furthermore, those socialist societies in the Third World which were created by revolutions have experienced their own difficulties. White (1983), in his introduction to a valuable collection of studies on the socialist developing countries, argues that 'they constitute a *distinctive* and *viable* mode of development, in terms of certain key social, economic and political indices, and – though this may be true to greater or lesser degrees – *preferable* to hypothetical capitalist alternatives in so far as the interests of the mass of the population are concerned'; but he goes on to recognize that while 'revolutionary socialism has many developmental achievements to its credit' it also 'embodies many basic problems, more or less common to its various national expressions, which are "internal" to this specific mode of development, and which cannot be attributed to objective constraints or external pressures'.

What emerges most clearly from recent studies of the developing countries is the need for a broad comparative perspective, which would also take account of the diverse relationships between these countries and the advanced industrial societies; and at the same time, a *sociological* perspective which would conceive the process of development in a comprehensive way, recognizing the complexity of its goals and not reducing them to a simple matter of technological and economic growth, however important this may be as an underlying factor in social change.

Types of Social Change

A first valuable step in dealing with the issues I have just raised would be the construction of a typology of social change. This would set in perspective the problems of development in the Third World and enable us to avoid at least one prevalent error, which consists in assuming that the industrial countries have attained a definitive form, while the developing countries are simply trying to catch up with them. It is much more accurate to regard the late-twentieth-century world as being involved in a general process of exceptionally rapid change, in which the transformations in one part of the globe influence profoundly the course of events elsewhere. Further, the working out of a typology would lead us on to still more general questions concerning social changes in past as well as present societies: for example, the development of Western capitalism, the rise and decline of earlier civilizations and empires. This would provide a wider basis for comparison and generalization, and would restore to sociology the kind of historical awareness which characterized its origins, but was then extinguished for a time.

Finally, in a period when large numbers of people have become more aware of the potentialities for change in present-day societies, and when there is at the same time a more critical view of the directions and implications of some kinds of change – notably what Gabor (1970) has called 'compulsive (technological) innovation' and 'growth addiction' – it would undoubtedly be useful to have even a very tentative scheme of classification which would indicate some of the causes, limits and consequences of social change. The formulation of such a scheme seems possible in terms of five major questions:

(1)   Where does social change originate? A distinction can first be made between *endogenous* and *exogenous* change, that is, change originating within or outside a particular society. In practice, the origin of change can only rarely be assigned wholly to one or the other category; but it is evident, as I indicated in an earlier chapter (Chapter 12), that war and conquest have played a large part in bringing about major social changes, and in the modern world the changes taking place in the developing countries have been provoked in large measure by Western technology which was introduced in most cases following colonial conquest. But in all societies, including those in which the initial impetus comes from outside, social change depends crucially upon the activities of various social groups within the society; and a major part of sociological analysis consists in identifying the spheres and groups that are principally affected, and the ways in which innovations are diffused from one sphere to another. It is in this context that, for example, Marx's theory of social change through class conflict, various elite theories, and Weber's analysis of the influence of a religious ethic have to be considered as important, if divergent, elements in an explanatory scheme.

(2)   What are the initial conditions from which large-scale changes begin? The initial conditions may profoundly influence the course of social change; it cannot be assumed, for example, that the formation of ancient empires, of feudal states, or of modern capitalist societies, occurred in precisely the same ways or can be accounted for in terms of a single broad and abstract generalization of the kind that Marx (1877) contemptuously dismissed as a 'historical-philosophical theory whose chief quality is that of being supra-historical'. In the present-day world, industrialization is a very different process in tribal societies (as in Africa) and in societies of ancient civilization such as India or China. It is different again according to the size and complexity of the society. The sociological analysis of industrialization as a particular process of change would be greatly helped by a typology of the developing countries themselves.

(3)   What is the rate of change? Social change may occur rapidly in some periods, or in some spheres, and more slowly, perhaps imperceptibly, in others. The rate of change may also be accelerating or decelerating. Ogburn, whose work was referred to earlier, showed that in industrial societies the rate of technolo-

gical change, as measured, for example, by the numbers of patents issued, has been increasing, and it has certainly accelerated rapidly since the Second World War. An important distinction is that between processes of gradual change and processes of revolutionary change (as a particular form of rapid change). In the economic and technological spheres it is not too difficult to identify revolutionary changes, and to trace their causes and effects. Gordon Childe (1956, ch. 5) has admirably described what he terms the 'neolithic revolution', the introduction of a food-producing economy; economic and social historians have documented and analysed in detail the phases of the modern industrial revolution;[5] and in recent years there have been many studies of the new 'scientific and technological revolution'. Social and political revolutions have been studied largely in historical, descriptive terms, but there has also emerged in the last few decades – stimulated by the revival of Marxist theory – a body of more comparative and analytical research (see Chapter 12 above). The twentieth-century social and national revolutions have been closely linked with war, but these connections have not been systematically explored, although one aspect of them – the important role of intellectuals as well as social classes in revolutionary movements – has received greater attention.

(4) To what extent is social change fortuitous, causally determined, or purposive? The principal distinction here is one which I shall discuss more fully in the next chapter in considering social planning. In one sense, of course, almost all social changes are purposive, since they result from the purposive acts of individuals. But such acts may have unintended consequences, because the individual actions are not co-ordinated, and may actually impede or distort each other; for example, in situations of conflict. In such conditions, which have been those of most societies until recent times, change may be causally determined, or there may also be quite fortuitous elements in it, but it is not purposive in the sense that it achieves the purposes of all, or most, of the individuals who are involved. Change may more properly be termed purposive in the case of modern societies, to the extent that a common purpose emerges and may be realized by degrees through a process of planned social change. Even here, of course, fortuitous events may have an influence, and there may be (since planners, like other people, lack omniscience) many unintended consequences. In any case, a common purpose is only very imperfectly achieved in most present-day societies, continuously disrupted by major social conflicts, particularly between classes; and one influential doctrine, expounded pre-eminently by Hayek

(1982), argues that a common purpose is unattainable in a 'free society' and that the only choice is between a totalitarian planned economy and an individualistic free market economy.[6] Nevertheless, it may be claimed that human beings do now have, in some respects at least, a greater control over both the natural and the social conditions of their life – the social sciences themselves being a product of the aspiration to guide social change in desirable (or desired) directions – though in other respects it may seem that humanity is driven ineluctably by the advance of technology, in its productive *and* destructive forms, towards some unintended and undesired end: that, in Emerson's words, 'things are in the saddle and ride mankind'.

(5)   What are the consequences of social change? It is evident that rapid social change is disruptive – giving rise to tension and conflict between generations and between classes and other groups whose position in the established social hierarchy is modified, and creating psychological stress in individuals who have to respond to entirely new situations – and revolutionary change is the most disruptive of all. But the outcome may be either good or bad: a society may fall into decay, or on the contrary rapid change, and especially revolutionary change, may release entirely new forces which produce a great creative explosion in many different spheres of life. Even when that happens, however, there are problems and costs. For two centuries now, and most of all since the end of the Second World War, there has been an enormous emphasis in social thought upon economic growth and technological progress, and although this was questioned by earlier thinkers – for example, in Weber's gloomy vision of a 'disenchanted', bureaucratized and mechanized world – it is mainly in the past two or three decades that critical evaluations of uncontrolled technological innovation and 'growth mania' have become more widespread and insistent. What appears most clearly from recent studies and controversies is that the notion of social change is still inextricably bound up with the ideas of development and progress, because the consequences of change – the problems and dangers that accompany it, ranging from the restructuring of the labour process to environmental damage and the menace of nuclear war – are necessarily the object of evaluative judgements which enter into all reflection upon the probable and desirable future of humanity. It is not the business of the sociologist as such to define a 'good society' or a desirable 'quality of life', but it is his or her responsibility to be aware of these issues, to set out as precisely as possible the alternative courses of change and their implications,

and to show what social forces are at work in producing one outcome rather than another.

Notes to Chapter 18

1 Karl Mannheim was one of the few sociologists to see the importance of the subject, which he discussed in an illuminating essay, 'The problem of generations' (1927b). Since I first wrote this comment (in 1962) the conflict between generations has become a major theme of discussion; the problem which it presents is that of understanding how the more or less universal phenomenon of youthful revolt can acquire, in certain periods, a very great and even preponderant influence in promoting social and cultural change, as it appeared to do in the late 1960s.

2 See also Marx's formulation of this idea in the exposition of his conception of history in Marx and Engels (1845–6, Vol. I, pt I, sect. A, 1)

> at each stage of history there is found a material result, a sum of productive forces, a historically created relation of individuals to nature and to one another, which is handed down to each generation from its predecessors, a mass of productive forces, capital and circumstances, which is indeed modified by the new generation, but which also prescribes for it its conditions of life and gives it a definite development, a special character.

3 Although there are evidently social influences upon art, as is argued in diverse ways not only in Marxist studies (Laing, 1978) but, for example, in Max Weber's essay on the development of Western music (in *Economy and Society*, 1921). For a general discussion of aesthetics and the sociology of art see Wolff, 1983.

4 See Gopal, 1949, and Mukherjee, 1957, ch. 1. Similar changes occurred in other Third World countries during the colonial period, for example, in Africa as a result of the growth of commercial agriculture and the erosion of tribal ownership of land (Lloyd, 1967, ch. 3).

5 The changes in the economic system and in social attitudes are vividly presented in Heilbroner, 1952, ch. 2; and see also Polanyi, 1944.

6 For a criticism of Hayek's argument see Bottomore, 1985, ch. 4.

Notes on Reading for Part V

The Idea of Progress

Bury, J. B., *The Idea of Progress* (1920).
Ginsberg, Morris, *The Idea of Progress: A Revaluation* (1953).
Nisbet, Robert, *History of the Idea of Progress* (1980).

Social Evolution and Development

Childe, V. Gordon, *Man Makes Himself* (1956), chs. 1 and 2.
Ginsberg, M., 'The concept of evolution in sociology' (1932).
Hofstadter, R., *Social Darwinism in American Thought* (1955).
Ritchie, D. G., *Darwinism and Politics* (1889).
Sorokin, P. A., 'Sociocultural dynamics and evolutionism' (1945).

A major criticism of evolutionary theories on grounds of logic and method is K. R. Popper, *The Poverty of Historicism* (1957).

The concept of development as used in recent discussions of 'developing countries' is examined from different points of view in:

Alavi, Hamza and Shanin, Teodor (eds.), *Introduction to the Sociology of 'Developing Societies'* (1982).
Aron, Raymond, *The Industrial Society* (1966), chs. 1 and 2.
Bernstein, Henry (ed.), *Underdevelopment and Development* (1973).

The literature on economic growth, in particular, is now very extensive, but the following books provide useful introductions to the main issues:

Agarwala, A. N. and Singh, S. P. (eds.), *The Economics of Underdevelopment* (1963).
Lewis, W. Arthur, *The Theory of Economic Growth* (1955).
Myrdal, Gunnar, *Economic Theory and Underdeveloped Regions* (1957).

And on some of the limits to growth in advanced industrial societies see the work of Fred Hirsch, *Social Limits to Growth* (1977) which has provoked much debate.

Social Change

Cowell, F. R., *History, Civilization and Culture* (1952).
    Provides a useful short exposition of Sorokin's concept of social and cultural change.
Ogburn, W. F., *Social Change* (1922).
Smith, Anthony, *Social Change* (1976).
Wilson, G. and M., *The Analysis of Social Change* (1945).

On the Marxist theory see Marx and Engels, *The German Ideology*

(1845–6), Vol. 1, pt 1, and the following studies:

Kiernan, V. G., 'Stages of development' (1983).
Shaw, William H., *Marx's Theory of History* (1978).

There is a large literature on particular historical transitions as well as on Marx's general concepts, some of which is cited in the text and in the works mentioned above.

PART VI

Sociology and Social Practice

19 Sociology, Social Policy and Social Planning

The Formation of Social Policy

Sociology was conceived by many nineteenth-century thinkers as providing the theoretical foundation for a comprehensive applied science. Such views were especially prevalent in France, where the idea of a natural science of society was transmitted from the *encyclopédistes* through Saint-Simon and others to Comte, who believed that sociology, as the summation of positive science, could establish universal laws of social behaviour by reference to which all disputes about social policy might be settled. The 'anarchy of opinions' would then come to an end in social matters as it had done in the case of natural phenomena. Durkheim, although he rejected much of Comte's sociology, was nonetheless a positivist in the Comtean tradition, who wished to establish an applied moral and political science on the basis of a theoretical science of society. Marxism, as it actually developed in the practice of many Communist parties, had much in common with Comte's positivism. There was the same appeal to historical laws, and the same claim that an elite instructed in the science of society could resolve definitively all practical social problems and guide mankind infallibly along the path of social progress.

At the present time few sociologists would regard their discipline as a developed theoretical science capable of being applied to social affairs in the way that theoretical physics or chemistry is applied to the control and transformation of the material world. They are deterred, in the first place, by the fact that after more than a century of sociological thought and research few, if any, important sociological laws have been discovered. In this situation the question of applying general laws can hardly arise. They may also doubt the value of the analogy between natural science and sociology in respect of their practical application; for it is inconsistent with our ordinary notions of ourselves as individuals, and with our respect for other human beings, to think of sociological principles being directly applied by 'experts' to the shaping of social life, as physical principles are applied to the construction of roads and bridges. For this reason, and for others to be discussed later, there can be no 'social engineering'. This is not to deny, however, that sociology can be of practical use in a number of different ways, and at different levels. In this chapter I shall first consider in general terms the contribution of sociology to social policy, and then examine its role in social planning; in the following chapter I shall discuss some of the sociological research which has aimed to provide solutions to specific social problems.

The first important contribution to be noted is that of *descriptive sociology*, which has provided more exact and reliable information upon those matters of social policy with which politicians, administrators and social reformers have to deal. Among the earliest sociological researches, especially in Britain, were the surveys (including official surveys) of poverty and other problems of urban life, from the mid-nineteenth century onwards. Such surveys, which became increasingly numerous, and particularly those of Booth (1891–1903) and Rowntree (1901) at the end of the nineteenth century, showed in detailed and rigorous fashion the extent and nature of poverty in an industrial society. Moreover, Booth and Rowntree were able to indicate some of the causes of extreme poverty: the lack of regular employment, and the accidents or illnesses suffered by wage earners. These and similar researches undoubtedly influenced social policy, and a later study by Rowntree and Lavers (1951) argued that the policies of the welfare state (in particular, the maintenance of full employment and more adequate national provision for the emergencies of illness or accident) had almost entirely eradicated primary poverty (i.e. an absolute lack of essential resources). In the 1960s, however, there was a rediscovery of poverty in the affluent Western societies (Harrington, 1962; Abel-Smith and Townsend, 1965), though these studies do not deal so much with 'primary poverty' as with the condition of social groups which have fallen below the general level of well-being, and the questions they pose concern the extent of economic inequality in the capitalist industrial societies (Townsend, 1979). In the 1980s poverty has increased considerably as a result of the economic crisis and mass unemployment, especially in Britain, and the documentation of its scope and effects will again, no doubt, ultimately affect social policies.

In a number of other spheres sociologists have provided essential data for effective policy-making. Population studies have not only furnished exact information on population size, fertility and mortality, but have also indicated some of the social factors responsible for demographic changes. Studies of social mobility, which reveal the extent and forms of mobility in different societies and show the connections between mobility and such factors as family size, educational opportunity, and the occupational and class structure, provide essential knowledge for educational reforms, besides contributing to the discussion of more remote ends of social policy.

But although the growth of sociological research since 1945 has added greatly to the body of precise information on social matters, our knowledge is still deficient. As Glass (1950) pointed out in the early days of postwar social research in Britain, important social policies are still formulated and implemented without any research into the ends or means proposed (as in the case of the New Towns policy, which established in an arbitrary fashion the size and density of the towns); and major social services are administered without much attempt to discover whether they meet the needs for which they were designed, or meet them in the most effective way, or indeed whether the needs themselves have not changed in a rapidly changing society. Similarly, Titmuss (1958) drew attention to the lack of social research which would 'identify and measure the more subtle and complex needs of today and their distribution among the different sections of the population'.

In few countries has social (as distinct from economic) research yet become firmly established as a normal part of government and administration; although it has gained a more prominent place in the postwar period. In India (as in other Third World countries) comprehensive planning favoured social research; thus the Research Programmes Committee of the Planning Commission played an important part in encouraging and sponsoring research in a number of fields which directly concern government planning,[1] and the Programme Evaluation Organization made a promising beginning with studies of the effectiveness of Plan projects in several areas.

Some similar developments may be noted in Western Europe. In Britain, for example, the Government Social Survey (established in 1941) made numerous surveys on behalf of government departments, and this work has been continued by the Social Survey Division of the Office of Population Censuses and Surveys; the Department of Scientific and Industrial Research sponsored much social research into industrial problems; and the Home Office established a research section to conduct studies in the field of crime and delinquency. The Danish Parliament established, in 1958, a National Institute of Applied Social Research to undertake a continuing programme of research on problems of social welfare. But much remains to be done if the social sciences are to make their full contribution to administration in modern societies. It would be useful, in the first place, to review the range of social data at present collected by governments, and to examine the use which is made of such information and the influence which it has upon social policy. This would provide a starting point for an extension and rationalization of government social research, which should ultimately lead to the establishment of national research centres. The function of such national research centres would be to conduct specific inquiries needed for policy-making, but also to collect on a regular basis information on the major aspects of social life, and to publish it in the form of surveys of social conditions. Most governments now collect basic economic information which they publish regularly along with general surveys of the economic situation. But it is essential, in a modern society, to extend this service to a much wider range of social questions, which should include crime and delinquency, dependency, housing, health, education, levels of living, family budgets and environmental matters. The value of such data collection and survey is shown by the United Nations *Report on the World Social Situation* (first published in 1961), but such international surveys would clearly be easier to compile and more comprehensive if there were more adequate publication of national data. In Britain a welcome beginning was made with the annual publication of *Social Trends* (beginning in 1970), and there have been similar developments in other countries (e.g. in the USA, the Federal Republic of Germany and France).

The role of the sociologist in policy-making also needs to be reconsidered. This is no doubt only one aspect of a more general problem concerning the relation between 'scientists' and 'administrators' in the multifarious activities of modern governments; but the position of sociologists (and of other social scientists, with the possible exception of economists) has been exceptionally disadvantageous. Those engaged in social research for government seem to have had, as a rule, little say in defining the scope of particular inquiries, or in relating the results to policy decisions. Their discoveries are simply used by those who have the main responsibility for policy-making and administration, and the latter may be as much influenced by the 'conventional wisdom' as

by the results of systematic inquiry, if they know nothing about
the background and further implications of the research.

The contribution of descriptive sociology should not be
limited to providing information which is useful at the stage of
formulating and introducing new social policies; it is equally
important in evaluating the operation and achievements of these
policies. But there are still few evaluation studies of this practical
kind. As a report by a Danish Government Committee on the
Establishment of an Institute for Applied Social Research
observed:

> It is the view of the Committee that the legislature, the administra-
> tion and the general public has not at hand sufficient material for
> analysis of the functioning of the social services, their effects on the
> individual and other effects, *inter alia* on the national economy. The
> material at hand does not give sufficient basis for judgment whether
> the means used, in money or in organization, are put to the best
> possible use and are invested in the most important points . . . (quoted
> in Friis, 1959)

A few research institutes in other countries have, in recent years,
undertaken inquiries in this field (for example, of the reactions
of individuals and families to re-housing in new areas, and of
'consumer' attitudes towards the health services and education),
but these are isolated instances, and there are few signs of any
systematic programme of research. It is surprising that even in
those countries which have embarked upon radical planned
changes in economic and social life, little advantage has been
taken of the opportunities for social experiments which would
allow a more exact evaluation of different policies. The use of
experiment in social affairs is, of course, limited both by its cost
and by the obligation to respect the interests and rights of those
individuals who would be affected by it, but there are many
spheres in which small-scale experiments could be made without
great expense and without harming individuals: for example, in
town planning, in the provision of education, in policies concerned with juvenile delinquency, in the treatment of offenders.
Indeed, some policies in these various fields are often referred to
as 'experimental', but in fact they almost always lack the essential
feature of an experiment, namely the systematic comparative
examination of the results produced by different courses of
action.

It is not only those who may be called professional sociologists
who make use of sociological knowledge. The social sciences
generally have begun to influence social policy in another way,
through their part in the education and training of those who are

concerned with the formation and execution of policy. Sociology now has an important place in the training of social workers, and it is becoming recognized as a useful element in the training of industrial managers, personnel officers, teachers, and public officials responsible for the administration of social welfare services or of publicly owned enterprises. The value of sociology for these occupations is not, in most cases, that it provides the individual with sociological principles which can be applied directly to the solution of practical problems. It is rather that the individual who has acquired a broad general knowledge of different types of social structure and culture, has studied in greater detail the structure and history of his own society, and has learned something of the methods by which data on social matters may be collected and evaluated is thereby enabled to form more reasonable judgements and to make wiser decisions in dealing with the social problems which he confronts.

The increasing use of sociological research, and the desire of sociologists themselves to make a practical contribution, raises questions not only about how sociology *can* be applied but also about how it *ought* to be applied. In the preceding discussion I have taken for granted that the social policies are themselves good or desirable. But this assumption conceals a host of problems, which should be briefly noticed, though they cannot be fully examined here. For my part I consider that sociologists in the practical application of their discipline are necessarily committed to the improvement of social life, or, in the language of earlier writers, to social progress; and that this commitment prescribes for them certain fields of inquiry while proscribing others. An analogy may be drawn between applied sociology and medicine, as has been done by Gouldner (1956) in an informative essay. Gouldner distinguishes between an 'engineering' approach and a 'clinical' approach in applied sociology. The former is characterized by the fact that the client's formulation of the problem is accepted by the sociologist, who is concerned only to discover efficient ways of solving the problem; the latter by the fact that the sociologist (like a doctor) is not restricted, and is generally recognized as not being restricted, to the client's own definition of the problem, which he may indeed regard as one of the symptoms of the underlying difficulties. In recommending the clinical approach Gouldner is concerned partly with the effectiveness of the method, and partly with the values which should guide applied sociological research. He does not, however, consider an important difference between medicine and applied sociology. The practice of medicine is founded upon the doctor's commitment, which is in the great majority of cases precise and unambiguous, to maintain health and combat disease. Applied sociology is not based upon any precise commitment, for 'social welfare' or 'improvement' may be matters not of direct and unanimous appraisal but of conflicting judgements. The terms 'social health' and 'social disease' (or 'social pathology') which are sometimes employed are ambiguous and largely inappropriate; for it is not so much the health of a society (defined perhaps as its ability to survive) as the quality of its life which is a matter of concern, and on the other side what are taken to be diseases may subsequently be seen as unavoidable disorders accompanying healthy growth,[2] or more commonly they may be differently evaluated by different observers.[3]

I do not wish to conclude either that there is no intelligible standard by which applied sociology may be guided; or, in the opposite sense, that it is the business of sociologists themselves to declare authoritatively what constitutes welfare or progress. It should be recognized, in the first place, that very often the difficulties I have mentioned do not arise; there is near unanimity on the definition of many social evils. But where there is no agreement sociologists can make a practical contribution by clarifying the points of controversy, by assessing in the light of facts the received interpretations of a social problem, and, especially, by viewing alternative social policies in relation to the structure of society as a whole. In the latter case, sociologists necessarily produce ideas and data which become materials for social criticism, because they are obliged to take account of the influence upon social policy of established inequalities in the wealth and power of different social groups, and to describe how, in turn, different kinds of policy work to the advantage or disadvantge of particular groups. The exclusive insistence, in much sociology, upon a rigorous 'scientific method' (often narrowly conceived in 'empiricist' terms) has tended to create an unduly conservative outlook; the existing framework of society is accepted as given, because it is too complex for scientific study, and all the resources of a truly 'scientific' sociology are then marshalled for the investigation of small-scale problems carefully isolated from the wider social structure. It is desirable, therefore, to emphasize once more as the distinctive feature of sociological thought that it attempts to grasp every specific problem in its whole social context, and to conceive of alternative social policies which affect the entire life of society.[4]

The critical function of sociology can best be seen in its least tangible, but perhaps most important, influence upon social life;

that which is exerted through the instruction of the general
public or, at least, of that part of the public which has a sustained
interest in social and political affairs. Here sociology provides a
framework of concepts, and a basis of exact knowledge, for the
intelligent discussion of political issues.[5] The usefulness of sociological inquiry from this point of view is admirably illustrated in
an essay by Titmuss (1958) on 'The social division of welfare', in
which he explores some of the assumptions which have guided
thinking about social policy in Britain, and particularly the
assumption about the extent to which social welfare plans have
been implemented and about the effects which the social services
have had in redistributing income from rich to poor. His analysis reveals the many difficulties which confront the modern
search for equality, and the ever-renewed sources of social
inequality and dependency. He is sceptical about the egalitarian
effects of the social services, since the latter are too narrowly
defined, and other types of collective provision which tend to
increase inequality, are left out of account. The three distinct
systems of social service (social, fiscal and occupational) taken
together are, he says, 'enlarging and consolidating the areas of
social inequality'. In other essays in this volume Titmuss examines the age structure of the population in relation to some
popular views on the burden of dependency involved by an
ageing population, and some of the problems created by the
conflicting standards of behaviour expected of the working-class
father in the family and in industry. These essays contribute
directly to informed public discussion of major issues of social
policy, and they are firmly grounded in modern sociological
thought and research.

Another example may be taken from the field of educational
policy. Discussions of education, in Britain and in other industrial societies, have had to take account of sociological investigations which show the connections between social class origin,
educational opportunity and achievement. In so far as public
policy, or the policies of particular social groups, aim to establish equality of opportunity in education, and to extend and
improve the national system of education, they must pay attention to the results of sociological research which show the
sources and mechanisms of inequality, and the factors in poor
scholastic performance, and which suggest ways of eradicating
them.

In this critical function, and as a source of deliberate social
change, sociology has differed greatly from social anthropology
which was, for a long time, closely connected with colonial

administration. Evans-Pritchard (1951, pp. 109–10) observed that

> if it is the policy of a colonial government to administer a people through their chiefs it is useful to know who are the chiefs and what are their functions and authority and privileges and obligations. Also, if it is intended to administer a people according to their own laws and customs one has first to discover what these are.

Firth (1956, ch. 7) also emphasized the help which anthropological studies can give to the administrator who has to deal with the problems of social change resulting both from internal development and from contact with the colonial power. Both writers acknowledged that anthropology could only be applied within the limits of the colonial government's settled policy.

It is also worth noting that social anthropologists and sociologists have stood in quite different relations to their subject matter. The members of tribal societies do not, on the whole, read the anthropological monographs which are written about them; whereas some members of industrial societies do read the works of sociologists. Thus a sociologist often arouses, and expects to arouse, some response in some of the people he is studying; and this not only influences his study, but also affects in some degree, however modest, public opinion and attitudes. It is the ending of the colonial empires, much more than the fact that so many tribal societies have now been exhaustively studied, which accounts for the transformation of social anthropological studies, and for the *rapprochement* between social anthropology and sociology in respect of theoretical work and policy research.

The practical influence of sociology may be wider than has yet been indicated. Beyond the public which has a sustained interest in social affairs, a larger section of the population may be led, through the media of mass communication and the educational system, to consider some social problems and issues of social policy in a more informed way, to recognize the conflicts of interest that are involved, and to take more seriously their participation in democratic decision-making. But this process has not yet gone very far. As I noted in a paper contributed to a seminar on 'Social research in the public sector':

> The problems here concern how effectively the diffusion of information takes place. Much government research is published, but I do not think that it is at all adequately discussed or disseminated by the mass media. Thus, I find it surprising that in Britain the annual publication of *Social Trends* is virtually ignored by the press and by television, although it would provide an excellent occasion for a

regular national stock-taking. This is only one aspect of a more
general neglect of long term political debate, and an excessive
concentration of attention upon immediate problems, which reflects
perhaps the trend towards technocracy indicated by Habermas. At all
events, one major problem in the flow of information gained from
social research seems to me to involve not only government, but the
mass media, and more broadly the whole climate of political life.
(Bottomore, 1978b, p. 5)

In the various ways I have outlined – by the exact description of
social problems, the search for causes and remedies, the training
of social workers and administrators, the education of public
opinion, the revelation of inequalities and privileges and of the
political controversies to which they give rise – sociology has in
fact contributed to the realization of an ideal which was formulated, in a manner too dogmatic and naive, by its founders: the
participation of all human beings in the control of their social
conditions of life, a self-directing humanity. In the following
section I shall briefly consider one of the most distinctive modern
manifestations of such self-direction, namely, the process of
planned social change.

Social Planning

There is some degree of social planning in all modern societies.
Up to the present it has been conceived largely in terms of the
control and direction of economic activity, and sociologists have
had a relatively small part in the process. This is the case even
where, as in the developing countries, the sociological aspects of
economic growth are particularly apparent. But the relevance
and importance of sociological knowledge is becoming more
widely recognized; there is now a considerable literature on the
social aspects of economic growth, and those economists who
have been particularly concerned with problems of economic
development (e.g. Lewis, Myrdal, whose writings were discussed in the previous chapter) have drawn extensively upon
sociological theory and research.

In the 1920s and 1930s there was considerable debate about the
possibility of 'rational calculation' and 'rational' economic planning in a socialist economy, initiated by critics of socialism
(Weber, 1921; von Mises, 1922; Hayek, 1935). This debate has
now largely subsided, as Brus (1964, p. 41) indicated:

post-war non-Marxist literature is very little concerned with the
question of economic calculation in a socialist economy. At most it is

interested in the usefulness of applying one form or another of this calculation and with the assumptions on which it ought to be based . . . The reasons for this shift of emphasis are not difficult to find. They issue from the eloquence of the economic experience of the socialist countries and from the changes which have led to an increase in the economic role of the state in some capitalist countries.

Attention has shifted to other, more sociological, questions about the functioning of a socialist economy, and about the operation and development of a planned society as a whole – questions which concern above all the phenomena of over-centralization and bureaucracy in relation to individual freedom, democracy, and in the economic sphere the efficiency of management and of production in general. At the same time, the problems of economic calculation have declined in importance with changes in the socialist planned economies themselves, first in Yugoslavia and more recently in other countries of Eastern Europe and in China, towards what has been called a 'socialist market economy'.

It is evident that until recently the role of sociologists in the analysis or implementation of planned social change was quite limited in both capitalist and socialist industrial countries, though they were rather more prominent in some Third World countries (and notably in India). For the most part they remained external critics, pointing to some of the reasons for difficulties and failures in the achievement of economic and social plans, as is well illustrated in the discussion by Ossowski (1959) of inadequacies and mistakes in Polish planning, and by studies of 'bureaucratism' such as that of Hegedüs (1976). But we should not suppose that sociologists will continue to be confined mainly to a critical role, important though this is, or that their studies will be largely restricted to the social factors in planned economic growth. An illuminating study by Ferge (1979) analyses 'societal policy' (defined as encompassing the sphere of social policy but also including 'systematic social intervention at all points of the cycle of the reproduction of social life, with the aim of changing the structure of society') in the development of Hungarian society, and indicates how sociologists can intervene positively in the construction and implementation of broad social plans; in this case with the aim of 'organizing life in a socialist way'. It may be expected that as the scale of economic and social planning increases – notwithstanding local and temporary reversions to less planned forms of society – sociologists (as well as other social scientists) will become increasingly involved; but if that is to occur they will need to devote a great deal more of their thought and research to the mechanisms and problems of planning, and in particular to what Mannheim (1950) called 'democratic planning', though in a broader sense than he envisaged, replacing the idea of a society shaped and run by 'experts' with that of a society in which people regularly and effectively organize and develop their own social life through an active participation in politics and in social research itself.[6]

There is a distinctive historical connection between sociology and social planning. The growth of sociology has been in part responsible for extending the notion of planning from the idea of a planned economy to that of a planned society. At the same time, sociology has responded to developments in political thought and practice. As Nehru (1960, p. 402) wrote, in connection with the discussions in the National Planning Committee in 1938:

> The original idea behind the Planning Committee had been to further industrialization ... But no planning could possibly ignore agriculture, which was the mainstay of the people; equally important were the social services. So one thing led to another and it was impossible to isolate anything or to progress in one direction without corresponding progress in another. The more we thought of this planning business the vaster it grew in its sweep and range till it seemed to embrace almost every activity. That did not mean we intended regulating and regimenting everything, but we had to keep almost everything in view even in deciding about one particular sector of the plan.

It is part of the business of the sociologist to aid in 'keeping everything in view', by defining clearly, and describing precisely, the interconnections between social phenomena of different kinds, thus making planning more effective and helping to avoid unintended and undesired consequences. While not necessarily a critic, he also provides the means of criticism. In both respects, he serves an end to which both sociology and planning have been historically committed: the growth of human freedom and rationality.

Notes to Chapter 19

1 See *Research for Planning 1955–59*. The research projects approved covered the following fields: land reform, agricultural economics, savings, investment and employment, small-scale and cottage industries, urban surveys, social welfare, public administration, macroeconomic aspects of development, decentralization and regional

development, resources for development, benefits of irrigation projects.

2 As Raab and Selznick, 1964, p. 5, observe:

> It is apparent that the absence of social problems is not necessarily the mark of an ideal society ... Nor does the intensification of social problems necessarily signify that a society is moving in a backward direction. The contrary may indeed be true. A society which permits no change and no progress tends almost by definition to have fewer social problems. In a changing society ... some social problems may be symptoms of a change for the better.

3 For example, the greater sexual freedom which has come to exist in many Western societies in recent times is regarded by some as a symptom of social decline, by others as a manifestation of a more rational and tolerant social order.

4 This view of the practical uses of sociology, which perhaps appeared rather eccentric in the later 1950s when I first expressed it, became almost fashionable during the radical decade of the 1960s, and although the radical wave has subsided to some extent the change of outlook in sociology has not been reversed. A critical sociology is now well established and this is to be welcomed, even though it may raise new problems. Sociologists should certainly not treat existing forms of society as unalterable, or celebrate society as it is, but neither should they set themselves up as inspired prophets, a temptation to which some perhaps succumbed in the heady days of student radicalism.

5 As Myrdal, 1953, argued:

> My thesis is that, while there was little participation on the part of social scientists in the actual technical preparation of legislation and still less in administering induced social changes, their influence was nevertheless very considerable, and that this influence was due in the main to their exposition and propagation of certain general thoughts and theories.

Myrdal mentions among those who influenced social policy in this way, Malthus, Ricardo, Marx, Darwin, Spencer and Keynes. Later, as he says, social scientists (and particularly economists) were drawn increasingly into administration; but he would not deny that the propagation of 'general thoughts and theories' is still one of the important ways in which they influence policy-making.

6 For one example of participation in research and planning see Krampe, 1978.

20   *Social Problems*

Although there is a variety of ways in which sociology may contribute to social practice, as I have endeavoured to show in the previous chapter, it is plain that many sociologists, and most of those who are engaged in social work, think of applied sociology pre-eminently in terms of its capacity to provide (or at least to suggest) remedies for particular social evils. The attempt has rarely been made, however, to show exactly how sociological principles, concepts or data have been used, or might be used, in a direct way to solve practical problems. The actual state of affairs may be illustrated from the experience of the International Sociological Association in undertaking a systematic review of the application of sociological knowledge in a number of different fields (1959, Vol. 2). The authors of the principal papers found so few instances of the direct and successful application of sociology to the different problems with which they dealt that they had to confine themselves for the most part to reviewing current research, or to reflection on methodological questions.

But even if it is impossible to point, as yet, to any problems solved with conspicuous success by means of sociological reasoning or research, it is still useful to consider what has been accomplished on a modest scale, and what may be expected and hoped for if sociological studies are intelligently developed. Let us begin by examining what constitutes a social problem. Raab and Selznick (1964, p. 4) define it as 'a problem in human relationships which seriously threatens society itself or impedes the *important* aspirations of many people'. They go on to say, about the first aspect:

> A social problem exists when organized society's ability to order relationships among people seems to be failing; when its institutions are faltering, its laws are being flouted, the transmission of its values from one generation to the next is breaking down, the framework of expectations is being shaken. The widespread contemporary concern with juvenile delinquency, for example, is only partly that delinquency is the doorway to crime or is a threat to personal safety and property. It is also a fear that society is failing to transmit positive social values to its youth . . . It is seen, in other words, as a breakdown in society itself.

On the other hand, Barbara Wootton (1959) defines more narrowly what she terms 'social pathology': it includes 'all those actions in the prevention of which public money is spent, or the doers of which are punished or otherwise dealt with at the public expense'. Her intention is to define the field of study as sharply as possible, and to avoid the difficulties which arrive from divergent subjective ideas of what are to be regarded as 'social problems'. But this definition restricts the field unduly, in that it refers only to actions, and not to situations, and includes only such actions as attract the attention of the state at a particular time. Thus it excludes from consideration many important situations and kinds of behaviour which are very widely regarded as constituting social problems: for example, poverty, some types or degrees of industrial conflict and, in modern times, war. I shall, therefore, adopt here the broader definition proposed by Raab and Selznick.

Among the great array of problems thus defined there are two – crime and delinquency, and industrial relations – which have been investigated with exceptional thoroughness; and the research carried out in these fields reveals very clearly both the difficulties and the potentialities of sociology as an applied science. Crime and delinquency have perhaps attracted more public attention than any other problem in the Western industrial countries during the past few decades, partly because of the continued increase in their incidence, partly because other problems (such as poverty) seemed to have declined in importance.[1] An examination of the achievements of sociological research in this sphere is greatly helped by the work of Wootton, already mentioned, which provides a very comprehensive review and analysis of research up to the late 1950s. Wootton selects twenty-one major investigations for consideration (on the grounds of methodological soundness), and finds that they refer to twelve different factors as being possibly associated with criminality or delinquency: (1) the size of the delinquent's family, (2) the presence of other criminals in the family, (3) club membership, (4) church attendance, (5) employment record, (6) social status, (7) poverty, (8) mother's employment outside the home, (9) school truancy, (10) broken home, (11) health, (12) educational attainment (1959, Ch. 3). She shows that none of these factors can be regarded as causes, in any strict sense, and arrives at the general conclusion that 'this collection of studies although chosen for its comparative methodological merit, produces only the most meagre, and dubiously supported, generalizations'. Similar views have been expressed by other investigators; thus Mack (1955) observes that the total of possible factors which may be specially connected with delinquency is limited only by the patience of the investigator and by the number of methods extant and professionally favoured at the time of the investigation. It is now generally accepted that all that these comparisons can establish is the fact of correlation, the fact that delinquency is frequently accompanied by defective home discipline and by temperamental instability, and by intellectual disabilities such as backwardness and dullness, and so on.

It now seems to be widely held that the main positive contribution of research in this field has been to show that many popular explanations of crime and delinquency are untenable. As Wootton observes:

> Up till now the chief effect of precise investigations into questions of social pathology has been to undermine the credibility of virtually all the current myths. Solid evidence that irreligion, or lack of interest in boys' clubs, or life in the squalor of a problem family or a mother's absence at work have the corrupting effects that they are said to have, or that the younger one embarks on a career of crime, the longer one is likely to stick to it, or that the delinquencies of the young are 'all the fault of the parents', or that problem families repeat themselves generation after generation – solid evidence for any of this is conspicuously lacking; and any evidence that can be found has a way of falling to pieces after closer inspection. (1959, p. 326)

Similarly, Hermann Mannheim (1954) writes, in the course of a short survey of American criminology:

> It was not only laborious, it was also courageous and unpopular to prove that it was in fact not the immigrant but the American-born white who was largely responsible for the high crime rate; that American society rather than the Negro had to bear the blame for much of Negro crime . . . And, lastly, it may have required more than just ordinary courage to show, as the late Edwin H. Sutherland did, that some of the most powerful American business enterprises were in fact 'habitual criminals' . . .

Such findings are useful, both in restraining public authorities (it may be hoped, though sometimes vainly) from inappropriate remedial action, and over a longer period in influencing public opinion, but they can hardly be said to provide a firm basis for practical measures to deal directly with the problems. Among workers in the field who have tried to enhance the practical value of their studies, two principal lines of thought can be distinguished. There are those who argue that students of crime and delinquency have so far only mapped out in a very general way the main areas of social life which produce delinquency, and that the next stage will be to distinguish different types of delinquency and to seek the specific causes of each type (Rose, 1958). This view implicitly re-states Durkheim's rule that every social fact has a single cause, and that where a phenomenon appears to have several causes this is an indication that we are dealing, not with a single phenomenon, but with several distinct phenomena, each one of which has its own specific cause.[2] But the rule is only re-stated, without considering its difficulties and without showing how it might actually be applied in the study of crime and delinquency. The difficulties have long been recognized in connection with Durkheim's own study of suicide; first, that there is something arbitrary in his distinction between different types of suicide,[3] and secondly, that the causal connections which he establishes are by no means as solid or convincing as might be wished. Most sociologists today would probably be more inclined to accept J. S. Mill's contention that social phenomena depend upon a 'complication of causes' than Durkheim's criticism of it; and the investigator of a social problem may feel that he would be helped more by some kind of vector theory than by a theory which involves a one-to-one relationship between a phenomenon and its cause. Unfortunately, although much social analysis is couched in terms of 'factors', 'forces' and 'pressures', which are alleged to produce a particular happening or condition, there has been little progress in measuring the various acting forces with precision, in order to make prediction possible. Moreover, the forces or factors involved may be so numerous and heterogeneous that their interconnections can never be properly disentangled.[4]

The second line of thought, recognizing these difficulties of causal explanation, proposes a different approach. It is well formulated by Wootton, in a passage which deserves to be quoted at length:

> Much of the research reviewed in these pages is inspired by the hope that the connections between various manifestations of social pathology and other specific phenomena may prove to be a cause-and-effect relationship; and that the elimination of causes will result in a cure. It cannot, however, be said that this type of enquiry has been very successful. The generalizations that have been reached are shaky; few of them are supported by the work of any considerable numbers of investigators; and even in those that do recur, the quantitative variations are apt to be very large. Many of these generalizations, moreover, are quite untenable as causes . . . By contrast, the record of experiments in prediction is much more encouraging, and is also rapidly improving. Yet, as has already been observed, the predictive factors used by some of the most successful enquiries are obviously far

removed from 'causes' as we have defined them. The demonstrably reliable findings of the Mannheim and Wilkins enquiry (1955), which shows that previous experience of an approved school or of probation, together with frequent changes of job, augur badly for an offender's post-Borstal record can hardly be interpreted to imply that the abolition of approved schools and of the probation system, or the enactment of a law forbidding employees to discharge themselves would improve the outlook. And, although it is true that the factors used by the Gluecks (1930) in their predictive tables (such as inconsistent discipline in the home) could more credibly be regarded as causes of delinquency, the validation of these is still awaited.

The moral seems to be that it is in their role as the handmaidens of practical decision that the social sciences can shine most brightly. Prediction may be a less ambitious goal than causation but it is certainly more often within the reach of our present capacities and techniques. Though still unable to say much about the why or wherefore of any given social events, we may yet be in a position to indicate which of a limited range of decisions is most likely to produce required results; and the reason for this is just the fact that the range of possible alternatives is so closely limited. The factors, for instance, which throw light upon the relative success of alternative methods of dealing with particular types of offenders are much more manageable than are the multifarious observations necessary to establish why people commit the crimes that they do. (1959, pp. 323–35)

Other social scientists have come to similar conclusions. Sargant Florence (1950) makes a distinction between 'applied science' and 'operational research':

When a science . . . is called applied it seems to assume that a body of general theory, principles or doctrine has been built up by 'pure' science . . . which is fairly certain. It is then only a question of applying the general theory by deduction to a particular case . . . Operational research, on the other hand, does not necessarily assume any theory or principle to be certain or reliable and deduce from it. The official definition of operational research as 'the use of the scientific method to provide executives with an analytical and objective basis for decisions' (First Report of the Committee on Industrial Productivity, 1949, p. 17, Cmd. 7665) clearly stresses method rather than doctrine.

And Wilkins (1955), who co-operated with H. Mannheim in the prediction study on Borstal training, has advocated an extension of prediction methods in operational research.

It is unnecessary to choose between these two approaches in the sense of excluding one of them entirely; for research can well be pursued along both lines. But in considering their relative importance in the whole strategy of research, two further points need to be made. In the first place, operational research is *not* applied sociology. It is a procedure which appears to depend upon commonsense or practical wisdom, rather than upon any specialized sociological knowledge or sociological mode of thought. Its connection with sociology consists chiefly in the use of techniques of inquiry derived from sociology, and of statistical methods which have been largely employed in sociological research. By all appearances it could well proceed in the absence of any sociological (or psychological) theories or descriptions. For in this case it is not, as Wootton claims, the *social sciences* which 'shine most brightly' as handmaidens of practical decision; it is only certain *techniques of investigation* which do so, while the social sciences (as bodies of theory and description) play little part. Even in the matter of practical guidance the contribution of operational research, at least in the form of prediction studies, is not quite so promising as has been claimed. For the ability to predict success or failure in a course of action does not always imply the ability to solve the social problem to which the action relates. The study of Borstal training, which Wootton particularly cites, is a case in point; for the social problem is constituted by the 'failures', and the successful prediction of failure provides no clue to its causes or, consequently, to the remedies.

Secondly, in the attempts to formulate causal explanations of crime and delinquency, extremely heterogeneous factors have been juxtaposed or associated. Thus, explanations may be offered which refer to a range of individual psychological characteristics (temperamental instability, mental backwardness, etc.), and to a variety of social circumstances (divorce, parental discipline, criminal environment, etc.). In this particular field of study the general problem of the relation between psychological and sociological explanation is very acutely posed; but there are few works in which the problem is even clearly formulated, and none, to my knowledge, in which a plausible theoretical model encompassing both sets of data has been constructed.

In the quarter of a century which has elapsed since the studies I have discussed here were undertaken there have been many changes in the sociological approach to crime and delinquency. But it does not seem that these amount to a cumulative development; thus Rock (1979, p. 52) observes: 'The sociology of crime and delinquency has developed fitfully. Indeed, it may be misleading to describe it as an example of clear development at all.' The changes in this field have reflected the new departures in sociological theory generally, and the emergence of numerous alternative paradigms, during the past two decades, with the result that theoretical, and above all methodological, disputes have had a pre-eminent place. One example is to be found in the rise of a 'radical criminology' in the early 1970s, influenced by phenomenology and also by Marxism, though some Marxists opposed this tendency and Hirst (1975, p. 204) roundly declared that 'There is no "Marxist theory of deviance", either in existence, or which can be developed within orthodox Marxism.' The Marxist writing in this field has become very diverse, but largely eschews any general theory and concentrates on the relation between crime and capitalism (Greenberg, 1981), developing themes which were familiar much earlier, concerning such issues as the 'crimes of the powerful' and the connection between competitiveness and crime. More recently 'radical criminology' as a whole has been strongly criticized from various aspects (Downes and Rock, 1982, ch. 10; Lea and Young, 1984, ch. 1); nevertheless, the more critical study of crime, delinquency, and 'deviance' in a more general sense, has been valuable in establishing more clearly and prominently the diversity of what is, or may be, treated as 'crime', in setting the individual and social costs of crime and delinquency in the context of other costs (for example, of traffic accidents or environmental pollution), and in assessing more dispassionately what is sometimes seen, via the mass media, as a 'rocketing' rate of crime (McDonald, 1976; Lea and Young, 1984). All this is useful in defining the extent of a particular social problem, setting it in the wider context of a social system, and perhaps in the longer term influencing public opinion and making possible more effective policies; but it does not provide either causal explanations or precise solutions.

The second field of applied research which I shall briefly consider is that concerned with industrial relations. The principal aim of research has been to discover the causes of industrial conflict, in the individual enterprise and on a national scale, and of other impediments to high productivity such as high rates of absenteeism, illness, and labour turnover. The same difficulties of causal explanation as in the study of crime and delinquency have been encountered, but there are additional difficulties which arise from the ramifications of industrial problems.

Before considering these questions I should like to take up again the point made earlier, that the principal contribution of sociology is generally seen as consisting in skilled investigation. This is very apparent in industrial sociology. The authors of a survey of sociological research in industry (Clémens and Evrard, 1959, p. 3) observed that:

it is often the case, no doubt, that to the firm which calls upon his services, the sociologist appears less as the possessor of a particular kind of knowledge which is capable of application, than as a person trained in the use of certain tools (interview, etc.), or indeed as one who has the advantage of appearing neutral to everyone concerned.

This is very close to the view advanced by Wootton according to which the contribution of the social sciences to practical life is found in a scientific attitude and in the use of certain techniques of inquiry. This conception is very prevalent. In the sphere of medical research, for example, it has been claimed that 'Many physicians approach sociologists, if they approach them at all, as I did, thinking of them as people with technical skill in interviewing and questionnaire construction' (Goss and Reader, 1956). But a contribution of this kind can only be regarded as a very minor part of applied sociology, more especially since these techniques of investigation are common to all the social sciences. Clémens and Evrard recognize this, and while admitting that there are few instances of the successful application of sociological principles to solve specific problems, they make a case for applied industrial sociology in respect of its contributions to improved organization. The contributions are of two kinds: first, studies of the social structure of business enterprises which make possible improvements in management, the system of communication, the constitution of working groups, and so on; and secondly, training courses for managers and supervisors. Clémens and Evrard (1959, p. 3) regard the latter as the more successful development:

> It is in the sphere of training for those who hold positions of authority in industrial life, that the most serious attempts to apply sociology in a systematic way are to be found. The ever more numerous training courses for managers, technicians and supervisors, or for trade union officials, constitute an important factor of social change in modern industry . . .

But this favourable assessment would not receive universal assent. As Whyte (1956) observes:

> To be sure, important changes in human relations have taken place in industry, but there is little reason to believe that they have come to any considerable degree through research and through training that has been based upon such research. There have been hundreds of thousands of human relations training programmes in industry. To my knowledge, only two of them have been subjected to the sort of solid research evaluation which would measure their effectiveness. In one case, an International Harvester programme, workers' reactions to the foreman who had been trained were slightly more negative after

the programme than they had been before. In the other case, Detroit Edison, there was a loss registered in one division which was more than counterbalanced by a gain in another.[5]

The inadequacy of applied research in industry is due, Whyte suggests, to the failure to take account of the wider social context of industrial problems. Similar criticisms were expressed more fully by Georges Friedmann (1946), who made an outstanding contribution to the study of problems of industrial work in relation to different types of economic and political system. Some of the principal difficulties of research in this field arise, then, from the fact that in investigating the causes which have produced a practical problem, we encounter a network of interrelated factors which extends far beyond the limited situation in which the problem itself occurs. The study of obstacles to greater productivity, of resistances to technological change, of ways to increase the efficiency of management, or of the prevention, limitation or peaceful settlement of industrial conflicts leads inescapably to the consideration of much broader questions concerning the property system, social stratification and occupational mobility, family structure, ideologies and cultural traditions. Thus a more recent account of the field of industrial sociology defines it as being concerned with how the economic subsystem is structured, and how it is related to other subsystems (Parker *et al.*, 1967).

From this perspective industrial relations have to be studied in the context of different economic systems (capitalist and socialist, the transitional economies of Third World countries), and of the history and culture of particular regions and nations. There is still relatively little comparative research of this kind, although there are some interesting limited comparisons, such as that by Gallie (1978) which examines the response of workers and trade unions to new technology in the oil industry in Britain and France, and also discusses more generally the diverse conceptions of industrial relations in advanced capitalist societies. One important question in a broader comparative perspective concerns the role of trade unions in capitalist and socialist societies respectively; a question which acquired great prominence with the rise of the Solidarity movement in Poland. Marxist social scientists conceive industrial relations in capitalist societies as an aspect of class relations, and industrial conflict as a form of class conflict; and trade unions are seen therefore as the independent organizations of a subordinate class (Hyman, 1984). The situation and role of trade unions in a socialist society – and particularly in the existing socialist societies of Eastern Europe – have been diversely interpreted (Hyman,

1983), from Lenin's definition of unions as 'transmission belts from the Communist Party to the masses' to the emphasis in more recent Marxist writing on the importance of independent trade unions in a pluralistic socialist society, in the context of debates about the emergence of a new class structure in the USSR and Eastern Europe (see Chapter 11 above).

This brief examination of two major areas of social problems to which much sociological research is devoted indicates that such research needs to be conceived and undertaken in a very broad framework, involving social policy as a whole and the various social interests and ideas which determine or influence it. In seeking to make their knowledge useful in practical social life, therefore, sociologists have to contend with two kinds of difficulty: first, that of establishing precise causal connections, and secondly, that of delimiting a problem without doing violence to its relations with important general features of the social structure and culture. The consideration of these difficulties leads, I believe, to a recognition that there are different types of social problem, varying both in their importance and in the extent to which they can be resolved. Some social evils are, in the strict sense, ineradicable. Durkheim argued that crime is a 'normal phenomenon' in human societies which could only be eliminated by social controls and sanctions so repressive as to destroy many other cherished values; and further, that each type of society has its own 'normal rate' of crime. What are seen as historically high rates of crime and delinquency in some modern industrial societies may therefore be the counterpart of the relative laxity of social control in these societies, and at the same time of a particularly strong emphasis in the culture upon individualism and competitiveness. Similarly, high divorce rates may be explained, in part, as the outcome of the pursuit by individuals of other ends – personal freedom, an ideal romantic love – which are in themselves good. In the developing countries, many social problems have to be seen at the present time as concomitants of the disturbing processes of industrialization and urbanization. It should not be concluded that in these cases social research is futile. Sociological studies may encourage a more realistic approach to such problems, and in particular restrain those immoderate moral denunciations which often exacerbate the difficulties. They may also, at the least, suggest means of diminishing the evils without harm to other social values, and more effective ways of dealing with their consequences; and they may go on to suggest a need for more radical changes in society.

There are other social problems which can be solved or which constitute such a grave danger to human society that a radical solution has to be sought. In the first category comes the problem of poverty in economically developed societies. Here, the solution requires not only an investigation and presentation of the facts, on a historical and comparative basis, but also the formulation of feasible policies (of which there might be several alternative versions) that would deal with the major factors creating poverty: mass unemployment and the specific character of the distribution of social resources among different groups in the population. In the second category, of supremely dangerous problems, the pre-eminent example, in this age of nuclear weapons, is war. No one is likely to suppose that sociologists alone, or sociologists together with psychologists and other social scientists, will provide a universally acclaimed solution. Equally, however, no one will contest that a war fought with nuclear weapons would be an immense and probably final disaster for humanity, that sociological and psychological research can at least contribute significantly to understanding how crucial situations of tension and conflict develop and so help responsible leaders to avoid them, and that sociologists ought consequently to make an exceptional effort to investigate the problems of war and peace, and to disseminate their findings as widely as possible. It is sad that so few have yet undertaken the task,[6] even though it is so formidable, so exposed to the incursion of political strife, and so little assimilable to the neat research designs of much current inquiry.

This last example illustrates very clearly a feature which I have tried to bring into relief at various places in this and the preceding chapter. Sociologists can rarely solve a problem directly or propose a policy which is exactly appropriate, even when they are sure what is wrong; for every solution of a problem and act of policy is a political decision. It expresses the resolve of a social group to maintain or to change a particular way of life, and to act in accordance with certain social ideals. Sociologists may supply information, elucidate the context of problems, point to causes or conditions, outline feasible policies, indicate the advantages and costs of alternative courses of action; in the longer term, their studies may, and I believe do, influence social ideals themselves. But in the last resort political decisions rest upon judgement, or political wisdom, and upon the interests of particular social groups. To suppose otherwise, and to assign sociologists the role of philosopher kings in modern dress, is to revert to the delusions of Comte's positive politics.

It may be well, at the close of this book, to restate my view, which informs all the preceding discussion, that it would be a misconception to suppose that the value of sociology culminates in its various detailed applications to practical life which we have just been considering. To the question, 'What is the use of sociology?' I would answer rather that it widens our sympathies and imagination, opens up new perspectives on social policy, and increases our understanding of other human beings outside the narrow circle of our own time, locality, and social situation, than that it simply provides means to discover the remedies for specific present ills. But these purposes are not radically antithetical and they are perhaps of equal practical significance in the long run. Most sociologists would like to feel that in all spheres of their work they are making some contribution to the improvement of social life, by extending knowledge and engendering ideas which will help human beings to struggle more effectively for the kind of society they desire.

Notes to Chapter 20

1   However, the reappearance of mass unemployment since the late 1970s has changed this situation, as have the arms race and the growing threat of nuclear war. As will be argued later in this chapter one of the fundamental tasks of sociology is to depict the whole range of social problems and to consider the relative significance for human well-being of different problems.

2   See *The Rules of Sociological Method* (1895), ch. 6. Durkheim in fact gives as examples of phenomena which appear to have several causes suicide and crime; and he argues 'if suicide depends upon more than one cause, this is because there are in reality several types of suicide. And it is the same with crime.' The application of the rule 'one effect – one cause' is shown in great detail in Durkheim's study of suicide.

3   That is to say, the distinction seems to be determined not by observable differences in the phenomena under examination, but by some preconception of the possible causes.

4   This may be the case, for example, if we conceive causation from the standpoint of a realist philosophy of science, according to which an underlying structure determines only tendencies and limits (see Chapter 3 above).

5   The article as a whole sets out admirably the problems of applied research and makes some excellent suggestions for more effective studies.

6   But the amount of research has increased significantly in the past decade with the growth of the peace movement; see Chapter 12 above.

Notes on Reading for Part VI

1 Social Policy

Coleman, James, 'Sociological analysis and social policy' (1978).
Douglas, Jack D. (ed.), *The Impact of Sociology* (1970a).
Douglas, Jack D. (ed.), *The Relevance of Sociology* (1970b).
Ferge, Zsuzsa, *A Society in the Making* (1979).
George, Vic and Manning, Nick, *Socialism, Social Welfare and the Soviet Union* (1980).
Lloyd, Christopher (ed.), *Social Theory and Political Practice* (1983).
Lynd, Robert A., *Knowledge for What?* (1939).
Marshall, T. H., *Social Policy* (1970).
Titmuss, Richard M., *Essays on 'The Welfare State'* (1958).
Titmuss, Richard M., *Social Policy: An Introduction* (1974).

2 Social Planning

The general sociological literature on planning is still quite limited, but the following works provide an introduction to various aspects of the subject:

International Sociological Association, Symposium on 'Sociological aspects of social planning', *Transactions of the Fourth World Congress of Sociology*, vol. II, pt II (1959).
Mannheim, Karl, *Freedom, Power and Democratic Planning* (1950).
Myrdal, Gunnar, *Asian Drama* (1968), Vol. 2, pt 4, 'A third world of planning'.

3 Social Problems

Merton, Robert K. and Nisbet, Robert (eds.), *Contemporary Social Problems* (1976). A comprehensive study which goes beyond narrowly defined problems to consider such issues as population, equality and inequality, the world of work, and collective violence. The introductory chapter by Merton sets out some of the fundamental issues involved in sociological approaches to the study of social problems.
Wootton, Barbara, *Social Science and Social Pathology* (1959). Still one of the most valuable surveys of applied social research.
See also the journal *Social Problems*.

Bibliography

Note: Date of first publication is shown after the author's name; dates of translations or more recent editions are given with the publication details.

Abel-Smith, B. and Townsend, P. (1965), *The Poor and the Poorest* (London: Bell).

Abercrombie, N., Hill, S. and Turner, B. S. (1980), *The Dominant Ideology Thesis* (London: Allen & Unwin).

Abercrombie, N. and Urry, J. (1983), *Capital, Labour and the Middle Classes* (London: Allen & Unwin).

Aberle, D. F. (1966), *The Peyote Religion Among the Navaho* (Chicago: Aldine).

Aberle, D. F. *et al.* (1950), 'The functional prerequisites of society', *Ethics*, vol. 60, no. 2.

Abu-Lughod, J. and Hay, R. (eds.) (1977), *Third World Urbanization* (Chicago: Maaroufa Press).

Adler, Max (1904), *Kausalität und Teleologie im Streite um die Wissenschaft* (Vienna: Wiener Volksbuchhandlung).

Adler, Max (1913), *Marxistische Probleme: Beiträge zur Theorie der materialistischen Geschichtsauffassung und Dialektik* (Stuttgart: J. H. W. Dietz).

Adler, Max (1927), 'Zur Kritik der Soziologie Othmar Spanns', *Der Kampf*, vol. 20.

Adorno, T. W. (1940), 'Husserl and the problem of idealism', *Journal of Philosophy*, vol. 37, no. 2.

Adorno, T. W. *et al.* (1950), *The Authoritarian Personality* (New York: Harper & Row).

Adorno, T. W. *et al.* (1969), *The Positivist Dispute in German Sociology* (London: Heinemann, 1976).

Agarwala, A. N. and Singh, S. P. (eds.) (1963), *The Economics of Underdevelopment* (New York: Oxford University Press).

Agassi, J. (1966), 'Methodological individualism', *British Journal of Sociology*, vol. 11, no. 3.

Alavi, H. (1983), 'Colonial and post-colonial societies', in Bottomore (1983).

Alavi, H. and Shanin, T. (eds.) (1982), *Introduction to the Sociology of 'Developing Societies'* (London: Macmillan).

Albertoni, E. A. (1987), *Gaetano Mosca and the Theory of Elites* (Oxford: Blackwell).

Albig, W. (1956), *Modern Public Opinion* (New York: McGraw-Hill).

Albrow, M. (1970), *Bureaucracy* (London: Macmillan).

Allport, G. W. (1954), *The Nature of Prejudice* (Cambridge, Mass.: Harvard University Press).

Almond, G. A. and Coleman, J. S. (1960), *The Politics of the Developing Areas* (Princeton, NJ: Princeton University Press).

Althusser, L. (1965), *For Marx* (London: Allen Lane, 1969).

Althusser, L. and Balibar, E. (1970), *Reading 'Capital'* (London: New Left Books, 1971).

Amin, Samir (1976), *Unequal Development* (New York: Monthly Review Press).

Anderson, J. N. D. (1968), *Family Law in Asia and Africa* (London: Allen & Unwin).

Anderson, M. (1980), *Approaches to the History of the Western Family* (London: Macmillan).

Anderson, Perry (1974a), *Passages from Antiquity to Feudalism* (London: New Left Books).

Anderson, Perry (1974b), *Lineages of the Absolutist State* (London: New Left Books).

Angell, R. C. (1941), *The Integration of American Society* (New York and London: McGraw-Hill).

Archer, M. S. (1979), *Social Origins of Educational Systems* (London: Sage).

Archer, M. S. and Giner, S. (eds.) (1971), *Contemporary Europe: Class, Status and Power* (London: Weidenfeld & Nicolson).

Arensberg, C. M. and Kimball, S. T. (1940), *Family and Community in Ireland* (2nd edn, Cambridge, Mass.: Harvard University Press, 1968).

Argyle, M. (1957), *The Scientific Study of Social Behaviour* (London: Methuen).

Ariès, P. (1960), *Centuries of Childhood* (New York: Knopf, 1962).

Ariga, K. (1956a), 'The contemporary Japanese family in transition', in ISA *Transactions*, vol. 4.

Ariga, K. (1956b), 'Problems of the Asian family system', in ISA *Transactions*, vol. 8.

Aron, Raymond (1936), *German Sociology* (London: Heinemann, 1957).

Aron, Raymond (1938), *Introduction to the Philosophy of History* (London: Weidenfeld & Nicolson, 1961).

Aron, Raymond (1950), 'Social structure and the ruling class', *British Journal of Sociology*, vol. 1, nos. 1–2.

Aron, Raymond (1955), *The Opium of the Intellectuals* (London: Secker & Warburg, 1957).

Aron, Raymond (1958), *War and Industrial Society* (London: Oxford University Press).

Aron, Raymond (1960), 'Classe sociale, classe politique, classe dirigeante', *European Journal of Sociology*, vol. 1, no. 2.

Aron, Raymond (1961), *18 Lectures on Industrial Society* (London: Weidenfeld & Nicolson, 1967).

Aron, Raymond (1962), *Peace and War: A Theory of International Relations* (New York: Doubleday, 1966).

Aron, Raymond (1965), *Democracy and Totalitarianism* (London: Weidenfeld & Nicolson, 1968).

Aron, Raymond (1966), *The Industrial Society: Three Essays on Ideology and Development* (London: Weidenfeld & Nicolson, 1967).

Aron, Raymond (1967), *Main Currents in Sociological Thought* (2 vols., London: Weidenfeld & Nicolson, 1965, 1968).

Atkinson, A. B. (1974), *Unequal Shares: Wealth in Britain* (rev. edn, Harmondsworth: Penguin Books).

Avineri, S. (1968a), *The Social and Political Thought of Karl Marx* (Cambridge: Cambridge University Press).

Avineri, S. (ed.) (1968b), *Karl Marx on Colonialism and Modernization* (Garden City, NY: Doubleday).

Ayer, A. J. (1982), *Philosophy in the Twentieth Century* (London: Weidenfeld & Nicolson).

Bachofen, J. J. (1861), *Das Mutterrecht* (new edn as Vols. 2–3 of *Gesammelte Werke*, ed. Karl Meuli, Basle: Schwabe, 1943).

Bailey, F. G. (1957), *Caste and the Economic Frontier* (Manchester: Manchester University Press).

Bailey, F. G. (1963), *Politics and Social Change: Orissa in 1959* (Berkeley, Calif.: University of California Press).

Balandier, G. (1967), *Political Anthropology* (London: Allen Lane, 1970).

Banfield, E. C. (1958), *The Moral Basis of a Backward Society* (Glencoe: Free Press).

Banks, J. A. (1954), *Prosperity and Parenthood: A Study of Family Planning among the Victorian Middle Class* (London: Routledge & Kegan Paul).

Banks, O. (1981), *Faces of Feminism: A Study of Feminism as a Social Movement* (Oxford: Martin Robertson).

Baran, P. (1957), *The Political Economy of Growth* (New York: Monthly Review Press).

Baran, P. and Sweezy, P. (1966), *Monopoly Capital* (New York: Monthly Review Press).

Barbour, Floyd B. (ed.) (1968), *The Black Power Revolt* (Boston: Porter Sargent).

Barraclough, G. (1964), *An Introduction to Contemporary History* (London: Watts).

Barrett, M. (1980), *Women's Oppression Today: Problems in Marxist Feminist Analysis* (London: New Left Books).

Barry, B. M. (1970), *Sociologists, Economists and Democracy* (London: Collier-Macmillan).

Basu, Sobharani (1957), 'Forest universities of ancient India', *Year Book of Education*.

Bauer, O. (1907), *Die Nationalitätenfrage und die Sozialdemokratie* (2nd enlarged edn, Vienna: Wiener Volksbuchhandlung, 1924).

Bauman, Z. (1973), *Culture as Praxis* (London: Routledge & Kegan Paul).

Bauman, Z. (1978), *Hermeneutics and Social Science* (London: Hutchinson).

Becker, H. (1932), *Systematic Sociology* (New York: Wiley).

Beetham, D. (1981), 'Michels and his critics', *European Journal of Sociology*, vol. 22, no. 1.

Beetham, D. (1983), *Marxists in Face of Fascism* (Manchester: Manchester University Press).

Bell, Clive (1928), *Civilization* (Harmondsworth: Penguin Books, 1938).

Bell, D. (ed.) (1963), *The Radical Right* (Garden City, NY: Doubleday).

Bell, D. (1973), *The Coming of Post-Industrial Society* (New York: Basic Books).

Bell, N. W. and Vogel, E. F. (eds.) (1960), *A Modern Introduction to the Family* (rev. edn, New York: Free Press, 1968).

Bendix, R. and Lipset, S. M. (1957), 'Political sociology', *Current Sociology*, vol. 6, no. 2.

Bendix, R. and Lipset, S. M. (eds.) (1967), *Class, Status and Power* (London: Routledge & Kegan Paul).

Benton, T. (1977), *Philosophical Foundations of the Three Sociologies* (London: Routledge & Kegan Paul).

Berger, P. and Luckmann, T. (1966), *The Social Construction of Reality: An Essay in the Sociology of Knowledge* (Garden City, NY: Doubleday).

Berle, A. A. (1955), *The Twentieth Century Capitalist Revolution* (London: Macmillan).

Berle, A. A. and Means, G. C. (1934), *The Modern Corporation and Private Property* (New York: Macmillan, 1947).

Berlin, I. (1954), *Historical Inevitability* (London: Oxford University Press).

Berlin, I. (1963), *Karl Marx*, 3rd edn (London: Oxford University Press).

Berlin, I. (1969), 'A note on Vico's concept of knowledge', *New York Review of Books*, vol. 12, no. 8.

Bernard, Jessie (1954), 'The theory of games of strategy as a modern sociology of conflict', *American Journal of Sociology*, vol. 59, no. 5,

Bernstein, H. (ed.) (1973), *Underdevelopment and Development* (Harmondsworth: Penguin Books).

Béteille, A. (1965), *Caste, Class and Power: Changing Patterns of Stratification in a Tanjore Village* (Berkeley, Calif.: University of California Press).

Beynon, H. (1984), *Working for Ford*, rev. edn (Harmondsworth: Penguin Books).

Bhaskar, R. (1978), *A Realist Theory of Science*, 2nd edn (Brighton: Harvester Press).

Bhaskar, R. (1979), *The Possibility of Naturalism: A Philosophical Critique of the Contemporary Human Sciences* (Brighton: Harvester Press).

Bhaskar, R. (1983), 'Dialectics' and 'Realism', in Bottomore (1983).

Bierstedt, R. (1978), 'Sociological thought in the eighteenth century', in Bottomore and Nisbet (1978).

Billig, M. (1982), *Ideology and Social Psychology* (Oxford: Blackwell).

Blau, P. M. (1956), *Bureaucracy in Modern Society* (New York: Random House).

Blau, P. M. (ed.) (1975), *Approaches to the Study of Social Structure* (New York: Free Press).

Blau, P. M. and Duncan, O. D. (1967), *The American Occupational Structure* (New York: Wiley).

Bloch, Marc (1928), 'A contribution towards a comparative history of European societies', in Bloch (1967).

Bloch, Marc (1931), 'Feudalism: European', *Encyclopaedia of the Social Sciences*.

Bloch, Marc (1939–40), *Feudal Society* (London: Routledge & Kegan Paul, 1961).

Bloch, Marc (1967), *Land and Work in Medieval Europe* (London: Routledge & Kegan Paul).

Bloch, Marc (1975), *Slavery and Serfdom in the Middle Ages* (Berkeley, Calif.: University of California Press).

Bloch, Maurice (ed.) (1975), *Marxist Analyses and Social Anthropology* (London: Malaby Press).

Bock, K. (1978), 'Theories of progress, development, evolution', in Bottomore and Nisbet (1978).

Booth, Charles (1891–1903), *Life and Labour of the People in London* (London: Macmillan).

Borkenau, F. (1936), *Pareto* (London: Chapman & Hall).

Bottomore, T. (1964), *Elites and Society* (Harmondsworth: Penguin Books, 1966).

Bottomore, T. (1965), *Classes in Modern Society* (London: Allen & Unwin).

Bottomore, T. (1967), *Critics of Society* (London: Allen & Unwin).

Bottomore, T. (ed.) (1973), *Karl Marx* (Oxford: Blackwell, 1979).

Bottomore, T. (1974), 'Social class and mobility' and 'Social differentiation and stratification', *Encyclopaedia Britannica*.

Bottomore, T. (1975a), *Marxist Sociology* (London: Macmillan).

Bottomore, T. (1975b), *Sociology as Social Criticism* (London: Allen & Unwin).

Bottomore, T. (1978a), 'Marxism and sociology', in Bottomore and Nisbet, 1978.

Bottomore, T. (1978b), 'Social research and democratic participation', in *Social Research in the Public Sector*. Supplement (Amsterdam: European Society for Opinion and Marketing Research, 1978).

Bottomore, T. (1979), *Political Sociology* (London: Hutchinson).

Bottomore, T. (ed.) (1981), *Modern Interpretations of Marx* (Oxford: Blackwell).

Bottomore, T. (ed.) (1983), *A Dictionary of Marxist Thought* (Oxford: Blackwell).

Bottomore, T. (1984a), *Sociology and Socialism* (Brighton: Wheatsheaf Books).

Bottomore, T. (1984b), *The Frankfurt School* (Chichester and London: Ellis Horwood/Tavistock).

Bottomore, T. (1985), *Theories of Modern Capitalism* (London: Allen & Unwin).

Bottomore, T. (1987), *The Socialist Economy: Theory and Practice* (Brighton: Wheatsheaf Books).

Bottomore, T. and Goode, P. (eds.) (1978), *Austro-Marxism* (Oxford: Clarendon Press).

Bottomore, T. and Goode, P. (eds.) (1983), *Readings in Marxist Sociology* (Oxford: Clarendon Press).

Bottomore, T. and Nisbet, R. (eds.) (1978), *A History of Sociological Analysis* (New York: Basic Books).

Bottomore, T., Nowak, S. and Sokolowska, M. (eds.) (1982), *Sociology: The State of the Art* (London: Sage).

Bouglé, C. (1903), 'Théories sur la division du travail', *Année Sociologique*, vol. 4.

Bouglé, C. (1908), *Essays on the Caste System* (Cambridge: Cambridge University Press, 1971).

Bouglé, C. (1925), *Les Idées égalitaires*, 3rd edn (Paris: Alcan).

Boulard, F. (1954), *Premiers itinéraires en sociologie religieuse* (Paris: Éditions ouvrières).

Bourdieu, P. and Passeron, J.-C. (1970), *Reproduction in Education, Society and Culture* (London: Sage, 1977).

Bowles, S. and Gintis, H. (1976), *Schooling in Capitalist America* (London: Routledge & Kegan Paul).

Braithwaite, R. B. (1953), *Scientific Explanation* (New York and London: Cambridge University Press).

Bramson, L. (1961), *The Political Context of Sociology* (Princeton, NJ: Princeton University Press).

Bramson, L. and Goethals, G. W. (eds.) (1964), *War: Studies from Psychology, Sociology, Anthropology* (New York: Basic Books).

Brass, P. R. (1965), *Factional Politics in an Indian State: The Congress Party in Uttar Pradesh* (Berkeley: University of California Press).

Braudel, F. (1955), 'Histoire et sociologie'. Reprinted in *Écrits sur l'histoire* (English trans. *On History*, London: Weidenfeld & Nicolson, 1981).

Braudel, F. (1979), *Civilization and Capitalism, 15th–18th Century* (3 vols., London: Collins, 1981–4).

Brewer, A. (1980), *Marxist Theories of Imperialism: A Critical Survey* (London: Routledge & Kegan Paul).

Briefs, G. A. (1926), *The Proletariat* (New York: McGraw-Hill, 1937).

Briggs, A. (1966), 'History and society', in McKenzie (1966).

Brinton, C. (1957), *The Anatomy of Revolution* (Englewood Cliffs, NJ: Prentice-Hall).

Broekmeyer, M. J. (ed.) (1970), *Yugoslav Workers' Self-Management* (Dordrecht: Reidel).

Brubaker, R. (1984), *The Limits of Rationality: An Essay on the Social and Moral Thought of Max Weber* (London: Allen & Unwin).

Brus, W. (1964), *The Market in a Socialist Economy* (London: Routledge & Kegan Paul, 1972).

Brym, R. J. (1980), *Intellectuals and Politics* (London: Allen & Unwin).

Bryson, G. (1945), *Man and Society: The Scottish Inquiry of the Eighteenth Century* (Princeton, NJ: Princeton University Press).

Buchan, A. (1966), *War in Modern Society: An Introduction* (London: Watts).

Burckhardt, J. (1860), *The Civilization of the Renaissance in Italy* (London: Phaidon Press, 1944).

Burgess, E. W. (ed.) (1926), *The Urban Community* (Chicago: University of Chicago Press).

Burke, P. (1980), *Sociology and History* (London: Allen & Unwin).

Burnham, J. (1941), *The Managerial Revolution* (Harmondsworth: Penguin Books, 1945).

Burnham, J. (1943), *The Machiavellians: Defenders of Freedom* (London: Putnam).

Burt, C. (1950), 'The trend of national intelligence', *British Journal of Sociology*, vol. 1, no. 2.

Bury, J. B. (1920), *The Idea of Progress* (London: Macmillan).

Butterfield, H. (1950), *The Origins of Modern Science* (rev. edn, London: Bell, 1957).

Cardozo, B. (1941), *The Nature of the Judicial Process* (New Haven, Conn.: Yale University Press).

Carlsson, G. (1958), *Social Mobility and Class Structure* (Lund: Gleerup).

Carmichael, S. and Hamilton, C. V. (1967), *Black Power: The Politics of Liberation in America* (New York: Vintage Books).

Carr, E. H. (1950), *The Bolshevik Revolution, 1917–1923*, Vol. 1 (London: Macmillan).

Carr, E. H. (1961), *What is History?* (Harmondsworth: Penguin Books, 1964).

Carr-Saunders, A. M. (1958), *Natural Science and Social Science* (Liverpool: Liverpool University Press).

Cassen, R. H. (1976), 'Population and development: A survey', *World Development*, vol. 4, no. 10/11.

Castells, M. (1976), *The Urban Question* (London: Edward Arnold).

Cauter, T. and Downham, J. S. (1954), *The Communication of Ideas* (London: Chatto & Windus).

Centre International de Synthèse (1930), *Civilisation, le mot et l'idée* (Paris).

Childe, V. Gordon (1956), *Man Makes Himself*, 3rd edn (London: Watts).

Chombart de Lauwe, P. *et al.* (1952), *Paris et l'agglomération Parisienne*, 2 vols. (Paris: Presses Universitaires de France).

Clémens, R. and Evrard, P. (1959), 'La Connaissance sociologique et son application à la vie industrielle', in ISA, 1959, vol. 2.

Coakley, J. and Harris, L. (1983), *The City of Capital* (Oxford: Blackwell).

Coale, A. J. and Hoover, E. M. (1958), *Population Growth and Economic Development in Low-Income Countries* (Princeton, NJ: Princeton University Press).

Cohen, R. and Wartofsky, M. W. (eds.) (1965), *Boston Studies in the Philosophy of Science* (New York: Humanities Press).

Cole, G. D. H. (1955), *Studies in Class Structure* (London: Routledge & Kegan Paul).

Coleman, J. (1978), 'Sociological analysis and social policy', in Bottomore and Nisbet (1978).

Collingwood, R. G. (1946), *The Idea of History* (Oxford: Oxford University Press).

Collins, H. (1982), *Marxism and Law* (Oxford: Clarendon Press).

Comte, Auguste (1830–42), *Cours de philosophie positive* (*The Positive Philosophy of Auguste Comte*, trans. and condensed by Harriet Martineau, 3 vols., London: Bell, 1896).

Comte, Auguste (1851–4), *System of Positive Polity* (4 vols., London: Longmans, 1875–7).

Cooley, C. H. (1909), *Social Organization* (New York: Schocken, 1962).

Coser, L. (1956), *The Functions of Social Conflict* (Glencoe, Ill.: Free Press).

Coser, L. (ed.), (1965), *Georg Simmel* (Englewood Cliffs, NJ: Prentice-Hall).

Coulborn, R. (ed.) (1956), *Feudalism in History* (Princeton, NJ: Princeton University Press).

Cowell, F. R. (1952), *History, Civilization and Culture* (London: Doubleday).

Cox, O. C. (1948), *Caste, Class and Race* (New York: Doubleday).

Crewe, I. *et al.* (1977), 'Partisan dealignment in Britain 1964–1974', *British Journal of Political Science*, vol. 7.

Crick, B. (1959), *The American Science of Politics* (London: Routledge & Kegan Paul).

Dahrendorf, R. (1959), *Class and Class Conflict in an Industrial Society* (London: Routledge & Kegan Paul).

Dahrendorf, R. (1965), *Society and Democracy in Germany* (Garden City, NY: Doubleday, 1967).

Dahrendorf, R. (1968), *Essays in the Theory of Society* (Stanford, Calif.: Stanford University Press).

Davis, C. (1980), *Theology and Political Society* (Cambridge: Cambridge University Press).

Davis, K. (1948), *Human Society* (New York: Macmillan).

Davis, K. (1966), 'The world's population crisis', in Merton and Nisbet (1976).

Davis, K. and Moore, W. E. (1945), 'Some principles of stratification', *American Sociological Review*, vol. 10, no. 2. Repr. in Bendix and Lipset (1967).

Dawe, A. (1978), 'Theories of social action', in Bottomore and Nisbet (1978).

Demeny, P. (1982), 'Population policies', in Faaland (1982).

Demerath, N. J. and Peterson, R. A. (eds.) (1967), *System, Change and Conflict* (New York: Free Press).

Derrett, J. Duncan M. (1968), *Religion, Law and the State in India* (London: Faber & Faber).

Desai, A. R. (1948), *Social Background of Indian Nationalism* (Bombay: Oxford University Press).

Desai, I. P. (1955), Symposium on 'Caste and joint family', *Sociological Bulletin*, vol. 4, no. 2.

Desan, W. (1965), *The Marxism of Jean-Paul Sartre* (Garden City, NY: Doubleday).

Desroche, H. (1955), *The Shakers* (Amherst: University of Massachusetts Press, 1971).

Dicey, A. V. (1905), *Lectures on the Relation Between Law and Public Opinion in England During the Nineteenth Century* (London: Macmillan, 1962).

Dilthey, W. (1883), *Einleitung in die Geisteswissenschaften* (new edn, *Gesammelte Schriften*, Vol. 1, Stuttgart: Teubner, 1959).

Djilas, M. (1957), *The New Class* (London: Thames & Hudson).

Dobb, M. (1946), *Studies in the Development of Capitalism* (London: Routledge).

Domhoff, G. W. (1967), *Who Rules America?* (Englewood Cliffs, NJ: Prentice-Hall).

Domhoff, G. W. (1970), *The Higher Circles: The Governing Class in America* (New York: Random House).

Dore, E. (1983), 'Dependency theory', in Bottomore (1983).

Dore, R. P. (1973), *British Factory, Japanese Factory* (London: Allen & Unwin).

Douglas, Jack D. (1966), 'The sociological analysis of social meanings of suicide', *European Journal of Sociology*, vol. 7, no. 2.

Douglas, Jack D. (ed.) (1970a), *The Impact of Sociology: Readings in the Social Sciences* (New York: Appleton–Century–Crofts).

Douglas, Jack D. (ed.) (1970b), *The Relevance of Sociology* (New York: Appleton–Century–Crofts).

Douglas, J. W. B. (1964), *The Home and the School* (London: MacGibbon & Kee).

Douglas, J. W. B. (1969), *All Our Future* (London: MacGibbon & Kee).

Downes, D. and Rock, P. (eds.) (1979), *Deviant Interpretations: Problems in Criminological Theory* (Oxford: Martin Robertson).

Downes, D. and Rock, P. (1982), *Understanding Deviance* (Oxford: Clarendon Press).

Dube, S. C. (1955), *Indian Village* (London: Routledge & Kegan Paul).

Dube, S. C. (1958), *India's Changing Villages* (London: Routledge & Kegan Paul).

Dumont, L. (1966), *Homo Hierarchicus: The Caste System and its Implications* (London: Weidenfeld & Nicolson, 1970).

Dupeux, G. (1954–5), 'Electoral behaviour', *Current Sociology*, vol. 3, no. 4.

Durbin, E. F. M. and Bowlby, J. (1938), *War and Democracy* (London: Kegan Paul, Trench, Trubner).

Durkheim, Émile (1893), *The Division of Labour in Society* (New York: Macmillan, 1933).

Durkheim, Émile (1895), *The Rules of Sociological Method* (Chicago: University of Chicago Press, 1938).

Durkheim, Émile (1897), *Suicide: A Study in Sociology* (Glencoe, Ill.: Free Press, 1951).

Durkheim, Émile (1898), Preface to *L'Année Sociologique*, vol. 1.

Durkheim, Émile (1903), 'Sociologie et sciences sociales', *Revue philosophique*, vol. 55.

Durkheim, Émile (1904), 'On the relation of sociology to the social sciences and to philosophy', *Sociological Papers*, vol. 1.

Durkheim, Émile (1906), 'The determination of the moral fact', in Durkheim (1924).

Durkheim, Émile (1909), 'Sociologie et sciences sociales', in *De la méthode dans les sciences* (Paris: Alcan).

Durkheim, Émile (1912), *The Elementary Forms of the Religious Life: A Study in Religious Sociology* (London: Allen & Unwin, 1915).

Durkheim, Émile (1922), *Education and Sociology* (Glencoe, Ill.: Free Press, 1956).

Durkheim, Émile (1924), *Sociology and Philosophy* (London: Cohen & West, 1953).

Durkheim, Émile (1925), *Moral Education: A Study in the Theory and Application of the Sociology of Education* (New York: Free Press, 1961).

Durkheim, Émile (1950), *Professional Ethics and Civic Morals* (London: Routledge & Kegan Paul, 1957).

Durkheim, Émile (1960), *Montesquieu and Rousseau: Precursors of Sociology* (Ann Arbor, Mich.: University of Michigan Press).

Durkheim, Émile and Mauss, Marcel (1913), 'Note sur la notion de civilisation', *L'Année Sociologique*, vol. 12.

Duverger, M. (1951), *Political Parties* (London: Methuen, 1959).

Eagleton, Terry (1983), *Literary Theory: An Introduction* (Oxford: Blackwell).

Easton, D. (1965), *A Systems Analysis of Political Life* (New York: Wiley).

Eckstein, H. (ed.) (1964), *Internal War* (New York: Free Press).

Eden, F. M. (1797), *The State of the Poor* (3 vols., facsimile reprint, London: Frank Cass, 1966).

Eisenstadt, S. N. (1963), *The Political Systems of Empires* (New York: Free Press).

Engels, Friedrich (1884), *The Origin of the Family, Private Property and the State* (New York: International Publishers, 1972).

Etzioni-Halevy, E. (1985), *The Knowledge Elite and the Failure of Prophecy* (London: Allen & Unwin).

Evans-Pritchard, E. E. (1951), *Social Anthropology* (London: Cohen & West).

Faaland, Just (ed.) (1982), *Population and the World Economy in the 21st Century* (Oxford: Blackwell).

Farmer, M. (1982), 'Rational action in economic and social theory: some misunderstandings', *European Journal of Sociology*, vol. 22, no. 1.

Fay, B. (1975), *Social Theory and Political Practice* (London: Allen & Unwin).

Ferge, Zsuzsa (1977), 'School systems and school reforms', in Kloskowska and Martinotti, 1977.

Ferge, Zsuzsa (1979), *A Society in the Making: Hungarian Social and Societal Policy 1945–75* (Harmondsworth: Penguin Books).

Ferguson, Adam (1767), *An Essay on the History of Civil Society* (reprint, ed. with an introduction by Duncan Forbes, Edinburgh: Edinburgh University Press, 1966).

Field, F. (ed.) (1983), *The Wealth Report: 2* (London: Routledge & Kegan Paul).

Fine, B. *et al.* (1979), *Capitalism and the Rule of Law* (London: Hutchinson).

Finer, S. E. (1958), *Anonymous Empire: A Study of the Lobby in Great Britain* (London: Pall Mall).

Finley, M. I. (ed.) (1968), *Slavery in Classical Antiquity* (Cambridge: Heffer).

Finley, M. I. (1973), *The Ancient Economy* (London: Chatto & Windus).

Finley, M. I. (1977), 'The Ancient City: from Fustel de Coulanges to Max Weber and beyond', *Comparative Studies in Society and History*, vol. 19 (corrected reprint in Finley 1981).

Finley, M. I. (1980), *Ancient Slavery and Modern Ideology* (London: Chatto & Windus).

Finley, M. I. (1981), *Economy and Society in Ancient Greece*, eds. R. P. Saller and B. D. Shaw (London: Chatto & Windus).

Finley, M. I. (1983), 'Ancient society' and 'Slavery', in Bottomore (1983).

Firth, R. (1939), *Primitive Polynesian Economy* (2nd edn, Hamden, Conn.: Shoe String Press, 1965).

Firth, R. (1951), *Elements of Social Organization* (2nd edn, London: Watts, 1956).

Firth, R. (1956), *Human Types*, 2nd edn (London: Nelson).

Firth, R. (ed.) (1957), *Man and Culture* (London: Routledge & Kegan Paul).

Firth, R. (1972), *The Sceptical Anthropologist? Social Anthropology and Marxist Views on Society*. From the Proceedings of the British Academy (London: Oxford University Press).

Fisher, B. M. and Strauss, A. L. (1978), 'Interactionism', in Bottomore and Nisbet (1978).

Fitzgerald, C. P. (1952), *The Birth of Communist China* (Harmondsworth: Penguin Books, 1964).

Flint, R. (1893), *History of the Philosophy of History* (Edinburgh and London: W. Blackwood).

Florence, P. Sargant (1950), 'Patterns in recent social research', *British Journal of Sociology*, vol. 1, no. 3.

Florence, P. Sargant (1953), *The Logic of British and American Industry* (rev. edn, London: Routledge & Kegan Paul, 1961).

Floud, J., Halsey, A. H. and Martin, F. M. (1956), *Social Class and Educational Opportunity* (London: Heinemann).

Forde, C. D. (1941), *Habitat, Economy and Society* (London: Methuen).

Foster, G. M. (1965), 'The peasants and the image of limited good', *American Anthropologist*, vol. 62, no. 2.

Fox, R. (1967), *Kinship and Marriage* (Harmondsworth: Penguin Books).

Frank, A. G. (1967), 'Sociology of development and underdevelopment of sociology', *Catalyst* (Buffalo), vol. 3.

Frank, A. G. (1969), *Capitalism and Underdevelopment in Latin America* (New York: Monthly Review Press).

Fraser, R. (ed.) (1968–9), *Work*, 2 vols. (Harmondsworth: Penguin Books).

Frazer, J. G. (1890), *The Golden Bough: A Study in Magic and Religion*, 3rd rev. edn, 13 vols. (London: Macmillan). Chapters 1–7 of abridged edn published as *Magic and Religion* (London: Watts, 1944).

Freeman, E. A. (1873), *Comparative Politics* (London: Macmillan).

Freud, Sigmund (1927), *The Future of an Illusion* (Standard edn, Vol. 21, London: Hogarth Press, 1962).

Freud, Sigmund (1933), Letter to Einstein. Reprinted in Bramson and Goethals, 1964.

Fried, M. (1966), 'On the concepts of "tribe" and "tribal society"', *Transactions of the New York Academy of Sciences*, Series III, vol. 28.

Fried, M., Harris, M. and Murphy, R. (eds.) (1968), *War: The Anthropology of Armed Conflict* (New York: Doubleday).

Friedmann, G. (1946), *Industrial Society* (Glencoe, Ill.: Free Press, 1955).

Friedmann, G. (1956), *The Anatomy of Work* (London: Heinemann, 1961).

Friedmann, G. (1966), *7 Études sur l'homme et la technique* (Paris: Gonthier).

Friedmann, J. and Wulff, R. (1975), *The Urban Transition* (London: Edward Arnold, 1976).

Friedmann, W. G. (1951), *Law and Social Change in Contemporary Britain* (London: Stevens).

Friedmann, W. G. (1959), *Law in a Changing Society* (2nd edn, Harmondsworth: Penguin Books, 1972).

Friedmann, W. G. (1961–2), 'Sociology of law', *Current Sociology*, vol. 10/11, no. 1.

Friedrich, C. J. (ed.) (1966), *Revolution* (New York: Atherton Press).

Friedrich, C. J., Curtis, M. and Barber, B. R. (eds.) (1969), *Totalitarianism in Perspective: Three Views* (London: Pall Mall).

Friis, H. (1959), 'The application of sociology to social welfare planning and administration', in ISA, 1959, vol. 2.

Frisby, D. (1984), *Georg Simmel* (Chichester and London: Ellis Horwood/Tavistock).

Fromm, E. (1932), 'The method and function of an analytic social psychology: Notes on psychoanalysis and historical materialism'. Translated, with other essays, in *The Crisis of Psychoanalysis* (New York: Holt, Rinehart & Winston, 1970).

Fromm, E. (1942), *The Fear of Freedom* (London: Routledge & Kegan Paul).

Fustel de Coulanges, N. D. (1864), *The Ancient City: A Study in the Religion, Laws and Institutions of Greece and Rome* (Garden City, NY: Doubleday, 1956).

Gabor, D. (1970), *Innovations: Scientific, Technological and Social* (New York: Oxford University Press).

Galbraith, J. K. (1971), *The New Industrial State*, 2nd edn (Boston: Houghton Mifflin).

Gallie, D. (1978), *In Search of the New Working Class* (Cambridge: Cambridge University Press).

Galtung, J. (1967), *Theory and Methods of Social Research* (London: Allen & Unwin).

Gamble, A. (1985), *Britain in Decline*, 2nd edn (London: Macmillan).

Garfinkel, H. (1967), *Studies in Ethnomethodology* (Englewood Cliffs, NJ: Prentice-Hall).

Gellner, E. (1958), 'Time and theory in social anthropology', *Mind*, vol. 67, no. 266.

Gellner, E. (1964), *Thought and Change* (London: Weidenfeld & Nicolson).

Gellner, E. (1968), 'The new idealism – cause and meaning in the social sciences'. Repr. in Gellner (1973).

Gellner, E. (1973), *Cause and Meaning in the Social Sciences* (London: Routledge & Kegan Paul).

Gellner, E. (1983), *Nations and Nationalism* (Oxford: Blackwell).

George, V. and Manning, N. (1980), *Socialism, Social Welfare and the Soviet Union* (London: Routledge & Kegan Paul).

Geras, N. (1983), *Marx and Human Nature: Refutation of a Legend* (London: Verso).

Gerth, H. H. and Mills, C. W. (eds.) (1947), *From Max Weber: Essays in Sociology* (London: Kegan Paul, Trench, Trubner).

Gerth, H. H. and Mills, C. W. (1954), *Character and Social Structure* (London: Routledge & Kegan Paul).

Gewirth, A. (1954), 'Can men change laws of social science?', *Philosophy of Science*, vol. 21, no. 3.

Gibson, Quentin (1960), *The Logic of Social Enquiry* (London: Routledge & Kegan Paul).

Giddens, A. (1966), 'A typology of suicide', *European Journal of Sociology*, vol. 7, no. 2.

Giddens, A. (1971), *Capitalism and Modern Social Theory* (Cambridge: Cambridge University Press).

Giddens, A. (1972), *Politics and Sociology in the Thought of Max Weber* (London: Macmillan).

Giddens, A. (1973), *The Class Structure of the Advanced Societies* (London: Hutchinson).

Giddens, A. (1976), *New Rules of Sociological Method* (London: Hutchinson).

Giddens, A. (1978), 'Positivism and its critics', in Bottomore and Nisbet (1978).

Giddens, A. (1979), *Central Problems in Sociological Theory* (London: Macmillan).

Giddens, A. (1981), *A Contemporary Critique of Historical Materialism*, Vol. 1 (London: Macmillan).

Giddens, A. (1984), *The Constitution of Society* (Oxford: Polity Press).

Gilmour, R. (1981), *The Idea of the Gentleman in the Victorian Novel* (London: Allen & Unwin).

Ginsberg, M. (1921), *The Psychology of Society* (London: Methuen, 1964).

Ginsberg, M. (1932), 'The concept of evolution in sociology', in Ginsberg (1956).

Ginsberg, M. (1934), *Sociology* (London: Oxford University Press).

Ginsberg, M. (1939), 'The causes of war', in Ginsberg (1947).

Ginsberg, M. (1947), *Reason and Unreason in Society* (London: Longmans, Green).

Ginsberg, M. (1953), *The Idea of Progress: A Revaluation* (London: Methuen).

Ginsberg, M. (1956), *On the Diversity of Morals* (London: Heinemann).

Ginsberg, M. (1958), 'Social change', *British Journal of Sociology*, vol. 9, no. 3.

Ginsberg, M. (ed.) (1959), *Law and Opinion in the Twentieth Century* (London: Stevens).

Girard, A. (1961), *La Réussite sociale en France* (Paris: Presses Universitaires de France).

Glasgow University Media Group (1976), *Bad News* (London: Routledge & Kegan Paul).

Glasgow University Media Group (1980), *More Bad News* (London: Routledge & Kegan Paul).

Glass, D. V. (1940), *Population Policies and Movements in Europe* (Oxford: Clarendon Press).

Glass, D. V. (1950), 'The application of social research', *British Journal of Sociology*, vol. 1, no. 1.

Glass, D. V. (ed.) (1954), *Social Mobility in Britain* (London: Routledge & Kegan Paul).

Glass, D. V. (1959), 'Education', in Ginsberg (1959).

Glotz, G. (1928), *The Greek City* (London: Routledge & Kegan Paul, 1965).

Gluckman, Max (1949), *An Analysis of the Sociological Theories of B. Malinowski* (Rhodes–Livingstone Papers, 16).

Gluckman, Max (1955), *The Judicial Process among the Barotse of Northern Rhodesia* (Manchester: Manchester University Press).

Glueck, S. and E. (1930), *500 Criminal Careers* (New York: Knopf; repr. Kraus, 1965).

Godelier, Maurice (1973), *Perspectives in Marxist Anthropology* (Cambridge: Cambridge University Press).

Goldmann, L. (1970), *Marxisme et sciences humaines* (Paris: Gallimard).

Goldmann, L. (1971), *Cultural Creation in Modern Society* (Oxford: Blackwell, 1977).

Goldthorpe, J. H. (1980), *Social Mobility and Class Structure in Modern Britain* (Oxford: Clarendon Press).

Goldthorpe, J. H. *et al.* (1968–9), *The Affluent Worker*, 3 vols. (Cambridge: Cambridge University Press).

Goode, W. J. (1966), 'Family disorganization', in Merton and Nisbet (1976).

Goode, W. J. and Hatt, P. K. (1952), *Methods in Social Research* (New York: McGraw-Hill).

Goodfellow, D. M. (1939), *Principles of Economic Sociology* (London: Routledge).

Goodman, Paul (1960), *Growing Up Absurd* (New York: Random House).

Goodsell, W. (1934), *A History of Marriage and the Family* (rev. edn, New York: Macmillan, 1947).

Goody, J. *et al.* (eds.) (1976), *Family and Inheritance: Rural Society in Western Europe 1200–1800* (Cambridge: Cambridge University Press).

Gopal, S. (1949), *The Permanent Settlement in Bengal and its Results* (London: Allen & Unwin).

Gore, Charles (Bishop of Oxford) (ed.) (1913), *Property: Its Duties and Rights* (London: Macmillan).

Goss, M. E. W. and Reader, G. G. (1956), 'Collaboration between sociologist and physician', *Social Problems*, vol. 4, no. 1.

Gough, K. (1960), 'Is the family universal? – the Nayar case', in Bell and Vogel (1960).

Gough, K. (1967), 'World revolution and the science of man', in Roszak (1967).

Gouldner, A. W. (1956), 'Explorations in applied social science', *Social Problems*, vol. 3, no. 3.

Gramsci, A. (1929–35), *Selections from the Prison Notebooks* (eds. Quintin Hoare and Geoffrey Nowell Smith, London: Lawrence & Wishart, 1971).

Granger, G. G. (1956), *La Mathématique sociale du Marquis de Condorcet* (Paris: Presses Universitaires de France).

Greenberg, D. F. (ed.) (1981), *Crime and Capitalism: Readings in Marxist Criminology* (Palo Alto, Calif.: Mayfield).

Guevara, Che (1960), *Guerrilla Warfare* (London: Cassell).

Gurvitch, G. (1945), 'Social control', in Gurvitch and Moore (1945).

Gurvitch, G. (1957), *La vocation actuelle de la sociologie* (Paris: Presses Universitaires de France).

Gurvitch, G. (ed.) (1958), *Traité de sociologie* (2nd edn, 2 vols., Paris: Presses Universitaires de France, 1962).

Gurvitch, G. and Moore, W. E. (eds.) (1945), *Twentieth Century Sociology* (New York: Philosophical Library).

Habermas, J. (1968), *Knowledge and Human Interests* (London: Heinemann, 1972).

Habermas, J. (1968–9), *Toward a Rational Society* (London: Heinemann, 1971).

Habermas, J. (1973), *Legitimation Crisis* (London: Heinemann, 1976).

Habermas, J. (1976), *Communication and the Evolution of Society* (London: Heinemann, 1979).

Habermas, J. (1981), *Theorie des kommunikativen Handels*, 2 vols. (Frankfurt: Suhrkamp).

Halbwachs, M. (1938), *The Psychology of Social Classes* (London: Heinemann, 1958).

Hallowell, A. I. (1953), 'Culture, personality and society', in Kroeber (1953).

Halsey, A. H., Floud, J. and Anderson, C. A. (eds.) (1961), *Education, Economy and Society* (New York: Free Press).

Halsey, A. H., Heath, A. F. and Ridge, J. M. (1980), *Origins and Destinations: Family, Class and Education in Modern Britain* (Oxford: Clarendon Press).

Hamilton, P. (1983), *Talcott Parsons* (Chichester and London: Ellis Horwood/Tavistock).

Hamilton, R. (1978), *The Liberation of Women* (London: Allen & Unwin).

Hamilton, R. F. (1967), *Affluence and the French Worker in the Fourth Republic* (Princeton, NJ: Princeton University Press).

Hans, N. (1958), *Comparative Education*, rev. edn (London: Routledge & Kegan Paul).

Hardach, G. and Karras, D. (1978), *A Short History of Socialist Economic Thought* (London: Edward Arnold).

Harré, R. (1979), *Social Being* (Oxford: Blackwell).

Harrington, M. (1962), *The Other America* (New York: Macmillan).

Harris. D. B. (ed.) (1957), *The Concept of Development* (Minneapolis, Minn.: University of Minnesota Press).

Harris, L. (1983), 'State monopoly capitalism', in Bottomore (1983).

Hatt, P. K. and Reiss, A. J. (eds.) (1957), *Cities and Society* (Glencoe, Ill.: Free Press).

Hayek, F. A. (ed.) (1935), *Collectivist Economic Planning: Critical Studies on the Possibilities of Socialism* (London: Routledge).

Hayek, F. A. (1952), *The Counter-Revolution of Science* (Glencoe, Ill.: Free Press).

Hayek, F. A. (1982), *Law, Legislation and Liberty*, 3 vols. in 1 (London: Routledge & Kegan Paul).

Heath, A. (1981), *Social Mobility* (London: Fontana).

Heberle, R. (1951), *Social Movements: An Introduction to Political Sociology* (New York: Appleton-Century-Crofts).

Hegedüs, A. (1976), *Socialism and Bureaucracy* (London: Allison & Busby).

Heilbroner, R. L. (1952), *The Great Economists* (London: Eyre & Spottiswoode, 1955).

Held, D. (1980), *Introduction to Critical Theory: Horkheimer to Habermas* (London: Hutchinson).

Herberg, W. (1955), *Catholic, Protestant, Jew* (Garden City, NY: Doubleday).

Herskovits, M. J. (1952), *Economic Anthropology* (New York: Knopf).

Hilferding, R. (1904), *Böhm-Bawerk's Criticism of Marx* (New York: Augustus M. Kelley, 1949).

Hilferding, R. (1910), *Finance Capital* (London: Routledge & Kegan Paul, 1981).

Hilferding, R. (1927), 'Die Aufgaben der Sozialdemokratie in der Republik'. English trans. in Bottomore and Goode (1983).

Hilferding, R. (1941), *Das historische Problem* (Ms. first published in *Zeitschrift für Politik*, New series, vol. 1, 1954).

Hill, R. (1958), 'Sociology of marriage and family behaviour 1945–56', *Current Sociology*, vol. 7, no. 1.

Hilton, R. H. (1969), *The Decline of Serfdom in Medieval England* (London: Macmillan).

Hilton, R. H. (1983), 'Feudal society', in Bottomore (1983).

Himmelstrand, U. *et al.* (1981), *Beyond Welfare Capitalism* (London: Heinemann).

Himmelweit, S. (1983), 'Domestic labour', in Bottomore (1983).

Hindess, B. (1984), 'Rational choice theory and the analysis of political action', *Economy and Society*, vol. 13, no. 3.

Hindess, B. and Hirst, P. Q. (1975), *Pre-Capitalist Modes of Production* (London: Routledge & Kegan Paul).

Hindess, B. and Hirst, P. Q. (1977), *Mode of Production and Social Formation* (London: Macmillan).

Hirsch, Fred (1977), *Social Limits to Growth* (London: Routledge & Kegan Paul).

Hirst, P. Q. (1975), 'Marx and Engels on law, crime and morality', in Taylor *et al.* (1975).

Hirst, P. Q. (1976), *Social Evolution and Sociological Categories* (London: Allen & Unwin).

Hirst, P. Q. and Woolley, P. (1982), *Social Relations and Human Attributes* (London: Tavistock).

Hobhouse, L. T. (1906), *Morals in Evolution* (London: Chapman & Hall).

Hobhouse, L. T. (1908), 'Introduction', *Sociological Review*, vol. 1, no. 1.

Hobhouse, L. T. (1911), *Social Evolution and Political Theory* (New York: Columbia University Press).

Hobhouse, L. T. (1912), *Liberalism* (London: University Press, 1945).

Hobhouse, L. T. (1913a), 'The historical evolution of property, in fact and in idea', in Gore (1913).

Hobhouse, L. T. (1913b), *Development and Purpose* (London: Macmillan).

Hobhouse, L. T. (1924), *Social Development: Its Nature and Conditions* (London: Allen & Unwin).

Hobhouse, L. T., Wheeler, G. C. and Ginsberg, M. (1915), *The Material Culture and Social Institutions of the Simpler Peoples* (London: Chapman & Hall).

Hobsbawm, E. (1959), *Primitive Rebels* (new edn, Manchester: Manchester University Press, 1971).

Hobsbawm, E. (1964), Introduction to Karl Marx, *Pre-Capitalist Economic Formations* (London: Lawrence & Wishart).

Hobsbawm, E. (1980), 'The revival of narrative: some comments', *Past and Present*, vol. 86.

Hodges, H. A. (1944), *Wilhelm Dilthey: An Introduction* (London: Trubner).

Hodges, H. A. (1952), *The Philosophy of Wilhelm Dilthey* (London: Routledge & Kegan Paul).

Hodgkin, T. (1962), *African Political Parties: An Introductory Guide* (Harmondsworth: Penguin Books).

Hoebel, E. A. (1954), *The Law of Primitive Man* (Cambridge, Mass.: Harvard University Press).

Hofstadter, R. (1955), *Social Darwinism in American Thought*, rev. edn (Boston: Beacon Press).

Hofstadter, R. and Lipset, S. M. (eds.) (1965), *Turner and the Sociology of the Frontier* (New York: Basic Books).

Hogbin, H. I. (1934), *Law and Order in Polynesia* (London: Christophers).

Hoggart, R. (1957), *The Uses of Literacy* (London: Chatto & Windus).

Holton, R. J. (1985), *The Transition from Feudalism to Capitalism* (London: Macmillan).

Homans, G. C. (1948), *The Human Group* (New York: Harcourt Brace).

Horkheimer, M. (1937), 'Traditional and critical theory', trans. in *Critical Theory: Selected Essays* (New York: Herder & Herder, 1972).

Horowitz, D. (ed.) (1968), *Marx and Modern Economics* (New York: Monthly Review Press).

Horowitz, I. L. (ed.) (1967), *The Rise and Fall of Project Camelot* (Cambridge, Mass.: MIT Press).

Horvat, B. (1969), *An Essay on Yugoslav Society* (White Plains, NY: International Arts and Sciences Press).

Horvat, B. (1982), *The Political Economy of Socialism* (Oxford: Martin Robertson).

Hoselitz, B. (1960), *Sociological Aspects of Development* (New York: Free Press).

Hughes, H. Stuart (1958), *Consciousness and Society: The Reorientation of European Social Thought 1890–1930* (New York: Knopf).

Hunt, Alan (1978), *The Sociological Movement in Law* (London: Macmillan).

Hunter, Guy (1969), *Modernizing Peasant Societies* (London: Oxford University Press).

Huntington, S. P. (1968), *Political Order in Changing Societies* (New Haven, Conn.: Yale University Press).

Hussain, A. and Tribe, K. (1981), *Marxism and the Agrarian Question*, 2 vols. (London: Macmillan).

Hutchison, T. W. (1981), *The Politics and Philosophy of Economics: Marxians, Keynesians and Austrians* (Oxford: Blackwell).

Hutton, J. H. (1951), *Caste in India*, 2nd edn (Bombay: Oxford University Press).

Hyman, R. (1975), *Industrial Relations: A Marxist Introduction* (London: Macmillan).

Hyman, R. (1983), 'Trade unions', in Bottomore (1983).

Hyman, R. (1984), *Strikes*, 3rd edn (London: Fontana).

Ibn-Khaldûn (1377–1404), *An Introduction to History* (3 vols., New York: Pantheon Books, 1958).

Ingham, G. K. (1974), *Strikes and Industrial Conflict: Britain and Scandinavia* (London: Macmillan).

International Sociological Association (ISA) (1954), *Transactions of the Second World Congress of Sociology* (London: ISA).

International Sociological Association (ISA) (1956), *Transactions of the Third World Congress of Sociology* (London: ISA).

International Sociological Association (ISA) (1959), *Transactions of the Fourth World Congress of Sociology* (London: ISA).

Issawi, C. (1955), *An Arab Philosophy of History*, 2nd edn (London: John Murray).

Jackson, B. and Marsden, D. (1963), *Education and the Working Class* (London: Routledge & Kegan Paul).

Jacobs, P. and Landau, S. (eds.) (1966), *The New Radicals: A Report with Documents* (New York: Random House).

Jacoby, R. (1983), 'Western Marxism' in Bottomore (1983).

James, W. (1902), *The Varieties of Religious Experience* (New York: Doubleday, n.d.).

James, W. (1910), 'The moral equivalent of war', in *Memories and Studies* (New York: Longmans).

Jameson, K. P. and Wilber, C. K. (1981), 'Socialism and development: editors' introduction', *World Development*, vol. 9, no. 9/10.

Janowitz, M. (1964), *The Military in the Political Development of New Nations* (Chicago: University of Chicago Press).

Jencks, C. *et al.* (1972), *Inequality: A Reassessment of the Effect of Family and Schooling in America* (New York: Basic Books).

Kabir, H. (1956), *Education in New India* (New York: Harper & Row).

Kamenka, E. and Erh-Soon Tay, A. (eds.) (1980), *Law and Social Control* (London: Edward Arnold).

Kapadia, K. M. (1958), *Marriage and Family in India*, 2nd edn (Bombay: Oxford University Press).

Karabel, J. and Halsey, A. H. (eds.) (1977), *Power and Ideology in Education* (New York: Oxford University Press).

Karim, A. K. Nazmul (1956), *Changing Society in India and Pakistan* (Dacca: Oxford University Press).

Kassof, A. (ed.) (1968), *Prospects for Soviet Society* (London: Pall Mall).

Katz, D. *et al.* (1954), *Public Opinion and Propaganda* (New York: Holt).

Katz, N. and Kemnitzer, D. (1983), 'Kinship', in Bottomore (1983).

Keat, R. (1981), *The Politics of Social Theory* (Oxford: Blackwell).

Keat, R. and Urry, J. (1982), *Social Theory as Science*, 2nd edn (London: Routledge & Kegan Paul).

Kechekyan, S. F. (1956), 'Social progress and law', in ISA *Transactions*, vol. 6.

Kelsall, R. K. (1957), *Report on an Inquiry into Applications for Admissions to Universities* (London: Association of Universities of the British Commonwealth).

Kerr, C. *et al.* (1962), *Industrialism and Industrial Man* (London: Heinemann).

Key, V. O. (1950), *Politics, Parties and Pressure Groups* (5th edn, New York: Crowell, 1964).

Kiernan, V. G. (1983), 'Religion' and 'Stages of development', in Bottomore (1983).

Kloskowska, A. and Martinotti, G. (eds.) (1977), *Education in a Changing Society* (London: Sage).

Kluckhohn, C. (1953), 'Universal categories of culture', in Kroeber (1953).

Knowles, K. G. J. C. (1952), *Strikes: A Study in Industrial Conflict* (Oxford: Blackwell).

Kohn, H. (1944), *The Idea of Nationalism* (New York: Collier Books, 1967).

Kolakowski, L. (1971), 'Althusser's Marx', *The Socialist Register*.

Kolakowski, L. (1978), *Main Currents of Marxism: Its Rise, Growth and Dissolution*, 3 vols. (Oxford: Clarendon Press).

Kolko, G. (1962), *Wealth and Power in America* (London: Thames & Hudson).

Konrád, G. and Szelényi, I. (1979), *The Intellectuals on the Road to Class Power* (Brighton: Harvester Press).

Kornhauser, A., Dubin, R. and Ross, A. M. (eds.) (1954), *Industrial Conflict* (New York: McGraw-Hill).

Korsch, K. (1923), *Marxism and Philosophy* (London: New Left Books, 1970).

Kosambi, D. D. (1956), *An Introduction to the Study of Indian History* (Bombay: Popular Book Depot).

Krader, L. (1975), *The Asiatic Mode of Production* (Assen: Van Gorcum).

Krampe, G. (1978), 'Social research in the field of new public technologies', in *Social Research in the Public Sector* (Amsterdam: European Society for Opinion and Marketing Research).

Kroeber, A. L. (ed.) (1953), *Anthropology Today* (Chicago: University of Chicago Press).

Kroeber, A. L. and Kluckhohn, C. (1952), *Culture*. Papers of the Peabody Museum of Harvard, 47 (1).

Kuhn, T. (1970), *The Structure of Scientific Revolutions*, 2nd edn (Chicago: University of Chicago Press).

Kühne, K. (1972), *Economics and Marxism* (2 vols., London: Macmillan, 1979).

Laing, D. (1978), *The Marxist Theory of Art: An Introductory Survey* (Brighton: Harvester).

Lakatos, I. and Musgrave, A. (eds.) (1970), *Criticism and the Growth of Knowledge* (Cambridge: Cambridge University Press).

Lane, D. (1970), *Politics and Society in the USSR* (London: Weidenfeld & Nicolson).

Lane, D. (1976), *The Socialist Industrial State* (London: Allen & Unwin).

Lane, D. (1982), *The End of Social Inequality?* (London: Allen & Unwin).

Lang, Olga (1946), *Chinese Family and Society* (New Haven, Conn.: Yale University Press).

Lanternari, V. (1960), *The Religions of the Oppressed* (New York: Knopf).

Larrain, J. (1979), *The Concept of Ideology* (London: Hutchinson).

Larrain, J. (1983), 'Base and superstructure', in Bottomore (1983).

Larrain, J. (1986), *A Reconstruction of Historical Materialism* (London: Allen & Unwin).

Laslett, P. (1977), *Family Life and Illicit Love in Earlier Generations* (Cambridge: Cambridge University Press).

Laslett, P. and Runciman, W. G. (eds.) (1967), *Philosophy, Politics and Society* (third series, Oxford: Blackwell).

Lea, J. and Young, J. (1984), *What is to be Done About Law and Order?* (Harmondsworth: Penguin).

Leach, Edmund (1957), 'The epistemological background of Malinowski's empiricism', in Firth (1957).

Leach, Edmund (ed.) (1967), *The Structural Study of Myth and Totemism* (London: Tavistock).

Leach, Edmund (1970), *Lévi-Strauss* (London: Fontana).

Le Bras, G. (1955–8), *Études de sociologie religieuse*, 2 vols. (Paris: Presses Universitaires de France).

Lefebvre, G. (1939), *The Coming of the French Revolution* (Princeton, NJ: Princeton University Press, 1947).

Leiss, W. (1972), *The Domination of Nature* (New York: Braziller).

Le Play, F. (1877–9), *Les Ouvriers européens*, 2nd enlarged edn, 6 vols. (Tours: Mame).

Lévi-Strauss, C. (1949), *The Elementary Structures of Kinship* (rev. edn, Boston: Beacon Press, 1969).

Lévi-Strauss, C. (1953), 'Social structure', in Kroeber (1953).

Lévi-Strauss, C. (1958), *Structural Anthropology* (New York: Basic Books, 1963).

Lévi-Strauss, C. (1962), *The Savage Mind* (London: Weidenfeld & Nicolson, 1966).

Lévy-Bruhl, L. (1903), *Ethics and Moral Science* (London: Constable, 1905).

Lewis, W. A. (1955), *The Theory of Economic Growth* (London: Allen & Unwin).

Lindsay, A. D. (1943), *The Modern Democratic State* (London: Oxford University Press).

Lindsay, B. (1941), 'Law', in O'Malley (1941).

Lippmann, W. (1922), *Public Opinion* (London: Allen & Unwin).

Lipset, S. M. (1960), *Political Man* (London: Heinemann).

Lipset, S. M. (1963), *The First New Nation: The United States in Historical and Comparative Perspective* (New York: Basic Books).

Lipset, S. M. (1968), *Revolution and Counterrevolution: Change and Persistence in Social Structures* (New York: Basic Books).

Lipset, S. M. (ed.) (1969), *Politics and the Social Sciences* (New York: Oxford University Press).

Lipset, S. M. and Bendix, R. (1959), *Social Mobility in Industrial Society* (Berkeley and Los Angeles: University of California Press).

Lipset, S. M. and Rokkan, S. (eds.) (1967), *Party Systems and Voter Alignments* (New York: Free Press).

Llewellyn, K. N. and Hoebel, E. A. (1941), *The Cheyenne Way* (Norman: University of Oklahoma Press).

Lloyd, Christopher (ed.) (1983), *Social Theory and Political Practice* (Oxford: Clarendon Press).

Lloyd, P. C. (1967), *Africa in Social Change* (Harmondsworth: Penguin Books).

Lloyd, P. C. (1982), *A Third World Proletariat?* (London: Allen & Unwin).

Lockwood, D. (1956), 'Some remarks on "The Social System"', *British Journal of Sociology*, vol. 7, no. 2.

Lockwood, D. (1958), *The Blackcoated Worker* (London: Allen & Unwin).

Lorenz, K. (1966), *On Aggression* (London: Methuen).

Louch, A. R. (1966), *Explanation and Human Action* (Oxford: Blackwell).

Löwe, A. (1935), *Economics and Sociology* (London: Allen & Unwin).

Lowie, R. H. (1920), *Primitive Society* (New York: Liveright).

Lowie, R. H. (1927), *The Origin of the State* (New York: Russell).

Lowie, R. H. (1936), *Primitive Religion* (London: Routledge).

Lowie, R. H. (1950), *Social Organization* (London: Routledge & Kegan Paul).

Löwith, K. (1932), *Max Weber and Karl Marx* (London: Allen & Unwin, 1982).

Luckham, R. (1977), 'Militarism: force, class and international conflict', *Institute of Development Studies Bulletin*, vol. 9, no. 1.

Luckmann, T. (ed.) (1978), *Phenomenology and Sociology* (Harmondsworth: Penguin Books).

Lukács, G. (1923), *History and Class Consciousness* (London: Merlin Press, 1971).

Lukes, S. (1973), *Émile Durkheim: His Life and Work* (London: Allen Lane).

Lukes, S. (1985), *Marxism and Morality* (Oxford: Clarendon Press).

Luxemburg, Rosa (1922), *The Russian Revolution* (Ann Arbor: University of Michigan Press, 1961).

Lynd, R. A. (1939), *Knowledge for What?* (New York: Grove Press, 1964).

Lynd, R. A. and H. M. (1929), *Middletown* (New York: Harcourt).

Lynd, R. A. and H. M. (1937), *Middletown in Transition* (New York: Harcourt).

McDonald, L. (1976), *The Sociology of Law and Order* (London: Faber and Faber).

Macdonell, A. A. and Keith, A. B. (1912), *Vedic Index of Names and Subjects*, 2 vols. (London: John Murray).

McGee, T. G. (1971), *The Urbanization Process in the Third World* (London: Bell).

MacIntyre, A. (1971), *Against the Self-Images of the Age* (London: Duckworth).

MacIver, R. M. (1926), *The Modern State* (London: Oxford University Press).

MacIver, R. M. and Page, C. H. (1952), *Society: An Introductory Analysis* (London: Macmillan).

Mack, J. (1955), 'Juvenile delinquency research: a cricitism', *Sociological Review*, vol. 3, no. 47.

McKenzie, N. (ed.) (1966), *A Guide to the Social Sciences* (London: Weidenfeld & Nicolson).

McKenzie, R. T. (1963), *British Political Parties*, 2nd edn (London: Heinemann).

McKenzie, R. T. and Silver, A. (1968), *Angels in Marble* (London: Heinemann).

McLellan, D. (1969), *The Young Hegelians and Karl Marx* (London: Macmillan).

McLennan, J. F. (1876), *Studies in Ancient History* (London: Macmillan).

MacNeil, R. (1970), *The People Machine* (London: Eyre & Spottiswoode).

Macpherson, C. B. (1965), *The Real World of Democracy* (Toronto: Canadian Broadcasting Corporation).

Macpherson, C. B. (ed.) (1978), *Property: Mainstream and Critical Positions* (Oxford: Blackwell).

Maine, H. S. (1861), *Ancient Law* (London: John Murray; Everyman's Library edition, 1917).

Maine, H. S. (1871), *Village Communities in the East and West* (London: John Murray).

Maine, H. S. (1875), *Lectures on the Early History of Institutions* (London: John Murray).

Maine, H. S. (1883), *Dissertations on Early Law and Custom* (London: John Murray).

Malinowski, B. (1926), *Crime and Custom in Savage Society* (London: Routledge & Kegan Paul).

Malinowski, B. (1930), 'Culture', in *Encyclopaedia of the Social Sciences*.

Malinowski, B. (1934), 'Introduction' to Hogbin (1934).

Malinowski, B. (1939), 'The functional theory', in Malinowski, 1944.

Malinowski, B. (1944), *A Scientific Theory of Culture and Other Essays* (Chapel Hill, NC: University of North Carolina Press).

Malinowski, B. (1948), *Magic, Science and Religion, and Other Essays* (Glencoe, Ill.: Free Press).

Mallet, S. (1963), *The New Working Class* (Nottingham: Spokesman Books, 1975).

Mandel, E. (1975), *Late Capitalism* (London: New Left Books).

Mann, M. (1973), *Consciousness and Action among the Western Working Class* (London: Macmillan).

Mannheim, H. (1954), 'American criminology: impressions of a European criminologist', *British Journal of Sociology*, vol. 5, no. 4.

Mannheim, H. and Wilkins, L. T. (1955), *Prediction Methods in Relation to Borstal Training* (London: HMSO).

Mannheim, Karl (1927a), 'Conservative thought', in Mannheim (1953).

Mannheim, Karl (1927b), 'The problem of generations', in Mannheim (1952).

Mannheim, Karl (1940), *Man and Society in an Age of Reconstruction* (London: Kegan Paul, Trench, Trubner).

Mannheim, Karl (1950), *Freedom, Power and Democratic Planning* (London: Routledge & Kegan Paul).

Mannheim, Karl (1952), *Essays on the Sociology of Knowledge* (London: Routledge & Kegan Paul).

Mannheim, Karl (1953), *Essays on Sociology and Social Psychology* (London: Routledge & Kegan Paul).

Mannheim, Karl (1956), *Essays on the Sociology of Culture* (London: Routledge & Kegan Paul).

Marcuse, H. (1941), *Reason and Revolution: Hegel and the Rise of Social Theory* (New York: Oxford University Press).

Marcuse, H. (1951), *Eros and Civilization: A Philosophical Inquiry into Freud* (Boston, Mass.: Beacon Press).

Marcuse, H. (1964), *One-Dimensional Man: Studies in the Ideology of Advanced Industrial Society* (London: Routledge & Kegan Paul).

Marcuse, H. (1965), 'On science and phenomenology', in Cohen and Wartofsky (1965).

Marett, R. R. (1912), *Anthropology* (London: Williams & Norgate).

Marković, M. (1983), 'Human nature', in Bottomore (1983).

Marković, M. and Petrović, G. (eds.) (1979), *Praxis: Yugoslav Essays in the Philosophy and Methodology of the Social Sciences* (Dordrecht: Reidel).

Marriott, McKim (ed.) (1955), *Village India: Studies in the Little Community* (Chicago: University of Chicago Press).

Marshall, G. (1980), *Presbyteries and Profits: Calvinism and the Development of Capitalism in Scotland, 1560–1707* (Oxford: Clarendon Press).

Marshall, G. (1982), *In Search of the Spirit of Capitalism: An Essay on Max Weber's Protestant Ethic Thesis* (London: Hutchinson).

Marshall, T. H. (1950), *Citizenship and Social Class and Other Essays* (Cambridge: Cambridge University Press).

Marshall, T. H. (1953), 'The nature and determinants of social status', *Year Book of Education*.

Marshall, T. H. (1956), 'General survey of changes in social stratification in the twentieth century', in ISA *Transactions*, vol. 3.

Marshall, T. H. (1970), *Social Policy* (London: Hutchinson).

Marx, Karl (1847), *The Poverty of Philosophy*.

Marx, Karl (1850), *The Class Struggles in France*.

Marx, Karl (1852), *The 18th Brumaire of Louis Bonaparte*.

Marx, Karl (1853), Articles on India in *New York Daily Tribune*, repr. in Avineri (1968b).

Marx, Karl (1857–8), *Grundrisse* (Harmondsworth: Penguin Books, 1973).

Marx, Karl (1859), *A Contribution to the Critique of Political Economy*.

Marx, Karl (1867), *Capital*, Vol. 1.

Marx, Karl (1877), Letter to the editor of *Otetshestvennia Sapisky*.

Marx, Karl (1905–10), *Theories of Surplus Value*.

Marx, Karl and Engels, Friedrich (1845–6), *The German Ideology*.

Masterman, C. F. G. (1909), *The Condition of England* (London: Methuen).

Masterman, M. (1970), 'The nature of a paradigm', in Lakatos and Musgrave (1970).

Mauss, M. (1925), *The Gift* (Glencoe, Ill.: Free Press, 1954).

Mayer, K. B. and Buckley, W. (1969), *Class and Society*, 3rd edn (New York: Random House).

Mayne, J. D. (1950), *A Treatise on Hindu Law and Usage*, 11th edn ed. N. C. Aiyar (Madras: Higginbothams).

Mayo, E. (1933), *The Human Problems of an Industrial Civilization* (New York: Viking, 1960).

Mead, G. H. (1934), *Mind, Self and Society* (Chicago: University of Chicago Press).

Mead, M. (ed.) (1953), *Cultural Patterns and Technical Change* (Paris: UNESCO).

Medick, H. (1976), 'The proto-industrial family economy: the structural function of household and family during the transition from peasant to industrial capitalism', *Social History*, vol. 1.

Meisel, J. H. (1970), *Counter-Revolution: How Revolutions Die* (New York: Atherton Press).

Merton, R. K. (1957), *Social Theory and Social Structure* (3rd edn, New York: Free Press, 1968).

Merton, R. K. and Nisbet, R. (eds.) (1976), *Contemporary Social Problems*, 4th edn (New York: Harcourt Brace Jovanovich).

Metcalfe, C. (1855), *Selections From the Papers of Lord Metcalfe*, ed. J.W. Kaye (London: Smith, Elder).

Meusel, A. (1934), 'Revolution and counter-revolution', in *Encyclopaedia of the Social Sciences*.

Michels, R. (1911), *Political Parties* (Glencoe, Ill.: Free Press, 1949).

Middleton, J. and Tait, D. (eds.) (1958), *Tribes Without Rulers* (London: Routledge & Kegan Paul).

Miliband, R. (1969), *The State in Capitalist Society* (London: Weidenfeld & Nicolson).

Miliband, R. (1983a), 'The state', in Bottomore (1983).

Miliband, R. (1983b), *Class Power and State Power* (London: New Left Books).

Mill, J. S. (1879), *A System of Logic*, 10th edn, 2 vols. (London: Longmans, Green).

Miller, M. V. and Gilmore, S. (eds.) (1965), *Revolution at Berkeley* (New York: Dell).

Miller, N. and Aya, R. (eds.) (1971), *National Liberation* (New York: Free Press).

Miller, S. M. (1960), 'Comparative social mobility', *Current Sociology*, vol. 9, no. 1.

Mills, C. Wright (1951), *White Collar: The American Middle Classes* (New York: Oxford University Press).

Mills, C. Wright (1956), *The Power Elite* (New York: Oxford University Press).

Mills, C. Wright (1959), *The Sociological Imagination* (New York: Oxford University Press).

Mingione, E. (1981), *Social Conflict and the City* (Oxford: Blackwell).

Mises, L. von (1922), *Socialism: An Economic and Sociological Analysis* (2nd edn 1932; new English edn, London, Jonathan Cape, 1951).

Mohiddin, A. (1981), *African Socialism in Two Countries* (London: Croom Helm).

Mohun, S. (1983), 'Division of labour', in Bottomore (1983).

Mommsen, W. J. (1974), *The Age of Bureaucracy* (Oxford: Blackwell).

Montesquieu, C. de S. (1748), *The Spirit of Laws* (New York: Hafner, 1962).

Moore, Barrington (1966), *Social Origins of Dictatorship and Democracy* (New York: Beacon Press).

Moore, W. E. (1946), *Industrial Relations and the Social Order* (New York: Macmillan).

Moore, W. E. (1951), *Industrialization and Labour: Social Aspects of Economic Development* (Ithaca, NY: Cornell University Press).

Moreno, J. L. (1953), *Who Shall Survive?*, rev. edn (Beacon, NY: Beacon House).

Moret, A. and Davy, G. (1926), *From Tribe to Empire* (London: Routledge).

Morgan, L. H. (1877), *Ancient Society* (Cambridge, Mass.: Belknap, 1974).

Morishima, Michio (1982), *Why Has Japan 'Succeeded'? Western Technology and the Japanese Ethos* (Cambridge: Cambridge University Press).

Morris, M. B. (1977), *An Excursion into Creative Sociology* (New York: Columbia University Press).

Mosca, Gaetano (1896, 1923), *The Ruling Class* (New York: McGraw-Hill, 1939).

Moser, C. A. and Kalton, G. (1971), *Survey Methods in Social Investigation* (London: Heinemann; repr. Gower, 1985).

Mouzelis, N. P. (1967), *Organisation and Bureaucracy* (London: Routledge & Kegan Paul).

Mukerji, D. P. (1948), *Modern Indian Culture*, 2nd edn (Bombay: Hind Kitabs).

Mukherjee, Ramkrishna (1957), *The Dynamics of a Rural Society* (Berlin: Akademie Verlag).

Mukherjee, Ramkrishna *et al.* (1977), *Scientific and Technological Revolution: Social Aspects* (London: Sage).

Mulkay, M. (1979), *Science and the Sociology of Knowledge* (London: Allen & Unwin).

Mumford, L. (1940), *Culture of Cities* (London: Secker & Warburg).

Mumford, L. (1961), *The City in History* (London: Secker & Warburg).

Murdock, G. P. (1949), *Social Structure* (New York: Macmillan).

Myrdal, Alva (1945), *Nation and Family* (London: Routledge & Kegan Paul).

Myrdal, Gunnar (1944), *An American Dilemma* (New York: Harper).

Myrdal, Gunnar (1953), 'The relation between social theory and social policy', *British Journal of Sociology*, vol. 4, no. 3.

Myrdal, Gunnar (1957), *Economic Theory and Underdeveloped Regions* (London: Duckworth).

Myrdal, Gunnar (1958), *Value in Social Theory* (London: Routledge & Kegan Paul).

Myrdal, Gunnar (1968), *Asian Drama*, 3 vols. (New York: Pantheon).

Myrdal, Jan (1965), *Report from a Chinese Village* (New York: Pantheon).

Nadel, S. F. (1951), *The Foundations of Social Anthropology* (London: Cohen & West).

Nadel, S. F. (1957), *The Theory of Social Structure* (London: Cohen & West).

Nagel, E. (1957), 'Determinism and development', in Harris (1957).

Narayan, Jaya Prakash (1959), *A Plea for Reconstruction of Indian Polity*, mimeo (New Delhi: Socialist Research Bureau).

Natanson, M. (ed.) (1973), *Phenomenology and the Social Sciences* (Evanston, Ill.: Northwestern University Press).

Nehru, Jawaharlal (1960), *The Discovery of India* (London: Meridian).

Nettl, J. P. (1965), 'The German Social Democratic Party 1890–1914 as a political model', *Past and Present*, vol. 30.

Neumann, Franz (1942), *Behemoth: The Structure and Practice of National Socialism* (2nd edn, New York: Oxford University Press, 1944).

Neurath, Otto (1931), *Empiricism and Sociology* (Dordrecht: Reidel, 1973).

Nieboer, H. J. (1900), *Slavery as an Industrial System* (The Hague; Nijhoff).

Niebuhr, H. R. (1929), *The Social Sources of Denominationalism* (New York: Holt).

Nisbet, R. (1967), *The Sociological Tradition* (London: Heinemann).

Nisbet, R. (1980), *History of the Idea of Progress* (London: Heinemann).

Nordlinger, E. A. (1967), *Working Class Tories: Authority, Deference and Stable Democracy* (Berkeley, Calif.: University of California Press).

Oakes, G. (1980), 'Introduction' to Simmel (1980).

Odegard, P. H. (1928), *Pressure Politics: The Story of the Anti-Saloon League* (New York: Octagon).

Offe, C. (1980), 'The separation of form and content in liberal democratic politics', *Studies in Political Economy*, vol. 3.

Offe, C. (1984), *Contradictions of the Welfare State* (London: Hutchinson).

Ogburn, W. F. (1922), *Social Change* (New York: Dell, 1966).

Ogburn, W. F. and Nimkoff, M. F. (1955), *Technology and the Changing Family* (Boston: Houghton Mifflin).

O'Malley, L. S. S. (ed.) (1941), *Modern India and the West* (London: Oxford University Press).

Oppenheimer, F. (1907), *The State* (New York: Free Life Editions, 1975).

Ossowska, M. (1971), *Social Determinants of Moral Ideas* (London: Routledge & Kegan Paul).

Ossowski, S. (1957), *Class Structure in the Social Consciousness* (London: Routledge & Kegan Paul).

Ossowski, S. (1959), 'Social conditions and consequences of social planning', in ISA *Transactions*, vol. 3.

Ostrogorski, M. I. (1902), *Democracy and the Organization of Political Parties* (London and New York: Macmillan).

Outhwaite, W. (1975), *Understanding Social Life: The Method Called Verstehen* (London: Allen & Unwin).

Outhwaite, W. (1983a), *Concept Formation in Social Science* (London: Routledge & Kegan Paul).

Outhwaite, W. (1983b), 'Culture', in Bottomore (1983).

Pahl, R. E. (1975), *Whose City? and Further Essays on Urban Society* (Harmondsworth: Penguin).

Panitch, L. (1980), 'Recent theorizations of corporatism', *British Journal of Sociology*, vol. 31.

Pareto, Vilfredo (1902), *Les Systèmes socialistes* (Paris: Marcel Giard).

Pareto, Vilfredo (1916), *A Treatise on General Sociology* (2 vols., New York: Dover, 1963).

Park, R. E. (1926), 'The urban community as a spacial pattern and a moral order', in Burgess (1926).

Parker, S. R. *et al.* (1967), *The Sociology of Industry* (London: Allen & Unwin).

Parkin, F. (1982), *Max Weber* (Chichester and London: Ellis Horwood/ Tavistock).

Parsons, Talcott (1937), *The Structure of Social Action* (New York: McGraw-Hill).

Parsons, Talcott (1951), *The Social System* (New York: Free Press).

Parsons, Talcott (1958), 'Some reflections on the institutional framework of economic development'. Repr. in Parsons (1960).

Parsons, Talcott (1960), *Structure and Process in Modern Societies* (New York: Free Press).

Parsons, Talcott (1966), *Societies: Evolutionary and Comparative Perspectives* (Englewood Cliffs, NJ: Prentice-Hall).

Parsons, Talcott (1971), *The System of Modern Societies* (Englewood Cliffs, NJ: Prentice-Hall).

Parsons, Talcott and Smelser, N. J. (1957), *Economy and Society: A Study in the Integration of Economic and Social Theory* (Glencoe, Ill.: Free Press).

Paterson, W. E. and Thomas, H. A. (eds.) (1975), *Social Democratic Parties in Western Europe* (London: Croom Helm).

Penrose, E. F. (1934), *Population Theories and Their Applications* (Stanford, Calif.: Stanford University Press).

Perroux, F. (1960), *Économie et société* (Paris: Presses Universitaires de France).

Peters, R. S. (1958), *The Concept of Motivation* (London: Routledge & Kegan Paul).

Piaget, Jean (1968), *Structuralism* (New York: Basic Books, 1970).

Pigou, A. C. (ed.) (1925), *Memorials of Alfred Marshall* (London: Macmillan).

Pirenne, H. (1914), 'The stages in the social history of capitalism', *American Historical Review*, vol. 19, no. 3.

Pirenne, H. (1925), *Medieval Cities* (Princeton, NJ: Princeton University Press, 1925; repr. Doubleday, 1957).

Pivčević, E. (1970), *Husserl and Phenomenology* (London: Hutchinson).

Piven, F. F. and Cloward, R. A. (1977), *Poor People's Movements* (New York: Pantheon).

Plekhanov, G. V. (1898), *The Role of the Individual in History* (London: Lawrence & Wishart, 1940).

Polanyi, K. (1944), *The Great Transformation* (New York: Rinehart).

Pollard, S. (1984), *The Wasting of the British Economy*, 2nd edn (London: Croom Helm).

Poole, A. L. (1946), *Obligations of Society in the Twelfth and Thirteenth Centuries* (Oxford: Clarendon Press).

Popper, K. R. (1934), *The Logic of Scientific Discovery* (London: Hutchinson, 1959).

Popper, K. R. (1945), *The Open Society and Its Enemies*, 2 vols. (London: Routledge).

Popper, K. R. (1957), *The Poverty of Historicism* (London: Routledge & Kegan Paul).

Popper, K. R. (1974), *Unended Quest: An Intellectual Autobiography* (London: Fontana/Collins, 1976).

Poster, M. (1978), *Critical Theory of the Family* (London: Pluto Press).

Poulantzas, N. (1968), *Political Power and Social Classes* (London: New Left Books, 1973).

Poulantzas, N. (1974), *Classes in Contemporary Capitalism* (London: New Left Books, 1975).

Pound, Roscoe (1945), 'Sociology of law', in Gurvitch and Moore (1945).

Prabhu, P. N. (1956), 'A study of the social effects of urbanization on industrial workers migrating from rural areas to the city of Bombay', in UNESCO (1956).

Qualter, T. H. (1985), *Opinion Control in the Democracies* (London: Macmillan).

Quételet, A. (1835), *Sur l'homme et le développement de ses facultés ou essai de physique sociale* (Paris: Bachelier).

Raab, E. and Selznick, G. J. (1964), *Major Social Problems*, 2nd edn (New York: Harper & Row).

Rabb, T. K. and Rotberg, R. I. (eds.) (1973), *The Family in History* (New York: Harper & Row).

Radcliffe-Brown, A. R. (1922), *The Andaman Islanders* (Cambridge: Cambridge University Press).

Radcliffe-Brown, A. R. (1952), *Structure and Function in Primitive Society* (London: Cohen & West).

Radcliffe-Brown, A. R. (1957), *A Natural Science of Society* (New York: Free Press).

Radcliffe-Brown, A. R. (1958), *Method in Social Anthropology* (Chicago: University of Chicago Press).

Radcliffe-Brown, A. R. and Forde, D. (eds.) (1950), *African Systems of Kinship and Marriage* (London: Oxford University Press).

Radhakrishnan, S. (1927), *The Hindu View of Life* (London: Allen & Unwin).

Radhakrishnan, S. (1947), *Religion and Society* (London: Allen & Unwin).

Rapoport, A. (1960), *Fights, Games and Debates* (Ann Arbor, Mich.: University of Michigan Press).

Redfield, R. (1955), *The Little Community* (Chicago: University of Chicago Press).

Reich, W. (1942), *The Mass Psychology of Fascism* (London: Penguin Books, 1975).

Renner, K. (1904), *The Institutions of Private Law and their Social Functions* (London: Routledge & Kegan Paul, 1949).

Reuck, A. de and Knight, J. (eds.) (1966), *Conflict in Society* (London: Churchill).

Rheinstein, M. (ed.) (1966), *Max Weber on Law in Economy and Society* (Cambridge, Mass.: Harvard University Press).

Richards, A. I. (1957), 'The concept of culture in Malinowski's work', in Firth (1957).

Richardson, L. F. (1960a), *Statistics of Deadly Quarrels* (Pittsburgh: Boxwood Press).

Richardson, L. F. (1960b), *Arms and Insecurity* (Pittsburgh: Boxwood Press).

Richta, R. *et al.* (1969), *Civilization at the Crossroads* (White Plains, NY: International Arts and Sciences Press).

Riesman, D. (1950), *The Lonely Crowd* (New Haven: Yale University Press; abridged edn. with new preface, 1961).

Rioux, M. and Martin, Y. (eds.) (1964), *French-Canadian Society* (Toronto: McClelland & Stewart).

Ritchie, D. G. (1889), *Darwinism and Politics* (London: Swan Sonnenschein).

Robertson, R. (1970), *The Sociological Interpretation of Religion* (New York: Schocken).

Robey, D. (ed.) (1973), *Structuralism: An Introduction* (Oxford: Clarendon Press).

Rock, P. (1979), 'The sociology of crime, symbolic interactionism and some problematic qualities of radical criminology', in Downes and Rock (1979).

Roethlisberger, F. J. and Dickson, W. J. (1939), *Management and the Worker* (Cambridge, Mass.: Harvard University Press).

Rokkan, S. (1961), 'Mass suffrage, secret voting and political participation', *European Journal of Sociology*, vol. 2, no. 1.

Rosas, P. (1943), 'Caste and class in India', *Science and Society*, vol. 8, no. 2.

Rose, A. M. (1952), *The Roots of Prejudice* (Paris: UNESCO).

Rose, Gillian (1984), *Dialectic of Nihilism: Post-Structuralism and Law* (Oxford: Blackwell).

Rose, Gordon (1958), 'Trends in the development of criminology in Britain', *British Journal of Sociology*, vol. 9, no. 1.

Rose, R. (1968), 'Class and party divisions: Britain as a test case', *Sociology*, vol. 2, no. 2.

Ross, A. M. and Hartman, P. T. (1960), *Changing Patterns of Industrial Conflict* (New York: Wiley).

Ross, E. A. (1901), *Social Control: A Survey of the Foundations of Order* (New York and London: Macmillan).

Roszak, T. (ed.) (1967), *The Dissenting Academy* (New York: Pantheon).

Roszak, T. (1970), *The Making of a Counter Culture* (London: Faber & Faber).

Routh, G. (1980), *Occupation and Pay in Great Britain 1906–79* (London: Macmillan).

Rowntree, B. Seebohm (1901), *Poverty: A Study of Town Life* (London: Macmillan).

Rowntree, B. Seebohm and Lavers, G. R. (1951), *Poverty and the Welfare State* (London: Longmans, Green).

Royal Commission on Population (1949), *Report* (London: HMSO).

Rudé, G. (1959), *The Crowd in the French Revolution* (Oxford: Oxford University Press).

Rudé, G. (1964), *The Crowd in History* (New York: Wiley).

Rumney, J. (1934), *Herbert Spencer's Sociology* (new edn, New York: Atherton Press, 1965).

Ryan, A. (1970), *The Philosophy of the Social Sciences* (London: Macmillan).

Sartre, Jean-Paul (1960), *Critique of Dialectical Reason* (London: New Left Books, 1976).

Saunders, P. (1981), *Social Theory and the Urban Question* (London: Hutchinson).

Sauvy, A. (1952–4), *Théorie générale de la population*, 2 vols. (Paris: Presses Universitaires de France).

Scase, R. (1975), 'Sweden', in Paterson and Thomas (1975).

Schäffle, A. (1875–8), *Bau und Leben des sozialen Körpers* (Tübingen: J. C. B. Mohr).

Schapera, I. (1956), *Government and Politics in Tribal Societies* (London: Watts).

Schapera, I. (1957), 'Malinowski's theories of law', in Firth (1957).

Schlatter, R. (1951), *Private Property: The History of an Idea* (London: Allen & Unwin).

Schmalenbach, H. (1922), 'Die soziologische Kategorie des Bundes', *Dioskuren*, vol. 1.

Schmoller, G. (1890), 'Das Wesen der Arbeitsteilung und der sozialen Klassenbildung', *Schmollers Jahrbuch*, vol. 14.

Schumpeter, J. A. (1927), 'Social classes in an ethnically homogeneous environment', in *Imperialism and Social Classes* (Oxford: Blackwell, 1951).

Schumpeter, J. A. (1942), *Capitalism, Socialism and Democracy* (5th edn, London: Allen & Unwin, 1976).

Schurmann, F. (1970), *Ideology and Organization in Communist China*, 2nd edn (Berkeley and Los Angeles: University of California Press).

Schurmann, F. and Schell, O. (eds.) (1967), *Communist China* (New York: Random House).

Schutz, A. (1932), *The Phenomenology of the Social World* (Evanston, Ill.: Northwestern University Press, 1967).

Scott, J. (1979), *Corporations, Classes and Capitalism* (London: Hutchinson).

Scott, J. (1982), *The Upper Classes: Property and Privilege in Britain* (London: Macmillan).

Scottish Council for Research in Education (1949), *The Trend of Scottish Intelligence* (London: University of London Press).

Scottish Council for Research in Education (1953), *Social Implications of the Scottish Mental Survey* (London: University of London Press).

Seddon, D. (ed.) (1978), *Relations of Production: Marxist Approaches to Economic Anthropology* (London: Frank Cass).

Senart, E. (1894), *Caste in India* (London: Methuen, 1930).

Sève, Lucien (1974), *Man in Marxist Theory and the Psychology of Personality* (Brighton: Harvester Press, 1978).

Shanin, T. (ed.) (1971), *Peasants and Peasant Societies* (Harmondsworth: Penguin Books).

Shanin, T. (1983), *Late Marx and the Russian Road* (London: Routledge & Kegan Paul).

Sharma, G. S. (1966), *Secularism: Its Implications for Law and Life in India* (Bombay: Tripathi for the Indian Law Institute).

Shaw, W. H. (1978), *Marx's Theory of History* (London: Hutchinson).

Shelvankar, K. S. (1940), *Problem of India* (Harmondsworth: Penguin Books).

Shorter, E. (1975), *The Making of the Modern Family* (New York: Basic Books).

Showstack Sassoon, A. (1983), 'Hegemony', in Bottomore (1983).

Simiand, F. (1912), *La Méthode positive en science économique* (Paris: Alcan).

Simiand, F. (1932), *Le Salaire, l'évolution sociale et la monnaie* (Paris: Alcan).

Simmel, Georg (1902), 'The number of members as determining the sociological form of the group', *American Journal of Sociology*, vol. 8.

Simmel, Georg (1903), 'The metropolis and mental life', in Hatt and Reiss, 1957.

Simmel, Georg (1907), *The Philosophy of Money* (London: Routledge & Kegan Paul, 1978).

Simmel, Georg (1908a), 'The problem of sociology' and 'How is society possible?' in Wolff (1959).

Simmel, Georg (1908b), *Conflict and the Web of Group Affiliations* (New York: Free Press, 1955).

Simmel, Georg (1980), *Essays on Interpretation in Social Science*, ed. Guy Oakes (Totowa, NJ: Rowman & Littlefield).

Sinclair, J. (1791-9), *Statistical Account of Scotland*, 21 vols. (Edinburgh: W. Creech).

Sivard, R. L. (ed.) (annually), *World Military and Social Expenditures* (Leesburg, Virginia: World Priorities).

Skocpol, T. (1979), *States and Social Revolutions* (Cambridge: Cambridge University Press).

Skocpol, T. (ed.) (1984), *Vision and Method in Historical Sociology* (Cambridge: Cambridge University Press).

Smelser, N. J. (1963), *The Sociology of Economic Life* (Englewood Cliffs, NJ: Prentice-Hall).

Smith, A. D. (1971), *Theories of Nationalism* (London: Duckworth).

Smith, A. D. (1976), *Social Change* (London: Longman).

Smith, D. E. (1963), *India as a Secular State* (Princeton, NJ: Princeton University Press).

Smith, W. Robertson (1894), *Lectures on the Religion of the Semites* (3rd edn, New York: Macmillan, 1927).

Sombart, W. (1902), *Der moderne Kapitalismus: Historisch-systematische Darstellung des gesamteuropäischen Wirtschaftslebens von seinen Anfängen bis zur Gegenwart* (2nd edn, 3 vols., Munich and Leipzig: Duncker & Humblot, 1924–7).

Sombart, W. (1930), 'Capitalism', in *Encyclopaedia of the Social Sciences*.

Somjee, A. H. (1979), *The Democratic Process in a Developing Society* (London: Macmillan).

Sorokin, P. A. (1937), *Social and Cultural Dynamics*, 4 vols. (New York: American Book Co.).

Sorokin, P. A. (1945), 'Sociocultural dynamics and evolutionism', in Gurvitch and Moore (1945).

Sorokin, P. A. (1959), *Social and Cultural Mobility* (New York: Free Press).

Southall, A. (1968), 'Stateless society', in *International Encyclopaedia of the Social Sciences*.

Southern, R. W. (1953), *The Making of the Middle Ages* (London: Hutchinson).

Spencer, Herbert (1850), *Social Statics* (London: Routledge & Kegan Paul, 1954).

Spencer, Herbert (1876–96), *Principles of Sociology* (3 vols., New York: Appleton, 1925–9).

Springborg, P. (1981), *The Problem of Human Needs and the Critique of Civilization* (London: Allen & Unwin).

Srinivas, M. N. (1952), *Religion and Society Among the Coorgs of South India* (Bombay: Asia Publishing House, 1965).

Srinivas, M. N. (1954), 'Village studies', *Economic Weekly* (Bombay).

Srinivas, M. N. (1960), 'The Indian road to equality', *Economic Weekly* (Bombay), 20 August.

Srinivas, M. N. (1965), *Caste in Modern India and Other Essays* (Bombay: Asia Publishing House).

Srinivas, M. N. *et al.* (1959), 'Caste', *Current Sociology*, vol. 8, no. 3.

Stalin, J. V. (1938), *Dialectical and Historical Materialism* (London: Lawrence & Wishart, 1940).

Stanworth, P. and Giddens, A. (eds.) (1974), *Elites and Power in British Society* (Cambridge: Cambridge University Press).

Steinmetz, S. R. (1898–9), 'Classification des types sociaux et catalogue des peuples', *Année Sociologique*, vol. 3, pp. 43–147.

Steward, J. H. (ed.) (1955), *Irrigation Civilizations: A Comparative Study* (Pan-American Union).

Stewart, Dugald (1854–8), 'Memoir of Adam Smith', in *Works*, Vol. 10 (Edinburgh: Constable).

Stewart, J. D. (1958), *British Pressure Groups* (Oxford: Clarendon Press).

Stockholm International Peace Research Institute (SIPRI) (1982), *The Arms Race and Arms Control* (London: Taylor & Francis).

Stone, L. (1979), 'The revival of narrative', *Past and Present*, vol. 85.

Strachey, J. (1956), *Contemporary Capitalism* (London: Gollancz).

Strauss, L. (1953), *Natural Right and History* (Chicago: University of Chicago Press).

Stubbs, W. (1874–8), *The Constitutional History of England in its Origin and Development*, 3 vols. (Oxford: Clarendon Press).

Sturmthal, A. (ed.) (1967), *White-Collar Trade Unions* (Urbana: University of Illinois Press).

Sumner, W. G. (1906), *Folkways: A Study of the Sociological Importance of Usage, Manners, Customs and Morals* (New York: Dover, 1959).

Sumner, W. G. (1911), *War and Other Essays* (New Haven: Yale University Press).

Szalai, A. and Petrella, R. (eds.) (1977), *Cross-National Comparative Survey Research: Theory and Practice* (Oxford: Pergamon Press).

Tabah, L. (1982), 'Population growth', in Faaland (1982).

Tawney, R. H. (1937), *Religion and the Rise of Capitalism* (2nd edn, Harmondsworth: Penguin Books, 1938).

Tawney, R. H. (1952), *Equality*, 4th rev. edn (London: Allen & Unwin).

Taylor, C. (1967), 'Neutrality in political science', in Laslett & Runciman (1967).

Taylor I. *et al.* (eds.) (1975), *Critical Criminology* (London: Routledge & Kegan Paul).

Taylor, John G. (1979), *From Modernization to Modes of Production* (London: Macmillan).

Taylor, John G. (1983), 'Underdevelopment and development', in Bottomore (1983).

Taylor, L. R. (ed.) (1970), *The Optimum Population for Britain* (London: Academic Press).

Tenbruck, F. H. (1954), 'Formal sociology', in Wolff (1959).

Terkel, S. (1974), *Working* (Harmondsworth: Penguin Books, 1985).

Thabault, R. (1945), *Mon village* (Paris: Delagrave).

Thomas, W. I. and Znaniecki, F. (1918–20), *The Polish Peasant in Europe and America* (2 vols., 2nd edn, New York: Dover, 1958).

Thrasher, F. M. (1936), *The Gang* (Chicago: University of Chicago Press).

Tilly, C. (ed.) (1975), *The Formation of National States in Western Europe* (Princeton, NJ: Princeton University Press).

Titmuss, R. M. (1958), *Essays on 'The Welfare State'* (London: Allen & Unwin).

Titmuss, R. M. (1974), *Social Policy: An Introduction* (London: Allen & Unwin).

Tocqueville, Alexis de (1835–40), *Democracy in America* (London: Oxford University Press, 1946).

Tönnies, F. (1887), *Community and Association* (London: Routledge & Kegan Paul, 1955).

Touraine, Alain (1965), *Sociologie de l'action* (Paris: Éditions du Seuil).

Touraine, Alain (1966), *La Conscience ouvrière* (Paris: Éditions du Seuil).

Touraine, Alain (1968), *The May Movement* (New York: Random House, 1971).

Touraine, Alain (1969), *The Post-Industrial Society* (New York: Random House, 1971).

Touraine, Alain (1973), *The Self-Production of Society* (Chicago: University of Chicago Press, 1977).

Townsend, P. (1979), *Poverty in the United Kingdom* (Harmondsworth: Penguin Books).

Toynbee, Arnold (1934–56), *A Study of History*, 10 vols. (London: Oxford University Press).

Trevor-Roper, H. R. (1957), *Historical Essays* (London: Macmillan).

Troeltsch, E. (1912), *The Social Teaching of the Christian Churches* (London: Allen & Unwin).

Trotsky, L. (1932–3), *The History of the Russian Revolution* (London: Gollancz; repr. Sphere, 1967).

Tumin, M. M. (1967), *Social Stratification: The Forms and Functions of Inequality* (Englewood Cliffs, NJ: Prentice-Hall).

Turner, Bryan S. (1978), *Marx and the End of Orientalism* (London: Allen & Unwin).

Turner, Bryan S. (1983a), 'Asiatic society', in Bottomore (1983).

Turner, Bryan S. (1983b), *Religion and Social Theory* (London: Heinemann).

Turner, Denys (1983), *Marxism and Christianity* (Oxford: Blackwell).

Turner, Roy (ed.) (1962), *India's Urban Future* (Berkeley and Los Angeles: University of California Press).

Tylor, E. B. (1871), *Primitive Culture* (Gloucester, Mass.: Smith, 1958).

UNESCO (1956), *The Social Implications of Industrialization and Urbanization* (Calcutta: UNESCO).

UNESCO (1957), *The Nature of Conflict* (Paris: UNESCO).

United Nations (1954), *The Determinants and Consequences of Population Trends* (New York: United Nations).

Veblen, Thorstein (1904), *The Theory of Business Enterprise* (New York: Scribner).

Veblen, Thorstein (1918), *The Higher Learning in America* (New York: Hill & Wang, 1957).

Vinogradoff, P. (1920), *Historical Jurisprudence* (Oxford: Clarendon Press).

Wach, J. (1944), *Sociology of Religion* (Chicago: University of Chicago Press).

Wallas, Graham (1908), *Human Nature in Politics* (London: Constable).

Waller, W. (1932), *The Sociology of Teaching* (New York: Wiley).

Wallerstein, I. (1974), *The Modern World System* (New York: Academic Press).

Wallerstein, I. (1980), *The Modern World System II* (New York: Academic Press).

Washburn, S. L. (1966), 'Conflict in primate society', in Reuck and Knight (1966).

Weber, Alfred (1935), *Kulturgeschichte als Kultursoziologie*, 2nd rev. edn (Munich: Piper).

Weber, Max (1904), ' "Objectivity" in social science and social policy', in Weber (1949).

Weber, Max (1904–5), *The Protestant Ethic and the Spirit of Capitalism* (London: Allen & Unwin, 1976).

Weber, Max (1915), 'The Chinese literati', in Weber (1947).

Weber, Max (1917), 'The meaning of "ethical neutrality" in sociology and economics', in Weber (1949).

Weber, Max (1919), 'Politics as a vocation', in Weber (1947).

Weber, Max (1920), *Gesammelte Aufsätze zur Religionssoziologie* (Tübingen: J. C. B. Mohr).

Most of these studies are now available in English; in addition to *The Protestant Ethic* see:

The Religion of China: Confucianism and Taoism (London: Allen & Unwin, 1952).

Ancient Judaism (London: Allen & Unwin, 1953).

The Religion of India: The Sociology of Hinduism and Buddhism (London: Allen & Unwin, 1958).

Weber, Max (1921), *Economy and Society* (3 vols., New York: Bedminster Press, 1968).

Weber, Max (1923), *General Economic History* (New York: Collier Books, 1961).

Weber, Max (1947), *From Max Weber*, ed. H. H. Gerth and C. W. Mills (London: Routledge & Kegan Paul).

Weber, Max (1949), *The Methodology of the Social Sciences*, ed. E. Shils and H. Finch (Glencoe, Ill.: Free Press).

Weiner, M. (1957), *Party Politics in India: The Development of a Multi-Party System* (Princeton, NJ: Princeton University Press).

Weiss, J. (1967), *The Fascist Tradition* (New York: Harper & Row).

Wellmer, A. (1969), *Critical Theory of Society* (New York: Herder & Herder, 1971).

Weselowski, W. (1979), *Classes, Strata and Power* (London: Routledge & Kegan Paul).

Westermarck, E. (1906), *The Origin and Development of Moral Ideas* (2nd edn, London: Macmillan, 1924–6).

Westermarck, E. (1926), *A Short History of Marriage* (New York: Macmillan).

White, G. *et al.* (eds.) (1983), *Revolutionary Socialist Development in the Third World* (Brighton: Wheatsheaf Books).

Whyte, W. F. (1943), *Street Corner Society* (Chicago: University of Chicago Press).

Whyte, W. F. (1956), 'Problems of industrial sociology', *Social Problems*, vol. 4, no. 2.

Whyte, W. H. (1956), *The Organization Man* (New York: Simon & Schuster).

Wiatr, J. (1964), 'Political sociology in Eastern Europe', *Current Sociology*, vol. 13, no. 2.

Wiener, M. J. (1981), *English Culture and the Decline of the Industrial Spirit, 1850–1980* (Cambridge: Cambridge University Press).

Wiese, L. von (1933), *System der Soziologie als Lehre von den sozialen Prozessen und den sozialen Gebilden der Menschen (Beziehungslehre)*, 2nd enlarged edn (Munich: Duncker & Humblot).

Wilkins, L. T. (1955), 'Some developments in prediction methodology in applied social research', *British Journal of Sociology*, vol. 6, no. 4.

Williams, Raymond (1958), *Culture and Society* (London: Chatto & Windus).

Williams, R. M. (1965), *American Society: A Sociological Interpretation*, 2nd rev. edn (New York: Knopf).

Willock, I. D. (1974), 'Getting on with sociologists', *British Journal of Law and Society*, vol. 1, no. 1.

Wilson, B. R. (1961), *Sects and Society* (London: Heinemann).

Wilson, B. (1982), *Religion in Sociological Perspective* (Oxford and New York: Oxford University Press).

Wilson, G. and M. (1945), *The Analysis of Social Change* (Cambridge: Cambridge University Press).

Winch, P. (1963), *The Idea of a Social Science*, rev. edn (London: Routledge & Kegan Paul).

Wirth, L. (1938), 'Urbanism as a way of life', repr. in Hatt and Reiss (1957).

Wiser, H. (1936), *The Hindu Jajmani System: A Socio-Economic System* (Lucknow; Lucknow Publishing House, 1958).

Wittfogel, K. (1957), *Oriental Despotism* (New Haven, Conn.: Yale University Press).

Wolf, Eric R. (1966), *Peasants* (Englewood Cliffs, NJ: Prentice-Hall).

Wolf, Eric R. (1970), *Peasant Wars of the Twentieth Century* (New York: Harper & Row).

Wolff, Janet (1983), *Aesthetics and the Sociology of Art* (London: Allen & Unwin).

Wolff, Kurt H. (ed.) (1959), *Georg Simmel 1858–1918* (Columbus, Ohio: Ohio State University Press).

Wolff, Kurt H. (1978), 'Phenomenology and sociology', in Bottomore and Nisbet (1978).

Wootton, B. (1955), *The Social Foundations of Wage Policy* (London: Allen & Unwin).

Wootton, B. (1959), *Social Science and Social Pathology* (London: Allen & Unwin).

Worsley, P. (1957), *The Trumpet Shall Sound* (London: MacGibbon and Kee).

Worsley, P. (1967), *The Third World*, 2nd edn (London: Weidenfeld & Nicolson).

Wright, G. H. von (1971), *Explanation and Understanding* (London: Routledge & Kegan Paul).

Wright, Quincy (1942), *A Study of War*, 2 vols. (Chicago: University of Chicago Press).

Wrigley, E. A. (1969), *Population and History* (New York: McGraw-Hill).

Wrong, D. (1967), *Population and Society*, 3rd edn (New York: Random House).

Yeager, R. (1982), *Tanzania: An African Experiment* (Boulder, Colo.: Westview Press).

Young, M. and Willmott, P. (1957), *Family and Kinship in East London* (London: Routledge & Kegan Paul).

Zeldin, T. (1979–81), *France 1848–1945* (Oxford: Oxford University Press).

Zetterberg, H. (ed.) (1956), *Sociology in the United States of America* (Paris: UNESCO).

Znaniecki, F. (1940), *The Social Role of the Man of Knowledge* (New York: Columbia University Press).

Zorbaugh, H. W. (1929), *The Goldcoast and the Slum* (Chicago: University of Chicago Press).

Zubaida, S. (ed.) (1970), *Race and Racialism* (London: Tavistock).

Index